Trust YOUR IMMORTAL Soul

A GUIDE TO SPIRITUAL LIVING

WILLIAM F. STURNER

Second (Revised Edition): 2016

Copyright © 2012 William F. Sturner
All rights reserved.

ISBN: 1463718624
ISBN-13: 9781463718626

Other Books by William F. Sturner

BIOGRAPHICAL

Love Loops: A Divorced Father's Personal Journey (1983)

CREATIVITY

AHA: Creating Each Day with Insight and Daring (2000)

LEADERSHIP AND ORGANIZATIONAL CHANGE

Action Planning (1974)

Impact: Transforming Your Organization (1993)

Superb Leadership: The 12 Essential Skills (1997)

MYTHIC SPIRIT TALES

The Three-Legged Deer: Exploring the Miracles of Nature (2010)

Kindred Spirits: Celebrating Angels, Mystics and Miracles (2011)

THE PSYCHOLOGY OF RISK AND CHANGE

Calculated Risk: Strategies for Managing Change (1990)

Risking Change: Ending and Beginnings (1987)

SPIRITUAL COMMENTARY

Mystic in the Marketplace: A Spiritual Journey (1994)

The Creative Impulse: Celebrating Adam and Eve, Jung and EveryOne (1998)

Other Dimensions

The Open Heart Sanctuary

1307 Copperwood Drive, Osprey, Florida 34229

wfsturner@mac.com

www.KindredSpirits.Us

Presenting

Mythic Spirit-Tales, and

Spiritual Commentary

For the Childlike,

the Curious,

the Loving

and the Spiritually Inclined

Dedicated

With Gratitude and Blessings

To the wondrous Archangel Gabriel

who never fails to evoke and protect,

and my loving Guardian Angel, Nathaniel,

who never fails to guide and enlighten.

Benozzo Gozzoli, *Angels*, c. 1459
The angelic realm: always available, always guiding, always loving.

In Appreciation

Who and What to Thank

We are all composites of our experiences. If we open to what our experiences offer us, and how those interactions impact on us – how they form us and shape us – then we begin to realize that everything and everyone we've encountered throughout life has helped to create who we are: our values, behaviors, skills and abilities, certainly our state of consciousness.

For example, despite all the disappointments and frustrations Holden Caulfield experiences in "The Catcher in the Rye", he ends up concluding that he misses everyone – even Ackley and the guy in the elevator. Why? Grappling with them – both his encounters and subsequent reflections - made him more aware of himself and his link to others, all of which, in some wondrous way, added to his understanding that he and Life were one.

You would now think I would list all the "stupid people" I have met and how much I learned from each encounter. But – given J.D. Salinger's interpretation, the term 'stupid' and its supposed negative connotation, applies only to the initial and fleeting impact. So I begin – and end - my list of salutations by giving thanks to the life process itself – to the many oppositions, blockages, disappointments and failures as well as all the people and happenings that at the time and since then have been experienced as helpful, joyful and affirming.

Looking at the total collage of people and happenings – years after – it is hard to decipher which was which. Some of my greatest disappointments redirected my path, for which I am now eternally grateful, and some of my so-called greatest mistakes have had very positive long-range consequences.

Experience - in general – not just the bright spots but also the series of twists and turns - are the stimulants of growth and development. Consciousness of who we are and what is most important only deepens and expands if we are open to receive - and absorb - the insights and lessons that life offers us. Facing the human analogs of a bridge that collapses, a sand storm that stops you in your tracks or a glad tiding that's washed away the next day: all these sources of experience and related spurts in consciousness, become, with reflection and adjustment, the wondrous creators of discernment, clarity, insight and thanksgiving.

So I begin my list of thanks by honoring *Life* itself– with all its intended and unexpected learning, and its the innate capacity to steer the boat to those places and persons who have contributed in one way or another.

I, you, all of us, are here for a reason – and the reason rarely has anything to do with who we are formally or what we seek overtly. Resumes filled with worldly accomplishments are helpful but only if they include both a rendering of one's loving intentions and one's contributions to creativity, understanding and joy.

Did you and I wish to create a profession, an organization, a family, a life – with the intention of uplifting anyone but our own immediate and material welfare? Did we deliberately – and frequently - intend to create love as we also sought to fulfil some sort of outer achievement? And was it our intention - in any one of a million ways - to give, restore, contribute, aid, heal, cure, empower others to feel good about themselves or help them transform a difficult situation into something that had a healthy, useful or creative impact on themselves and the world?

Domenico Ghirlandaio, *Choir Singing in Celebration of the Coronation of Mary*, 1504
Ah - the choir: symbol of celebrating all aspects of life and all
who contribute to its fullness.

Or did we ever employ our God-given — but increasingly bloated egos - for anything other than self-interest, protection or aggrandizement? Has life only been about us — the would-be 'number one' — or have we used it to deliberately help others, to serve 'it', the situation or the relationship - even at a sacrifice to our immediate wants and needs? Have we acted with the conscious intention of affirming and growing the state of our Soul?

And what has been the impact of our intentions and actions? Have they furthered the cause of love and justice, helped to heal and cure, served to educate and encourage learning, fostered acknowledgment of the inner soulfulness of all human beings, and diminished the plight of the sick, the poor and the hungry?

These are the key questions. Our reflections and answers tell us whether we have embraced, served and thus learned from the Life process, or reveal that we have attempted to use it's opportunities to cushion and fortify our egos and material welfare, learning as little as possible about ourselves and Life while contributing the minimum in the process.

As you will see, it is the intent of this book to further the cause of the Soul by encouraging all of us to affirm our identity as immortal Souls — spiritual beings who have incarnated on Earth in order to learn deeper and more loving states of consciousness, to act as effective ambassadors of the Spirit, to celebrate and give thanks for the opportunity to serve, create and contribute.

It is the flow of *Life*, with all its gifts and challenges - that presents our capacity to learn, develop and mature — and then slowly but surely affirm and abide by its lessons. As such, my life has given me the same opportunity given to each of us: to embrace it — all of it, the so-called highs and lows - with as such love and joy and as I can muster. And for that I am most thankful.

CONTENTS

Dedication vii
In Appreciation ix

Section One: Overview 1
   1. The Essentials 3
   2. Outrageous 14
   3. "Breaking News" 25
   4. Dealing With The Consequences. 38

Section Two: Soul Identity 43
   5. The Spiritual Experience 45
   6. Accepting The Challenge 61
   7. On Being Fully Alive 70
   8. Everyday Awareness 74

Section Three: Spirituality. 87
   9. What Is Spirituality?. 89
  10. Cultivating Our Spirituality. 103
  11. Affirming Our Spiritual Core 123
  12. No Limit or Lack 142
  13. The Spirit of Everyday 157

Section Four: The Process of Incarnation 179
  14. Reincarnation. 181
  15. The Soul-God Relationship 198
  16. Manifesting Your Spirituality. 209
  17. Everything Converges 222
  18. The Challenge of Change 234

Section Five: Nurturing the Soul 247
    19. Creating Soul Consciousness. 249
    20. Practical Spirituality 275
    21. Prayer 293
    22. Meditation 317
    23. Contemplation 331
    24. Angelic Beings 343
    25. Asking for Guidance 357

Section Six: Extensions of the Soul 363
    26. Cells in the Kosmic Body 365
    27. Religion and Spirituality 387
    28. The Soulfulness of Art 419
    29. Choosing And Creating 434
    30. Sacred Partners 449

Appendix: Outline of Our Soul Identity 463
The Author 469

SECTION ONE

Overview

CHAPTER 1

THE ESSENTIALS

This is a book on spirituality – a practical set of guidelines for living a loving and inspired life. There is no organization to join. No monthly fees to remit. No shoulds, mandates or compulsory creeds and rituals. It is all begins and ends with Trust – trust in your innate connection to the Divine, and trust in your immortal Soul and its remarkable God-given empowerments.

The assertion of one's spiritual identity has ancient roots and all sorts of modern extensions. It is the basis for any and all religious beliefs and practices. When the assertion – "I am an immortal Soul"- is understood fully and asserted with both love and gusto, it is the sure antidote to any person or group who suggests you need to practice your innate spirituality according to their views and prescriptions. Spirituality is open and free. The specifics of 'how and when and why' – are all up to you for you are already everything you need to be to make such choices. You – an immortal Soul – is the spiritual person who determines whatever spiritual practices you think will enhance your love and compassion for yourself, others and God.

Trusting In Yourself

Trusting in yourself - because you are an immortal Soul – is an incredibly powerful statement. You are not a sinner, a dependent, a wanderer, a waif, among the lost or an indentured servant to some religious tribe. You are an immortal Soul – a person who is empowered to complete the ministry and mission that you chose before incarnating, the set of life challenges and contributions that now enable you to enhance your capacity for love, creativity and understanding.

Your lead. Your choice. Your life. Your affirmation that there is a revered alternative to either going it alone or continuing to rely – out of habit or guilt - on the religion of your childhood. Asserting one's innate spirituality does not preclude joining a church group if there is something in its beliefs, ceremonies and social network that enables, deepens and/or extends your spiritual identity.

But like any relationship, it is best to enter into it with a clear sense of who you are versus connecting with another (person or organization) in order to find out who they prefer you to be, or what it will take for you to be accepted. Asserting your identity first produces clarity and focus. Any selected add-on could then make a positive contribution to deepening or extending that core identity. Joining any organization, including a religious one, prior to affirming and understanding the depths of your identity as an immortal Soul, could render you vulnerable to the needs and wishes of anyone willing to fill your vacuum with their preferences and prescriptions.

A Spiritual Blending of Tradition

The spiritual perspective presented here champions the creativity and immortality of your Soul, and thus offers you a very affirming and loving approach to everyday life - one that honors and expresses the everyday realities and practical empowerments of your Soul. It confirms a universal community of the Spirit but contains none of the requirements and judgments associated with many or most institutionalized religions.

"TRUST" is a very modern version of what the sacred sciences call 'syncretism' – the combining of elements from different traditions into a creative expression of Universal Spirituality. It champions such living realities as reincarnation, the life everlasting quality of your Soul, the power of your Soul to create its own reality, your direct access to God (free of any intermediaries), the pre-eminence of love and compassion, our role in co-creating the universe, and of course, the continual presence of God, your Guardian Angel and a host of other angelic helpers.

"TRUST" honors the role organized religions play in the lives of its participants. As an affirmation of the spiritual roots of all Life, however, the spiritual approach prospers everywhere. The alternatives include, of course, the one you are already in – whether that be individuality with or without communal links to kindred spirits, or a regular or loose connection to a religion or religious setting. Wherever your Soul seeks and finds the setting that enables it to prosper and express itself as an advocate of love and compassion, therein is your spiritual mooring or Soul-home.

By re-empowering the individual, literally interpreting the immortality of the Soul, and consolidating the perspective of several traditions into a new and somewhat daring spiritual amalgam, we run the risk of being deemed heretical by the straight and narrow advocates of some organized religions. That's unfortunate - for what is affirmed here merely highlights what spirituality shares in common with both Eastern and Western traditions.

This set of affirmations is also more than a blend of ancient and modern wisdom. Many of the insights stem from personal involvements, the experiential insights of the mystics, the realities uncovered by Jungian psychology and the everyday spiritual encounters conveyed by both the revered and relatively unknown. The consolidation includes the following:

- We don't just state but fully apply the Hindu philosophy of re-incarnation: as immortal Souls we return to the physical realm repeatedly, each time as a new person with a new set of challenges.

- We don't just write about the Judeo-Christian principle of the immortality of the Soul: we apply it to life's many challenges and opportunities, celebrating our ability to progressively incarnate in vary guises and circumstances, each with a mission to transform and spiritualize the physical realm.

- We don't just ponder the empowerments of the Soul: the immortal Soul embedded in our bodies creates and attracts the circumstances we need to develop and extend our capacity for love and compassion. There are no accidents or coincidences.

- We don't just pay lip service to the unconditional love of God: everything we intend and do is communicated to God and feeds into His/Her continuous creation of the Kosmos (the whole shebang).

- We are not separate from a transcendent God: we are cells in the kosmic and universal organism of God and thus integral parts or aspects of Divinity.

- We don't just talk about the presence of God: we honor the capacity of our Souls to invoke His/Her guidance directly – without need of clerical or ceremonial intermediaries.

- And we don't just paint and sculpt images of Angels: the Archangels, our Guardian Angel and a host of other angelic spirits are ever-present, always ready to respond, guide and protect us.

Spirituality and Organized Religion

Religion as 'organized religion' can be traced back to the series of avatars or holy men and woman who, after learning now to emulate the loving God in and through their multiple incarnations, were empowered by God to appear as special messengers throughout human history. Thus the wondrous appearances – in various guises - of such avatars as Zoroaster (Zarathustra), Sophia, Dionysus, Buddha, Moses, Jesus, Mohammed – all of who had remarkable spiritual gifts and experiences which in turn generated insights of enormous value to the development of humankind. Unfortunately - despite the protests and warnings of such holy men and women – their experiences were often transformed by some of their overly anxious followers into 'the way' versus 'a way'. When surrounded by structures and belief systems, the words and actions of these holy people were slowly but surely transformed - by those loving power and structure - into religious systems, complete with required theologies, codes, rituals and hierarchies. The experiences of the original avatars thus became the basis for promulgating the doctrines and mandates of institutionalized religion; rather than honoring the original avatars as models of spiritual living, the more doctrinaire of the followers viewed 'their' holy person as *the* idol, worshipped 'him' as 'the Holy One' and formed an institution to prove it.

Yet each codified religion – based on the experience and teachings of its inspired avatar – offered an aspect of the truth as it was then known and which has since served its community well. History tells us, however, that many lapsed into theological chutzpah and proclaimed to possess 'the one and only truth' – applicable to all times and cultures. The proponents of a broader and indeed deeper view of innate 'Spirituality', as outlined here – as well as the more open minded participants of the many organized religions - realize that an infinitely Loving God is much too big, too inclusive by nature, too compassionate in practice and too multidimensional in reality to ever be contained within the constructs of any one historical institution.

It is important to realize, then, that all religions are merely partial inflections of the broader base of spirituality and the general, non-codified belief in God. No one of history's many religions can represent the entire field of The Spirit. Such groups cannot be either the total or the only representatives of God. They may reflect that portion of divine wisdom that was or still is particularly relevant to their times and adopting culture, but still they are local and fragmentary. When pure or sacred energy is poured into the molds of historic and cultural preferences it assumes only the local form into which it is cast.

Such significant but limited castings may reflect divine energy and meet the needs of a particular people during a given historical period. But no one of them is or can be the totality of divine energy Itself. That is why consolidating the essence of several of them seemingly inches closer to the totality while meeting the needs of those who hunger for a third way between isolation and organized religion. All spiritual practices – including those of organized religion - are only examples of divine energy. And if any one of them meets your needs and fulfills your aspirations, so be it. That is cause for celebration. This book is hardly anti-religion – for it reveres them all and finds aspects of the divine in all of them.

The distinctions between the generic practice of spirituality and the institutionalized and specific forms of religion are raised only to rectify the assumption that any one of history's religious constructs expresses the totality of the divine presence. A historical imprinting of some portion of divine energy is very different from the whole of Divine Presence. Affiliate if you wish, of course, for old-time sake, the social interaction and support, the beauty of a ritual or your belief its is claims. But it does seem best to at least begin with - and then build on – a solid grounding in your innate spiritual nature and the reality of your immortal Soul.

> PLEASE NOTE: Most of the ten images reprinted in the book were produced for or within a particular religious tradition - especially that of Christianity and the Medieval and Renaissance periods of the West. They are not used to support any specific religious belief or the specific interpretation of the organization that commissioned them. Rather all the images used here are intended to illustrate that which is archetypal or generic, and thus serve merely as examples of the kinds of experiences shared in common by all spiritual traditions. See Chapter 28, "The Soulfulness of Art", for a fuller explanation of archetypal images.

The Third Way

What we here call 'spirituality', then, is that innate and universal impulse to honor, communicate with and experience the guidance of a Loving God, and to do so in one's own way, however individualized – freed of codification, hierarchy and intermediaries. To be spiritual is to be instinctively 'religious' – honoring one's personal connection to God and loving Life in and through both intent and practice. Spirituality is innate and internal and thus precedes and is independent of one's participation in an organized or institutionalized approach. It is the basis for each historical and cultural religion and is and always will be the successor to any codified set of religious beliefs and practices.

So there is a third way. The spiritual alternatives are no longer confined to being a participating member of an organized religion versus the alleged vacuum of the non-participant or apostate. Organized religion is only one way of expressing your instinctual desire and need to be 'religious'. It is only one aspect of universal Spirituality. You are and always will be an immortal Soul! Given that status and empowerment, you are literally in an empowered position to embrace and express your spiritual heritage in any way you wish, and then get on with the business of completing your partnership with Life.

The open hand, the blended knee, the sense of awe, the expression of love and joy, the gratitude for one's life (whatever and wherever it is) – are among the many ways one can encounter and express the presence of the ubiquitous, loving and creative essence of God.

The Spirit Manifest

Spirituality, then, is manifest throughout the universe in everything from planets, to people, to institutions, to technology and poetry. God – here also referred to as Prime Source, Prime Spirit or Spirit (thus 'Spirituality') - is not a divinity that is separate from the universe It creates. Rather it is manifest or immanent in each aspect of its creations. God or Spirit is an all-pervasive and primal energy, *the* life force that both creates and pervades the entire Kosmos.[1] No matter which group or religion or institution or creed attempts to bottle or attempt to envelop It with its limited perspective, Spirit, or spiritual energy, is everywhere

---

1   A Greek term used by the Pythagoreans and resurrected by Ken Wilbur - meaning the totality of everything and implying total inclusiveness. See Ken Wilbur, *A Brief History of Everything* (Boston: Shambhala, 1996), p. 19. Kosmos thus denotes the entire physical, cultural, psychological and spiritual universe, from mind to matter - from buttons to operas, squirrels to humans, ideas to tall buildings, ants to computers, literature and music, art and religions, the stars and teddy bears - everything that has been and is in the process of being created throughout the entire the universe. Thus the Kosmos includes the physical realm of the cosmos, the biosphere or all life forms, the psyche or expressions of the mind, and the *theos* or domain of the Divine.

and in everything – and no container or creed can possibly grasp no less express It in It's entirety.

This divine, creative energy is reflected in everything for it *is* everything. It is expressed in the micro universe of quarks and neutrinos, the macro universe of black holes and galaxies, and the meso (or middle) universe including all the life forms and creations evident on Earth – from bacteria and microbes, the incredibly diverse array of plants and animals, and everything the human mind has ever expressed through its art, music, architecture, technology, philosophy, psychology, religion and all the related institutions.

Moreover, this divine energy pervades your life, my life and every form of life that exists. It is evident not only on and through the activities of this planet but throughout the rest of the cosmos – culminating in the non-material realm of Pure Spirit, the abiding home of the immortal Soul, the angelic hosts and God, aka Prime Source or the Totality.

Your Immortal Soul

The major agent of this ubiquitous or ever present divinity and Its capacity for continually creating the Kosmos, is the immortal Soul, namely all of us. Each Soul is both a particle and the partner of Spirit. The connection is integral, the Soul being in essence a cell in the Cosmic Body of Spirit. We – as immortal Souls – are in a sacred partnership with the immortal and Divine Spirit. It, the Totality or God contains, includes – and as we shall see - depends as well on us: you and I are organic cells within the total life force or organism of divinity. We are Harriet and George in the everyday material world. We are also the Souls that inhabit those temporal incarnations. As immortal Souls, we are integral aspects of It, particles of the universal life force known as the Loving Spirit of God.

As immortal Souls or aspects of divinity, we are empowered to incarnate in material form in order to complete one more creative mission on behalf of eternal creativity. When we incarnate on Earth – as all of us who now inhabit the Earth have - we become God's agents of creation in the material universe. And even in our incarnational or material form we continue to be "made in the image of God" as the Hebrew Bible intuits in Genesis 1:27.

Sandro Botticelli, *Birth of Venus*, ca 1482
An image that reflects and honors the universal archetypes of love and creativity.

The Soul – your Soul and mine, or more accurately, *you and I* – are likenesses of God, agents of divinity, responsible for infusing divine life into the physical realm. We are here for a purpose. You and I – in our current circumstances – are here to infuse love into everything we think, feel, sense and encounter, thereby transforming and uplifting the Earth.

In sum, we are – each and all - immortal Souls who are now Soul-incarnates in material form. We chose to come to Earth in order to learn how to Love more fully through circumstances we selected. We did so in order to fulfil a transformational mission, developing and expressing our divine consciousness as we add to Spirit's continuous creativity.

History's Revered Messengers

So Yeshua ben Yosef or Jesus was an incarnation of his immortal Soul – just as you and I are emanations of our Souls. Yeshua was once a concrete embodiment as the historical and biological child of Joseph and Mary. His physical appearance may have changed since 33 ACE (the archeological term meaning 'After the Common Era') because his Soul may have taken on a series of new roles or manifestations since then. Unlike his temporary incarnations or manifestations, however, his Soul – like ours – is immortal. So he – like the Souls of everyone who has ever existed in material form – is still very much alive. So are the Souls of those the world once knew as Krishna, and Moses, and Buddha and Basho, and Confucius and Plato – as well as Abraham, Socrates, Eckhart, Mandela, ML King, Mother Theresa, Hildegard von Bingen, Mary, John the Baptist, Maimonides, Mohammed and the legions of others the world rightly considers saintly or sacred. Their earthly manifestations may have passed but they – as immortal Souls – have not.

The essence of such avatars – again like you and I – is their identity as immortal Souls. Given the contributions they have made during their various incarnations, they are rightly considered holy, special messengers or Master Teachers. They used their various incarnations to perfect and express their capacity for empathy and compassion and thereby personified the presence of the *Divine*.

We each have the same potential. So be patient. This may very well be the lifetime in which you and I really learn how to love. The settings and roles in which we are now placed may be the ones that enable us to truly appreciate, honor and value everyone and everything we encounter as opportunities to create love and express compassion And we can and will make such contributions as we uncover our central reality: we are immortal Souls and as such are sacred partners with God.

Obviously, the spiritual energy and counsel of any and all Souls are always present – whether currently manifest in incarnated form or serving on "the Other Side". The counsel of Yeshua and Buddha and all the other Master Teachers – like that of the Archangels and our Guardian Angels - are always present. All we need do is ask for their guidance, remembering that God, the Angelic hosts, and the Souls of the spiritual leaders that once graced the Earth – are immortal and thus still very much alive and willing to assist us.

Divinity, then, in all its forms and aspects - is alive and well - and living in your house. You are a divine Soul here living the outline of a script you composed and agreed to before you assumed your current physical form and took up residence in the mind and body you choose for this lifetime's incarnation.

What's Next?

Does all this seem mysterious? Is it new, or have you already experienced the presence of your Soul and sensed your immortality? Moreover, do these ideas ring a bell or strike a chord? Do they resonate even though you might not fully understand it all – yet? Moreover, are you encouraged to remember *who you really are* and awaken to the reality that you are indeed – like all of us - an immortal and divine being, a servant to and messenger of God?

If you wish to learn more about the nature of your current incarnation and your ongoing partnership with Prime Source,

- if you seek to develop your full capacity for Love and creativity,

- if you want to experience divinity, talk with your Guardian Angel and feel the guidance being offered to you daily by the Angelic Hosts and Avatars,

- if you wish to understand how your intentions not only create your life story but contribute to the unfolding of the entire Kosmos,

- then, please, walk with us to the next chapter. In hardly any time at all, you will be able to affirm your gifts and your mission this time around. You might even begin to experience your sacred identity with a renewed sense of grace and fullness.

CHAPTER 2

OUTRAGEOUS

What is proposed here may appear to some as being as outrageous as any religious claim on the market.

Let's put the term 'outrageous' in perspective. Consider, for example, that the world of religion already is - and has been for centuries - awash in the outrageous: the alleged creation of the world in seven days, the parting of the Red Sea, the walking on water, the talking to Krishna, the bodily absorption into an unseen heaven, the Holy Ghost impregnating a married but virgin woman, God or Brahma present in the trinity with Shiva and Krishna, the presence of the Creator God in a wafer. What could be more truthful to the believer, yet preposterous - and outrageous - to those of a different persuasion?

Trying to explain belief in a supernatural God through everyday language is in itself a very difficult task. It is also impossible to recount one's direct experience of the sacred without being accused of silly exaggeration and possible delusion. Stay within the now acceptable 'delusions' of traditional religion, however, and there is no fuss. But walk beyond those boundaries and actually champion the immortal Soul as our inner and everyday reality and identity and you run the risk of being dismissed by those who do *not* believe in God and being condemned by those who *do*. Yet it is the affirmation of our immortal Soul and now our current incarnation in time and space – as our core identities - that makes this book supposedly *radical and outrageous*.

The Incarnation was not a single historic event in the calendar of Christianity or the special preserve of one sacred avatar or manifestation of the divine. It is a process by which each of us - as immortal Souls –

continually choose to assume a physical form in the material world. The Christian belief in the incarnation of the divine in the form of the historic Yeshua, now called Jesus, is surely a reflection of this revered archetype or universal happening. Incarnation is how we all got here, on Earth, with the personal features, abilities and challenges we chose before 'descending' into material form. Incarnating from the realm of Pure Spirit is the prototype of a common, everyday experience. Visit the birthing ward of any hospital and there you will find the most recent expressions of the incarnational process.

If Jesus and Moses and Buddha and Mohammed were children of God so are we. Their incarnations and special roles do not make the rest of us orphans or so many pounds of chopped liver. Rather we are their brothers and sisters. We are all equal. We are all Souls. We are all immortal - derived and from the same divine, unified Father-Mother spirit creator.

Our Souls have incarnated in the 21st century in the same way Jesus did in the first century. And the process is ongoing, as acclaimed daily in the appearance of every new born - the millions of immortal Souls who each minute of every day choose once again to re-enter the material realm, ready to complete one more mission on Earth and thereby contribute to the further extension of God's loving consciousness.

Remember Who You Really Are

Throughout this book, then, you will be encouraged to constantly "remember who you really are" — to remember above all that you are a divine being, an aspect of God, an immortal Soul who has chosen to have a human experience.

In so remembering and affirming your identity as a Soul, you put your immediate and mortal life into a much larger and deeper context. To recognize oneself as an "Immortal Soul" who is now residing in a mortal body for a human lifetime is to affirm the ultimate identity. Think through its implications - and life becomes both sacred and understandable. Acceptance of the title of 'Immortal Soul' is cause for both celebration and the assumption of enormous responsibility.

Outrageous? Yes – relative to the religious beliefs whose outrageousness are now – and finally - deemed acceptable after many years of themselves being deemed 'outrageous'. Remember: the only difference between those teachings and those espoused here, is that the former are now protected by tradition, familiarity and presumed orthodoxy, while this synthesis of ancient spiritual beliefs lacks only familiarity and the approval of those who currently control what is and what is not deemed acceptable. If a religious belief is finally tolerated by society because its sponsor or religious group acquires status and power, then it loses its formally 'outrageous' quality. If not, it is dismissed - if not condemned as blasphemy. Many religions have long espoused belief in the Soul and the afterlife. Spirituality, however, treats both not as singular historical events but as metaphors that point to on-going and universal processes.

The perspectives presented here do not exclude the viewpoints and practices of any person or group. It simply asserts its right to make a different interpretation and be included under the umbrella of equal opportunity 'outrageousness' yet acceptability. It simply wishes to be affirmed as possible and not condemned or dismissed simply because it is different, audacious or guilty of extending a few existing beliefs beyond current limits. In short, by presenting the principle of the immortal Soul as our core and universal identity, we wish to be no more confronting, preposterous and unlikely than any other religious viewpoint now controlling the field.

Who is the Biggest Blasphemer?

Obviously, what is anathema to some can be a blessing to another, and what is a core practice to many, may be deemed silly, irrelevant or passé to another. Many institutional religions take their work, structures and belief systems so seriously that they reject as heretical anything that is not within their immediate and literal perspective. As the Catholic doctrine of transubstantiation may seem outrageous to Protestants, so may the Lutheran primacy of "faith" appear to the Moslems as immature and unnecessary. Surely the Buddhist sitting in meditative zazen appears strange to Orthodox Jews, just as the celebration of Passover may be meaningless to Native American Indians. Every individual or specific viewpoint seems to believe in a certain something that others think of as either 'nice', nonsensical, misleading or heretical.

Few organized groups, however, seem to display the tolerance and compassion of the Dalai Lama who when asked about his religion, replied that his religion "is kindness". Few have the wisdom of Carl Jung to see all religious expressions as images of the central archetype, namely the archetype of the psychological Self, the unifying center, the deepest and highest essence of Life itself. This is the core that embraces and unifies the conscious and unconscious realms.[2] It equates to what the religious communities refer to as 'God'.

And few have the insight of Joseph Campbell to know that any religion that assumes their interpretation of the divine to be the one and only literal truth – thereby directly or by inference negating or superseding any other viewpoint - fails to realize that all religious expressions are culturally and historically bound: each is a local, cultural and historic inflection of a universal experience of the extra-ordinary, the spiritual, the sacred or what Jung called the Self.

To paraphrase the insight attributed to Hermes Trismegistus in the *Hermetica*, "God is the supreme energy whose center is everywhere and whose circumference is nowhere."[3]

The process of spirituality means practicing one's particular beliefs in such a way as to move beyond any specific or man-made structures, and viewing one's specific beliefs and practices as convenient, practical or cultural derivatives of generic archetypes. All religious practices and organizations adopt their own applications of such archetypal themes as God, prayer, ceremony, creed, the Soul, birth, death and immortality. But none of the forms adopted by any religion are the archetypes themselves, only local inflections or expressions of the Divine. They may suit the values and history of the group and its leadership – with its particular ways and institutions - but they are still only that local

---

2   C.G. Jung, *Memories, Dreams, Reflections* (New York: Vintage, 1965), p. 398.
3   *Hermetica: The Greek Corpus Hermeticum and the Latin Asclepius*: New English Translation (Cambridge, England: Cambridge University Press, 1995).

group's historical and cultural estimates, examples or approximations of the universal.

The reality of Prime Source, as Creator of the entire Kosmos, is much too gigantic, deep, awesome and complex to be summarized by any one denominational viewpoint or preferred ritual or image. It is and would be the height of audacity to assume that any human words, theories, interpretations of history - no less some fragmentary glimpse of a selected image of the archetype of God - could do justice to such cosmic dimensions.

God may exist in a church, temple, stupa, or landscape; be served in a hundred and one rituals; and be affirmed by hundreds of differing traditions. Other peoples' ways of honoring the Divine need not undercut one's chosen way of doing so, unless one feels a need for one-ups-man's-ship and protecting their insecurity by proclaiming exclusivity. In fact, when viewed with an open, loving and understanding frame of mind, awareness of the varied ways of acknowledging God should actually complement and reinforce everyone's particular way of honoring the universal Spirit.

The Modern Amalgam of Spirituality

The amalgam of ancient and modern beliefs outlined here contains none of the trappings of formalized religion: there's no hierarchy, no formalized doctrines, no set rituals and ceremonies, no intermediaries between you and your God, and no *codification cops* to protect you from the ravages of free exploration and open debate.

This set of experiential perspectives is simply one - but surely not the last - re-statement of spiritual insights that have long circulated in various forms. Many of its insights are reflected in total or part by the writings and spiritual traditions inspired by the likes of Zoroaster, Buddha, the writers of the Psalms, Hermes Trismegistus, Jesus, Bruno Giordano, the spiritual alchemists, the Native American Indian and a variety of other indigenous peoples, the poet Rumi, Rudolf Steiner, the Rosicrucians, Emanuel Swedenborg, the mystics of all religions,

Einstein, Ken Wilber, Jane Roberts, Gary Zukav and Eckhart Tolle. They are each different reflections of what is known as "the perennial wisdom" that is inherent in all spiritual traditions.[4]

And they all hint at, inquire into and even salute the pre-eminence of what we here refer to that *inner voice* that impels us to embrace what is sacred in each of us. This spiritual impulse creates the intention to express love as the underlying and foundational theme of Life, which in turn leads to the honoring of God as the creator of the impulse to love oneself and everyone we encounter.

Once this *inner impulse, love* and *Prime Source* are experienced and affirmed, it becomes a matter of personal choice which set of practices, beliefs, rituals and ceremonies best fit the needs and traditions of given individuals and groups. There need not be any restrictions on one's personal or organizational beliefs, and no condemnations of those adopted by others. Affirm the basics of the spiritual impulse, love and God – then add any custom or tradition to that basic frame you think helps to infuse those principles into your life, and you have your brand of spirituality.

The belief in incarnation, for example, as an ongoing, repetitive and continual process – happening as often as a child is born anywhere in the world – obviously stems from the Hindu and Buddhists philosophies of the East and has little in common with the allegedly exclusive historic incarnation attributed by Christianity to Jesus as the Son of God.

In the East, however, the individual Soul can be lost in the shuffle, either absorbed by the lockstep of the caste system on the earthly level, or subsumed by an amorphous and all-pervasive Spirit in the spiritual realm. Remembering and celebrating who you are as an individual Soul in the cosmic body of God – on the other hand champions the individuality of each Soul as an interactive part of and partner with Divine

---

[4] See, for example, the compilation of Aldous Huxley, *The Perennial Philosophy* (New York: Harper and Brothers, 1945).

Source. It also affirms and glories in the role each of us plays as conscious co-creators with the creator God.

Individuality Within the Totality

Including the individuality of each Soul within a unified totality known as God is akin to affirming the integrity of each cell in a cosmic body while acknowledging that the total body is still greater than the sum of its individual parts. Psychologically it matches Carl Jung's principle of individuation – the impulse of each individual to attain indivisibility or wholeness within the realm of the Collective Unconscious. And it supports the insights of philosopher Alfred North Whitehead[5] and paleontologist Teilhard de Chardin,[6] who viewed Divinity to be both immanent in matter and yet transcendent to it as its creator and Prime Source.

This 'spiritual amalgam', then, presents an updated version of the *perennial wisdom* referred to earlier. It combines ancient, recurring and modern insights from both the East and West that together affirm the primacy of love, the immortal Soul, the continual processes of incarnation and re-creation, the experience of God as the source and promulgator of Unconditional Love, and the presence of Divine Energy in every aspect of the universe. Many of the specifics will be explored in depth in separate chapters.[7] Until then, here is an overview and summary of this spiritual amalgam's most significant points of view:

---

5   See Roy Wood Sellars, "Philosophy of Organism', in Paul Arthur Schilpp (ed.), Vol. 3, *The Philosophy of Alfred North Whitehead* (LaSalle, IL: Open Court, 1991). Whitehead used the term, "panentheos", in which divinity is all-inclusive and universal (pan), both transcendent to and creator of matter (theos), yet is simultaneously immanent in every particle of the physical and mental Kosmos ('en').

6   Teilhard de Chardin, *Activation of Energy* (New York: Harcourt, 1976).

7   The sources of this amalgam include many scholars and mystics. Among the most influential are C.G. Jung, principally his *The Archetypes and the Collective Unconscious* (Princeton: Princeton University Press, 1959 [Bollengen Series XX, 1980]; Joseph Campbell, *The Masks of God* (New York: Viking, 1959-1964); the channeled messages of *Archangel Gabriel* by Karen Cook (Benu Too, Inc., P.O. Box 14343, Albuquerque, N.M., 87191, www. benukcook@gmail.com); Pierre Teilhard de Chardin, especially his *Toward the Future* (New York: Harvest, 1973; Evelyn Underhill, *Mysticism* (New York: Image, 1990); and Alan Watts, *The Way of Zen* (New York: Mentor, 1957).

Also see Ken Wilbur, *The Spectrum of Consciousness* (Wheaton, IL: Quest, 1982); and the works of Jane Roberts, especially *The Nature of Personal Reality* (New York: Bantam, 1976)

❖ God or Divine Source – as the Supreme Being - is the essence of life, the Creator of the physical universe, the abiding and spiritual energy of the Kosmos, the energy that is immanent in everything yet also its progenitor and propagator.

❖ Everyone and everything is an aspect and expression of God. We as individual Souls are integral parts of that integrated Divinity – immortal cells in that divine organism.

❖ God is the essence of both masculine and feminine traits and as a totally unified Being can rightfully be referred to as Prime Source or the Creator, and through such pronouns as He, She or It.

❖ The essence of our identity is 'an immortal Soul'. Our material embodiment serves as our temporary home for a given lifetime in time and space. As Archangel Gabriel has often said: "Humans are divine beings having an earthly experience".[8]

❖ We – as divine and thus immortal Souls – have and continue to incarnate in the material realm in order to deepen and expand our capacity to love. We design our own learning goals while still on *"the Other Side"*, and then choose the specifics of our life story once we incarnate and take physical form on the material Earth (or elsewhere in the universe).

❖ During our incarnations we are able to seek guidance from God, the various members of the angelic realm including our Guardian Angel, and the Avatars and Master Teachers (all of whom learned to personify unconditional love and thus attain individuation or wholeness during their many earlier incarnations).

❖ Divine guidance – as both requested and gifted - may be received during meditation, contemplation, prayer, night dreams, and via the intuitions, hunches, internal nudges and premonitions we receive in the course of everyday experience.

---

8   Archangel Gabriel, also known as Benu (an Egyptian terms meaning 'Teacher' and 'Doorway'): Channeled Messages by Karen Cook, Albuerquerque, NM.

- As spiritual beings we are inherently endowed with free choice – which we exercise in the realm of Pure Spirit before incarnating, throughout our incarnation and upon our return to the spirit world.

The Rest of the Reality

So far, so good. Now for restating the realities that some may deem beyond even the acceptable limits of outrageous.

- Each of us – as an indivisible and immortal Soul - is divine by nature for we are all cells in the Totality or the universal organism called God.

- Each Soul chooses what it wishes to experience and learn during each segment of its development. Those choices become the Soul's 'contract' or set of goals – which may be fulfilled in the realm of Pure Spirit, or for the more adventurous, in the incarnated or material state, here on Earth or elsewhere in the universe.

- For those reading this - who obviously have chosen to incarnate here on Earth – you are now involved in translating the outlines of your 'contract' into a lifetime of specific choices. Thus any one, including you, who earlier may have incarnated in India as a beggar, and then chose a military career with the French Air Force, may now be pursuing his/her new learning objectives as an accountant living in suburban Chicago.

- When we choose to incarnate, we also choose the outline characteristics of our placement, parents, talents, dysfunctions, perspectives, body type, challenges and dominant issues and patterns of our life.

- Once incarnated, however, we make our specific choices within that outline of intentions, consciously and unconsciously choosing to support them, negate them or ignore them. We thus are free to fulfil, modify or negate what we chose earlier as our learning objectives. Free will and choice are always the dynamics that govern human and thus spiritual development.

❖ Whatever the choice of time, place and circumstance, each incarnation is designed to help the Soul develop its potential to become whole and indivisible like God the Father and Mother. The process is like that of any human development: we begin as children yet possess the potential to become full adults – physically, mentally and spiritually – exercising our power to deepen and expand our consciousness as we proceed through life.

❖ There are no accidents. We are responsible for creating our life – progressively from outline, to specifics, to details. We choose and attract (specifically or through intention) everything that happens to and for us – including the details of how we will actually live and construct our life story. We both overtly create the circumstances needed to complete our choices as well as attract to us the people, circumstances and challenges we need to manifest our desires and intentions.

❖ Everyone now reading this book has obviously decided to incarnate on Earth. This placement on Earth is considered one of the most difficult assignments because of its complexities - which include the need to integrate such polarities as time and space, masculine and feminine, reason and emotion, spirit and matter, and life and death.

❖ The experiences of incarnation are designed primarily to help individual Souls achieve greater degrees of lovingness and the psychological maturity associated with spiritual wholeness. Our individual and collective incarnations thus serve the Totality or universal organism of the kosmic God. Through incarnation, Souls have the opportunity to infuse spirit into matter, activate love and expand understanding, and add to - or detract from - the level of spiritual consciousness of the Kosmos.

❖ During sleep, the cell-Soul is able to travel to, learn from and serve the needs of other cell-Souls - many of whom may be working in other portions or dimensions of the total kosmic organism.

- ❖ We 'incarnates' also communicate our thoughts, images, intentions and experiences directly to the Godhead as we experience them. We thus have the potential to contribute to the adjustments God makes to the continuous unfolding of the Kosmos.

- ❖ The primary dynamic of this seamless web of divine creation is the intention and experience of unconditional love. The subsets and processes of being loving include: 'no judgment', 'awareness', 'a higher (or deeper) consciousness', 'sensitivity', 'empathy' and 'compassion'.

- ❖ The life of the incarnated Soul (you and I) is not viewed as a battleground but is, in Huston Smith's [9] terms, 'a playing field', a school, a learning laboratory in which we are given the opportunity to infuse divine love into every one of our images, intentions, actions, experiences and situations.

In conclusion, each of us is a spiritual being, literally an immortal Soul, involved in both extending and learning from our spiritual universe. We are an integral part of a spiritual collaboratory[10] that includes God, you, me, the Angelic Hierarchy, the Avatars, and Master Teachers, and every thing, living consciousness and Soul entity that exits in the entire universe.

---

9   Huston Smith, *The World's Religions: Our Great Wisdom Traditions* (New York: HarperCollins, 1991).
10 A word coined by my cosmologist friend, Gus Jaccaci, Unity Scholars, New Gloucester, ME 04260

CHAPTER 3

"BREAKING NEWS"

Beep-Beep-Beep: May We Please Have Your Attention ...

"Please realize the body in which you are now located is only temporary. It is also wearing down - and will continue to fade in looks and endurance. Take good care of it in the meantime, of course. But please accept – and begin to deal with the reality - that you will eventually decide to let it go."

"But – not to worry: you, as an immortal Soul, will live forever – and once you have let go of your current embodiment, you will most likely re-incarnate into the physical realm relatively soon, repeating the process tens if not hundreds, even thousands of times, each time choosing another body and set of circumstances within which to learn the lessons you choose."

Background Information: As a Soul - an *immortal* Soul – you are only meant to keep your current embodiment for a little while, on average anywhere from 50-90 Earth years, which, of course, amounts to only a few mille-seconds in terms of eternity. And so it has been with each of the minds and bodies you – and all of us - have created and adopted over the eons of time.

Yet each material lifetime or incarnation of your Soul has a purpose; each is intended to accomplish one or more definable goals and learn to be more and more like the loving God. With time, of course, you will – as you always have – then let go of your body and return it to the Earth. You, the continuing you, the immortal you, the everlasting Soul – then returns to the purely spiritual realm where you assess your spiritual progress and get ready for one more assignment in the world of three dimensions.

Defining Who You Are

Everything depends on how you define yourself. If you consider yourself to be only a composite of bones, tissues and nerve endings – all of which quickly decompose when the brain stops functioning and the heart stopped beating – then life as you know it is finite and strictly bounded: there is birth, then a lifetime, then death. At that point, based on your beliefs, you will either disappear or spend the time you earned either in hell, purgatory or heaven.

Whatever your theological assumptions, however, you probably are opting to maintain your current form in healthy condition and extend your vital signs at least one more decade, year or day. Despite your best efforts, however – taking vitamins, regular exercise, eating a moderate diet, driving defensively – it is known fact that the body parts wear down and, at some juncture, the mechanism stops. That's when fear and anxiety emerge.

Look at all the ways society has invented to allegedly stave off the demise of the body: lotions, injections, freezing, preserving bones in a grave, rampant hypochondria, and the rush to empty the store shelves of any food, palliative, drug or alleged antidote at the slightest hint of pending difficulty. Actions designed to "save this life – for it is all I have" – are understandable but only if you implicitly or overtly assume that life really is 'over' when you surrender your body. In such cases, the assumption is: once my lovely nose, runners' legs, wondrous complexion, firm handshake, quick wit and brilliant smile are gone, then so am I: gone, over, caput.

Begrudgingly, you may face the inevitable by purchasing a plot in a cemetery – a last ditch effort perhaps to preserve your bones and insure your eligibility for a promised resurrection and life eternal. No matter what you believe in or what precautions you take, this reality called 'death' still haunts the best of us as a fearful mystery. Even if you believe in some religious aftermath, letting go of that which has served as the container of your identity - is still a scary proposition.

Heeding the 'Beep'

But if you heed the 'beep' of the 'breaking news' – the one that opened this chapter with the reminder that you are indeed an immortal Soul – then based on what you sense, intuit or have experienced, you know you are more than your temporary mind and very fragile body. As the logo of the 'YMCA' reminds us, there is also and foremost – the Spirit – which we here refer to as your immortal Soul - the field of energy that willed and formed your current incarnation, that is available to guide it every minute of everyday, that is your true identity, and that *is you* even after you finally let go of your current embodiment.

And 'immortal' means 'immortal'. Your body may pass but you, the Soul, never will. It is the abiding you, the entity that now looks at from your eyes, the consciousness that makes your choices, the particle of divinity that has the opportunity, with each new incarnation, to learn more and more about love and thus act with greater compassion.

There is a big difference between assuming you are only the temporary mind and body, and acting as if you are an immortal Soul. The former assumption – the mortal one - encourages you to strive, protect, cling, and if need be, panic if anything – no less death – challenges the welfare of that revered profile of yours. Meanwhile the latter conviction – regarding your immortality - continues to whisper "Trust" and "Be Not Afraid" even if the body is imperiled.

What Was That - Again?

You – the reader - may now be saying to yourself: "I got it, I understand, it makes sense." But others may be shaking their heads – wondering: "What did I just read? This stuff violates all my childhood beliefs. I think I need to hear that again – broken down into bite-size chewables."

Those of you who choose to join the first group, those who believe in the durability of your immortal Soul, now have the option to read on and obtain a full explanation of this basic message – or skip the rest of this chapter and move on immediately to Chapter 4.

As to the puzzled, the doubters, the head-scratchers and potential nay-sayers – you definitely are urged to read through to the end of this chapter. The fuller explanations that follow will either resolve some of your questions and doubts, challenge you to the very core, and/or invite you to affirm your highest potential. Either way, it probably would be best to read on.

The Immortal Soul

You, the real you, the 'essence' you, that immortal ball of energy that continues to create or incarnate as one material person after another - is actually a divine particle in the cosmic being called Prime Source or God.

You are not eternal for you were conceived by God – yes, God – eons ago, created to be His/Her/It's (remember: God cannot be confined by gender) agent and – together with all your colleagues - bring spiritual values to every corner of our ever-expanding cosmos. So little 'you', little ole mortal you with a name and birth date and all sorts of earthly agendas and involvements, is also a manifestation of big or everlasting 'You – the immortal Soul'. At your core, your deepest and more profound level – you are a godlike being who has been empowered to incarnate in the physical plane in order to learn how to love unconditionally and thereby spread God's spirit upon the Earth.

And there you thought you were just the V.P for Eastern Sales, or the mother of those three beautiful children, or the best mechanic or seamstress in the county. Or perhaps you were thinking you did not amount to much - assuming you were not making much of a contribution or having an impact on anyone or thing. Haw! No, no, no – there is a lot more going on – within and around you – lots more. And lo and behold you are not only an integral part of it: you are a dynamic center fulfilling the most wondrous, earth-shattering adventure possible.

Awakening

With this reminder, with this re-affirmation of the immortality of your Soul, with the ensuing awareness that everyone you have and will ever meet is also an immortal Soul, with the understanding that we Souls all rotate onto Earth in order to complete a mission related to the themes of love and enlightenment - with all these truisms you may have heard about but never fully absorbed or affirmed before – with it all comes an opportunity to attain a fuller awakening.

Suddenly everything you have ever heard, and intuited and experienced – begins to make sense. It all fits. This life, your sense of life 'before and after' this particular incarnation, the reason for your current existence, your faint recollections of distant memories, the knowledge of having been in similar situations before (but where and when?), the instant attractions or repulsions you feel to some people and events, as well as all fleeting images that bleed through (from past lives) but which you try to ignore or dismiss because they do not fit into some mundane definition of who you are – all of it begins to fall into place.

There is an explanation for all of it, namely the cycles of continuous re-incarnation you have experienced as many different people facing many different situations - all of them having taken place before you chose your current face, interests, placement and challenges.

The immortality of the Soul holds the key. It unlocks all the doors. Zow, Holy Mackerel and "Oh My Goodness" – as my grandmother used to say. It – our shared soulfulness - is the key that unlocks all doors. The recognition of your spiritual identity may have been stirring in you for years. But you have denied it, sloughed it off – perhaps fearful of embracing such an empowering enormity for fear of being audacious or presumptuous.

Transformations in Process

Such a muffled or delayed affirmation is understandable. When you decide to incarnate, you agree to forget who you really are; if not, completing your human assignments would be a cakewalk if you were instantly aware of your true identity. So - like all good Souls – you and I have agreed to long bouts of temporary amnesia during our stays on Earth.

We maintain an inkling of our spiritual roots, however, and continue to search for meaning – on our own or with a religious group, participating in rituals that honor Life, God and the unseen, even turning instinctively to prayer and meditation in times of need and confusion. The Soul's amnesia when coupled with human free will, however, makes living on Earth a genuine challenge. In the course of a lifetime, we may alternate between cultivating our spiritual impulses and neglecting them. We may – through reflection and meditation - recall inklings of our true identity and even uncover the contents of the learning agreements, or we might not. That is the human dilemma, and that is why reaching clarity at some juncture as to who we really are is so significant. The Soul seeks recognition. Without it - we instinctively know - we risk negating the promise of a lifetime.

When we awaken to our spiritual reality, however, we discover that the rewards of the Earth are to be earned by and through our human embodiments. Although guided – if requested by our inner Soul - the all-too-human aspect of our being continues to face all the challenges and temptations that govern the physical arena. The spiritualization of the Earth apparently was intended by God to be earned - and earned after a substantial slog by each individual personality during each successive incarnation, through one generation after another.

The development of the human race itself has indeed been a substantial and long slog but not without substantial signs of progress. Through human effort and growing sensitivity, the Earth has been transformed, with each generation of human change agents building on the progress of their ancestors, each deepening and extending their individual skills as they deepen and extend the spiritual transformation of the Earth. Look at the progress the series of human civilizations have made – especially considering the fact that spiritual or eternal time envelops our centuries as if they were virtual seconds. In the physical realm, for example, consider the difference between the harsh world of the hominoid "Lucy' 2.7

million years ago in comparison to the conditions we face as the latest reflections of the species Homo Sapiens. Over the millennia, tools were made, the body evolved and learned to walk erect, and hunting and foraging communities were formed. It was only 200,000 years ago that the Neanderthals – sensing another realm - were inspired to bury their death, and today we are blessed with – among many others - the sophisticated rituals and moral philosophies of Christianity, Judaism, Islam and Buddhism.

As to our current realities,[11] despite the continued emergence of war, greed, mass murder, holocausts and gulags, we have also come a long way: endemic religious wars, Inquisitions, the incessant witch hunts and discriminations practiced against woman and non-whites, and centuries of judgmental theocracies have been substantially minimized and even neutralized by the spread of democracies, a greater sense of tolerance, and the growing moral indignation of public opinion and world leaders.

Political bodies, aid agencies, courts and codes of justice, as well as the more enlightened individual states and international bodies, have also increasingly condemned the kinds of heinous crimes that were once lauded or simply accepted. War and avarice have not disappeared and the world has in just this century suffered through the disasters of Stalin, Hitler and Mao. But unlike the days of Genghis Khan, Attila the Hun, the conquistadors in the Americas, and the colonists of Asia and Africa world opinion has increasingly voiced its mortal indignation over such atrocities, intervened to mitigate the worse offenses and taken action to stave off and prevent such catastrophes in the future.

And unlike any time in human history, the international community has sent massive amounts of aid to those harmed by war and natural disasters. Given the rise of the telephone, then television and now electronic communications, what were once local tragedies – like

---

11 For example, see Steven Pinker, *The Better Angels of Our Nature: Why Violence Has Declined* (New York: Viking, 2011) for an historical analysis of how the emergence of nation-states, the influence of state and local governments, the rise in moral standards and the general patterns of society have had civilizing effects and brought about the decline in deaths from war, murder and cruelty. Also see Strobe Talbott's *The Great Experiment* (New York: Simon & Shuster, 2008) for a summary of the historical growth of communal, regional and international communities and how they have aided and abetted the sharing of resources, and the attainment of nuclear control, disarmament, negotiated peace settlements and the proactive resolution of pending conflicts.

Katrina, the tsunami in Indonesia, the earthquake in Japan and the drought in Somalia - are now not only known throughout the world but responded to with an outpouring of individual prayers and contributions, and enormous amounts of assistance provided by nation states and numerous international communities.

And never before has there been such organizations as Doctors Without Borders, a truly international Red Cross, and a Habitat, Audubon and Greenpeace fighting for the preservation of wildlife and the environment. And look at the number of organizations like Care and the Salvation Army that now serve such groups as children, the homeless, veterans, the poor and the displaced. And then there's the advent of numerous action groups fighting activities and policies that damage the environment and the communities of international scientists investigating such dangers as global warming and the depletion of the ozone layer. Greedy, ignorant, insensitive, egotistical, aggressive and warlike individuals, organizations and national leaders still exist, of course, but increasingly their actions are being blocked and their harmful impact minimized by the force of world opinion and both national and international policy.

The Spiritual Process

And look at the consequences of our individual spiritual awakening. It is synonymous with becoming aware that we are decision makers, creators of our own reality. As humans, we have been endowed with capacity to choose. We don't just inherit or instantly unwrap a finished lifetime. We explore and discover. Our process is not automatic or pre-determined but evolutionary and creative. Now that is magnificent - not just as an outcome but also as a process. It makes all of us co-creators in the continual unfolding of the universe. Each of us is intended to awaken over time to a sufficient understanding of our individual spiritual identity, and the desire to fulfil a spiritual mission that makes a contribution to something much larger than our own immediate welfare. Such cumulative upgrades in our individual sensitivities are then - sooner or later - transmitted to and reflected in the intentions and actions of our community organizations, nations and international agencies.

And perhaps most important: God uses what we create in our individual lives and communities as inputs to Her continual re-creating of the Kosmos. God intends and transforms as we intend and transform. So when we affirm our identity and use our empowerments to spiritualize what is in front of us each day, we produce the data needed by God to elevate and amalgamate the material and spiritual realms. Our intentions and subsequent actions help to enhance the spiritual evolution of our planet and in so doing support the process of bringing more and more of heaven to the Earth.

The Consequences

As the process of mutual transformation proceeds, our everyday concerns become significant only in so far as they relate to recognizing and affirming our basic identity. We begin to see everything as an opportunity to express our spiritual essence – namely, to learn how to love, become compassionate, and adopt attitudes and actions that help others and add to the world's welfare.

The immortality of the Soul also means we have plenty of time to get it right: we have had and will continue to have multiple lives or incarnations to make and perfect our contributions, infinite opportunities to bring God's essence of love and compassion into material form. Having multiple incarnations to attain our goals and develop our spirituality is not an excuse to relax. Rather it is an encouragement to do the task in front of us, not to rush it but do it 'right'. So this lifetime, and every lifetime of every Soul, is very important indeed. The universe is not complete and neither are we. We are responsible only for seizing on the opportunities offered to us now.

Our Contributions

As immortal Souls, why do we willingly create and assume a successive series of material forms, working to increase our own spirituality as well as the people and situations we encounter en route? There are three principal reasons.

One, so we can – slowly but surely - learn how to become whole, more like the totally loving God that created us as immortal Souls. We learn to emulate the fullness of God's love (since God and Love are synonymous) by living each successive incarnation with greater depth of empathy and compassion. We, as immortal Souls or 'cells' in the universal body of Spirit, thereby earn the right – with each incarnation - to become healthier, more whole, more loving, more Godlike.

Two, by learning how to love more thoroughly - by learning to create love in every conceivable situation that might arise in everyday, material reality - we become healthier beings, increasingly able to contribute to the overall 'health' of the Totality. In the physical body, for example, a few 'bad' cells can weaken a particular organ or bone and jeopardize the entire organism. It is the same with the spiritual organism: as cells in that Kosmic Body, our intentions and behaviors have the power to contribute to or undercut the operative health of the Totality.

Three, by seizing on the continual opportunity to become more loving with each incarnation, we become more effective agents of the loving God who created us. By activating our capacity to convert our experiences and life circumstances into loving situations, we become increasingly able to help God fulfil His/Her/It's intention to spiritualize the entire universe.

Soul by Soul, incarnation by incarnation, situation by situation, cell by cell, opportunity by opportunity, piece by piece - each of us has multiple options to contribute to the ongoing spiritualization of the whole shebang.

Zow: is this a lot or what? But *this is who we are*: immortal Souls. *This is how things work* – as immortal Souls we provide a direct connection between the spiritual realm and our everyday material realities. We *help to spiritualize the universe* as we use our human incarnations to handle our everyday challenges and opportunities with love, compassion and creativity.

The Process of Incarnation

Let's say a few more words about the central process of incarnation. A full chapter on the subject will follow later in the book.

As a Soul - prior to your taking on and residing in your current body – you, like any Pure Spirit, lived on "the Other Side", the eternal residence of God or Prime Source, the same realm to which you will return whenever you decide to surrender the body you are now using to express your current life themes and goals.

The process is otherworldly but very simple. Every once in a while, you like every other Soul, decide to take the ferry – via the process of re-incarnation (or re-embodiment) – from "the Other Side" to someplace like the Earth. You choose a body-type and select the outline of a lifestyle, and are then birthed into a setting of your own choosing where you then set about the task of fulfilling your 'learning agreement'. That agreement, drawn up by you while still on "the Other Side", contains the general outline of the talents you bring to Earth, the life situations and challenges you will face, and the things you want to learn while here.

As the outline of your life in the physical realm unfolds, you will also face many temptations to forget the terms of your agreement and treat your time in the physical world as an opportunity to do little but seek what glitters. Temptations – big and little – to over-extend your ego will always arise; it is of the nature of the polarized physical world (male-female, forgive-revenge, me-other, hot-cold and so on).

So why do any of us decide to return to such a complex world filled with mixed, difficult agendas, especially if life as a purely spiritual being on *'the Other Side'* is comparatively comfy? There are no mortgages to worry about in the realm of Pure Spirit, or romantic difficulties to resolve, or chest colds and broken bones to cure? And instead of nosey neighbors or dysfunctional families and overbearing organizations, the untrammeled Soul on "the Other Side" has the option to schmooze when it wants - that is, when not enthralled by the heavenly choirs and the wisdom of the Angels. Given all this, why would any Soul want to go back to working on a set of challenges in a comparatively alien environment? We know the schlep - to and on the Earth - is at best a mixed bag. Yet we go anyway. Why?

Incarnate – Again?

Well – all God's creatures, all God's Souls, all of us, are, as noted, integral aspects of Divinity and the Spiritual Reality. We simply are not intended, wherever we dwell, to sit around and eat either spiritual Twinkies or material Bon Bons. Wherever we are – on the side of Pure Spirit or on this material side – we always know we have some work to do, work that will enable us to become more like God, become more effective agents of spiritual change and thus healthier cells in the total organism of God.

Of course, there are also challenges on 'the Other Side' in also converting the norms love and creativity into living realities. But the heavier lift, the work of applying those ideals to 'everyday' realities is on this material side. The overall purpose of Life is to insure the Kosmos becomes a more loving place for its many inhabitants and life forms. Thus the material and the spiritual are intertwined, the realms of Pure Spirit and material reality are two complementary aspect of the same universe. You/I/we - all Souls – in both our spiritual and material capacities - are the agents of that unity. Incarnation – whereby the Soul assumes a physical presence – is the spiritual process that enables the Earth and any material realm to be sanctified. At the moment, the Earth – or our everyday physical reality – is the specific material place we have chosen to learn how to be whole and develop our capacity for empathy and understanding.

Although immortal, you and I – as Souls - are not complete. We are of God but we are not God – meaning we still have a lot to learn about being compassionate and creative – especially in the everyday activities of the physical realm. The best way to deepen one's capacity to cultivate such a divine impulse is to face the daily (if not minute by minute) challenge of living by those standards in a land known for its enticements to do otherwise.

As you know, incarnating on Earth is no easy assignment, yet we have chosen it as the arena for working through the general outlines of our life scripts. Surely generation after generation has done so feeling confident it can accomplish its mission while here. As the title says: "Trust Your Immortal Soul." The sub-titles might be: "Stop Hesitating and Doubting Yourself", and "You Are Doing Exactly What You Chose to Do".

Got it? It sounds complicated but it is really very simple. The process of re-incarnation explains everything. And it puts responsibility where it should be: on each of us. We wanted it, we are living it, and we are creating or attracting all the challenges we need in order to learn the lessons we want to learn. We Souls were created to think and act big. And we assume responsibility for attaining goals that are higher and deeper than our human egos can fully realize on their own.

Alas, however well we're doing in our current embodiment on Earth, we need periodically to fortify ourselves by affirming the immortal status of our Souls. As Souls we never die. We always live to choose another lifetime – whether it is to study and learn in the spiritual universe or apply and learn in the material one. Either way, we are hard-wired to seek experiences that will deepen and extend our capacity to love and create and understand, and thereby become more like our divine sponsor.

CHAPTER 4
DEALING WITH THE CONSEQUENCES

Every writer on spiritual themes refers to *the Soul*. Yet few seem to take it seriously or seek to understand its profound implications on everyday life. Your health, the incredible functioning of your brain, the continual pumping of your heart, the presence of your family, your job and career, and even your capacity to delight in your favorite foods – all exist, all function, all are possible because of the presence and significance of your Soul.

This is the central reality of life: each of us: you, me, everyone – is an immortal Soul. We don't have a Soul. We are a Soul. Contrary to popular assumptions, therefore, we are not just human beings who may or may not choose to have a spiritual experience while on Earth. We are spiritual beings who have chosen to incarnate on Earth in order to have a material or earthly experience. And although we may surrender our human bodies after a lifetime on Earth, our Soul always lives on.

Shedding our outer material costume does not affect our core identity. Our temporary identity, these wondrous but temporary conglomerations of tissue and nerves we call our bodies, are, of course, mortal. But our core identity is that of an immortal Soul – which always lives on – forever.

It – your Soul and mine – is the entity that chooses to incarnate in bodily form, and it is the entity that decides to let the embodiment go when it has served its purpose. It, the Soul, is forever. You and I are immortal Souls. That is the basic truism of life. Everything else is merely an extension of this startling reality.

Our daily life takes on a new dimension when viewed from this spiritual perspective. Suddenly all the events, all the feelings, all the triumphs and disappointments, all the trials and tribulations, hopes and dreams – must be viewed in the context of the Soul creating and attracting people, events and experiences that help it fulfil its learning contract. We each started in the realm of Pure Spirit – and will return there after living the kind of material life we chose for our physical reality of Earth.

Hint: this is no Heaven or Hell. There is a period of reckoning upon death of the body - after an incarnation has been terminated - when the Soul undergoes a life review and re-experiences both the compassionate and the unloving moments and incidents it created in the last incarnation. But the purpose of the review is not to punish our Soul but to help it to realize the impact of its earthly decisions and learn from them. It is then in a better position to calibrate its goals more finely in the next learning cycle or incarnation. More on this process later.

The Soul Chooses

We choose the *general outlines* of life before we incarnate. We choose and attract all the *specifics* of life once we live in the incarnated state. Then we choose and attract - on a minute-by-minute, day-by-day basis - the *particulars* that enable us to attain, neglect or undercut our intended mission. And, of course, we choose when we wish to surrender the body and end a particular embodiment on Earth. We choose it all and we are each responsible for it all. There is no good or bad luck, no coincidences, no tragedies, and certainly no 'he or she - or God - made me do it'.

1. We choose and attract it all, in order to learn potentially from it all. The specific learning objectives of any given embodiment will vary greatly from Soul to Soul, dependent on the progress made in earlier incarnations. But they all revolve around three basic themes: learning to love more deeply and extensively, achieving a greater depth of awareness and understanding (regarding the essence of Divinity and

the divine nature of the universe), and using our creative empowerments to contribute to the evolution of the Kosmos.

2. The means to these major ends also become learning objectives. They can include such processes as taking responsibility, living in the now, learning how to pray and meditate, becoming increasingly emphatic, exploring innovative options, attending to the needs of others, fostering good will, serving the welfare of the greater community, learning how to be a unique individual yet doing so within community, becoming a person of integrity in the face of challenges presented by individuals and groups, propagating a spiritual perspective, and in so many and varied ways – celebrating Life by living one's particular life with dedicated sense of peace, joy and thanksgiving.

3. The themes and dramas of our incarnated lives thus reflect the choices we, as Souls, made regarding our placement, life circumstances and the type of person we wished to be. All the things we now take for granted – our personalities and our life experiences – have a spiritual purpose that are directly related to the learning objectives we choose before coming through the birth channel. Our everyday lives are nothing but opportunities to complete the spiritual adventure that we designed.

4. Consciously or unconsciously, we choose and attract circumstances that confront us and challenge both the terms of our mission and the ways we chose to attain them. Once incarnated, God and the devil are indeed in the details – and we can act on our good intentions or allow them to dissolve in the face of difficulty. This is how obstacles and why challenges to our deepest preferences often become the means to our personal growth and development.

5. As immortal Souls, we are each an aspect of God. We are likened to cells in a Total Organism that is of kosmic proportions. All of our earthly experiences are significant for they are used by God to adjust, transform and continuously create our ever-expanding universe or Kosmos. As immortal Souls, as cells in the kosmic and universal Body of Prime Source, we are co-creators of God's continuous creation.

6. When we have completed the work outlined for a given incarnation in the material realm, we surrender our bodies and transit back to the realm of Pure Spirit. Our progress is reviewed and evaluated, after which we resume our studies and prepare to choose - when the 'time' is right - still one more incarnation, one that serves both the needs of our individual Soul as well as the loving intent and creative preferences of Prime Source.

That's the whole story. Read on for all the particulars, learning more about your core identity as a Soul, and figuring out how well you're handling your current assignment.

SECTION TWO

Soul Identity

CHAPTER 5

THE SPIRITUAL EXPERIENCE

Everyday Inklings and Invitations

Ever notice…that every once in a while…you get an inkling of another existence, another realm, a different or enhanced identity.

A word…a setting…an experience - triggers the memory of something otherworldly. It appears suddenly and leaves just as quickly: glimpses or intuitions of something beyond the ordinary - so powerful that they are difficult to forget.

But you often feel you must forget such inklings because there is no way 'it' or 'they' make sense. You reason that such sudden glimpses of and into another extraordinary universe are silly, extraneous 'whatevers' that popped up from the recesses of your mind, or reflected something you read in a book, heard on TV or dreamt after eating too much and too late.

Yet you keep recalling how the experiences surprised if not startled you. And they evoked memories of related experiences – all of them partial, unexplainable, out of the ordinary. There was the time, for example, when you sensed a hidden curtain had opened and you were able to peek into another universe. Then, as suddenly, the scene was gone and the curtain closed. There was also that recurring image and the 'answer' you received from 'that voice' that penetrated the noise of the crowd. And there is that feeling you often get along your spine and in your hands – a sudden pulsation of intense energy that seemed as if an angelic being was at you side.

Gradually you realize that although you've dismissed or rationalized each individual experience as 'strange' and 'out of this world', each encounter stirred a deepening resonance. Finally you allow yourself to accept the reality that each of these varied entrees evokes a linkage to another realm. Taken together they definitely have a cumulative effect – convincing you that something very significant and *real* is going on.

- ❖ There was that time when you imagined yourself in very different clothing, from a different time, in a setting that seemed to come right out of a movie.

- ❖ On another occasion, for a millisecond, you saw those imaged people walking toward you and then fusing with you - as if we were aspects of the same person.

- ❖ Then there was the time the word 'intergalactic' stirred your long held interest in the star Arcturus and the constellation of Cassiopeia - and somehow you 'knew' you had been to both.

- ❖ And, oh yes – that recurrent glimpse of a particular dream, the one in which you sense yourself flying - the radiant blue Earth on the horizon growing larger and larger as your Soul returns to your sleeping body.

Such experiences accumulate, and you know you can no longer dishonor them. They are parts of your experience: intimations of another realm, commentaries on a larger and deeper universe, revelations of an extra-ordinary and purely spiritual dimension. And you read, and converse with friends, and slowly begin to put the pieces together, realizing it is entirely possible that a world beyond the ordinary does indeed exist and that your current persona needs to be viewed within a much larger context.

Despite your daily preoccupation with your Earthly identity, you begin to grapple with the notion that the roots of your identity are multiple, maybe even intergalactic. You may exist on several levels – past and present. Your Soul has and continues to assume many faces. Your partnership with God and the Kosmos feels multi-faceted, multi-colored and utterly fantastic.

Overwhelmed, you might weep…or your body sakes. Can it be? Your mind is swirling - dazzled by the open-ended implications. "Ah: slow down," you say. "I'd best go easy, maintain stability, invoke a clear-headed rationality." So you slowly resume regular breathing - yet you are still unsteady, you stumble, stopping again and again to scratch your head and stretch your shoulders. You bath your face in cold water…and sit still for a while…until you feel grounded…again…and yet now emboldened to give thanks for the growing realization of who you *really* are.

So you reflect and think - and perhaps even write something like this in your Journal.

"It took be a long time to accept the reality that is being revealed to me in various ways and circumstances. At first, I resisted the glimpses that emerged during my reveries, my meditations, my extraordinary experiences, and my flights of controlled fancy. I even refused to abide by the cumulative invitations I received from a host of experiential encounters, and all the intuitive insights I gleaned from follow-up reading and meditation."

"Why the resistance? Is it the fear of being ridiculed? Is it ignorance or am I too busy to consider anything that might disturb the habitual or predictable patterns of my life? Did I really want to consider why I – and apparently many others - had these experiences, felt these impulses? Am I ready to consider the possibility of changing my perspective, of redoing and enlarging - if not revolutionizing - my concept of who I am and why I am here?"

Personal Acceptance

Here is a bit of my personal journey – clues as to how I began to answer these questions and collect and collate the bits and pieces that led to my writing this book.

I was born, as most, into a family that had a religious tradition. The Sturners – my father's side of the family – were not only Roman Catholic, they were numerous, and, like the religion they espoused, were much more insistent and determined than my Methodist mother. My brother and I thus were raised in the Catholic family tradition – a close kit group of fun loving people whose love of life, work ethic and the Catholic faith were solidified by the strong Irish roots of my paternal grandmother (Dublin) and the French-Germanic background of my paternal grandfather (Alsace-Lorraine).

So any newborn obviously had to bear the forename of someone already in the family. My mother was willing to go along with most rules but all of them. She insisted on naming my bother 'Robert' with his second name of 'Joseph' - which the family quickly transformed into 'Bobby-Joe' in deference to my father and paternal grandfather. 'William' was fine because it was the name of an uncle (the youngest of my five uncles) but even it was further subsumed by family tradition when I was given the second name of 'Francis' and was called 'Billy-Frank' in deference to my godfather, 'Frank Sturner'.

The Early Years

Thinking back, I now realize that although I went to confession and Mass every week, my brother and parents tended to stay home. They encouraged my devotion, especially when my resolve slackened since I had obviously become, without realizing it, the designated family 'church-goer'. So aside from my mother's periodic Novenas (weekly church meetings for a particular devotional purpose), I had assumed the role of carrying the family name to the altar each week.

The system of organized religion fit me well for I was a solemn and insecure kid: I liked and was good at being steadfast and so participated rigorously in the mandatory rituals. Apparently it was my assigned role to 'be good' – at home, in school, and at church. So I regurgitated, on cue, the right phrase at the dinner table, the correct answer at school, and appropriate prayer while on bended knee.

Among my most vivid boyhood memories was the insufferable heat in the church during Mass – all year round. The church – an Italian Geographic Parish named 'Immaculate Conception' in the north-central Bronx - was always overheated and poorly ventilated, exacerbated in the winter months by the tradition (to save seating space, I guess) of keeping your heavy jacket on throughout Mass despite the packed house (we called it the 'Sunday Subway'). During the summer months, the dedication to heat and humidity was continued via the inexplicable need to keep the windows tightly shut.

Despite the 'weather' and the interminable sermons, I followed the Mass with my own daily missal. If I was going to do something, I concluded, I might as well do it right – an attitude I brought to every aspect of life. Part of my diligence, I now realize, was to compensate for my parents comparative neglect of Sunday Mass and my brother's cavalier approach to both it and school; he already was 'somebody' – an acclaimed baseball player and acknowledged hero to the neighborhood. Me? I still had to try harder, be smart, stay on the straight and narrow. It was my perceived niche.

Although both religious and brainy, I never really grasped the essence of what was going on every Sunday from 10-11:00 o'clock. I loved listening to the literally 'little, old Italian women' sing in their high-pitched voices, as they arrayed themselves along the altar railing, veiled and all shrouded in black. Now that was the 'old' days when the priest had his back to the congregation most of the time, so even when you could hear him it was in Latin or what we referred to as "Lumbo-jumbo".

The rest of the time in Church was consumed by long-winded admonitions to live by one rule or another and repeated appeals for more money. It was and still is amazing to me that I - and the entire congregation - did not at such times cry out or at least walk out. As if by design, decorum was saved and attention replenished in the nick of time by the ringing of the altar bells. The anticipation and appearance of the Eucharist muffled any smoldering discontent and converted inner exasperation and outer stupor into memorized acts of piety and devotion.

Opening Up

As a function of age and growing curiosity, my willingness to accept rote learning, compliance and obedience were gradually supplemented by questions, reading and explorations. The more I studied, the more questions I asked, the more I realized that I was ensconced in an echo chamber in which search and discovery were limited by Papal proclamations and the opinions of Cardinal Spellman, the then very conservative steward of New York Catholics. By the time I was in college, my doubts and protestations had gone beyond crossing my fingers while taking a pledge not to see the film, 'Blue Moon'. I did not reject my religion or my practice but I started to pull away. It may not sound very dramatic now but it certainly felt that way at the time: I started to skip confession every Saturday and even occasionally missed the prescribed Sunday Mass.

In graduate school, I studied – among other things - constitutional law, and knew enough to boldly and publicly oppose the Cardinal's call for aid to parochial education. That quickly led to my being severely censured and condemned by my colleagues in the Solidarity, a Catholic action group that literally urged and expected me to follow every whim of the Cardinal – and thereby surrender my capacity to think in the process. Censured, I left the group the next week. I am not sure who was more relieved.

I saw Enrico Fellini's film, 8 ½, soon thereafter and it had a profound effect on me; Marcello Mastroianni stove to make sense of his life – first within the rules and latticing of the Church and then - "Oh my God": outside of its structures (despite the threat of eternal damnation). Confusion reigned: he was unable to make any decisions regarding his marriage, his religion or the film he was directing. He lapsed into reverie, and in reliving earlier scenes from his life, became a delightful, risking-taking and decisive child again. Suddenly everything changed: life became meaningful – even joyful.

The story ends with all the main characters of his life – he as a little boy and as an adult, his mother, wife and lovers, the circus clown, even the members of his movie crew – joining hands to dance merrily around a center ring to the joyful tune of circus music. Life, that is, Mastroianni's life, suddenly made sense, especially when understood with an attitude of thanksgiving and celebration. Wow! What joy. What freedom. What openness to life's natural unfolding and varied experience! Be not afraid. Embrace everything. Ahhh! Marcello's journey was soon to become my story as well. This was the early sixties. I was approximately 26-27.

Once my fear of and acquiescence to external constraints to real inquiry was set aside, I turned my attention to the more positive dimensions of my spiritual identity. I had been releasing 'the outer shackles' of prescription and habit. Now I was about to reclaim responsibility for creating my own fate.

But I did not know what to do next. After all those years of rules and structures, I did not know what or how to affirm the personhood I yearned to discover and express. By letting go of the old persona, I had become a blur. I was now relatively free but unformed and greatly undernourished both emotionally and spiritually. My love of rituals continued but now it took the form of informal prayers while walking in the woods or meditating by a stream. Most important, I longed to be guided by a loving God, not the judgmental one I listened to and feared during my childhood, teens and early adulthood.

Exploration and Discovery

Following the lead of Ira Progroff, [12] I began to write about my feelings and experiences. Soon I was creating and compiling my first journal - which served to legitimize my growing experience of myself as a spiritual being, not strapped to a theoretical God but internally linked to 'the Other' as a process and a living presence.

Around the same time, a copy of Carl Rogers' little pamphlet, "A Therapist's View of Personal Goals" [13]- was given to me by my then girlfriend, Lisa Flynn (Lisa: where are you, what happened to you? I want to thank you again and again for this piece by Rogers. I still have it!). That booklet was a turning point for me. At first, I read it with hesitation. Then I read it again and again – and it opened door after

---

12 Ira Progroff, *At a Journal Workshop* (New York: Jeremy Tarcher, 1977).
13 Carl R. Rogers, *On Becoming A Person* (New York: Houghton Mifflin, 1961), Chapter 9.

door. My searches led to discoveries, which in term led to affirmations. Inwardly, I even began to hear a faint and loving roar.

Rogers encourages the reader to seek and fulfil his/her own sense of being unlimited. The invitation to be a potentiality – rather than a fixed point on someone else's predetermined plan - was startling news. I could unfold, become, evolve – and in monitoring the journey, discover who I was and where and what I wanted to do. Here finally was someone who not only told me that I could become a multi-faceted person but who also encouraged me to affirm versus fear my own development. Suddenly, both my head and my heart were sending the same message: I had the right – a God-given right – to jettison everyone else's admonitions and definitions and, instead, embrace a path 'I' chose, one that reflected my needs, my talents, my values, my images of potential.

It took a year or more for all of this to sink in and take hold. But by then I knew I was able to cut my own path up and into what I once considered an unassailable mountain. And the new plateau had a vista that was grand and alluring. With each step, the authoritarian codes and restrictions of others gave way. What had once been a clearly defined and repetitive path going around the base of the mountain was becoming a jagged but joyful one – one that had some lilt in it as it gradually began to ascend. I was now exploring and discovering and opening up, rather than repeating and following and closing down. I was becoming my own decision-maker.

So I considered the Episcopalians and Reform Judaism. Both were still decidedly 'religious' and filled with their own sets of rules – but each was also intriguing simply because they were new. For a while, the beliefs and practices of the Buddhists and the Unitarians also intrigued me for they seemed more spiritual versus religious in nature, were more broadly defined and more loving in mood and more receptive to personal add-ons. Yet all of them were still systems - not on the scale of Roman Catholicism's detailed structures but still filled with predetermined scaffolding.

So I still yearned to discover or construct something that lay between the heavy structuring of my past and that lost and disorientated feeling that frequently accompanied my new mode of experimentation. I continued exploring but was still on guard - warning myself repeatedly not to adopt someone else's mooring simply because I was spiritually lonely. Learning how to straddle the abyss between alleged security and creating my own amalgam was a dilemma I struggled with on a daily basis - that is until I slowly but finally internalized the insights of Rogers and put all my energies into learning how to trust in myself. Finally, I felt free to both shed and search simultaneously, and even began to enjoy my freedom to just be, taking to heart Manuel Machado's marvelous advice: "Pilgrim, there are no roads. Roads are made by walking."[14]

The books on values clarification published in the sixties, and the conferences inspired by the work of Carl Rogers and Virginia Satir (such as the American Association for Humanistic Psychology) in the seventies put me in touch with other explorers. Zen and the Christian mystics were soon on my radar screen - alluring because they emphasized the immediacy of experience and cultivation of one's inner life.

Then years of training in Gestalt psychology – with its accent on completing unfinished business, and enacting one's images versus endlessly analyzing them – helped free me from the smoldering anger I felt toward the Church and my regret at having lived so long with its imprints and limitations. Regular sessions with Gestalt therapists also encouraged me to fill the gap by trusting in my own promptings, intuitions and experience.

Shortly thereafter, in the late 1970's, I was exposed to the work of Roberto Assagioli [15] and 'Psychosynthesis' and I knew a new world was at hand. 'You are not a solemn child, or a creature of the Church, or determined in any way,' was his message. "You are a center of pure self-consciousness."

---

14 *Antologia Poetica* [Poetic Anthology], (Madrid: The Editorial Alliance, 2007); and *Des Dichas de la Fortuna* [The Words of Fortune], (Madrid: Espasa Calpe, 1991).
15 Roberto Assagioli, M.D., *The Act of the Will* (New York: Viking Press, 1973); and *Psychosynthesis* (New York: Viking Press, 1976).

Affirmation Time

The capacity to affirm my Soul and assert my existence as an immortal Soul, was not far behind. The Existentialists – especially Kierkegaard – solidified my growing confidence in my desire to choose my own life. The writings and presentations of Joseph Campbell, the famed mythologist, introduced me to the archetype of spirituality and the inner search for spiritual identity as expressed in the great myths of all traditions. And Carl Jung[16] provided me with the framework for exploring the connection between the ego - and its persona - and the 'Self' and its many and diverse images of the archetypal center we call "God".

I was en route to returning home – back to God again – but this time via a route borne of my inner needs and experiences, my own growing integrity, and my emerging sense of discovering and even nurturing a 'center' that was opened-ended, experiential and still under development. God was no longer 'The Almighty' – but referentially referred to as 'The Essence', 'The Center', 'The Self', and 'The Loving and Affirming God'. And He or She was no longer out there, to be possibly accessed only through sets of intermediary priests, doctrines and sacraments. He or She could - and was now encountered – in here, directly, through a series of interior, intuitive and meditative experiences.

Next came Jane Roberts[17] who spoke not of the codes and rituals of structured religion but of a universal creative energy. In her recorded conversations with the angelic Seth, she reiterated the convictions of the mystics: each of us is an integral facet of God or the Kosmic Spirit; each of us is an immortal Soul empowered to create our own spiritual experience.

---

16   C.G. Jung's autobiography, *Memories, Dreams, Reflections* (New York: Vintage, 1965) is still the best introduction to his work.
17   See in particular, Jane Roberts, *Seth Speaks* (New York: Penguin, 1974).

THE SPIRITUAL EXPERIENCE 55

Lorenzo di Credi, *The Annunciation*, c. 1480-85
Symbol of an archetypal calling - to affirm our spiritual identity,
make our next contribution and fulfill our intended mission.

The cumulative impact of all these experiences was now clear to me: there was and is no one answer for everyone, no one book or revered master, no one doctrine or way of life that fits all. Three cheers for the Catholics – and all the other religious institutions - who find in their systems what they consider historically true and worth passing on as deposited knowledge to each successive generation. It had become clear to me, however, that the glory of any spiritual perspective was not be gained by mouthing a hand-me-down set of beliefs that were exulted because it was deemed valid by one's ancestors. I was now learning to trust the integrity of what I had uncovered personally - based on the revolutionary awareness of my own experience, vitality and integrity.

If we were all children or particles of Prime Source, then we each possess the power to create a life that is personally meaningful to us. Others may choose different points on the spectrum. As long as they all revered and practiced Universal Love, then they - although different in the particulars - are all of one kind. It now seemed obvious to me that there were many, many, many paths up, around and into the mountain.

Finally, I was able to differentiate, edit - and then affirm as desired. Each successive discovery seemed to reveal at least a bit of a spiritual truth. And, most importantly, I realized that if I followed only that which was imprinted at birth, which I was taught to accept and honor as my mandated inheritance, which I had perpetuated simply because it was prepackaged and convenient, then there was a good chance I would wander - not up to the heights and into the depths of the mountain - but thoughtlessly, habitually and sluggishly in the same groove. Granted: that same marked trail, if embraced not out of convenience or fear but expanded, customized or adapted to accommodate one's own needs and discoveries, could also meet the test of integrity. That - I realized - was the key: whatever is created by the sweat and toil of one's own investigations, that honors the integrity of one's own needs and experiences, was to be honored and embraced - even though it was not evident to well meaning parents, self-serving moralists and those who were officially ordained.

The routing of one's spiritual growth and development was not to be imposed - on an adult no less a child - for it emerged and was consciously constructed cumulatively over a lifetime. New invitations to explore and discover one's spiritual calling arrived with each new stage and circumstance of life - each new experience creating an opening for and receptivity to the next, and the next, and the next insight, expansion and point of depth. The spiritual journey is like a treasure hunt: one clue leads to the next, each resonance building on the other. Some never go in search for they are told at birth that there was no need. Some seek treasures but stay within the original confines. Others branch out and cross into areas formerly considered 'forbidden', thereby uncovering all sorts of treasures – none of which ever become available to those who, very early on, mapped what they assumed (and perhaps secretly hoped) was the final frontier.

Some seekers do initiate spiritual journeys but only short ones over only familiar territory. Others – with great intentions but too many mundane commitments - quickly grow weary. Still others rise from their couches only as long at it takes them to find a lawn chair or hammock. Many, however, push on in both spurts and long explorations – always following the fresh breeze, always sensing there are new and more glorious vistas just beyond the horizon.

A Total Experience

As the years unfolded, each exposure to a new idea, each deepening of my experience, each beckoning to explore even further - filled me with excitement. Given words would jump off the page, images would compel me to draw, and intuitions would inevitably lead to the computer where the keyboard and resident Muse would inspire the next paragraph.

Occasionally a given insight would literally jolt me. A particularly powerful 'awareness' would also be accompanied by a felt infusion of energy. At times, in response to something I read or in the midst of prayer or meditation, tears would flow, or my head would literally rock.

I might be inspired to dance. Sometimes I would walk around as if in a daze. Frequently, my head, neck and shoulders would quake. And sometimes my entire body would shake, head to toe – often uncontrollably. Whatever I received or generated a particularly powerful thought, image, intuition, whatever – I was simultaneously prompted to express it outwardly in some tactile action or response. My senses thus confirmed the inner significance of the awareness and instantly baptized it by name: tears might flow, I would occasionally fall and lie prostrate on the ground, then rise in thanksgiving to hold my arms aloft in a figure Y, dance spontaneously, and then just sit on the carpet for a long while in silence – my body in a constant 'hum'.

Something significant clearly was happening - but I could not explain the experience or crystallize the insight; something was being registered but specific understanding often escaped me. I definitely was in a new territory. I was not scared but often I was puzzled, elated, surprised – overwhelmed even, and very, very grateful.

So I continued to follow the clues, the openings and the invitations. Spirituality became the dominant theme of my desired learning – in the books I read and the workshops I offered and the conferences I attended. My focus became not religion but spiritual practice, spiritual psychology and the spiritual traditions that produced them. So I read Plato's dialog, *Phaedo* dealing with the immortality of the soul, the Gnostic Gospels, the books of Alan Watts on Zen, Dominic Crossan's works on Jesus, many of the writings of Alfred North Whitehead, the books by Elaine Pagels and everything ever written by Joseph Campbell. And, of course, I underlined the words of the mystics of every tradition. [18]

---

18   Benjamin Jowett [Trs.], *The Four Socratic Dialogues of Plato* (Oxford: Clarendon Press, 1949). Elaine Pagels has written a series of illuminating texts, including *The Gnostic Gospels* (New York: Random, 1979); *Adam, Eve and the Serpent* (New York: Random, 1988); and *The Gnostic Paul* (Harrisburg, PA: Trinity Press International, 1975). Also see Marvin Meyer (Translator), *The Secret Teachings of Jesus* (New York: Random, 1984); and John Dominic Crossan, *Jesus: A Revolutionary Biography* (San Francisco: Harper, 1993).

For Joseph Campbell, see his *Transformations of Myth Through Time* (New York: Harper & Row, 1990); *The Inner Reaches of Outer Space* (New York: Alfred Van Der March Editions, 1986); his four volume series on *The Masks of God* (New York: Viking, 1959-1964); and *The Power of Myth* [with Bill Moyers] (New York: Doubleday, 1984).

I chatted with friends and various spiritual channels about both the identifiable and the unseen forces that formed and affected their daily lives. I organized and offered tens of workshops on psychological and spiritual development. I wrote several books on my insights and experiences. And through prayer, meditation and monitoring my day and night dreams – I was able to transform clusters of insights and glimpses into an ever deeper trail of awareness and understanding.

Support Group

Then there was the counsel I received periodically from:

- my many readings with my dear friend and mentor, Linda Ward, a master of astrology, numerology and the Kabbulah; [19]

- the wondrous and continuous advice I received from Archangel Gabriel as he speaks to the world through the medium Karen Cook; [20]

- the experiential insights of Rudolf Steiner, the German mystic and seer whose life and work stimulated the movement known as Anthroposophy (the knowledge of the spiritual nature of humankind);

- the clear evidence provided by psychologist Michael Newton, whose interviews of people at the Soul level - here and on 'the Other Side' – have been summarized in his two epoch making books; [21]

As to the process philosophy of Alfred North Whitehead, see his *Adventures of Ideas* (New York Free Press, 1967); *Process and Reality* (New York, Free Press, 1978); *Modes of Thought* (New York: Macmillan, 1938); and *Religion in the Making* (New York: Macmillan, 1926).

The readings on the mystics included Richard Woods [Editor], *Understanding Mysticism* (New York: Image, 1980); Alan Watts, *The Way of Zen* (New York: The New American Library, 1957); Helena Blavatsky, *The Secret Doctrine* (London: The Theosophical Publishing Society, 1897); Thomas Merton, *Mystics and Zen Masters* (New York, Noonday Press, 1961); and G. de Purucker, *The Esoteric Tradition*, Two Vols. (Pasadena, CA: Theosophical University Press, 1935).

19   Kabalistic Life Planning Services, Linda-Ward, klpslindaward@gmail.com
20   The channeled messages of *Archangel Gabriel* by Karen Cook: www. benukcook@gmail.com
21   *Journey of Souls* (St. Paul, MN: Llewellyn Publications, 2001); and *Destiny of Souls* (St. Paul, MN: Llewellyn Publications, 2002).

- the writings of Eckhart Tolle, Gary Zukav, Fritjof Capra, Thomas Merton, the Transcendentalists like Emerson, and The Course on Miracles;

- the encouragement of the thousands of inspired participants who offered so much during and after my workshops on "The Spiritual Journey" - presented annually for some twenty years at the one, only and 'original' Creative Problem Solving Institute of Buffalo, New York. [22]

In other words, I gradually discovered that I - like you – am, in the words of Archangel Gabriel, "a spiritual being having an earthly experience". We can't say that often enough. This 'lifetime' is actually a wondrous expedition in which each of us has allegedly 'gone fishing' for meaning and earthly significance - never realizing that we're already sitting on the wondrous whale known as 'the immortal Soul'.

---

22 See the author's *Mystic in the Marketplace* (Buffalo, NY: Creative Education Foundation Press, 1994) for the details of the perspective, design and music used during these three-four hour workshops.

CHAPTER 6

ACCEPTING THE CHALLENGE

It is not easy being a Soul ensconced in a human body. The difficulties of the earthly incarnation are many. In fact, the life of the incarnated Soul is one of continuous challenge; the average lifeline consisting of tests and periodic adaptations that involve and deeply affect the body, mind and Soul.

Such challenges – and their related opportunities for spiritual awareness – are evident at every stage of development, the impulse to mature physically and mentally being matched at each turn with a related urge - and capacity - to develop and express a nagging awareness of spiritual consciousness. The tension between the incarnate's mental, emotional and bodily needs and constructs, and its spiritual impulses, is not unlike E.T. loving of his life on Earth yet also yearning to return home.

Combining the material and spiritual also raises issues of competition: the desire to explore, be creative, to honor the deep and loving instincts of the Soul, are all periodically neutralized if not blocked by the at times misguided intentions of others – parents, teachers and the ministerial class – who in devotion to their roles want to protect each child, student and parishioner by imposing on them their personal set of do's and don'ts. When carried too far, such deliberate molding encourages – if not demands - the incarnate to follow and obey versus explore and discover.

The Influence of Others

From the day of our birth, our parents try to guide us by teaching us what to avoid and what to embrace. Don't climb on the table! Don't put your hand near the fire! Look both ways in crossing the street! Always remember to wash your hands! Love him: he's your brother! Pay attention at school: to get ahead, you must get good grades!

Such advice is invariably motivated by love and the result is usually protective and nurturing. But if those good intentions become 'pushy', continuous and authoritative, if they extend into overly influencing a young person's mate, college, career, religion and perspective, then they teach the child – and evolving young person - how to respond to external forces versus helping him/her to do what is most essential: develop one's inner life, trust in one's inquisitive and creative instincts, respond to one's inner yearnings and interests, customize one's own development and, in the process, learn how to approach the world with reverence, compassion and a desire for inclusiveness.

External authority often has an agenda, and although couched in the lingo of 'advice', it can encourage the child – and a young adult and even the adult – to seek that which allegedly guarantees safety and security at the expense of service, making a contribution and taking responsibility for creating one's own life. If overemphasized - which is often the case in capitalistic societies in which external success, getting ahead, making money, buying frenzies and surrounding oneself with 'stuff' – the admonitions of external authority can out-compete, if not suppress, the need for the individual Soul to respond to deeper inner needs and cultivate universal values.

The older the child, the greater the possibility of being exposed to the multiple options championed by diverse groups and other cultures – especially in this age of travel, relocation, television, computers and electronic communications. But the physical and psychological desires of youth – on average - hardly tilt them in the direction of seeking and experiencing the deeper dimensions of the spirit. Being 'number one', graduation, finding a job, pursuing a career, dealing with dating-mating-marriage-and parenting priorities, and managing the finances needed to make all that possible, can easily become the major concerns of the human persona from the teens to the thirties and forties – and even beyond. When in pursuit of success in the external domain, the deeper issues of spirituality, love, compassion and trusting one's inner impulses and images can easily be ignored or overwhelmed by family, peer group and societal pressures and the assumption that 'success' is best attained through popularity, professional success and amassing large sums of money as fast as you can.

Some parental, familial and environmental values even denigrate the essentials of a Soulful life. "We don't associate with people who…." "Your father would appreciate it if you followed in his footsteps and also become a…." And "you must remember to do X, avoid Y, and never think of doing Z" – admonitions which can destroy independent judgment, service, creativity and following one's inner counsel and light.

In just a few years, the baton of authority is shared with teachers and schools, religion and ministries - and later with diverse communities and professions. Each component of the socialization process brings the newcomer closer and closer to attaining acceptance and measured growth within the established frameworks: *following in another's footsteps* and *being successful* are too often encouraged, whereas creativity and challenging the status quo tend not to be raised at all.

Society's representatives are everywhere and none too shy – raising the danger that each new apprentice will be more prone to adopt each successive set of values and behaviors presented to them rather than seek to develop their own capacity to discover who they are and where and how the wish to thrive.

Applying Maslow's Hierarchy

Granted, most of these repetitive cycles of 'assistance' can intend – in the immediate context – to be loving, protective and useful. The recipient, however, the one on whom this cumulative coaching is heaped, also tends to follow Maslow's hierarchy - naturally seeking values and related activities that first insure survival, then safety and then belongingness. Once those needs are taken care of, the average person then seeks to meet their needs for self-esteem, then self-actualization and finally self-transcendence.[23]

If overbearing and manipulative, external authority can exploit the fears and concerns of those still mesmerized by the needs of the lower half of Maslow's hierarchy. Rather than opening new vistas, encouraging independence and exalting spiritual values as ways of proceeding up the hierarchy, many individuals and organizations – familial, economic, political, social and religious – exploit our natural desires to attain survival, safety and belongingness, and thus do whatever they can to insure that we always feel at least a little vulnerable, unprotected and like an outsider – no matter what we have achieved.

As means to those ends, such individuals and organizations can deliberately perpetuate dependence and subsistence living, punish those who challenge the status quo, impose detailed structures, encourage group-think, always provide definite answers versus motivating clues; prescribe methods and set strict boundaries versus explorations and creative problem solving; insist on following orders versus trusting in group process; and prefer building on the status quo versus stimulating creativity and innovation.

It is no wonder that lectures and courses on "Leadership" are so popular: each generation loves to talk 'Leadership' to counterbalance how much time and effort it actually spends on instilling 'followship'. Never having experienced being the creators and thus leaders of one's fate, it is no wonder many people surrender to the early and easy grooves, become docile note-takers and eventually proclaim their 'armchair leadership' of alleged adventures. By the time the average young citizen is ready to be out on their own, many have been armed with more admonitions than empowerments, and encouraged to fulfil roles that denigrate their

---

23   Abraham H. Maslow, *Motivation and Personality* (New York: Harper & Row, 1954); and *Religions, Values and Peak Experiences* (New York: Viking, 1970).

creativity, minimize their decision-making powers, ignore their inner life and dismiss any intention to contribute to something larger than themselves.

If we are indeed immortal Souls, then we have incarnated on Earth with needs and impulses that go far beyond someone else's sense of what we are supposed to know and do. These deeper imperatives include cultivating a sense of love for self and others; a belief in the integrity and spiritual empowerment of every person; and a celebration of each person's capacity to know - and act on – whatever serves their spiritual desires and inclinations.

The Journey

Even if you and I know, or at least concede, that we have incarnated here on Earth many times before, we know as well that we agreed each time to temporarily set aside our full awareness, live fully within the limited embodiment and sustain only an inkling of our identity as immortal Souls. This also means we surrender our power to recall what we have experienced and learned during prior incarnations. If not – as noted earlier – dealing with the challenges of the material realm and learning the lessons of the current incarnation would be a walk in the park.

During incarnation, however, we humans do manage to maintain our instinctive desire to honor Spirit and harbor some sense at least of our spiritual identity – witness humankind's unbroken history of founding one religious and spiritual tradition after another. As to actually experiencing our true identity and having easy access to God, that is most intense in early childhood - when the memory of our spiritual essence is still vivid, and in the later stages of life - when memory of one's original home is in the process of being reactivated.

Depending on one's development, however, many people are still able to display marked spiritual empowerments at any age and stage of life, and most have a mystical encounter and experience several bleed-throughs from "the Other Side" in the course of a lifetime (although not many are willing to admit it - out of confusion, humility or fear of ridicule).

What's a Soul to Do?

In terms of eternity, any given incarnation for 20-40-80 or more years is but a wink. In earthly terms, however, if can often seem like an eternity - especially during difficult times. Life as an incarnate can be experienced as overcoming one obstacle after another – during which we only vaguely remember the promptings of our Soul essence. Thus we constantly face the challenge of putting the pieces together in some meaningful pattern as we attempt to overcome our temporary amnesia. It takes a lot of determination, cultivation (through affirmation, prayer, meditation and contemplation) and trusting in our glimpses of 'the Other Side' to regain that vital sense of having and being a spiritual center. Rather than learn how to do 'it' (love, service, compassion, prayer, etc.), we usually find it is easier to simply learn something about such spiritual methods, and then get on with our earthly tasks and challenges.

People read about Gandhi all the time but how many of us are able – within the short time-span allotted – to emulate his spiritual approach to life. That does make the rest of us 'bad'. It does suggest, however, that many more of us know about and admire him (or Yeshua, Mary, Nelson Mandela and the many sacred figures of every religion, culture and historical period) but far fewer are able to activate their spiritual core fast or fully enough to think and behave like them. Many of us do so in part - and in many significant ways - but lack full engagement. Most of us seem to live most of the time fully immersed in material reality, flirting intermittently with our true sense of self – and even then it can take a pending catastrophe to get us that far.

Yet glimmers of our true identity do periodically reassert themselves. It is during these best of times that we are openly motivated to seek God, cultivate His/Her presence and guidance, and commit to a lifestyle of love and compassion. Thank goodness such inklings of our spiritual identity do bleed through on occasion - in our dreams, perhaps during walks in nature, at the cry of the newborn, while gazing at the stars, during prayer and mediation, in a thousand and one ways that reconnect the embodied Soul to its origins and destiny.

We even invent imitations of that reality to console us - like the umpteen spiritual philosophies and religious practices that have always dotted the human landscape, and our tendency to project our own sparks of divinity onto the best among us and thereby enshrine them as surrogates for Prime Source. Yeshua, Sophia, Athena and Zarathustra are thus elevated to the status of 'God' – versus being the enlightened Souls they were able to become.

So we struggle, and we experience ups and downs – personally, professionally and spiritually. We grope and wander, sometimes failing to rise to the occasion as instinctually desired, and at other times, choosing deliberately to convey true empathy and attain a deep understanding of the spiritual nature of the universe. Either way, we experience the difficulties and the joys of integrating our human psyche with our divine Soul – learning as best we can how to honor ourselves and love others under very trying conditions.

Obviously, we need to develop our human egos if we are to establish our individuality and complete our earthly missions. But we also run the risk of allowing the ego - with its many plans, roles and achievements - to become overly developed and then bloated. If so, the ego is tempted to out-shine and out-compete other egos. It is at such times that it (you and I) begins to project its power needs and sense of divinity onto an external and judgmental God, while simultaneously projecting its own shadow (our unwanted and perceived 'negative' traits) onto both others and an imaged external and wicked Devil. If so, the Soul's inner light or awareness is blocked. One's dark or 'shadow' side is denied and thus gains control precisely because it not acknowledged. Such an imbalance - obeying the dictates of an over-extended ego and ignoring the counsel of the Soul - can invite a series of disappointments and difficulties.

Rekindling the Spark of Awareness

Remember the drawing of the toddler leaning over the crib of the newborn. S/he doesn't attempt to guide or advise the baby. It is the other way around. "Tell me," the child whispers to the newborn. "Tell me about God. I am beginning to forget."

And we do forget because the Soul gets immersed in - and acts through the ego and its coordination of our involvements with matter. But there is always the danger that this usually protective ego – coordinator of our mind, heart and body – begins to think its material role is paramount and exclusive – and thus runs the risk of becoming over extended. A bloated ego is capable of conjuring up exaggerated images of its own power and capacity to amass great material riches, which, of course, tends to muzzle if not obliterate the already faint whispers of our Soul.

Whenever the ego grows so successful in its pursuits, it not only begins to grasp and protect its earthly enrichments; it tends to seek more and more. If anything, the psyche works to attain balance. Thus a bloated ego will often attract enough failure and dislocation to evoke a new or enhanced receptivity to therapy, service, prayer, and the desire for spiritual community (including a religion).

As we re-member remnants of our origins or destiny, we begin to put things back in focus and rekindle our awareness of our real and abiding supra-identity. Over the long haul, most of us learn to do the work of integrating both sides: the material arena of the ego and the spiritual realm of the Soul. In fact, many go so far as to integrate both and even transform the physical through the intentions and wisdom of the Soul. The body and mind, the heart and the Soul can and do work together: the ways of the world are not denied but are recalibrated by our spiritual impulses. Ultimately, we realize the faint whispers from the Soul – as cultivated with prayer and meditation – can become a clear and consistent voice.

So let us not only accept but also joyfully honor the challenges that arise throughout our life situations. Remember: we chose those challenges so we could grow in awareness through them. The sweet - and the sour - are both filled with opportunities to learn and ascend in consciousness.

May we also listen to and abide by the counsel of those social leaders and spiritual elders who have proven they are wise and loving. But may we also - with each advance in our spiritual maturity - learn to resist the temptation to believe more in others than we do in our selves. It is also only right that we learn to honor the sacred nature of our own Souls and thus bow down to no one but Prime Source Itself. "Never give up your power," says Archangel Gabriel - [24] for we are integral parts of a loving God, immortal Souls here to learn how to integrate the human and the divine and thereby contribute to the continuing spiritualization of the Kosmos.

---

[24] 'Messages Channeleled' through Karen Cook, benukcook@gmail.com

CHAPTER 7

ON BEING FULLY ALIVE

Feel it? Sense it? Listen. Look around you. Over there. Just outside the window. And at your finger tips. Stop for a second and become aware of what you see, hear, sense.

Life: abundant, pulsating, renewing, ceaseless life. There is fecundity everywhere, by and within every being and thing. Every weed, tree, dog and human being is in the midst of churning, seeking, mating, combining, infusing, receiving, changing or giving birth to the new.

Clouds, rain, the mountain brook. The sap of life always unfolding, prompting the next seed, bud, bough, person.

If only we would shed the blinders – release the plugs – and notice the sway of the trees, the buoyancy of flowers, the emerging abundance of wild grasses and shrubs.

Ever notice the birds? They are always in movement: wings flutter, necks stretch, beaks peck, legs scratch, dig and bounce – instant by instant. So many colors, so many squawks, so much laughter and so many reflections of Life.

Mysterious yet ever so real – life unfolding, incessantly, its lingering footprints in the snow, the cuts in the bark, the sudden cracks in the seeds – there, see the punctures in the berries and the scrapings along the new shoots and barks of trees.

If only we would relinquish our stare - and notice what is actually unfolding in and along the ponds, the rivulets and the incoming tide: would that we could open wide with each gill, claw and howl; witness that dash of red, the white and blue tail; listen to the flap of long black wings;

actually notice the varied insects as they crawl, hop and nod; watch the swiveling eyes of the turtle as it's neck stretches - then quickly recedes.

If only we could detect the kaleidoscope called the core of a flower. If only we would look below the surface – ooze with foam, sway with rockweed, hang on like a barnacle.

If only we could see how the skin salutes the sun, the eye honors the moon, the mind observes the overlapping orbits, and the imagination distills the incessant birth of suns.

Bored? Try engaging the pulse of life unfolding, non-stop, 24-7 – everywhere. Enter the universe of becoming - whenever you wish – any and everywhere it is flowing - including its incessant pulsations along, around and within every particle of you.

All and Instantly

It is amazing to realize that you, an immortal Soul, are capable of participating in each of the following realities simultaneously.

One, be totally involved in this moment, here on Earth.

Two, be aware of the fact that you – like each of us - is an immortal Soul here to learn more about love and our own capacity for creative wholeness.

Three, be conscious of the intergalactic nature of our surroundings, that beyond our neighbourhood, nation and continent is an entire Earth, circled by a moon, both in orbit around a sun, an integral system which itself circulates on the rim of a galaxy which is only one of billions of galaxies in an ever expanding universe.

Four, be able to communicate – via the mind and the heart - with other Souls on Earth as well as those who have incarnated in other extra-terrestrial life forms.

Five, be able to experience other dimensions of reality, dimensions that are timeless yet instantly accessible, multiple yet immaterial, real yet beyond exact measurement.

And six, be capable of interacting - through intuition, prayer, meditation, contemplation and direct communication with the other facets of the One and the Kosmic: from people to animals, trees and flowers, insects and bacteria, and even Angels. Every aspect of the universe is an aspect of God and thus may be addressed as 'thou'. Everything is holy. Everything is part of the whole. None of 'It' is less than magnificent. None of 'It' is an impersonal 'it'. We are related to all of It because we an integral aspects of It.

In short, you, like us all, are endowed as a spiritual being, able to experience the Now, the Soul, other Souls in other forms and placements, any of the multiple dimensions, and Prime Source Herself. Such insights and empowerments are not self-executing while your Soul is embodied in the material world. But they can be activated through prayer, meditation and contemplation, and any time you choose intentions and actions that are caring, inclusive, empathetic or compassionate.

That, ladies and gentlemen, is our common birthright. Such is the reality – and potential glory - of being an immortal Soul.

It's Starting to Come Together

Consciousness = the awareness that you are a sentient or reflective Being who is aware of your thoughts, feelings, intuitions, needs and ability to act on the impulses and insights generated by those capacities. Thus you can hug her, thank him, reach out, invite, smile, be joyful, sad, apologize, give praise – and be aware of what you are doing and with what intention.

You can also focus on that tree, listen to that person, solve a problem by thinking about it, image the desired events of tomorrow, recall memories, feel the warmth of the sun, sense the presence of Spirit, taste the sweetness of that apple – and be aware of the fact that you are having each those experiences.

Spiritual Consciousness = being aware of:

1. Your impulse and capacity to express unconditional love,

2. Your identity as an immortal Soul, one who never dies although you shed the temporary body you have chosen once it has completed its assigned lifetime in the physical realm,

3. Your essence as an aspect of Divinity, a cell in the Kosmic Presence, and

4. Your embodiment now in a material person, placed somewhere on the planet Earth, facing the opportunities and challenges you – as a Soul - chose before incarnating.

Which Brings Us to An Important Question

What have you learned today that was a mystery yesterday, that is still winking at you, inviting you to affirm the deepest part of you, something you sense you have experienced before but which is still mysterious and difficult to explain so less share with others – a special inkling that keeps encouraging you to accept some new reality and go on a new adventure?

All and Everything

all the varied phenomena in the universe

reflect and resonate as the same reality

variations on the same storyline

pages in a divine testament

aspects of the Essence

the Ever-Present

Kosmic Soul

of God

CHAPTER 8

EVERYDAY AWARENESS

Aperture of the Eye

Your eyes have openings to the light that gives them the capacity to determine the width and depth of your sight. They have an aperture that allows you to place an object in your line of vision. The view of the chickadee, for example, is condensed and narrow, enabling it to focus best on what is immediately in front of it - and thus enhance its ability to see and feed on tiny seeds like fennel.

The owl has a wider range of sight. Sitting high in the branches of a tree, it can take in much more than the chickadee. It has a much wider angle of inclusion and sees much more than what is immediately in front of it. In one glance it can see the chickadee, the tree in which the chickadee has landed and a good part of the wooded area around the tree.

The eagle has an even wider view or aperture. From its perch on the hilltop it can see the chickadee, the tree, the observing owl, and a large part of the forest and the river running through the valley.

Then there are the enhanced views accessible to the human eye - aloft progressively in a single engine airplane, a transatlantic jet and then a spacecraft – each view enabling it to take in a wider context. With the aid of telescopic lenses, the human eye an also look back into time and see the light emitted by a distant galaxy millions of light years ago.

Each increase in aperture creates a wider and more inclusive stream of light. And each increment progressively available to the chickadee, the owl, the eagle and human beings - with all our enhancements - are able to penetrate deeper and farther. This leads us to the realization that the aperture of pure Spirit – with its infinite power to see and penetrate - is able to see everywhere and everything all at once, the entire expanse of Life from alpha to omega, including and beyond time and space.

The sighting capacity of God, and the spiritual hierarchy S/He created to administer the universe (such as the Archangels and Angels) is an all-inclusive scale called 'infinity'. And infinity is best imaged - not as a straight line with an implied past and future - but rather as an all-encompassing spiral. There are no endpoints to infinity or Divinity yet our image of the archetype of God is one of being – at one and same 'time' - the center, the totality of the spiral and its cutting edge. God, it would appear, is not only the creating source of the universe but also its continuous energizer and incessant seeker of an ever-widening and ever-deepening spiral. Prime Source thus is everywhere and is present in everything. And It is omniscient precisely because it is All-Seeing: its aperture is infinite.

Any part, aspect or spark of Divinity – such as our immortal Soul as a facet of The One – can, when true to its full empowerment, also see, understand or gain access to the divine lens. The aperture of the immortal Soul has the capacity to encompass all 360 degrees in all directions when mystically illuminated even while incarnated in the material world. Its divinely inspired vision can also encompass other dimensions as well. If regular human consciousness can play at and even master the chessboard, then it appears that it can cultivate its divine perspective and learn to master multi-dimensional chess as well. You and I – as aspects of the divine organism – also possess the powers of the divine aperture. When we activate that empowerment through prayer, meditation and contemplation we too can learn to envision everything on the kosmic chessboard simultaneously.

What we normally experience as mortal life unfolding sequentially, one minute at a time, from birth to death, from the vantage point of the human lens, can be transformed when we activate our divine empowerments and its extraordinary aperture. The spiritual perspective - with its infinite sight from its eternal mountaintop — has the potential to make everything accessible to it: the fennel, the chickadee, the tree, the forest, the hawk, the eagle, the planet, the solar system, the spiraling sets of lifetimes, the incarnations of all Souls - the entire past, present and unfolding nature of spiritual Reality, ad infinitum.

God can see all of eternity at a single glance precisely because Its aperture is infinite. Our earthly Avatars, saintly personalities and Ascended Masters - human beings who have led exemplary lives and thus attained full awareness of the ubiquitous presence of the God Force — have proved themselves capable of seeing through the divine lens in the course of their cumulative incarnations. Through their elevated and expanded states of consciousness, they were able to activate their Soul's capacity for enlightenment and transformed their initial, mortal and narrow view of the universe into the depth and breadth of the divine.

It is true of all of us. As we cultivate our Soul empowerments with love and thanksgiving, as we raise our awareness, as we shed the conditioning and illusions of our earthy limitations - we activate and manifest the gifts of our divine heritage. Like the mystics before us — we can ascend to the spiritual heights and depths. As enlightened Souls we are empowered – with each incarnation - to see and understand more and more of Everything. We attract experiences that enable us to learn how to love more fully and unconditionally and thus become more God-like. And slowly – and sometimes suddenly – we do enough and reach deep and high enough to realize who we really are: immortal Souls with infinite apertures.

Through awareness, affirmation and practice, we consciously reconnect to our Source, and appreciate the essence of *everything*, including who we are, why we are here, and what we can now achieve. There comes a mystic point where we are enabled to see glimpses of it All in a nutshell - when the reach of our spiritual aperture is revealed in the blink of a penetrating eye.

Notice the Difference

Notice

the difference

between saying "I Am"

and saying "I am a parent'

or "I'm an engineer"

Or identifying yourself

As anything in particular.

'I Am' is unadorned, unmodified. It is not a third party 'something else'. It is not a third person, or an add-on. The affirmation of 'I Am' is not an insignificant designation of some fleeting role. And it's not a temporary conduit - for just this moment or lifetime. It is the signal of immortality - affirming a sacred Soul, now embodied, spiritual at the core. It is Complete unto Itself yet is also a part of a Universal Being.

'I Am'

Is pure

It is Present

It is complete

It's of the Essence

It is the emergent Gestalt

It is Pure Self Consciousness

It is a whole one within the Universal ONE.

It is Me. It is you. It is EveryOne. It is true on this earthly side. It is equally true on 'the Other Side'. It affirms All of us as integral parts of the kosmic Whole. More than mere mortal, yet still micro within the macro. Right here and always: The Unlimited "I Am." Say it: "I Am". Once more with feeling: 'I Am'.

Image of Self

How do you see yourself?

Like the rest of us, you are probably - at given moments and on given days – feel less than fully confident, trusting and positive: annoyed at one thing or another, impatient now and then (especially when in a car), getting a bit discouraged when your best efforts have been blocked, feeling frustrated when your confidence is frayed by everyday realities. But if you treat earthy challenges as peripheral and of no lasting impact on your core identity, then the universe will cooperate in supporting your continuing development. If, however, you allow a set of negative outer experiences to diminish your sense of who you are, then you suppress your capacity to activate and realize your full potential.

There is a big difference between having a so-called negative experience (shit happens) and internalizing that event and your alleged less-than-perfect handling of it, versus becoming conscious of your so-called lapses, learning from them and then re-affirming your capacity as an immortal Soul for self-correction and growth through awareness.

In fact, it is a good idea to anchor your desire to let go of some nagging memories by using words and actions which actively demonstrate your decision to let them go and get on with life. It really is easy. Simply say the words 'let go' as you literally use your hands to sweep your body, arms and legs – as if you are swiping away some lint or dust. It does not totally erase the memory, of course, but it does put it in perspective, causes you to laugh, symbolizing the fact that you are no longer holding onto it.

Happiness

What makes you happy? What makes you smile? What triggers those wondrous feelings of appreciation? The responses vary person to person. But everybody's got something that makes them feel good. What are yours?

It not only helps to remind your Self of the things that make you happy. It helps even more to seek out those experiences, to put yourself in situations where you can be in the company of whatever or whoever pleases you. This is not the same as fantasizing about winning the lottery or meeting Mr. or Ms. 'Right'. If you are not happy now, no amount of money will make you feel happy or whole, and no fantasy person or event can transform you from being dour to being joyful.

Determining what is important to you, what brings you joy - involves more than satisfying the cyclical reoccurrence of a physical need or desire. What if you want to have sex, then after participating in sex, you feel good or at least satisfied – at least for a while. When you are hungry and then eat, that physiological desire is satisfied – as least until the next meal. Many things bring us happiness in and for the moment. But are there other kinds of experiences - of things, relationships and situations - that fulfil at a deeper level and sustain a sense of inner thanksgiving and joy.

Imagine you are the Creator of a magnificent universe filled with people, flowers, ice cream and joyful ways of connecting with nature, events and other people. Despite all the wondrous options you have created in this imaginary world, however, the recipients think only of what is allegedly missing at any given moment. They complain, they mope, they alternatively curse the day and the night and they either ignore or denigrate the gazillion options you presented them. Instead, they spend their time focusing on what was not available in the form and timetable desired by their fluctuating moods.

If you were the Creator, how would you feel if these were the kinds of reactions you received to the universe of infinite possibilities you had created? Sad, right? So how do you imagine God feels? Why not make yourself happy - and in the process, make God happy too – by seeking out the wondrous things and people that are available to you. And remember to begin and end with a note of thanks, for all the big and the little things - especially the ginormous gift of being alive.

Energy Exchange

Let's begin where we always begin: with our breathing.

Inhale...fully...now exhale and let go.

Inhale again – this time opening your hands and spreading your arms out in front of you. Slowly exhale, lower your arms ... and smile. Ahhhhhh! Isn't that wonderful? What else could you possibly want?

Ah: but there is more. Now add content to your life breath by imaging an energy or experience. Give it a name: just a one or few word label – like 'joy', 'insight', 'allowing', 'focus' or 'gratitude' – a something you wish to both receive and gift to others. Then deliberately choose to bring that energy to yourself. Bend your knees gently and extend your arms downward slightly as you inhale and *scoop* the desired energy up and into you as you slowly extend your arms upward to form the figure 'Y'.

Hold your breath gently for a few seconds, *absorb* the desired energy and allow it to cascade gently down your arms and into your body.

Then bend you knees slightly again as you lower you arms and extend them in front of you, *gifting* that same energy back to the universe.

Complete this simple exercise at least once a day, preferably in the morning to give the day a focus. If you think of it but cannot act it out immediately (because of your surroundings), then 'image' it: feel yourself *scooping* the desired energy as you inhale, extending your arms upward and *absorbing* that energy in for few seconds, and then *gifting* it back to the universe as you exhale fully. Choose three or four themes – like love and joy, healing, trust and gratitude or whatever is you need or want to affirm in life – *scooping, absorbing and gifting* each one in succession. The entire exercise might be completed in less than a minute.

Ideas that Could Make Me Squirm…or Celebrate

Living one's life fully – and thus spiritually - is not a matter of completing a series of designated chores in as short a time as possible and then watching your favorite program on TV. It is not a race up the hill, a contest to see who is King or Queen of the Mountain, or a way of proving who is Number One. Doing a lot, doing it quickly and proving you are better-taller-faster-smarter than someone else is not what the spiritual journey is all about.

Read the following statements to yourself and see how each one 'feels'. If you feel uneasy or resistant to any or all of them, if any of them makes your squirm or feel uncomfortable, then it may be an indication that you still have work to do (just like the rest of us!).

If, on the other hand, you agree with a given statement – then you may be one of those wondrous individuals who is "open to learn, grow and develop". Ready? Here are the cues:

- "I choose to experience life at my pace and on my own terms."

- "Everything is a learning experience."

- "There are no winners or losers – only people who allow themselves to integrate and learn from their experiences and those who resist such learning.'

- "I wish – at least over the long haul – to align my choices with my intentions, my actions with my words."

- "I can discern the general outline of my learning agreement or ministry (the one I completed while still on "the Other Side") by tracing the patterns in my life: both the challenges and the opportunities I attract."

- "If the theme of a given challenge has emerged time and again, then it is obvious I have not learned the intended lesson or how best to handle that situation. Until I do, I will continue to attract variations on the same theme."

- "If the intensity of an issue subsides or disappears then it may mean I am learning how to handle it more effectively. Thus it would help to retrace my steps, reflecting on what I intended and how I actually handled given situations."

- "I will live for as long as it takes for me to fulfil my learning objectives and my over-all mission in life."

If you want to dig a bit deeper, use a blank sheet of paper to note your responses in five areas.

One and two word responses are all that's needed - although you obviously can write as much as you want.

1. "I have learned a lot by responding to such challenges as…by…"

2. "I realize I've avoided or undercut such opportunities as…by…."

3. "There are arenas in which I still have some important work to do and contributions to make. They include…."

4. "I have responded creatively and effectively to a host of challenges (such as….) by doing such things as…."

5. "The following kinds of opportunities have emerged in my life again and again:…"

That Was Fun: Let's Do More

How do you react to the following statements? Accept, embrace, question, disagree?

- "I realize this lifetime is not a competition with or against myself or any one else. Rather it is an opportunity for me to learn the attitudes and actions needed to grow spiritually and fulfil my potential to create more love and express more gratitude."

- "I choose, and attract into my life, the challenges and opportunities that will help me to learn, grow and develop."

- "Life is not a race against others, and there are no comparative winners or losers. There are only those who do or do not wish to learn their lessons, expand their consciousness and deepen their capacity to love."

- "I sense I may not yet have learned everything I want to, in which case I will not hide from the next set of challenges but choose to learn from them."

- "En route, I will partner with others, listen to and commune with them, and encourage and assist them as best I can. In being of service, however, I cannot diminish or surrender my own values and empowerments, or deny my obligation to live my life according to my own lights and intentions."

- "I am responsible for my own growth and development. I am not here to please or placate another, feel guilty for not doing so, or serve another's needs if it involves disobeying my own inner voice."

- "*Learning my lessons* may not always be supported by or have a positive impact on others. In fact, learning such lessons as self-affirmation may present challenges for others. I will be mindful of such impacts and do what I can to assist others to learn with me during such encounters. But I will not take care of others at the sacrifice of my own development or do their work for them. I will nourish patience, assistance and understanding but never at the expense of my own integrity and sense of worth."

- "I am the writer, producer, director, the lead and supporting characters - as well as the lighting director, costume designer, curtain puller and 'reviewer' - of this drama called "My Life".

Giving Versus Mere Doing

"Its not how much you do, but how much love you put into the action," said Mother Teresa. Simple actions, undertaken with a loving intent, have a greater impact on you, others and the situation than anything done out of habit or sense of duty. Intention makes all the difference. And the most effective impact is the one motivated by love.

The person receiving a gift of any sort - a package, greeting or service of some kind – not only benefits from the formal contents that is received but is also affected by the way that something is presented. The impact of a small gift intended with love and joy is magnified a hundredfold just as a so-called 'big' gift is negated by indifference or resentment.

A meal always tastes better if it is prepared with Grandma's love versus Cousin Adrian's snarl. The car rides better if worked on by Good Old Larry rather than the guy with the clip on his shoulder. Even your computer responds better and faster to whiz kids from 'We Do Care' versus da guys from 'We're Smart. You're Dumb. Step Aside'.

The giver, of course, always shares in the graces created by his/her intention. What we create tends to circle on back to us – not immediately or necessarily from the same person. But like energy does inevitably boomerang on back to the sender - which makes giving with a loving intent the perennial winner in any cost-benefit analysis. With love, everyone gains. It epitomizes the ultimate in a meaningful and mutually beneficial bottom line.

Human and Divine Relations

Find warm and loving people, and you feel like you are at home – no matter where you are. When you greet another, it re-enacts Michelangelo's depiction of God's reaching out to receive Adam and giving birth to that relationship. When a person looks you in the eye, it is God honoring your presence. When you warmly extend your welcome to another, or say 'hello' with interest and earnest, it reflects the spiritual greeting of 'Namaste' - "I honor the divinity in you".

When you ask 'how are you today?' – and mean it - you show respect and concern. When you respond to such a greeting, not with a bland 'fine' or 'not bad' or 'okay' but with an affirmation such as 'wonderful,' 'joyful', 'grand' or 'outrageously blessed' – you express the celebration of your sacred Soul.

When you serve the other, it is akin to God serving you. As you smile, you become an expression of God's delight in openness and gratitude. With each extension of hospitality, you join in God's continuous creation of life. As you interact and share, you create and exchange the divine energies of trust and love. As you hug goodbye, you communicate unity and continuance. When you wave, you know the connection will recycle. When you let go, you create space for another face to appear in your window. When you allow your door to swing open, you invite divinity to reappear in the form d'jour.

Being Honest

Not every day is a good day spiritually. But the days in which everything goes smoothly may be among the worst – that is, if you are not instinctively prone to give thanks and live in that moment. If not, one's nonchalance can be seductive - inviting us to do little but float, snooze and become presumptuous – living in a state of semi-consciousness, not particularly alert to oneself or anyone or anything else.

On the other hand, it is the really tough days that are fraught with the greatest opportunities to develop our spiritual consciousness. Difficult days force us to be alert and choose deliberately – not something that compounds negativity - but a course of action that stops a downward cycle, puts difficulties into perspective, and jump-starts a more positive dynamic.

During difficult times, it is best to take a deep breath and let whatever it is – go with your exhalation. Ask yourself: 'does even my justifiable annoyance outweigh the larger imperative to react spiritually'? Or, being reflective, you ask: 'what difference will this passing difficulty make in three hours or three months'?

So it helps to keep as 'cool' as possible as soon as things get 'hot', thus enabling us to keep tabs on and honestly assess what happened, make amends if necessary (there's no statute of limitations on apologies or expressions of regret), realize how we would have preferred to handle the situation, and then recommit to applying the highest spiritual ideal in the future. The standard is not perfection but honesty and taking responsibility – high spiritual bars indeed.

As we take responsibility, we also learn to recommit; as we become more conscious, we sharpen our spiritual resolve; as we stop protecting our ego, we resume projecting the highest intentions of the Soul. Catching oneself, confronting oneself and forgiving oneself are acts of profound spirituality. Everyone – including us - deserves our honesty, our love and our compassion.

SECTION THREE

Spirituality

CHAPTER 9

WHAT IS SPIRITUALITY?

Hmmm: exactly what is Spirituality?

Obviously, the reactions vary widely. The conservative religionist may consider 'Spirituality' to be a watered-down if not distorted version of 'true religion'. Most, however, more properly associate Spirituality with an individualized way of being 'religious' without any overriding connection to a formal 'religion' or organization. One's spiritual beliefs and practices could include a loose affiliation with an organized religion and some of its rituals and observances. But most seem to be unaffiliated for their beliefs are more generic - consisting usually of a composite of values and activities based on one's personal experience rather than adherence to the more codified systems presented by organized religions.

Thus there are many variations on Spirituality – given its basis in individual choice. Most associate it with some aspect of the human potential movement: friendly people who embrace diversity, no longer practice their parents' traditional religion, trust more in their own experiences, and therefore create their own way of being 'religious' and honoring the Divine. Depending on the person, all sorts of religious beliefs, philosophical assumptions, and traditional, ancient and New Age insights may enter into one's religious practice.

Beyond the core belief in a loving God and honoring the immortality of the Soul – the particulars vary immensely from person to person. Spirituality is thus a huge if not kosmic tent with as many center rings as there are practitioners. It clearly affirms oneself as being 'religious' or 'spiritual' but does so by celebrating one's individualized approach – which may include some of the beliefs and practices of an organized religion or two but not adhering to any organizational codes or rituals simply because they are prescribed.

Looking for simplicity, flexibility and tolerance for individuality, many have come to embrace 'Spirituality' because it allows for personal choice, and a mixing and matching of a range of activities and perspectives. Like children meeting at the playground, they are drawn spontaneously to kindred spirits – in this case to those who share their reverence for life and are as loving, open and free flowing as themselves.

People who consider themselves to be Spiritual easily align in spirit with the mystics of every tradition; view the likes of Emerson, Gandhi, Mother Teresa and Martin Luther King as kinfolk; feel free to communicate with Moses, Yeshua, Buddha and Mohammed; bypass any alleged intermediaries by speaking directly with the ever-present Creator God; discover supportive Angels everywhere; treat the institutionalized ways of honoring God as potentially helpful but not mandatory; and place primary focus on living a life that is reverent, joyful, reflective and loving.

There are no codes, edicts, shoulds, hierarchy, intermediaries, regulations, prescribed rituals and ceremonies, judgment, sin or heresy, rites of induction or expulsion, heaven and hell, catechisms, the devil, governing board or councils, formalities, officialdom or assumed beginnings and endings – only love, God, creativity, free choice, service, community, self-esteem, wonder, thanksgiving and the urge to make contributions in the course of everyday living.

A Tentative Outline of Spirituality

Diversity by its very nature can create a centrifugal force that causes elements to lose gravitational pull and thus leave the orbit of the center. The key to Spirituality, however, is centripetal: it is centered in the belief of a Loving God – which of course will then attract related but varied add-on beliefs to it. No surprise here. This book summarizes the cluster of spiritual beliefs espoused by this author and many of my friends or kindred spirits. You may agree with some and not others. So be it. They are presented here as a point of departure, however, to encourage you to clarify the core and the extensions of your attraction to Spirituality and your way of honoring God.

- Spirituality affirms the primacy and practice of love and compassion.

- It views all of us as immortal Souls and cells in the Totality called God.

- It understands that each of us has chosen to incarnate to the physical realm as an opportunity to perfect our capacity to love and become more like God.

- It views Life as a dynamic and ongoing process in which our experiences are used by the Creative God Center as S/He continuously adjusts and recreates the Kosmos.

- Prayer, meditation and contemplation are effective ways of communicating with, and enlisting the guidance and support of God and the Angelic Hosts.

- Free will and free choice reigns throughout and for all.

- We choose, create and attract everything we experience. There are no accidents or coincidences. Each of us is totally responsible for everything that occurs to us.

- There are no predetermined or recommended rituals and ceremonies, no catechisms, no intermediaries, and no external controls or governing boards.

- The core of Spiritual beliefs and practices can be adapted to or mixed and matched with aspects of any traditional religion that serves the values and needs of the individual.

- Spirituality is centered in love but is open-ended and highly individualistic thereafter — and is thus adaptable to a wide variety of beliefs and practices.

- If a group affiliation does emerge, the core energy is still person-to-God, not person to an intermediary and certainly not individual or person to a group or organization.

- Being facets of God or Divinity, our Souls and thus our temporary incarnations in the material domain, are innately spiritual by nature. They are grounded in the individual impulse to love, honor, thank and emulate the Creator Spirit.

- Spirituality possesses ancient roots, is and has been universal, admits of all personal moorings and combinations, has open-ended boundaries, and is grounded consistently in compassion, creativity and understanding the spiritual nature of the Kosmos. It is and has always been the basis for the formalized and organized religions that have followed it. Its foundational nature, simplicity and inclusiveness, suggests it will soon overcome the parochial concerns and structures of its institutionalized offspring, and once again be honored as the world's foundational approach to the sacred.

The Spiritual Perspective

'A loving and reverent freedom' is a good way to summarize the spiritual perspective.

Conversely, here are some of the pieces of that mixed bag that Spirituality is not: 'We live but once, need to avoid being tempted into sin en route by an external devil, sponsor male superiority and dominance, believe in absolute truth of our own beliefs and practices, feel totally justified in attempting to convert others to adopt our faith, speak to God (exclusively or primarily) through an ordained clergy (preferably males, and exclusively male in some religions) who we believe have been ordained to set and control adherence to our prescribed set of beliefs and practices, and henceforth are either rewarded for our conformity by going to heaven or punished for our sinfulness by being assigned to purgatory or hell."

As noted, but bearing emphasis: spirituality intertwines very easily with the mystics of every religion; Plato and the Neo-Platonists like Plotinus; Emerson and the American Transcendental Movement; the lives of Gandhi and the Dali Lama; the findings of quantum physics; the writings of Gibran and Saint-Exupéry; the insights of Psychosynthesis and the inspirations of Roberto Assagioli; the remarkable explorations, discoveries and affirmations of C.G. Jung and Depth Psychology; the advocates of the primacy of love in every tradition; the Hindu philosophers of incarnation; the mindfulness of Zen Buddhism; and the many contributors to the Perennial Philosophy.

Many people have gradually given themselves permission to ignore or reject portions of the religion bequeathed to them at birth. Why? They learned that such conditioned responses were either too restrictive, irrational or simply no longer relevant. Many others cut ties to their childhood religion because they found their church's attitudes on marriage, sexuality, male dominance, restricted entrance into the clergy and certain social issues to be inconsistent with their sense of equality, fairness, justice and love.

One way or another, millions have chosen to exercise their freedom from institutionalized religion. In the course of minimizing their old religious allegiance or forsaking it entirely – they obviously did not instantly go to hell. In fact, the opposite happened: despite (inappropriately) feeling twinges of guilt and even regret after so many years of conditioning, they knew they had to move on – thereby affirming that their spiritual identity resided within and was not bequeathed by any group or institution. At last they were free to build on their innate spirituality, live according to their own individualized values and create their own amalgam of beliefs and practices.

These are the people who have or are in the process of building a new foundation, one built on free choice and relevance - mixing and matching the main tenets of Spirituality with selected aspects of the many organized religions and philosophies (including any of their many variations) if they served them well. Having assessed the spiritual landscape, honored their own emerging needs and understanding, and no longer feeling guilty or restricted, they have or are now in the midst of adopting an individualized collage of spiritual or 'religious' practices that honors what is true and helpful to them.

And they are finding what they hoped for: a third option – no longer accepting any institutional judgment that they are heretic, damned or pitied as 'having fallen-away'. And that 'third way' is increasingly a position of affirmation of oneself as a spiritual person, and a commitment to whatever mosaic one has formed through their experience. Assurance is embraced when people realize they do not need an external permission to honor God, the primacy of love and the innate goodness and immortality of every Soul – but can do so simply by affirming their innate spiritual identity. Not only is there no need to apologize for their individualized approach. Having created it, it's time to realize they have every right to celebrate it.

Not adhering strictly to the codes and practices of a particular religion does not mean a person is not 'religious'. In fact they may be more so because they have crystallized their own composite out of their own experience. In fact, 'religious' and 'spiritual' are really the same thing. The term 'religious' is so directly related to institutionalized religion, however, that the individualistic 'spiritual' people tend instead to affirm themselves as 'spiritual'.[25] Given the nature of their journey, they might best be referred to as folks who live a life of 'free, individualized and committed 'Spirituality'.

Having left their religion of birth, in part or totally, many initially feel alone, on their own, perhaps even an outsider simply because society – especially many traditionalists – tend to think of them as

---

25 It is interested to note that the American Heritage Dictionary's definition of 'religion' includes the following: "A *personal* or institutionalized system ground in belief and worship."
The same dictionary includes the following in its definition of 'spiritual': "of or belonging to a church or *religion*; sacred" – in short, *religious*.

being outside the pale: non-religious, blasphemous, heretical or living in sin. Admittedly, after depending on the boundaries, doctrines and routines of organized religion, a person can feel – in the absence of all that scaffolding - like they are spiritual orphans. But once one begins to accept, enjoy and then flourish in the absence of the old dictums and authorities, the general tenets of Spirituality begin to feel like what they are: a religious or honoring attitude and practice, not codified or even consistent but at heart reverent and spiritually committed (perhaps as never before). The only difference now is that one is spiritually empowered – not through a group – but through one's awareness and experience of their innate spiritual nature.

Now this does not mean that many people do not continue to flourish as members of a traditional religion – especially as many review and renew their faith during their adult years. If that fits their needs and understanding, more power to them. But it should be obvious that organized religion has never, and undoubtedly, will never occupy the entire field of religious or spiritual activity. Look at how many people practice a traditional religion only once in a while – and yet sustain their capacity to be 'religious' by being the best person they can be, believing intensively in an ever-present God, living according to the principle of love and reinforcing that foundation with a mosaic of supportive actions and rituals. The particulars of the individualized mosaic may vary from person to person. Yet if grounded in love of God and the Golden Rule, then one surely deserves to be celebrated as having personally forged one of the gazillion variations on the theme of reverent and loving Spirituality.

So if you – although unaffiliated or only a part-time practitioner of an organized religion – consider yourself to be spiritually oriented, then you are far from being 'nothing' in religious terms. If you believe in a Creator God and adhere to the principles of love and compassion, then you are indeed 'a wondrous Soul'. If you are spiritually attuned in belief and practice then you are already there! Add all or part of a formal religion if you want – but the essentials are already in place!

What is wonderful about the phenomenon that we shall call 'Free and Committed Spirituality' is that it welcomes all the individual and group variations on the themes of reverence for God and commitment to being a loving, contributing and creative person. If you live according to the commandments to love God[26] and practice the Golden Rule[27] – then you are automatically included within and under a huge, multi-colored canopy, the one with no side panels or revolving doors, the one that guarantees universal entry, inclusion, admiration, affirmation, celebration and loving appreciation - 24/7/52.[28]

Spirituality Explored

Spirituality, then, is not a religion with a set creed, code, sacraments, rituals and governance structures. It is moreover is not an organization and thus is not governed or controlled by any group or norm. It does not tell people *what to do* (content) but does provide guidance on *how to behave* (the process) – in this case from a loving perspective. And it does not recommend or require anyone do or become anything in particular. It only encourages all of us to become increasingly aware of *ourselves as immortal Souls,* our many gifts and empowerments, the universal invitation to contribute to others, and how much love we are capable of creating, sharing and receiving.

Moreover, the practice of Spirituality is not confined to any cultural tradition or geographic area. It is not synonymous with the ways of North America or Asia, this planet, *our* solar system or even this galaxy. It is as universal and ubiquitous as God Itself. It also includes the continual transit of incoming and then returning Souls - and the angelic beings that guide and escort them. It recognizes the divine consciousness innate

---

26 "'You shall love the Lord thy God with all your heart, with all your Soul, and all your mind'… And…'You shall love they neighbor as yourself.' On these two commandments hang all the law and the prophets." Matt. 22: 34-40.
27 A saying of Yeshua of inestimable ('golden') and universal importance, which is part of the 'Sermon on the Mount': "In everything, do unto others as you would have them do to you." (Matt. 7:12). Also see the 'Sermon on the Plain' (Luke 6:31).
28 Paul's summary of the centrality of honoring God and practicing love also serves as a fundamental point of departure. "If I speak in the tongues of mortals and of Angels, but do not have love, I am a noisy gong or a clanging cymbal." And the cadence continues: without love, nothing we do or say makes any sense or any difference. See 2 Corinthians, 13: 1-13.

in every person and enables each of us to access the multiple dimensions of the spiritual realm that exists 'within' and thus on 'the Other Side.'

Spirituality affirms 'godliness'. And the affirmation of God and expression of love form the précis to the Everything, the All, to God the Creator and the universal presence. The Archangels, the Angelic Hosts, the holy Avatars that continue to incarnate on Earth and throughout the universe, the Ascended Masters and you and I – are all of the same divine substance, extensions of each other, all reflective dots and varied levels of consciousness in the holographic, infinite and ever-expansive reality called Life.

I Am That I Am, and *I Will Be as I Will Be* (Ex. 3:14) - is the essence of Spirituality. We are each and all part and parcel of the All, the sacred IT, the Totality, God, Divine Love. The spiritual person is capable of experiencing the reality that each of us is a reflection and aspect of the divine, and thus a co-creator of the ceaseless unfolding of the entire Kosmos.

No secret hand sake - just an attitude of love, a belief in the immortal Soul, the direct experience of God, an acceptance of humankind's diverse ways of communicating with God, and a commitment to contribute what we each can, as often as we can.

Say That Again...

Spirituality is the perspective that understands we are first and foremost immortal Souls, and that our Earthly identities are simply incarnations of the Soul in bodily form. The 'I' with whom we usually identify is actually an immortal Soul having a planetary experience.

The Soul is the Big I as well as the Big or Third Eye that both guides and monitors the choices of the psychological ego (little I). It is you, the Soul, that chooses the physical you - your general body frame, emotional makeup, the way your mind operates, the challenges you have and will face, the ways you handle yourself as a distinct personality, your visions of your future, and now - your increasing awareness of your spiritual roots and Soulful identity.

By incarnating, you – the Soul - have taken on the trappings of your particular incarnate's mental, emotional and bodily formats. You have chosen to manifest yourself in a bodily form that serves as your material agent in the physical realm. Your role, as a Soul (during this and any past or future incarnation), is to infuse your divine impulses of love and creativity into your earthly interactions and thereby transform matter into Spiritual happenings and experiences.

An over or exclusive identification with the incarnated aspects of your Soul's physical expression (the material 'I', persona or ego), can undercut your ability to understand your pre-eminence as a Soul and your commitment to achieve a spiritual mission on Earth.

Even if you, as an incarnate, feel you have tended to over-identify with the ego – perhaps frequently yearning to be 'number one' or incessantly seeking one external achievement after another – you will, sooner or later, come to grips with the reality of your core identity as an immortal Soul, begin to heed its call and attend to the deeper spiritual realities that beckon to you.

As you must realize, there are points in life when the ego matures, stops its striving, becomes content in guiding the mental and material aspects of your incarnation, increasingly admits the primacy of your identity as a Soul, and begins to aid the Soul by supporting its focus on deeper, spiritual concerns. There is a world of difference, for example, between the ego's drive for sexual activity and the Soul's impulse to parent and nurture a family. Ever notice that most people will grin and become a little giddy at the slightest mention of sex but are reverent when they hear of a pregnancy and are downright awed and teary-eyed at the sight of a newborn. The former is the perspective of the ego; the later is that of the Soul.

The Process of Affirming the Soul

Slowly the ego is able to hear and heed the invitation of the Soul to relinquish its preoccupation with external achievement and the construction of an impregnable future. The Soul and its incarnation then begin to work in tandem; the attention of the Soul-filled incarnate is unified and begins to focus on living with compassion in the present. With age, maturity and experience, the old and predominant desires to attain 'something' are softened and broadened to include the intention to appreciate and honor the role and significance of literally everything.

The search for such things as 'protections' and 'increases' and 'achievements', and even the use of such words as 'ladders', 'success' and 'acceleration' - give way to living more in the now and attending to and appreciating *this and that* versus attaining *This and That*. There emerges a greater trust in the natural life process – versus seeking or wanting to obtain something that bolsters the ego and placates it with some material gain. Trusting in life – and your immortal Soul - usually activates a greater sense of immediacy, depth of knowing, patience and loving appreciation for whatever is. Any preoccupation with the body and its ego is also naturally and gradually diminished through the aging process. Slowly but surely we all come to realize that the transformation of the body is only decades – if not years - away.

The ego, having done its work admirably by giving direction and energy to getting the incarnate established in the world as a distinct and stable if not 'successful' individual, gradually learns to relinquish its leadership role and allows itself to respond to the prompting of the Soul. And lo and below, the mind and body are delighted with the new inputs and vistas and begin to anticipate graduating to a more loving and forgiving plateau. And it is not surprising – given the natural coordination of body, mind and spirit - that the point where we yearn to climb fewer mountains, we are simultaneously less and less able to do so physically.

As proportions change, tired muscles need firming and new spiritual ones need flexing. Our energy resources begin to realign. The signs are everywhere. The body begins to reflect the same changes being envisioned by the mind: priorities shift and we begin progressively to let go of the needs and priorities associated with earlier periods in life. Old agendas are released and energy is redirected to support new interests and capacities - sure signs that the work of the ego and its coordination of the body have begun to acknowledge the predominance of the Soul and bow to its priorities.

Of course, the changes in the body are indications of a reality that youth never considers, namely that it will not and is not intended to last forever. Realizing 'the fact' of our pending mortality has a way of encouraging us to re-evaluate what is really important and realign our vital interests accordingly. Both developments reflect the natural recalibration of the mind and the body, and their conceding pre-eminence to the Soul. The outer increasingly makes more room for the inner, and the past and future begin to give way to the present - indications the incarnate is becoming increasingly aware that it is now intended to serve the impulses of the Soul more fully.

Trading Body for Soul

The changes in tone and emphasis, however, do not occur without initial and considerable resistance. As children we can't wait to say we are seven when we are only six and a half. And seven and a half is much greater than seven - don't you know. And then to be eighteen or twenty-one; is there a greater joy! But turning thirty is too much of what used to be a good thing. And 'oh my gawd': turning forty is feared, and becoming fifty to many is like getting old. As to being sixty or seventy – forgetaboutit!

Look at Facebook. The youth champion their age. The folks in the middle are shy. The so-called 'aging' list only the month and date of their birth – apparently thinking that denial is now the best way of staving off the inevitable.

Of course we know we are kidding ourselves – and soon adopt the role of mentoring, a interim term for would-be contributors of acquired depth and knowledge. Eventually, retirement is not avoided by many but anticipated and embraced with great gusto: finally we will have time to do all the things we neglected when we pursued the diagonal path. Go to a play? Certainly. Go away for the weekend? Why not? Forget about the Jones? Who are they? Follow the footnote, read a book outside of my field, walk gently through the forest? Yes, yes, yes.

Relax, smell the flowers, give thanks? Of course: such are the natural fruits and inclinations of the retiree – who may or may not yet be in the process of conceding substantial influence to the Soul.

So the full admission of and blossoming of the Soul presents another – perhaps life's greatest – opportunity, one that encourages us to fully cultivate our soulfulness and honor our spirituality. Love becomes the dominant word and energy - for home, for grandchildren, for the new computer or book, for gardening, for contacting old friends, for sending spontaneous greetings and intending love to a stranger, to actually taking that long talked about visit to the sacred sites versus finding more ways to work longer hours to attain more titles and glory.

The focus shifts from achievement to developing an authentic lifestyle, to finding a synthesis that enables us to manifest our spiritual identity by contributing something meaningful and of direct communal value. Of course, all these reflections of the Soul are evident throughout every period of our lives – in the many contributions we make at work, in the home, in the community. But those earlier periods also contain an energy pattern that competes with the spirit; the healthy ego exists and is expected to establish a clear presence in the world even as the Soul is exerting its desire to spiritualize what the ego is creating.

Given the nature of the physical domain, the ego is weakest in infancy, begins to assert itself in childhood, is confused but adamant in puberty, and then is relied on as the young person weaves his/her way through the personal and professional challenges of adulthood. The Soul is obviously ever-present yet supports the increasingly assertive role the ego needs to play in attaining and sustaining the incarnate's sense of psychological and physical identity. The spiritual impulse seeks expression throughout life yet it slowly shifts dominance with that of the ego as the natural aging process unfolds. Of course the physical and the spiritual are joined throughout life and are always functions of each other, yet with time, the physical is increasingly reminded that it serves at the pleasure of the Soul and increasingly gives way as physical mortality looms.

And so with each passing year, the mentor-retirees go to more of their grandchildren's plays and ball games than they ever did for their children. They volunteer more, stop more often to greet a neighbor, even begin to enjoy walking along the shops versus racing through town in a new car. In short, the determination and vigor of youth for external achievement is gradually complemented and informed by the desire to just be as loving and appreciative as we can. They begin to express more fully that which may have been suppressed during their task-oriented youth, or for which they did not have the time as a busy adult. Spirals begin to replace straight-line projections. Well-rounded becomes a desired attribute of the mind, the spirit – and the body as well. We ease up, take inventory and make more room for the true Self.

Welding it all together, uniting everything we already are and are becoming, and giving it some final form during this incarnation - is spiritual work. Look at the wondrous contributors and combos: ego attainments and the spiritualizing influence of the Soul; the material or external manifestations and the inner inspirations of the soul; the special perspectives and vigor – the particular agendas and processes - of adolescence, youth, middle-age and aging; the continual birthing, building and the letting go experienced by the mind, body and spirit; the challenges and the pains associated with each developmental period; the cycles of letting in, letting go and the moving on; the work and insight needed in learning how to love oneself and as well as others; and the silliness, heartbreak and the joy of all of it – everything energized, extolled and celebrated under the canopy of what we here affirm as 'the spiritual impulse'.

CHAPTER 10

CULTIVATING OUR SPIRITUALITY

Declaring one's spirituality is one thing. Activating it and keeping it alive and well is quite another. Here are a number of suggestions on how you can cultivate your spirituality - as your core identity and as the perspective you bring to all of your encounters.

The Value of Play

There would seem to be no greater or effective way to participate in the essence of spirituality than to lose oneself in the moment of 'play' – the sheer joy of interacting with the world – whether it be with children, friends, or those you meet as you glide through the day.

Among the sounds of Spirit is laughter.

Among the signs of heaven is joy.

Among those who walk with God are the playful.

It is one of the reasons we like to be around children: they smile and laugh with such ease and gusto. They are capable of such intense involvement. The live in the eternal moment with each recurring smile, giggle and adventure.

Our All-Important Lens

The lens we wear determines what we see. It brings the outer world into focus. In a larger, figurative sense, our lens is our perspective, our point of view, our way of interacting with the world. What we 'see' or experience, and how we 'see' or experience it, mirrors our inner interests and values. We tend to notice extensions of who we already are. And, as an old Salada Tea tag line said: "What we see depends mainly on what we look for."

The issues, events and energies that attract our attention, and the way in which we then interpret those happenings, reflect our priorities and values as well as the structures of our mental, emotional and spiritual make-up. Our lens not only reveals who we already are and wish to be. It also selects what we wish to attend to and how we intend to experience it.

Perpetually sad people, for example, are obviously wearing *sad lenses*. Most may experience a given event as neutral or even positive but it will be another downer to anyone wearing sad lenses. Of course, we all encounter some events and situations as sad but when sadness becomes a chronic response to almost everything and everyone, then it's clear our perspective is shrouded by a predetermined mind-set.

The same process works for the chronically adventurous – those who tend to see or yearn to see everything as an invitation to experience something new. Ditto for the joyful, the loving, the bewildered, the easy-going, the sexually dominant, the egotistic, and all the other lenses that may dominant a person's encounter with the world.

Each of our lenses are at least partially shaped, tilted or 'cut' in such a way that they attract into view examples or extensions of our dominant issues. Our perceptions mirror our sensors. The outer lenses express the inner ones. We tend to see, perceive and experience according to the perspective we bring to any given situation.

Except for a totally upending experience in which everything we *know* is transformed, we all tend to continue perceiving what we have been conceiving. We tend to experience the events of the outer world according to our pre-established or learned patterns of our internal world. We construct extensions – and indeed proof - of the mental and emotional structures that already exist within us. We find evidence for what we already *value*.

So a few significant questions: Have you inspected the state of your lens recently? What do your patterns - in how you experience people and events - tell you about how you tend to see and interpret those experiences?

Have you cleaned - no less updated - your perspective recently? If so, have you broadened your repertoire and strengthened your multiple powers of perception so you might increase the variety and range of what you see, hear, experience? Most important, what do your recent and current experiences tell you about the state of your spiritual lens? You may have affirmed your spiritual identity. But have you also dusted off your perspectives and correspondingly aligned your identity with the depth and expanse of your Soul?

Of course, we all have multiple smudges on our lenses – each one creating a different way of experiencing an event depending on the history of who and what is involved. "I never get angry,' you might say, "but around Uncle Louie or Aunt Dora, all I see and experience is (....) and (....)."

Did you realize that in addition to choosing to affirm your spiritual identity, you also have the power to activate your spirituality as the creator of all your future experiences? In fact, do you realize that unless you align your perspective with your spiritual identity, any negatives experiences you do not process, transform and integrate could potentially undermine your best intentions?

Do you realize you also have the right - and the responsibility - to deliberately choose a dominant lens that is spiritual in content (affecting what you seek) and process (how you seek it)? Thus it is wise to approach what you experience, think, sense or discover - from a spiritual, meditative and/or contemplative perspective. Everything, *everything* – in a spiritual universe - has a spiritual underpinning and thus possesses potential for spiritual learning and advancement. A spiritual perspective insures that you increasingly experience the world as a reflection of your sacred consciousness.

Spirit in the Mundane

This issue of perspective raises all sorts of other questions. We pose some of them now deliberately to poke, challenge and invite you to think this spirituality stuff through to its natural conclusions. For example,

- How do you spot the presence of the spiritual in the mundane?
- How do you notice the angelic in any given person?
- How can you become aware of the eternal in the everyday?
- How can you identify the spiritual intention of any person or its presence in any particular situation?

First, find something like a park bench or seat in a café - and relax. Close your eyes for a few seconds and allow yourself to draw fresh air into your lungs.

Then close your eyes as you give yourself a gentle command to receive an image or word that feels sacred, godly or loving. Focus on whatever you receive – no matter how unclear or fragmentary - and then allow your imagination to fill in whatever details seem right.

Then slowly open your eyes – and quietly observe whatever or whoever passes in front of you. Allow your spiritual antennae to pick up on anything that is or unfolds. Don't force it. Simply allow it. Then for the rest of the day, be open, to such experiences as:

'Ahhh – look there: that person's aura suddenly appears – so rich, so rosy, so vibrant.'

'I felt a field of energy emanating from that flower!'

'I am sure there is something special going on with that dog. There, that frisky one – the one with that extra bounce in its step. It is so happy to be romping around in the rain, so proud to be carrying its leash in its mouth…while its 'owner' struggles to cover his own head and dash for cover.'

'Look on that baby's face, its stare, its giggle, its exuberant giggle.'

'Ah: that elderly woman who sits across from me most days at the luncheonette, the one who greets everyone by name. There is definitely something special about her. I wonder....'

'I just realized that when my Uncle Louis comes to town, I don't even want to stop to say hello: I instinctively want to hug him, and thank him for all the attention he has paid to me over the years. That means I need to let go of my annoyance with him over his grumpy behavior. Strange, perhaps, but I just realized it's a challenge to convert the lingering tension between us into something nice, something kind and loving. I will therefore lead with my spirituality versus perpetuating a negative memory.'

'And excuse me, but do you hear the blue jays squawking! Watch that goose nonchalantly sauntering through the traffic. Have you noticed how the trees give various forms to the wind? And look at the trust and love being communicated between that elderly couple walking hand in hand.'

So much, so many signs of Spirit to see, hear and acknowledge. It all depends on what you bring to the situation, how receptive you are, and how intent you are in noticing and honoring the constant display of spiritual energy.

Spiritual Awakening

Spiritual awakening is not a thing but a process.

It does not have a defined content but is a free flowing energy.

It is not a conclusion but a way of continuing.

It is not a noun or object but an active verb.

It is not a sentence but an aid to completing one.

It is not an end-point but a constant beginning.

It never stagnates for it's always beckoning.

It can't be saved but can be cultivated.

It connects to larger vistas and wider contexts.

Spiritual awakening reveals the Kosmos as infinitely deep and vast.

It inclines us to be humble and appreciative.

It activates feelings of awe and wonder.

It is infinitely elastic, expansive and inclusive.

It enables us to create love, joy and a sense of abundance.

It helps us seek wholeness and holiness.

It motivates us to discover our identity with the One.

It is realized through intention and receptivity.

It can be activated anytime - by any person, group or culture.

Spiritual awakening is available everywhere, all of the time.

It is invisible yet flows within all living things.

It is most available through our everyday encounters.

It vibrates and resonates…and can send tingles down your spine.

It deepens our insight into what may have been out of sight.

Spiritual awakening prompts us to honor all contents.

It motivates our otherness to seek our togetherness.

It spurs our parts to seek our center.

It insures that our core will embrace our parts.

It is present wherever there is attention.

It pops into awareness each time we smile or give thanks.

Raking Leaves

Driving my car, coming around a curve, I spot someone in front of a house. Slowing down, I stop to observe…an elderly man…raking leaves near and along his driveway.

He's wearing a checked red hat with pull-down earmuffs. Nearby is a large dustpan and a trash can. His rake is golden bamboo.

The rake makes a 'whishing sound' on the grass that has grown brown. Then shrill sounds – scrape, scrape, scrape - emerge from the asphalt.

The leaves clump together as he makes a mound here and then another there. Only a few leaves escape although some continue to swirl at the edges.

The man looks up, adjusts his hold on the rake, then bends slowly but fully at the waist.

Scoop, pour, tap. Scoop, pour, tap.

Upright, he pauses…and sighs.

One hand rests on the rake, the other waves to a neighbor walking by.

Seated - I intentionally bow my head…ever so slightly.

I realize I am smiling - as I silently give thanks…and drive on.

Being Real, Celebrating Something

I go to a few annual conferences each year, and usually the lead question is "How are you?", and "How was your year?" In a business sense, that translates into "How successful were you at your work?" More generically it means, "How's life been treating you?"

Such questions, of course, are simple extensions of saying "hello". It might elicit news of something really good ("got that contract at JCN's" or "the office with the window is now mine"). It could also be a real downer (something like "my dog died" or "the consolidation led to my demotion and less pay").

But other than experiencing the extremes, the usually polite and discrete "fine" or "just great" allows the interaction to continue and perhaps – just perhaps – explore something that generates real contact.

If asked this year, I will not succumb to either a boastful, woeful or banal response. I will tell them the truth but I will also affirm something. "I have been working on patience" (with the optional add: 'and have made real progress"). Or, "I have made great headway in becoming less judgmental" (again with the option of also sharing some examples… if asked). Or, "I have become very grateful for my excellent health." Any of those responses may stop the conversation – or it may lead to sharing something about the important issues of life.

What I hope never to say or hear again are such phrases as "fine", "okay", and "not bad". Platitudes and clichés are mere throwaways, signifying nothing.

"Hello George: it is wonderful to see you again. You look great. How are you?"

"Fine." Plop.

So this time, I will persist. "Fine"? Please tell me: what does that mean? How about 'fantastic', or 'blessed' or 'outrageous" or "fundogamundo" - anything that suggests the blood is moving, that you are involved with life and you have not turned into a pumpkin, manikin or automatic recording."

"Did you have too much coffee today?" might be one response to my attempt to provoke a genuine interaction. "No – I simply encourage you to identify the kind of energy you've attracted into your life recently, and find something to affirm or celebrate."

"Hmmm," the other might say. "I'll have to think about that."

"Of course: I am happy to see you again and just want to encourageage some meaningful exchange – no matter how brief. I hope I did not come on too strong."

"I understand. By the way: 'Namaste'." [29]

"Ahhhh! Thank you! 'Namaste' to you as well.

Jean-François Millet, *The Gleaners*, 1857
Looking, finding, making a contribution – bit by bit.

You Don't Have to Be Perfect

When you are really into your spirituality, affirming the full reality of your immortal status and your sacred role in life, then you know:

---

29 The greeting, 'Namaste', was made famous most recently by Gandhi. It is a Hindu phase used in both meeting and departing from another, usually with a slight bow, with the option of simultaneously folding your hands gently as if in prayer. There are many interpretations; they all mean the same thing: "The divinity (the immortal Soul) within me honors the divinity (or immortal Soul) in you."

You don't have to strive any longer.

You don't need to follow any set of rules.

You don't need to search for your so-called 'higher self'.

You don't need an intermediary to talk with God.

You don't have to feel guilty about being playful and spontaneous.

You don't need to fear anything or anyone.

You can simply trust your immortal Soul and its empowerments.

You also don't have to pass a test, take a lie detector, study for a spiritual S.A.T., be initiated, follow a given code of conduct, obtain anybody's approval, learn a terminology or catechism, fear life, fear death, fear the future, second guess, rehearse the past, be concerned about being judged insufficient, be anxious, fret or worry, prepare, try to be perfect or even muster a desire to be 'better'.

Like a Buddhist monk wearing the circle of completion on the sash of his/her robe, you currently are everything you will ever be - although you may not fully realize it…yet. So relax, go easy, know that you are loved, and know that you have the ability to complete your mission and fulfil the terms of your learning contract with distinction.

You are an aspect of God whatever you do and wherever you wander. Never doubt that you are here for a reason, here to contribute, here to create, here to manifest wisdom and joy. And you are also exactly where you are meant to be, doing what you wanted to do, dealing with the challenges you agreed to, and contributing what you promised.

If you want to change any part of your experience – defuse your difficulties or intensify your sense of achievement - then alter if not transform your thoughts and images. You have the capacity to do so. If you prefer something different or new, then alter your perspective. Change your intentions and you create a new experience.

Ultimately, you are here to experience the power of the divine that is embedded in you. That gives you the power to create and recreate your life. You are here as a divine representative, to experience your divinity within a human context. You are here to experience eternity in the everyday by learning to live freely – and creatively - in the moment.

Happy journey – although you are already home...placed, by your own accord, in one of God's infinite number of divine hostels.

You Never Know

When you see crutches or a wheelchair, it is sure sign the person has suffered a setback. A bowed back, a limp, or pronounced scar are other signs that the individual has experienced - and perhaps is still experiencing - difficult times.

But what of the walking wounded, the folks who have suffered a lost of a job, loved one or their own health – yet bear no outer signs of their hardship? We easily empathize with those whose difficulties are outwardly visible. But unless we know a person, we may inadvertently – and nonchalantly - pass by many others who are troubled by invisible emotionally scars or difficulties.

When in doubt: be sensitive to the look and sound of everyone. Just in case, notice, greet, attend to, smile at, wave to, or just say something nice – to whomever you meet – no matter what their external state appearance. In fact, many who silently suffer an illness or from fear and anxiety do not display any dramatic signs of their difficulties. But if you attend closely you might notice a subtle 'something' in their bearing, speech or facial expression that suggests distress.

You never know who needs what. Your formal greetings and informal blessings could make a difference. Even if you are mistaken - and the people you meet tomorrow are all healthy and well – be assured that everyone can always profit from a little extra interest, recognition and honoring.

Wonders With Words

The derivation and composition of words can be very revealing.

Look at the word, 'enjoy'. The prefix, *en*, has its roots in Middle English, in French and ultimately in the Latin *in* – which means to put into or onto - as in *encapsulate;* to go into or onto – as in *enplane;* to cause to be - as in *endear;* or to intensify - as in *entangle*.

The American Heritage Dictionary describes the noun *joy* as that which is the source, object or expression of pleasure and satisfaction. Thus *enjoy* literally is the putting into, going into or causing a state of pleasure. It invokes the transitional verb, *rejoicing:* "to fill with ecstatic happiness, pleasure or satisfaction," the prefix *re*, like *en*, being an *intensifier*.

Let's switch to the word adventure. Here the prefix *ad,* from the Latin, means toward. And the noun, *venture*, like the intransient verb, translates as taking a risk or dare. Put them together and we have the activity of braving or proceeding into, moving toward and participating in that which is potentially daring, dangerous, risky and exciting.

And just look at the impact certain suffixes have on the common stem *theo* or God. Add *cracy* and you have *theocracy* or government by the clergy. Use *logy* and you have the study and knowledge of God. Try *morphic* and the combo attributes divine traits to other things or beings, just as *anthropomorphic* ascribes to them a human trait, personality or form.

The suffix *machy* and the word *theomachy* apply to the epic poems of Homer where the gods battled each other. Finally, tack on the suffix *phany* to obtain theophany and you get a term that denotes a divine manifestation or the appearance of the divine to a human being.

Words are indeed wondrous, not to be thrown around loosely and certainly not be ignored. Becoming aware of how we create meaning takes us deeper into the creative process itself. It is through words and sentences that we create meaning and convey consciousness. It's as if each utterance is preceded by the gentle command, 'open sesame'. It's a refection of the biblical intent, "And God said let there be...." (Genesis1: 6). And to insure the intention to create is manifest as desired, each choice of wording seems to be followed by the whisper, "so be it", and "God saw that it was good".

One more time: *A* when joined to *ware* creates a synonym for watchful. Add *ness* and the combination equals *awareness*, the process by which we become conscious and insightful – one of the most effective ways we have for reawakening our *awareness* of our own identity.

Words as Evocateurs

More on words as cultivators of spirituality.

There are certain words and phrases that have a special and vibrant energy. Just seeing or saying them evokes energy, encourages us to expand, prods us to act. They resonate with adventure. They invite discovery. They affirm and evoke insight and awareness. Here are a few such evocative word-symbols. Feel free to add your favorites to the list.

Audacity	*Outrageous*		Lovely
Adventure	DELIGHT		*I can and will...*
Abundance	C r e a t i v e	WONDROUS	
	Empowered	*NEW*	Bravo/a!
ZOW	I Love to ...	COURAGE	

Add Your favorites :

_____   _____   _____

_____   _____   _____

Worth Repeating

The following quote from Buddha is worth repeating at least several times a week. It is even worth putting a copy on your refrigerator. And it's certainly worth reading aloud, frequently with resolve and gusto.

believe nothing

no matter where you read it

or who has said it,

not even if I (Buddha) have said it,

unless it agrees with your own reason

and your own common sense

Insighting

Our vision usually concentrates on whatever is immediately in front of us. Move the head or the eyes - and what we see changes. Except in moments of sustained concentration – as in reading a book or tallying numbers – our heads and eyes move substantially and ceaselessly as we switch our attention from higher and lower, to the right and the left, producing thousands if not millions of fleeting and fragmentary images every minute - most of which are discarded from memory as soon as they are received. Such is the process of 'out-scoping': our sightings of the outer world unfold in a kind of mindless whirl until we focus on what we're looking for or that which captures our attention.

There is another way of seeing and understanding, however, called 'in-sighting'. In-sighting involves the conscious choice to investigate what is behind the visually obvious. It goes deeper and searches for meaning. Rather than being exploratory or random, in-sighting distinguishes us from the other mammals. It is what makes us sentient or self-aware. It is the other half of being a homo sapien sapien – humans who are aware that they are aware. It leads to understanding and reflecting, for example, not just on the facts but their significance.

Checking the newspaper to see when the sun rises is an example of out-scoping, the process that satisfies the information-seeking function. On the other hand, getting up early and climbing to a hilltop to experience the moment when the revolution of the Earth produces a sunrise is the result of in-sighting: the choice to experience and participate in something of internal and symbolic significance.

Consider the following interweaving of *observations about* (out-scoping) and *reflections on* (in-sighting) a set of astronomical realities. The Earth spins on its axis at 25,000 miles a day while flowing in an elliptical pattern through a sea of space at an average velocity of 66,672 miles per hour. It hurtles 95 million miles from sun before heeding the pull of its elliptical path and coming back to within 406 thousand miles of its gravitational center.

Meanwhile our planetary system is moving within and at the tip of one of the spiral arms of the Milky Way galaxy as it whips along at 540,000 miles an hour. We, this Earth, the planetary system, the Milky Way and the expanding cosmos – are all moving at astronomical speeds and yet are bound together as facets of an interdependent system – a reality that is difficult to comprehend without being humbled into silence, awe and reverence.

Ditto the wonders behind the arrival of spring and the flowering of crocuses and the early bulbs. Ditto the vast and complex ecologies of the Earth. Ditto the facts of sexual union, then the laughter and elation of the sexual experience, the joyful tears that greet a pregnancy and the sense of thanksgiving and wonder that accompanies the awesome process of birth. Ditto for both the facts and the symbolism surrounding the lungs and the process of breathing, surpassed perhaps only by the facts - and the poetry - that attempt to make sense of the incredibly rhythmic chambers of the heart. It is the same for the out-scoping wonders of the retina, and the incredible insights created by the inner eye. There is no end to such wondrous happenings.

We may be informed by the factual descriptions of how life operates. But we are also awed by their magnificence – and mystery – as we celebrate such phenomena in our reflections, meditations, sacred stories and songs.

The results produced by out-scoping the basic facts are very different from the spiritual and poetic in-scoping of their significance. The former attempts to describe what happened while the spiritual-poetic responses attempt to comprehend how and why Life and its physical phenomena unfold as they do. What can be perceived and understood by the outer lens – using words and numbers - are facts about the externals. What the internal or reflective lens focuses on and seeks to reveal – using metaphors and silent honoring – is insight into the sacred nature of Life.

In being true to themselves, the two approaches make enormous contributions. But the inevitable gap between the two is still very, very wide indeed: one looks for answers about the concrete, material functions of the universe while the other ponders the clues to the inner workings of Life itself.

This, You, Now

Whatever you are doing in your life - right now,
   Whatever you are experiencing,
      Whatever project or problem you face,
         Whatever the theme or focus of those issues,
Know at the deepest part of you
   That you have been training
      For exactly *this* -
         All your life!
The convergence
   Of you and 'it'
      Has happened
         For a reason.
The timing is perfect:
   'It' is why you are here.
      The tributaries are assembling,
         And the river is reaching its outlet.
And there you are –
   Prepped and aware
      At the helm of the boat
         You've been building all your life.

Who Lives in Your House?

Your body may be likened to your house.
    Your Soul is the one who lives in that house.
Your body is the residence.
    Your Soul is the resident.

Your eyes are like the two windows on the top floor.
    Your mouth could be the front door.
There are all sorts of analogies,
    Another play on the theme of 'Inner and Outer'.

The inner always creates,
    The outer radiates.
Intentions burn,
    Creations shine.

Whatever you call the shell – the body,
    house, vehicle, personality -
It is the occupant - the Soul who
    directs, resides, drives and chooses.

Whoever commissions and builds the house
    Furnishes it and makes it into a home.
And that's you: the presiding spirit,
    The residing Soul, Divinity's local representative

Reflecting The All in your time and space
    Infusing your essence
Into every lamp and doorway
    Activating the energy of your embodiment.

Things to Consider

Let's – for simplicity sake - put all this stuff into several aphorisms - that summarize it all.

1. You can choose to see beauty or you can wait for someone to tell you what's beautiful.

2. When in doubt, practice how it feels to be angelic.

3. Are you happy to be alive or are you putting life on hold until you find something to be happy about?

4. Is it possible to become better or worst when you are already divine?

5. Are you living your truth? Not spouting it - but living it?

6. You are becoming a better person or merely uncovering who you already are?

7. What is your unique expression? What is your special contribution? What do you sense is your particular mission?

8. Realize that as you release the pain and shoulda-woulda-couldas of the past, and let go of other people's prescriptions for your future, you enter into the present - where you can now be genuinely and fully creative, any way you want.

9. God made everything simple. We humans think it's cool to make it complicated.

10. When you remember who you really are, everything begins to make sense.

11. If you attend to the process of experiencing everything in the moment, you suddenly realize that you and your experience are the same.

12. Holding onto beliefs, attitudes or behaviors that are negative and thus self-defeating is like holding your breath. Blow them out, let them go, and get on with the joy of taking chances - creating your life versus waiting for something to happen.

13. The very 'formally' religious often moralize, need to have the last word, display great assurance, tend to judge and demean other belief systems, love legal distinctions and seem always to be

mouthing something from one holy book or another. The 'simply' religious or spiritually inclined tend to live and let live, listen attentively, bow equally to both the allegedly 'ordinary' and 'supposedly' august, and love to dance with ease and abandonment.

You Become

Cultivating your Spirituality means you become:

- What you image
- Reflections of the expressions you use (plus and minus)
- An embodiment of the thoughts you project
- An expression of your feelings
- Manifestations of the images you nourish
- A walking demonstration of how you smile
- A personification of how you greet people
- What you focus on
- A mirror image of your energy patterns
- What you value and intend
- The personality you adopt in dealing with challenges
- The identity you nurture in your mind's eye, and
- What you affirm and celebrate.

Whatever you think, and image, and feel, and do - you become - to your obvious regret or enhancement. So be careful – and be carefree. Do not carry your burdens – or those of others – as supposed badges of honor. You are - and become - an elongation of your thoughts and intentions. So play to the positive, the best, the spiritual. Do the math; it all adds up - for better or worst. You become your cumulative image of yourself. You become you. You become who and what you cultivate and thus create. You mold yourself with every feeling, intuition, action and stirring of your imagination.

Choose wisely – and with loving and joyful intentions – for you are, in each and every moment, involved in creating both your *incarnated life* and revealing the state *of your Soul*

CHAPTER 11

AFFIRMING OUR SPIRITUAL CORE

Enlightened

When the label on Paul Newman's 'Light Honey Mustard' encourages us to 'Lighten Up!" - then it is time to take the issue of "light" seriously. Of course, Newman is urging us to lighten up on calories and fats, do with less, cutback on our food intake in order to reduce our weight and overall density. His intent clearly is to sell a product that presumably is good for us because it will help us become and feel 'lighter'.

What wonderful metaphors for spirituality. We'll take our cues wherever we can find them. Encountering Newman and 'Light Honey Mustard' at the grocery is a veritable gift from heaven. It is always useful to play with any idea or experience that stimulates greater awareness – in this case, something that is apparently yearning to be recognized and expressed. The theme of spirituality is obviously front and center. As such, it operates like an emotional and mental magnet, attracting to it any ideas or experiences that tease the idea into awareness. Any stimulus or cue will activate the flow of energy. If the seeker is open, and the attraction proffered, the connection will be made. When this happens, all any of us has to do is play with the intake, amplify it and associate with it as freely as possible.

So the focal point is admittedly 'spirituality'. And the stimulating jolt has arrived in the form of the word 'light' appearing on a bottle of salad dressing. Let's see what we discover.

Personally, the connections with lightness include staying in good physical shape, going to the gym, cutting trails on my property, hiking, exerting in order to work up a good sweat, staying flexible and burning those calories. I have been slim all my life but I have had to take precautions: advanced middle age does slow the metabolism and allow the waistline to inch up versus down.

Being 'light' is also angelic, capable of flying high - including the enlightened and imaged stratosphere of 'heaven'. Being light on one's feet also means being able to dance the polka and the waltz. Recalling childhood, I realize that Plastic Man, my comic book hero of old, was so light and elastic he could – all at the same time – be eating pasta in Italy with his right hand, rummaging through a book in Moscow using his left hand, and booting the bad guys into jails right here in America.

Then there are the mental associations: a little bit of thought yields a goldmine of connections. The dictionary, for example, offers a range of interpretations of 'light'. 'To move easily and freely' is one; 'to be cheerful free of worry' is another; approaching life with 'a light heart' is third. When we add the suffix, 'en' and obtain 'enlighten', the plot thickens (yet shines more light): 'to shed light on' sounds downright spiritual, and the alternative, 'to make or become brighter' - as in "being seen or becoming more visible and evident" - brings us close to the essence of the enlightening process. The ultimate impact is revealed in the dictionary's final denotation: 'to relieve or be relieved of care or worry'.

Thus highlighting the letters 'en' as a prefix - as in 'enlighten' - converts the meanings 'in or into' the light. As a suffix, 'en' becomes "lighten" or 'becoming or causing' light. Adding 'en' as both a prefix and suffix gives us 'enlighten', or that which 'gives light' or renders us 'informed'.

To be 'enlightened', then, is to attain 'spiritual or intellectual insight', and 'be freed from ignorance or prejudice'. The fuller term, 'enlightenment', becomes a state of being 'enlightened' or "informed" by the light, able to move into or attain knowledge of the light, and to become like God or the Light.

Sacred literature and religious sermons speak of "moving toward the Light", a synonym for God, who in the Hebrew Bible created "light" on the first day with the creative affirmation of "let there be light" and differentiating it from "the darkness" (Genesis. 1:3). The Bible says God created the planetary and starry expressions of light on the third day: "And God said: 'Let there be lights in the dome of the sky [stars] to separate the day from the night'", adding that "God made the two great lights - the greater one to rule the day [the sun] and the lesser light to rule the night [the moon]" (Genesis 1:14).

As both the Hebrew and Christian Testaments unfold, the connotations of light are transformed from an exterior phenomenon to that which is both interior (enlightenment) and that which is the essence of God. Among the many references to light in the Hebrew Testament are such phrases as: "The Lord and the light are my salvation" (Ps 27:1); may you "walk before God and the light of life" (Ps 56:12); "let us walk in the light of the Lord (Isa. 2:5), and "the Lord shall be your everlasting light" (Isa. 60:19).

Such invocations of the light are supplemented in the Christian Testament with references to "your whole body will be full of light (Mt. 6:22); "true light which enlightens everyone" (John 1:9); "As long as I am in the world, I am the light of the world" (John 9:5); and "they need no lamp or sun, for the Lord God will be their light" (Rev. 22:5).

People of a more generalized, or non-denominational tradition have since ancient times affirmed what is common to all spiritual approaches - namely "love", "enlightenment" and "praising the Lord". When signing off letters and e-mails many people today use the words "in light and love". The connotations seem always the same: "light" points to the state or at least the desire - for one Self as well as others - to be 'in the light', enlightened, informed, and being at one with the sacred or the enlightenment of love.

Aha: look at what we have wrought. Between Paul Newman, personal associations, and leafing through the dictionary and both halves of the Bible, we have uncovered an array of ideas and experiences that were associated with a word, which when amplified stimulated our (and hopefully your) imagination. Shopping for salad dressing will never again be just a mundane experience.

Do You Realize...

Do you realize that as you become more conscious of your spiritual identity and divine mission, you activate more of your natural power to:

- Be telepathic, knowing that you can send mental messages to those you love, and to all the others to whom you feel especially well attuned.

- Travel out-of-body during the night, perhaps waking with the knowledge of having been in another time zone, in a different country, in the setting of an earlier incarnation, even traveling to a distant galaxy – even recalling a glimpse of your blue planet in the distance as you scurried back into the third dimension and awakened with the alarm.

- Recognize your ability to be clairvoyant, able to anticipate events and experiences.

- Become a conduit for healing by first quietly centering your Self, and then asking that you receive and convey healing energies to others.

- Directly invoke the blessings and guidance of God and any of the Angelic Hosts (including Archangels, your Guardian Angel and any of the assisting Angels) as well as any of the Ascended Masters (those Souls who have - after countless incarnations - attain divine consciousness).

- Transcend time and space, move into the fourth and fifth dimensions and beyond, and walk among and commune with the Angels and other loving spirits in the realm of Pure Spirit

All these and more are among your empowerments. As you activate your sense of your own divinity they will become more pronounced and your capacity to recognize and fulfil your earthly mission will be greatly enhanced.

Essence and Container

Your body is highly significant yet it is only the container for your essence. It serves as a temporary vessel for the abiding energy of the Soul. It is the form or vehicle you have chosen to register and gather the lessons of this lifetime on Earth.

Yet the body is only the packaging, the outer covering, the external manifestation created and utilized by the Soul to help increase its awareness and complete its earthly tasks.

As your vessel, the body needs to be treated well – filled with chicken soup, nourished with fruits and vegetables, cared for regularly with soap and water, replenished with sound sleep, occasionally covered with soothing oils, and dressed in the style and cloth that reflect and create your desired moods and identities.

The true role of the body is best revealed symbolically in the many ways we use containers to protect and support the energies of everyday life: a particular glass for drinking water, a favorite cup for our tea, 'that' pot for the stew and 'this' one for soup, 'the' special box for the chocolates, and of course 'these' shoes for 'this' outfit.

As to the body itself, there is the obvious skull to contain the brain, the chest cavity to house the heart and lungs, and veins and arteries to channel the blood. For everyday living, there's the crib for the child, the chair near the TV, the shed for the tools, and the sanctuary for the meditative and prayerful.

Each of these forms is functional and designed to contain, accommodate, protect and express. The perfume spray is different from the gasoline tank, which surely is different from the human lung. The size, contour and functions of each vessel are fashioned to serve the essence of what the container stores and dispenses. A house helps us to create a home. A chalice facilitates a transformation. The body in turn serves to ground the sacred and manifest the creations of the Soul.

Walk On

There is much to love in the Buddhist attitude: *Decide, act...and walk on.*

We in the West tend to procrastinate, weigh this option and that, study and plan and rethink everything as if the fate of the universe depended on it. We harbor regrets about the past, worry about the future, and create all sorts of anxieties in our desire to perfect, maximize and optimize. Ah, the 'fretting' and sweating we express over what to do, how to do it...and when.

Becoming stymied by options is understandable. But harmony is best attained the way a practitioner of Zen Buddhism views the alternatives, selects, and then walks on.

Folks who endlessly pursue perfection get caught in a world of their own making - their endless rounds of 'but', 'then again', 'why' and 'if only' constantly blocking action. Such hesitation amplifies the tendency to regret the past and magnify unfounded anxieties about the future, both of which blur the option to live in the present.

A person centered in Spirit naturally takes a Buddhist saying to heart:

If you sit, sit. If you stand, stand. But don't wobble.

The Soul Chooses, Guides and Allows

Who is making these decisions? The Soul – is the chooser of the incarnation, its learning contract, it skills and challenges, its personality and its preferred ways of operating. Once incarnated, however, the Soul operates through the temporary mind and body that is formed in the material realm. It also enables what we call the 'ego' - the embodiment's center or psychological identity - to guide and coordinate the earthly activities of the incarnation.

The brain and its networks of synapses comprise the physical circuitry needed to gather and store the data coming from the senses. The heart is linked to the nervous system as the selector of values and emotions. The ego is the active agent of the combined functions of the incarnate person or personality.

It is thus the Soul who occupies the central role and position in creating the incarnation, and which once formed, becomes the Soul's agent in achieving Its next or desired level of spiritual consciousness. Once embodied in the material realm, the Soul operates through the incarnate's body and mind and its component energies and functions, guiding it during its relatively brief stay on Earth to attain the level of creativity, altruism and service that's consistent with its learning objectives.

But once the incarnate is given the challenges and difficulties outlined in the Soul's learning contract, it is free – as an embodied ego-personality – to meet or even exceed the goals set for it. It can also undercut those goals by allowing itself to become bloated, over-bearing and egocentric, fail to resist and manage the snares and temptations of the material world, and thereby vitiate the good intentions of the learning contract. Free will always reigns.

In other words, the decision-making and behavioral apparatus of the physical person is as able to exercise free will as the Soul itself, and thus can choose to act in ways that meets or denigrates the Soul's spiritual potential. It is capable of activating the Soul's most enlightened levels of consciousness as well as displaying the ego's dimmest understanding of its spiritual potential.

The empowerment of the Soul, your Soul, to choose what it wants to learn and how, as well as how it wishes to handle its incarnation's life circumstances - is complete and plenary. But the full nature of our identity and the contents of our contracts are usually hidden to us during our incarnations – lest it become so easy to complete that it has no additive value.

As a consequence, not every incarnational personality gets to realize the full extent of its Soul power. In fact, we – as personalities - may never become aware of our identity as anything but an ego, never affirm an awareness of our Soul nature, and never fully activate our spiritual empowerments. It is indeed unfortunate that many people also never understand how they attract experiences that fortify their relatively uncreative and unthinking lifestyles.

So many immature, young, insensitive and uniformed Souls – despite their best intentions - allow their incarnates to coast once the basic needs of their physical wellbeing have been satisfied. With its immediate ego needs gratified, and its patterns and habits fortified, some incarnated beings may include some religion in their lives - just to hedge their bets or because a tiny bit of their Soul identity exerts itself and bleeds through. So they are nice and obliging with everyone, and even buy a plot with a view in the nearby cemetery - just in case in turns out that having a body to resurrect makes it easier to get into heaven. Other than that, many live in their own encapsulated worlds, resigned to making it through, staving off even the thought of death for as long as they can.

Fortunately and understandably, advanced Souls do encourage their incarnates to affirm and express the Soul's spiritual essence. They help them adopt lifestyles that activate and express spiritual identity, make substantial contributions, fulfil their learning contracts and both deepen and expand their state of consciousness.

If We Really Did Believe

- in the life of the immortal Soul, then why do we devote so much real estate to cemeteries?
- in life after death, then why do we clutch at and hold on to the dying?
- in Spirit, then why do we spend so much time seeking material possessions?

- in giving thanks, then why is there such a national frenzy to acquire more and more – and do so the very day after a nation celebrates Thanksgiving?

- in the love of God, then why do so many put so much emphasis on wanting vengeance, on seeking the death penalty, on using war to settle disputes?

- in the Sermon on the Mount, then why do we revere competition, winning and wanting to be number one?

- in the simplicity of Yeshua, then why are there so many churches filled with so much stuff, so many things, so much gold and jewelry, so many ornate displays of material wealth - all while there are so many in need of the basics?

- in the model of Yeshua and Mary and the sacrifice of the disciples, then why do the churches allegedly founded in their names sustain privileged hierarchies with elevated titles and who live in mini-palaces and dress so ostentatiously?

- in the lifestyle of Yeshua, then why don't all priests, clergy and ministers wear sandals, and plain robes, get married (like all the Apostles) and either fish for a living or beg for their sustenance?

- in the eternal Soul, then why do so many spend so much time and money slimming, tanning and buffing the body – thereby reinforcing the primacy of the body and the incessant need of the ego-centered to seek and revere their image in a mirror?

- in the United States as a 'Judeo-Christian" or 'religious' nation, then why is the United States involved in so many disputes, so many wars, so much wrangling for money and power – seemingly always pursuing treasure (Iraq) but holding back when innocent civilians are being hunted down and killed (Rwanda, Darfur)?

- in the beauty and indispensability of the Earth, then why are we so tolerant of polluters and those who misuse our land and waterways for purely material profit?

- in God, then why do we allow the vocabulary of the ego to dominate our conversations - with incessantly proud references to *me* and *my,* and *us versus them*?

- in a *christed* or holy person, then why has Christmas become the epitome of and the rallying cry for untrammeled hedonism?

- in a loving God, then why do so many religions outwardly boast or inwardly insinuate that their way is the only way and they alone possess exclusive entree to the realm of the loving God?

Affirming Yet Still Struggling

Affirming our spiritual identity does not mean the struggle is over. In fact, one of its potential impacts is to increase our awareness of the many spiritual challenges that lay – often hidden - in every situation. No longer blind or disinterested, we become increasingly aware of the opportunities to express our spiritual intentions - in a host of situations that earlier we did not see, acknowledge or act on.

And those opportunities are everywhere: in how we greet the world upon waking in the morning, in the way we treat the many clerks and waiters and waitresses who weave in and out of our day, how we handle perceived slights and the proverbial finger from a passing car, how we affirm versus aggress, how we politely confront an injustice versus remaining silent, and how we take a stand or walk away from actions of prejudice, insensitivity and disdain.

None of us is pure - making life on Earth a tightrope walk even on the best of days. All of us experience the continual seesaw between slippage from our best intentions and rededications to live by the standards we raise for others. But what happens to the bar, the standard and the vision - in the meantime? Does it not seem that the bar is getting lower, the standard dimmer and the vision more obscure as our compromises grow more numerous and avoidant? And it is not true that we learn to mouth one more platitude each time we allow our motivations and actions to follow the lowest common denominator.

Hypocrisy is a very slippery beast so it is sorrowful to admit that it often resides in our own house. Is this a theme - or set of topics - for our perennial, semi-serious set of New Year's Resolutions? Perhaps. But how long do our reclaimed outlooks and promised behaviors last? Ever note how many people crowd the gyms in January, and come March, are never be to seen again. It is no different in the realm of the Spirit: we mean so well around the holidays but subsequently seem willing to lose our way in the crowd. Maybe it will be different this year. Maybe we really will believe, affirm and act accordingly – more often than not.

Rules for Gaining and Radiating Depth of Soul [30]

1. Soulful people are the same people at work as they are at home.

2. They are integrated, their outer activities expressing their inner values.

3. By being soulful, they (*we, you*) are able to activate the soulful energies of others. They personify the very best in the human spirit and thereby stimulate the emergence of similar aptitudes and abilities in others.

4. Soulful people possess integrity because they have worked at it - finally *getting it together* after years of slipping and sliding like the rest of us.

5. Soulful people have earned their place in the world. They have cycled through many iterations of the spiral, with many incarnations revisiting related issues time and again - but each time with a greater degree of insight and awareness.

6. Soulful people seize on the opportunities to perfect *what* they do and *how* they do it. Over time they learn how to live with full involvement and enthusiasm despite the reappearance of conditions that once blocked and discouraged them.

---

[30] A substantial rewrite of an essay that first appeared in the author's book on *Superb Leadership: The 12 Essential Skills* (Melbourne Beach, FL: Helicon, 1997), pp. 154-155. For an update on the author's activities, see www.KindredSpirits.Us

7. People with depth of Soul seek creative and innovative goals that prove helpful to their own development, others – and, due to the cumulative ripple effect - the unfolding of the universe.

8. Soulful people are agents of creation, central players in a gigantic unfolding that promotes not just *their* immediate family, community or organization - but Life itself.

9. Soulful personalities choose and vigorously pursue commissions that generate love and heightened levels of consciousness. Inspired by visions of love and inclusion, the soulful among us activate others to follow their lead and thereby enliven circumstances for everyone. They are able to foster new developments that nourish the Earth because they are attuned to the needs of the common good.

10. Soulful people do not often spout their belief in love and God publicly, or make a spectacle of their spiritual practice. But they do speak with loving intention and act with integrity. They are the servants of inclusion and midwives of compassion.

Intention

Intention is what moves the world; it is what transforms an idea into a reality. No matter what we do, no matter when or where, no matter how quiet or demonstrative our delivery, it is our intention that creates the energy needed to express what is desired. A positive intent – like love and being helpful - is intended to elevate, uplift, and accent the positive. A negative intent - reflected in the method used or the outcome desired - deliberately wishes to be abusive, disempowering or denigrating to others.

Our intentions initiate, direct and energize the impacts of our actions. Our body language, tone, words and actions communicate our intentions. A negative intention can even degrade what is potentially positive – such as a bouquet of flowers given with a grunt, or loving words uttered with self-centered bravado.

Scientist-poet Buckminster Fuller entitled one of his books, *I Seem to Be a Verb*.[31] Intent is like the verb; it's what brings the object and subject together; it creates the energy field and generates the action. In an English sentence, the verb rarely positions itself first or last. It is usually placed in the middle where it becomes the conduit for the intended energy and impact.

Remember this when you next get ready to say or do something – however innocent or significant. Double check: what is your intention? What is in your heart? Is what you are about to say or do self-serving and minimizing of the other? Or do your words and actions emerge from a loving heart, from the core of your Soul?

Knocking on Doors

It is easy to make a decision when you follow a few simple rules:

- Knock only on the doors that interest you or to which you are intuitively drawn.

- Walk only through the doorways that open to you.

- Don't bother any longer trying to find your way around the obstacles, or knocking on doors that are barred, display no windows or reveal many locks.

One of the most significant truisms in spiritual literature is the saying attributed to Yeshua in Matthew (7:7-8): "Ask and it will be given you; search and you will find; knock, and the door will be opened for you. For everyone who asks - receives, and everyone who searches - finds, and for everyone who knocks - the door will be opened."

Note, however, that the injunction advises us to knock (with confidence) on a door, not knock our heads repeatedly against it. And despite the positive nature of the invitation to 'knock', it would be silly to think that Spirit would then respond on demand or in a way that suits our individual timetable and limited view of our own needs.

---

31 Buckminster Fuller, *I Seem to Be a Verb* (New York: Bantam, 1970).

Many doors do not open automatically or as desired. Rather they open on their own timing - suggesting that Spirit does know best; what we think we need may not be in our best interests at that time we're making the request. Recall the phrase: "Watch out what you wish for. You could get it and regret it." So it is best that we not knock as if we're having an arm wrestle with God; it is not our way or no way, or our will against Hers. It is more a matter of: "rightful requests being supported at the most propitious time – and in a way that best enhances the Soul and not a whim of a demanding ego".

So be assured that your knocking has indeed been heard. But we must realize that it may take time to make all the arrangements; we are not God's only client. If any of us now resided in the domain of Pure Spirit, we would be astonished by the sheer volume of the knocking coming incessantly from millions of earthlings. The roar is surely constant and thunderous. And many people are knocking for something that may be the exact opposite of what you and others are requesting.

Such a reality check would help us realize that to get what we request may involve God having to open and close – and maybe even move or bust down - a number of doors belonging to the many others involved or affected by our request. Our latest petition may need to be evaluated in terms of the vast number and complexity of wishes already posted on the 'Big Board'. If you think those in the tower of any major airport are juggling as fast as they can, think what the coordinator of Cosmic Traffic Control is going through every second of every day.

So it could be that God's hand has just reached for our name and number, and some spiritual energy (like your Guardian Angel) has been alerted to marshal forces in our direction. It could also be that a host of angelic spirits will soon be working on all the arrangements needed to grant not only your immediate wish but also the deeper and longer lasting one of which it is a part.

And it could be that lots of folks are experiencing minor to major changes in their lives in order to accommodate your knock! So let's be patient and understanding. We are only a part – surely a significant part but still only a miniscule part - of an enormous and complex ecology of interlocking doors, systems and Souls.

Besides, the impact we request in our latest knockings may not really serve our interests; it may serve only that which is immediate and material rather than our long range and spiritual essence. And some of our requested impacts could involve negating an important aspect of our learning contract; the delay may be God's way of giving us a chance to think things over and even change our mind – for our own benefit.

If we truly believe we are Souls and are part and parcel of God, then it would helpful to remind ourselves to trust that a loving parent will not mislead or deprive it's children. Nor will He/She allow them to forego learning the lessons they agreed to in their contracts.

Besides, life with a capital 'L' is not designed to comply with our view of our narrow earthly needs. Rather it is more an issue of how our individual and combined lives can serve Spirit, and how our life experiences contribute to the growth of God's Collective Consciousness. It is also possible that some of our requests, although not honored, and some of our experiences, although we did not desire or request them, occur because they are essential to our growth and also add to the continuous development of the universe.

So, please, continue to knock, of course, but do so with total trust in the process. And if the responses are slow in coming or are different from what you wanted, don't take it personally. But do take it spiritually. To insure a closer alignment of your requests relative to the greater good yours as well as God's and the universe - meditate just a bit longer and perhaps more frequently before framing your next request.

If it surprises you that one particular door opens while others do not, then it may be best to go on the adventure that is offered rather than willfully trying to kick in a door that will not yield easily. Persistent and willful pushing may temporarily get a door to crack open slightly but at a price: 'getting your way' may produce some temporary gains but always at the price of inflating the ego and negating trust in Spirit.

Rarely does pushing on anything produce the quality attained from earnestness and simple humility. The former may appease the earthly identity but the latter honors God's total reality and Her preferred way of hearing and honoring requests of all her children.

Neither More Nor Less

There are lots of people who say they want to be 'more' spiritual. That's not possible. We already are full spiritual beings.

We might want to meditate more often, kneel more or dance more, read more books on spiritual themes or devote more time to just being nice or contemplating the mysteries and glories of life. Either way, whatever we increase or neglect, whatever we do or don't do, our essence – and thus our potential impact - always remains spiritual.

This is not just semantics. This is the central issue regarding our core identity, and how it is affirmed or negated by the descriptors we adopt. We denigrate the presence of our innate spirituality by wanting to *increase it*; the phase suggests we believe we are less than fully spiritual already. 'Wanting to be more' spiritual begets the negative connotation that we are *less* than that at the moment.

The same thing happens with such phrases as the 'higher Self'. We each are already and always will be a total Self; there is no 'lower Self' that can invoke a 'higher Self'. To use such language or invoke such imagery only impugns the reality of who we each are and always will be, namely an integrated, empowered and fully spiritual Self. That identity deserves to be affirmed – always - and without reservation. It is the point of power for creating or attracting everything we experience. Tinker with that affirmation and you change and distort your identity, your impact and your reality.

Of course, it is helpful to strengthen our awareness of our soulfulness - doing things to activate our spiritual empowerments, and deliberately choosing intentions and activities that enhance, deepen and extend our spiritual consciousness. But realize that such wondrous activities begin with at least an implicit affirmation: "As an immortal spiritual being, I activate and fulfil my spiritual identity by doing the following: …(fill in the blank)."

Loving Self

We confess our love and appreciation to many people and for many things. Saying 'I love you' is a bit risky at the beginning of a romantic relationship - but somebody finally has to take a chance and utter the magic words first. It can be an unnerving time - as George Costanza on the Seinfeld show once testified. For those of you who missed that show, George uttered the magic words while sitting in the driver's seat and spooning with his beloved. He did not know she was deaf in her left ear. She, allegedly not hearing him, 'ignored' the comment. George took in personally. The rest was down hill.

But saying such words of endearment to your children - and your established mate - is a way of reconfirming the commitment. Among good friends the phase is usually reserved for tearful goodbyes, or when difficulties or stress motivate you to solidify a connection. And surely your dogs and cats, and pets of any sort, receive such endearments regularly. It is during such times parrots are worth their weight in gold.

But rarely - if ever - do we confess our love for the Soul peering out of the mirror, that person with your nose and lips, the twinkle in your eye, the person with the lines created by both joy and disappointment, that one who has learned to take very good care of others but who too often takes him/herself for granted.

Sure - guys buy gadgets for themselves, woman go crazy in shoe stores and both take themselves out for a good meal when accompanied by family or friends. "Good night, I love you," we say afterwards. "I love you too, my dear friend," is a frequent response. But when the meeting or gathering is over, when individuals and couples go their own way, when the kids are asleep, when you brush your teeth that evening and your hair in the morning, who of us remembers to share such endearments with one's soulful self. "Yeah-yeah – I know that you know, that I love you! It's implied. Of course I love myself. Why do I have to say it?" Hmmmm. Ever try using that rationale on another?

If you want your love for others to develop, if you want your love to grow more and more inclusive, if want to express your gratitude and commitment to others freely and frequently, then start to include your self in your endearments. "I really do appreciate you," s/he says to the face in the mirror, "I don't tell you often enough and I usually take you for granted. I assume you know I love and appreciate you but I never seem to tell you directly. Today I am starting something new. And look: you're smiling already! So: 'please know that I really do appreciate you and love you.' Wow. That feels good, and I can see that is really making you happy too."

Golden Linings

A disaster occurs: there's a hurricane, tsunami, tornado and the twin towers collapse. People are killed, homes destroyed, community and individual lives disrupted, property losses in the billions of dollars. Lamentation follows: tears, funerals, disarray and a sense of momentary hopelessness. Earthly tragedies cannot be denied nor should memory of them ever be suppressed. Anguish has to be acknowledged, and it needs an outlet and a voice.

Amidst the incredible challenge presented by a disaster, however, there emerges a countervailing dynamic in which people are stirred to come together, help one another, pray as one and rebuild in community. Communal bonds are inherent in living near each other but it often takes a major loss or threat to activate it. Until there is a genuine and demonstrable loss or threat, we tend to lead 'bubble' lives, insulated from each other, separated by internal moats. We live in a community but hardly act like one – that is until disaster strikes.

But when something serious does happen, when someone or many are hurt, when a wide area is affected, the old fences collapse and are immediately replaced with an inclusive sense of 'we' and 'us'. Attitudes that once signaled 'keep out' and 'private' tend to evaporate. Walls are rendered permeable and barriers fall; attending to 'my property' gives way to interaction and a sense of common space and responsibility.

The fireman risks his life to save ten others, and the house on the hill turns into a hospital and soup kitchen; political carping diminishes (at least for the moment) and the nation, and the international community, mourns the losses incurred by people who used to be 'others'; thousands of people send money, food and clothing half way around the world; many get in their cars and volunteer to remove debris, rebuild homes and do whatever needs to be done.

None of these communal awakenings can nullify the initial tragedy. But the separations between people – the busyness of life that begets the invisibility of others, and the hardened boundaries created by fear and suspicion dissipate when some one or a community suffers a loss. The psychic barriers come down. The subdivisions become one. The barricades become bridges. Old and the new sections meld together. The people who were strangers yesterday become neighbors today. Even strict family loyalists become more trusting and inclusive of others. For weeks if not months, people greet and meet, wave and inquire, smile and hug, look each other in the eye and listen to each other as they share and cry and work to recast their lives.

Who was it that said that it takes a real tragedy to create a real community? Dark clouds, golden linings. So much lost. So much gained. So much suffering. So much love.

CHAPTER 12

NO LIMIT OR LACK

Coming Out of the Closet

When you affirm your spirituality and go public with the news, it does indeed feel like 'coming out of the closet'. You may have declared yourself - to yourself - but had never declared it so emphatically and publicly, making it a celebration of yourself and often a revelation to others.

However modestly you may live, sooner or later you say or do something that reveals to others that you are not just another non-descript swallowed up by the generalities of the main stream. If you go public with your spirituality, you may be considered unique, strange or at least different from what others may have assumed. Going public can also be risky for many old friends and loved ones may prefer things are they were.

People in the West who suddenly declare they are born-again Christians, Muslim, Sufi or Hindu for example, must also experience a similar tipping point - and then both an exhilaration and sense of risk when they announce their relatively unique identity in a traditional Judeo-Christian culture. Yet such people usually declare their conversion or commitment within a group or congregation that shares in and thus encourages that declaration of identity.

It can be very different for those of us declaring a belief in a relatively unique amalgam of spiritual ideals. There is no preformed community to greet or support us. And most of us are introverts to begin with - sociable loners who love people and gatherings but prefer to express our spirituality alone in prayer, meditation and contemplation. We mix and match affiliations with various individuals and groups, social and religious, but tend to practice our brand of spirituality alone, not in community.

However modest we may be leading our lives, our subtle or overt declaration that we believe in continuous incarnation, for example, inevitably attracts surprised looks and scornful glances. Being 'liberated' in spiritual terms, however, means not being limited by anyone else's fears, needs or perspectives, or their definition of how a good person, citizen, 'Christian' or god-fearing person should think or behave. Still it's risky. Adopting a belief centered in love – sounds fine, but add in reincarnation, the divinity and immortality of the Soul, and a God that is still developing, learning and creating – and you have what many consider an unusual if not threatening combination.

But forming one's own spiritual mosaic – as centered in this case in a loving (not a judging) God and the Golden Rule – is what spirituality is all about. One's own experience is the basis for one's beliefs and practices, not inheritance; they are best formed through deliberate individual choice versus a continuance of an institutional approach bequeathed at birth. My version, as noted, builds re-incarnation, the immortality of the Soul and the developing organism called the Creative God into the mix. It also includes many of the approaches espoused by traditional religion – for the canopy of spirituality is a broad-based and inclusive amalgam of religious philosophies and practices.

Yet whatever your individualized mosaic, deviating from the structures and strictures of formalized religion – and professing and affirming your choice – still feels like risky business. Here in the West there obviously is no fear of arrest or suppression – as there has been throughout history all over the world. But there still are religious condo cops. Say nothing and no one asks or seems to care. Go public – and eyebrows – are raised. "Say what?' is not untypical. So, not needing a stump or a soapbox, you simply do your thing. But writing a book and telling all: now that will surely invite some stares and strange looks (especially among those who think they know me). Yet I sense it will also attract salutations and notes of 'thanks' from friends, family and strangers who have been on a similar path but who may not have admitted it yet or claimed their right to do so.

As for this newly declared exponent of personal spirituality, the exhilaration is now there but it has been preceded by a good deal of fear and hesitation. The inner dialogue has done something like this:

"Few people know I have been thinking this way and many will be shocked and perhaps pull away. I know my ideas are different from most – and surely a challenge to many. No heaven, no hell, no devil - and continual reincarnation in their place? What will x, y and z think?!"

"Besides, we practitioners of spirituality are not members of an organized community in which people quickly or easily extol their views in common. Most of us have only a handful of friends who share related or similar views. Some may even be part of an ongoing network in which people trade e-mails and attend the same conferences. And some discover there are kindred spirits - in their immediate area no less - only after they say or do something that reveals their devotion to some form of spirituality."

"There is a price to be paid for declaring adherence to a set of beliefs that many could consider strange. It could mean going it alone (what's new?), and absorbing the strange looks of some family and friends. It could also involve linking with others of like mind. In the interim, thank God for the several 'spiritually-oriented' friends who live nearby, and of course, e-mail: the larger spiritual family is scattered but very supportive. And, of course, most will probably yawn and simply go about their business."

"Actually, I sense the biggest impact of declaring myself will be on me personally. I now can, and will, embrace my spiritual identity with greater oomph and clarity. And now that I have organized my beliefs and experiences and gone public before God and everybody - in book form no less – I feel a renewed sense of integrity, vibrancy and centeredness I never realized before."

Liberated and Unlimited

When we recognize and declare our spirituality – subtly or more overtly (as in writing this book), it creates a sense of relief, elation and 'liberation'. The theme may be an old and continuing one but the declaration of primacy, identity and focus is new and thus very liberating. It also gives new meaning to our earthly responsibilities for they are henceforth more consistently viewed through this more authentic prism. Such a clear commitment can affect everything one values, does and supports – including what time and energy one contributes to what projects and causes.

In my own case, a new sense of core identity emerged once I dealt with the concern of being labeled as different and potentially shunned because of it. Declaring that I – like everyone else – was an immortal Soul has opened up whole new vistas. A new sense of integrity has emerged. The words and actions of my public persona are no longer muted but now reflect the more intensive spiritual impulses of my inner or true self. And my open declaration of my new identity - in my books and workshops – both reflect and create a greater commitment to spiritual causes and issues of social justice.

Now, being clear and open and proud does not resolve problems and challenges. And it does not eliminate the need during incarnation to live temporarily within a limited environment or deal with some of the confined perspectives and staid priorities of the greater culture. But we also we come to realize that anyone, group or environment that negates our experience, dismisses our sense of worth as an immortal Soul or judges our beliefs, needs to be politely heard and then gently challenged in turn. If all fails, then we simply search for some common ground – however great or minimal.

It is essential, however, to continue affirming belief in the Soul incarnate - when so asked - and stay true to the focus on prayer, meditation, direct communication with God and Her angelic hosts. Being 'liberated' is thus a state of consciousness that centers itself in trust – trust in self, God and the universe. Given the nature of our divine Soul, we each have immediate and unlimited power to claim liberation from whatever hinders our spiritual identity and growth. Claiming that right is not an aggressive act but an assertive one. And it is best stated simply, firmly and with love - love for others, but especially love for oneself as a conscious celebrant of liberated spirituality.

When activated, the energy of liberation is not brash and cocky but quietly confident and assured. One knows his/her incarnation came through the biological parents and into the social milieu that one selected personally, and thus continues to honor those choices as the source of both supportive activities and challenges. But the Soul is also empowered to overcome any tendency within the incarnate's family or social circles that seek to delimit its integrity, diminish its consciousness or compromise its mission on Earth.

The affirming Soul knows it is a member of a larger incarnated community and is, of course, willing to complete its chosen work within those natural restrictions and boundaries. But it is not beholden to any communal codes that violate the norms of love, the integrity of individuality, and the diversity that is the glue of any real community. The liberated Soul knows it is not superior to any other person (or Soul) yet knows as well that it is divine in nature and thus inferior to no one and equal to all challenges.

As the Soul incarnate activates full awareness of its true nature, it knowingly lays claims to an integrated identity of two aspects. It is aware of being an incarnated person living in a material reality. It also affirms itself as an immortal Soul who has chosen a physical form in order to spiritualize the earth in the name of love. It can then fully appreciate and gives thanks to God for the opportunity to intertwine the everyday and the eternal as it quietly, persistently and joyfully goes about the business of fulfilling its spiritual mission.

Consequences

There is a world – if not universe – of difference between our experiences of limit in the earthly domain and the continuing realities of the immortal Soul. In part, we chose the limitations we experience on Earth in order to deepen our appreciation of hardship, disappointment and difficulty and in the process learn something more about compassion and empathy.

But we must be careful not to confuse the difference between experiencing the limiting effects of earthly living with our continuing sense of being an empowered and immortal Soul. As incarnates, we must not allow our experience of occasional limit to call into question the reality of the Soul's immortality, or to tarnish our capacity to surround our temporary setbacks on Earth with life experiences that emphasize joy and contribution.

So while we may learn from challenges it is important not to elevate difficulties into virtues. Many parents, religions and organizations, for example, have conditioned us into thinking that limit and lack are good in themselves because they help to build character. A suffering and sacrificial God is the idolized figure for Christians. Some very radical Islamists suggest that martyrs are ushered immediately into heaven. And pain has long been the fate and lament of the Jews. Even Pope John Paul II, when asked if he would relinquish his papacy due to his long illnesses, gave suffering a 'positive' spin when he said, "Jesus did not come down from the cross" – the inference being, "Neither will I for I too am meant to suffer like Jesus."

Many children learn to get attention through real and feigned illnesses. And some parents learn to use guilt and fear of abandonment to obtain obedience from their children and pity for themselves. Many lovers don't want mates who are responsible and mature but prefer somebody in need of their care or direction. Unfortunately, there are also a sufficient number of folks in the mating game who want above everything else to be cared for and guided - even though their alleged provider may be an egotistic lout and general no-goodnik.

Pressures to imprint images of self-doubt envelop the human experience. With some parents, we never seem obedient enough. In school: we are never smart enough. In religion: not good enough. At work: not fast, assertive, quiet, or respectful enough. And socially many are often reminded that they are not pretty, handsome, tall or thin enough.

Even though we are children of God – true reflections of the Divine – we can - as incarnated human beings easily fall prey to many of these negations, affecting not only our identity as creative and capable human beings but inferentially having a negative impact on our Souls as well.

If we experience a human lack in attitude, ability or agility, then we need to take responsibility for it and not seek out options that invite us to perform poorly. Techies go to computer school while the artistic seek outlets that allow expression of their talents. No one should want to place him or herself in a position to fail.

But a demonstrable record of chronic unemployment, difficulty in working with others, or consistently being unable to manage or hold onto a home, a relationship or one's income suggests it may be a good idea to revisit the family, social and organizational tapes to see which negative psychological image was foisted on who. Clues to the presence of self-limiting scripts can be detected in how one describes others (negative projections), one's body postures, and one's attitudes toward new and untried activities.

Want to double-check? If you are having chronic difficulties negotiating your experience on Earth, ask a friend to mimic your words and behaviors. Ask them to do a caricature of how you walk and how you interact with others. Let them do 'you' - for you. Watch and listen, and then reflect on the words, tones and behaviors they use to imitate you. Discounting any exaggeration that goes with doing caricatures, do any of the portrayals of you suggest a perspective and pattern of behavior that is self-limiting or self-defeating? Has society convinced you that it is only human to doubt yourself and denigrate your abilities? If so, that image will inevitably seek to replicate itself by creating or attracting evidence that such an interpretation is true.

On the other hand, perhaps you – like all of us - agreed to come here to experience some forms of limit. If so, be careful not to have the human experience of limitation diminish your sense of having chosen that experience in order to learn something valuable. You have no reason, however, to allow any temporary human limitations to degrade your identity as either a empowered human being capable of creating life in your own image, or as an immortal Soul who is using the experiences of its physical incarnation to learn how to love and thus spiritualize the material domain.

Life on Earth is intended to teach us what life is like – positive and negative – and then use those experiences to make life better for ourselves and others. It is like the television program that features chief executives taking lowly jobs in their own organizations in order to gain greater insight into its operations, and greater appreciation for the people who complete its tasks on a daily basis.

So experiencing lack and limit is not the same as feeling or believing you are lacking and limited. The former may represent an opportunity to learn compassion. The latter is a human construct that diminishes the power of your identity. No problem, of course, with the former; it is called 'life'. There are major issues, however, if you allow your earthly experiences to blur, tarnish or obliterate your awareness of your innate human creativity and the empowerments of your immortal Soul.

The dialogues – and at times tussles - between the world and the human ego, and the ego and the Soul, are constant. It is very important then – whatever challenges you may have chosen, not to be worn down into thinking less of yourself as a human or a Soul. It might help to periodically reintroduce your ego to your Soul and vice versa, so they can remind each other of their mutually supporting roles: one experiences so the other can learn, and its the positive creativity of one that is most loved and appreciated by the other.

Lack and Abundance

How then do we tactically prevent the temporary limits we experience on the material domain from causing us to negate or forget our empowerments as an immortal Soul?

First, we have to realize that 'lack' is more a state of mind and then a material reality. If you think of yourself as being limited, less worthy, unable - whatever it is - you create and attract conditions that confirm that self-fulfilling prophecy. It is the same with 'abundance': if you consider yourself as already having abundance, then you create and attract what you experience as abundance. Both, of course, are relative terms. 'Lack' as compared to what? 'Abundance' in comparison to what real or imagined state? You can always find someone who has greater or less 'lack' or 'abundance' of whatever commodity or trait you can identify. Thus the preeminent influence of your *state of mind*.

Would winning the lottery bolster your sense of abundance? Yes – for finances and material goods. But would such a windfall be automatically converted into the inner feeling of abundance or would it only set off the next stage of seeking more of something else? And would any of it necessarily bring you love, understanding or that vital sense of contentment? Would losing money affect anything other than a temporary sense of material lack? Some people live in a comparative hovel and give thanks for their abundance. Others live in a penthouse yet continue to seek more riches.

The foundation for the sense of abundance in the human domain is being thankful for whatever tangible things, like a house and car - and intangible energies, like love and family - exist in your life. If you begin with a lament, you propagate the sense of lack, inevitably attracting people and situations that re-enforce the negative label you give to your experience.

When you start the day with a sense of appreciation and thanksgiving, you strengthen your feeling of inner support and activate a sense of overall wellbeing. You are then likely to attract circumstances and experiences that solidify that feeling. You attract what you honor. You create what you image and affirm.

Yes...~~But~~...And!

Here's another potential pitfall. We all do it. We say something descriptive, even affirming and then add the dreaded word...'but'.

The impact of 'but' – used anywhere in a sentence - is to take exception to what has already been stated. "I really like you in that suit...but". The latter condition negates the former affirmation, the after thought – the adverb 'but' undercutting the power of the verb 'like'. If that is what is intended, so be it. Often we simply don't know how to pay a simple compliment or describe something without overextending ourselves and squeezing in an unsolicited critique.

How about finding another word that supports the original intent by facilitating more of the same? How about using the word 'and' instead of 'but'? "I really like you in that suit...and I also like you in tan." Or, even stronger, "I love your sense of humor...and I also love your easy approach to life." The initial statement stands; so does the follow-up. The 'and' statement both reinforces the initial comment and adds to it.

These are not huge things, perhaps, in a world that includes crime, war and ethnic cleansing. They are significant, however, in every day relations with family, friends and colleagues...*and* what could be more important? Why inadvertently leave the impression of diminishing what is being communicated by sneaking in a 'but' - when you have the opportunity to honor 'this' *and* also 'that'.

Stop and Let

Stop

- carrying other people's burdens.
- trying to save someone from the lessons s/he must learn.
- insisting that others follow your lead, do your bidding or think as you do.

- being manipulative – maneuvering to make things happen your way.
- being so will-full.
- complaining.
- tolerating circumstances or hanging around with people who do not support or energize you.
- neglecting to find the time to explore what really fascinates and intrigues you.
- evaluating yourself and constantly taking your own psychological temperature.
- judging – anyone or anything.
- being fearful and worrying about everything.

Let

- others feel their empowerment.
- go of anything that does not serve your best interests.
- your imagination soar.
- others know how you feel.
- the day's events evolve - once in a while - versus trying to make things happen.
- yourself knock on doors that interest and excite you.
- yourself walk through doors that open and walk by those that don't.
- others make their own decisions and live their lives without your comment, approval or evaluation.
- the events of the day flow through you: bless them and then let them go.

- yourself ponder the mysteries of the universe: the innocence of a child, the workings of DNA, the incessant reality of the heart beat, the workings of the atom, the hum of an expanding universe, and the seed that is about to blow free and begin its journey of choosing, growing and becoming.

Lighten the Load

Spiritual energy is light, not heavy. Why then do we often experience this world as burdensome and heavy? Ah: we return once again to how the human mind works. Rather than many of our experiences operating as throughputs – images, thoughts and feelings progressively registered, integrated, stored, shed or acted upon – we allow many of them, especially so-called 'negative' ones, to linger and accumulate. The bin in which we store memory of our undesirable experiences not only grows large, it increases in density. By saving and inwardly savouring them, we empower any allegedly negative experience to smoulder and become a deep-seated resentment.

Such negative recalls weigh heavily on the mind and feel like incessant burdens - especially if little things cause us to relive them again and again. Each negative memory has the internal weight of a heavy stone. And each stone feels like it has been placed in a big sack along with the other cumulative junk. Worst of all, we feel obligated to carry that sack around wherever we go. And none of it ever seems to get sorted or discarded. Nothing ever seems to get thrown away; its as though we love to wallow in anger, regret, anxiety and self-pity. Consequently, the sack gets heavier and heavier.

This is one sure way of becoming psychologically obese. Anyone have a clue - as to what to do? Anyone have a hint as to what attitudes and actions might lighten the load? Is anyone interested in opening the bag and getting rid of some of this stuff? Anyone thinking of ways to put the bag down, open it up, examine what is in it and begin throwing some stuff out?

The theme of 'getting lighter' is not really important if you assume you were meant to be a beast of burden: things happen, they accumulate, and you learn to carry on. In fact, life without carting around a big heavy bag might feel strange after all these years.

But there is that other aspect of you, namely that empowered *soulful aspect* - that needs its adopted mind to be as light as possible. It does not want its incarnation to be weighed down by any sense of bondage, drudgery, limitation or heaviness. The incarnate needs to honor earthly gravity but does not need to invent, attract and carry heavy loads to prove it. Dense, immense and intense is not the destiny of the spirit's embodiment or among the attributes of enlightenment. To lighten up means to bulk down.

Best shed some stones…soon. Open the bag, spill some out, and deliberately choose some for immediate discard. Some throwaways can be added to the trash, some put on the curb, some dumped down the toilet, still others taken directly to the dump.

Some may also be great for flinging or skipping on a lake or pond. It is all in the wrist: flick and they are gone. Getting into the rhythm of tossing things away can be very cathartic and great fun. Being delighted by the number of skips you create is even better. And there's that exuberant realization that you'll never have to lug *that one* around again.

Loss and Learning

Being hurt in an accident, contracting a disease or facing a personal loss of any kind are not the kinds of things you find on anyone's wish list. A diminishment of the mind or body is always tragic – tragic that is, from the viewpoint of the mind and body, from the separate 'me' that identifies primarily with the embodiment portion of the incarnation.

But what is true on the ego-personal level is not necessarily the case on the Soul level. From the vantage point of the Soul, there are no coincidences, accidents, misfortunes or life-and-death situations that are not part of one's learning agreement. All such marker events – both their type and timing - are agreed to in advance, and incorporated into one's agreement prior to incarnation. At the Soul level, such occurrences are considered desired learning experiences — perhaps for learning forbearance, compassion, courage, or simply letting go of the 'things' related to the body in order to better cultivate the concerns of the Soul.

Of course, the ultimate letting go for humans is death — which is usually experienced more intensely by those left behind. The Soul of the departed returns home with intentions of review and integration while the human family and friends of the deceased usually suffer a deep sense of loss. The cycle of debilitation and death is especially horrendous if it involves a child, one's mate or a beloved parent.

Yet the greater truth is that every loss of life, limb and property - is willed or at least conceded — in order to learn a lesson. Learning to appreciate oneself, another, a job, home, family and friends – can include difficulties; giving any of it up and feeling its loss is one of the most profound and painful of all human experiences.

We cannot forget, however, that we are primarily immortal Souls temporarily clothed in human bodies - having deliberately decided not to have any human experience but the one that we – as Souls – designed, agreed to and are now living.

We choose to incarnate (again) in order to get involved in the activities of the physical plane, broaden and deepen our depth of experience and thus enhance our ability to both learn and express love and compassion. We also realized that we, as Souls, would inevitably need to lose many of our family members, friends and colleagues to sickness and then death. As incarnates we understandably experience those losses with great sorry and regret.

Yet at the level of the Soul, we know such losses are only temporary, part of the overall learning agreement we designed and agreed to. The Soul accepts and even appreciates the role that death of the body plays in the life cycle. If we can summon that awareness during those times when we read or hear of 'tragedies' or experience the death of a loved one, it may – just may – help to cushion the sense of loss and put our grieving into a spiritual context.

At the Soul level, we are able to anticipate and accept the larger spiritual circumstances that inevitably involve our friends and loved ones shedding their physical embodiments. We also know their Souls are immortal, that as immortal beings they never really die, that their Souls are always available for counsel and solace, and that we will indeed meet again - face to face - when we too let go of our earthly experience and pass back 'to the Other Side".

CHAPTER 13

THE SPIRIT OF EVERYDAY

Everyday Equals

Don't put gifted spiritual leaders on a pedestal
and assume they are so much better than you.
They are revered because they acquired
their level of awareness through experience
- something you are accumulating as well.

Messengers like Basho, Socrates, Rumi and Gandhi
were not born masters.
They started as children,
innocent yet unsure and incomplete–
humbled by time and place like us all.

History now tells us
they overcame their obstacles,
worked through their issues,
and earned their mastership
- millimeter by mile.

They learned how to ascend by learning
how to descend into everyday living.
So erect pedestals to no isolated person or thing.
Rather honor each, all and everything
As expressions of the presence of God.

> The Avatars uncovered their inner light,
> then shared it and became enlightened.
> So revere, if you will, the attributes of elevated Souls
> but look its bearers
> straight in the eye.

> If you need initially to look up
> then climb the invisible ladder
> only false humility erected,
> meeting them directly
> as they stand to greet you
> on common ground.

Extra-Ordinary

It is difficult, it is hard, it seems downright impossible at times. I am referring to the need to live our ordinary lives in extraordinary ways. Few of us are rock stars, famous architects, accomplished musicians, scientists, entrepreneurs or even politicians. We don't have a television talk show or ever appear on Broadway. Our names are not listed anywhere but on the tax rolls. And sometimes even our children forget that we have lives – even a history and a first name - like real people.

Given our lack of visibility, our potential impact seems limited. There are times when nobody – or at least very few – seem to listen to our viewpoint, heed our words, are inspired by our interpretations or are encouraged by our actions. We may rise to importance, here and there: occasional and momentary big fish in very small ponds. But our impact - in comparison to the headline personalities – often seems invisible and non-descript.

Yet our call to the spiritual perspective encourages us to live according to a vision that is extraordinary, that goes beyond the traditional or normal ways of thinking and acting. It beckons us to go deeper into ourselves, to nurture the inner life through prayer, meditation and contemplation – and with spontaneous yet-oh-so significant acts of joy and kindness. And it calls on us to exceed the ordinary by elevating our everyday intentions and creating just a little bit of empathy for one more person.

When we affirm and act on our spiritual heritage, we aim higher than the general norms used by society. In so doing, we also seek to attain something deeper than notoriety and material success. We are, by gosh, immortal Souls living in the land of mortality, who when acting with love and compassion are capable of transforming everything we engage.

When we think and behave like the sparks of divinity we are, we use our spiritual empowerments to create loving and joyful encounters so extraordinary that they far exceed any possible worldly attainment. Not many learn about the extra bounce in that person's step or the healing of another's suffering after encountering a Soul like you who had their spiritual jets turned on full. Many a headline is written every day on the hearts of those so graced by the natural transfer of healing energy that is deliberately intended by one immortal Soul for another.

Spirituality: Counterweight to the Mundane

Both the mundane and spiritual realms celebrate sheer talent. But to what use is that talent put? The spiritual point of view defines 'impact' in terms of quality and service. But society's exaggerated emphasis on power, position, good looks, money, sex appeal and a glamorous lifestyle – merely perpetuate the alleged value of the lowest common denominators.

Recall that psychologist Abraham Maslow studied human nature and uncovered the workings of what he called 'a hierarchy of values', the set of values that motivate the average human being throughout life. The base value is concerned with survival. The second looks to insure one's physical wellbeing and success. Third strives for belongingness or acceptance by others. The fourth, Maslow called 'self-acceptance' or affirmation, and the fifth is 'self-actualization' or the desire to activate one's full potential. Maslow in essence later added a sixth factor, one that he called 'self transcendence' which is akin to the perspective we refer to here as 'spiritual'.[32]

As a counterweight to the basic motivations, self-transcendence or spirituality encourages us to affirm our divine standing, pursue a loving mission and heighten our state of consciousness in the process. Spirituality beckons us to transcend society's accent on outer beauty and monetary success by transforming otherwise neutral and ordinary situations into opportunities for caring, giving and compassion.

This is the province of the soulful. As noted, one's spiritual contributions do not appear on the front page or as the lead items in the evening news. Those arenas are reserved for stories that emphasize power, money, sex and such peculiar attention-getters as an 'old man bites a young dog' - with the millions of soulful but 'significant trifles' being summarized on page 72 and used only as sentimental fillers.

But look at how vast the arena of the extraordinary is, and how closely its contents are concerned with helping or serving specific people – today, now, as we speak. Waving 'hello' to a neighbor, for example, becomes an 'extraordinary' deed when we instill our greeting with a loving intention, especially if that 'hello' is the only one received that day by the elderly lady who lives across the street. Offering your hand to a friend becomes more than an automatic gesture if it is complemented with a greeting that both meets the eye and affirms the divine presence of the other. Spontaneous compliments which notice the cut or color of the coat, the sparkle in another's eye, or the strength or warmth of their presence can also become transformative events which convert habitual rituals into real contact.

The list of possibilities for doing something extraordinary - in and through everyday events and encounters - is endless. So many happen 'everyday' that we often forget their power. Anything that helps build the confidence of another, that let's them know you like their company, appre-

---

32   The first five factors in the hierarchy are outlined in *Toward a Psychology of Being* (New York: John Wiley & Sons, 1968). What is here referred to as the sixth, namely 'self-transcendence' is affirmed later in *Religions, Values and Peak Experiences* (New York, Penguin, 1980). Maslow's hierarchy of values was also outlined below in Chapter 6, "Applying Maslow's Hierarchy".

ciates their input or enjoys their perspective, that simply notices them and attends to their presence and needs – is a spiritual act. Any look, greeting, gesture, telephone call, e-mail or tweet that affirms another, that's delivered in a loving way - meets the standard of spiritual quality and depth.

All we really have to do is trust our intuition and silently send something as readily available as our loving and joyful (or even healing) intention to anyone we sense might need or appreciate it. Think of an affirming message: intend it and then mentally send it. It will be delivered and received immediately. Bing-badda-boo-badda-boom. No headlines will appear in the local newspaper but banners will fly in heaven.

Intending spiritual energy is a lot like prayer: it is focused on sending energy but not necessarily focused on any desired outcome. When you send loving or healing energy to a stranger you sense could use a lift, you do not need to know anything about them for them to receive and absorb the energy you send. Intending spiritual energy is simply a gift from one Soul to another, making it available to them to use in any way they wish.

Will any television program praise you for what you have done? Not likely. Will your income rise? No. Will the recipient use the infusion of loving energy in time of need? Most likely. And will you feel good about yourself – knowing you have done something significant to aid another without asking for anything in return? Absolutely.

All you need do - to create the extraordinary and thus become extraordinary - is be who you are, a loving spirit in human clothing, an ascended master in training, an immortal Soul ready and able to gift your love, joy and sense of thanksgiving to any and all any way you want, wherever you want and whenever you feel called to express your transcendent nature and create the extraordinary.

In, Out and In Between

What is the difference between stillness, solitude and silence?

'Stillness' is a state of consciousness. It is an *inner* experience – when the normal busyness of the mind is quieted and we become fully present and aware. Stillness can occur during meditation, at the sight of a new born, walking in the woods, or anywhere you encounter the sacred. In 'stillness' one's Soul reigns supreme. Nothing in particular happens but everything significant is clear and present. If the busy brain *records*, and the inquiring mind seeks to *know*, it is the 'stillness' of the Soul that instantly *understands*.

'Silence' is the *outer* counterpart of *stillness*. It is what you 'hear'. It is no sound, a hushed atmosphere, when you become vividly aware of your breath and don't even want *it* to make a sound. You can sense wondrous 'silence' on a winter's day when the snow falls gently to the ground and onto the tips of your nose and eyelids. For others it arrives with twilight and a cup of tea. If evoked by inner 'stillness', silence can befall you in a bus, at a cafe, even while walking on a street as you notice - but do not necessarily care not to hear - vendors selling their wares.

The *in between* that links the inner 'stillness' with the outer 'silence' - and vice versa - is the catalyst called 'solitude'. 'Solitude' is not loneliness - for that is a malady of the ego. It does not involve a group consciousness or acting in accordance with any group norms. It is the mark of the true individual, the celebrant who revels being in the moment and experiencing a deep sense of *presence* – that which unifies what is both inside and out. As the *in between* or connector, 'solitude' not only provides the link between the inner state of *stillness* and the outer experience of *silence*. It is also the catalyst of both.

Like its aspects, the sense of 'solitude' may last for seconds, minutes or days, depending on the context of your life. It does need to be cultivated, however, by periodically doing 'nothing', meditating, taking a walk in nature (to insure your solitude is not out-competed by ordinary busyness), and contemplating the divine in and through an outer-and-inner encounter with some aspect of the universe.

Think of an equilateral triangle. The initial slanting side of *Stillness* connects to the oncoming slanting tip of *Silence*, and each is connected and anchored by the foundation of *Solitude*. The space enclosed is the triangle of spirituality. Within it, we are able to convert our experiences into moments of deep spiritual awareness.

You might even imagine yourself looking down from a balcony onto the first floor where three people have joined hands to form a human triangle. With arms outstretched and leaning backwards ever so slightly, the three persons - or states of being - become a balanced and interdependent field of energy. Many architects, most notably Frank Lloyd Wright, used such a technique to support the rotunda and other circular portions of a building.

So it is with the triad of Stillness, Solitude and Silence. When examined separately, they are the three interdependent parts of a triangle. When experienced, they are each extensions of one another. When viewed spiritually, they merge and become one continuous process - encompassed by the circle of wholeness.

Listen

Communicating with others is part of God's work - and yours as well. So here are some rules of thumb for dealing with other people – especially during times of difficulty. These suggested guidelines focus on the theme of honoring *the other*: being present fully for them, standing witness to their experience, and certainly resisting the urge to analyze, judge - or do their work for them.

First, truly listen to the other. Everyone has a story. You may not want to hear it over and over again; you can always draw that line later. Initially - just listen attentively. You might ask some questions to clarify issues. You might even paraphrase on occasion to make sure you understand and assure the speaker you are able to follow what he/she is communicating. Otherwise, be quiet and listen – actively and with respect. We all need to share and clear out our emotions on occasion - and it is good to have a friend who is a good listener on hand when those times arrive.

Second, don't judge, correct or scold. Just listen and *give witness.* The most supportive energy a person can receive – especially in times of difficulty – is to have another person simply be present for them and thus honour them and their experience.

Third, resist the temptation to give advice – unless asked, and even then, resist playing 'answer man' (or woman). You might – if asked - help the other sort through their feelings by reporting back what you think you heard or the patterns that seem evident to you. Again, if asked, you might encourage the other to think of potential remedies – asking such questions as "what do you need now?" and "what are your best alternatives"?

Fourth, the list of things that are sure to make matters worst - in the short and long run - includes doing the other's work for them. Your ability to assist immediately is best confined to listening, helping the other sort through their feeling and assisting them in identifying and taking whatever actions are then necessary.

In times of need, what another needs most is to reclaim their power to decide and confidence in taking care of themselves. So short of a pending catastrophe (and that's hardly ever) - never, never try to save the other with your alleged ability to restructure and take over their life. All a distressed person needs is a well-meaning authoritarian or well intentioned but intrusive 'helper' who thinks they need to rush to someone's side if that person appears shaky or begin to cry; that's likely to make matters worse by undermining their integrity and inviting dependence on you. Rather, it is always best to help another regain confidence in their ability to think clearly and make their own decisions.

Fifth, resist as well your ego's desire to play Junior Freud or take on the role of Mr. or Ms. Smarty Pants. Leave the analysis to the analysts. Your role is to be a friend with a big ear, and a tiny-tiny mouth that stays closed most of the time, and a helping hand when asked.

Sixth, you can be of assistance by helping the person contact friends and relatives, physicians and counselors – but only as a supplement to their own efforts and only if they are unable to complete a list of tasks on their own.

In sum: open your heart, put a zipper on your mouth, sit still, be attentive, grow big ears, and only move your hands and legs to help as requested. If you can do that, and only *that*, you will earn your friend's deepest appreciation for one, being present; two, allowing them to share and unwind; three, honor their power to sort things out and then choose what they want to do next; and four, support their desire - and ability - to regain their balance and confidence in themselves and their decision-making process.

Collaboratory

Gus Jacacci, a spiritual visionary and phrasemaker extraordinaire, has combined the words 'laboratory' and 'collaboration' to create the new, creative unity of "collaboratory".

All our efforts, certainly our best, are works in process, on-going laboratories of experimental learning. Whether our interactions are with children, a spouse, friends or co-workers - our individual energies seek a collaborative form, a synergistic coming together with others of like mind. The result is not a union but a meaningful connection of formerly separate entities; not a homogenized blending but a mutually supportive linkage of different elements. Individuality is thus preserved if not celebrated - yet each contributor becomes a significant part of a new, enhanced and hyphenated-whole.

The exchange is mutually nourishing: collaborating allows us to do things we could not do – or do as well – by ourselves. It also produces resonance, affirmations of our best intentions being echoed in the words and actions of others. We swap old stories and create new ones as we forge new bonds of celebration and mutual esteem.

Co-laboratories with others create synergy, one and one producing three or sixteen, each addition to the effort magnifying the process exponentially. They can evolve at home, on the job, in the community - anywhere creativity and productivity are valued. E. M. Forster captures the energy perfectly. "Only connect', he writes. "Only connect the prose and the passion, and both will be exalted, and human love will be seen at its highest. Live in fragments no longer. Only connect, and the beast and the monk, robbed of the isolation that is life to either, will die." [33]

Live Your Truth

If you are smart, be smart – but keep it to yourself, at least most of the time. When communicating with others – be smart only when asked or invited. It is never wise to act like 'Mr. or Ms. Know-It-All', displaying your knowledge, which, even if true, makes you sound like Cliff on *Cheers* with all his "Little Known Facts".

If you are pretty or handsome, be pretty or handsome but not a poser, or a show-off, or a person who acts like your external profile is tantamount to having a great Soul. Katherine Hepburn was once asked why she always looked like she was posing. Her response: "Of course. I am an actress" – in other words, "I" am the one to be seen and admired.

If you are cheerful, be cheerful but don't drive every one crazy with a ceaseless grin or an endless rendition of 'you've-got-to-hear-this-one'. And true humour - spontaneous remarks that are really funny – has nothing in common with ridicule, poking fun at another or looking down your nose with a sneer.

If you play the trumpet, then charm, smooth and excite us with your horn but please not at two in the morning or over breakfast.

If you are a lover of many things, then be a lover - and let us feel your inclusive energies in easy doses minus the flailing about, exuberant gestures and self-absorbed glee.

If you possess a clue to the Truth, then please live that truth and be that Truth. But, please, no sermons, admonishments, judgments, pamphlets or missionary zeal.

If you are a partner of God, then allow His or Her presence to emerge naturally, in little but significant ways - not with pontification

---

[33] *Howard's End* (London: The Folio Society, 1910/1973).

at dinner or the business luncheon, and surely not with a loud knock, a pamphlet or shouts of 'hallelujah'.

Really smart, attractive, cheerful, gifted, loving, insightful and graceful people don't push 'it' or themselves. The just are who they are - without pomp and theatrics, a lot like God and the mystics. And spiritual people tend not to pray on street corners and in large stadiums but exude love and lightness, naturally, through their unassuming presence. The talented and the people of depth just flow – sans testimonials, hoopla and canned prayers and applause.

No Complaining…Please!

Complaining is the ultimate slippery slope. It begins with a mildly egotistical premise and ends with a bloated conclusion.

Its most vocal practitioner is the self-centered individual who thinks everything that is not going well is worth broadcasting with a snarl. It is also common among the 'quiet' victims – only they complain more with frowns, pursed lips, sighs and frowned expressions of "what else could possibly happen"? Such an attitude, of course, has the effect of doing just that - inviting 'something else' to happen that further drains or disappoints them. And so the syndrome feeds the cycle that fulfills the prophecy.

The emotional logic of feeling aggrieved - and thus entitled to complain - goes something like this: There are standards. If those standards are not met, then I have a right to complain since I am in the best situation both to set the standards, and to judge whether or not the other person is meeting them. The 'world' or 'they', should know what I need - and if it or they do not know, then my ego has a right to feel wounded and label their actions stupid, insensitive or gross.

Complaining starts with the "I" or a normally balanced ego getting pulled out of whack. Once inflated, the insecure ego is easily deflated. Since it is larger than it has a right to be, it grows thin-skinned. Bloated beyond normal, it sucks up all the air in the room. Too expansive for any one person, it is impossible not to bump into it. The inflated balloon and the pinprick are perfect complements to one other.

Is there a spiritual problem with the chronic and habitual complainer? Of course: when the ego is exaggerated, the Soul is diminished. Enshrine 'the little one' and you neutralize or denigrate awareness and the role of the 'big' one.

What are the positive alternatives to complaining – especially if you feel you really have been wronged and have good reason to complain?

1. If your complaint is the consequence of a legal or contractual matter, then pursue your case as the law allows. But pursue it calmly and coolly – not as a David looking for a Goliath.

2. If it was a personal matter - a perceived snub or discourtesy – then share your feelings directly and as soon as you can. If that option is not available, arrange a meeting to clear up the unfinished business before it festers and grows into resentment.

3. If 'the finger' speeds by - bless the car and the occupant, and let it go. Remind yourself that it is up to you to choose your dramas and involvements; don't let the anger of others determine your agenda or change your intentions and energy patterns. Are you an incarnated Soul - here to create love, light and joy - or not?

4. Ask for guidance – in prayer or meditation.

5. If tugged into having a justified grievance (you really were wronged) – you have every right to deal with it. But then get on with it. Telling your story over and over again, and at higher and higher octaves will wear out your friends. Do some 'Soul' searching into why your ego was so bruised and why it now needs so much soothing. Was it 'this' situation alone that really affected you, or has it triggered a set of cumulative issues - perhaps unearthing something long buried and bruised?

6. Give yourself credit: an incident or two with certain people could have been very hurtful and it is normal to fume to whoever will listen – especially if the offending party is not available and is reluctant to meet. The key here is to insure your grievance is confined to a given situation or person and does not become

the basis for endemic complaining. Localized anger may be more than appropriate. But allowing one situation to affect your attitude toward everything in life would be doing yourself – and your family and colleagues - a great injustice.

7. It is also important to take responsibility for your reactions and feelings. Not everyone would have felt slighted; the fact that you did may have as much to do with your history and your makeup as the incident itself. Taking responsibility for one's part in creating a difficult situation is a sure sign of someone who is strong, loving and spiritually adept.

Opinions and Judgments

There is a big difference between having an opinion and proclaiming a judgment.

An opinion is a temporary statement that expresses responsibility for its likes and dislikes. It does not judge or condemn someone or something. The person with an opinion accepts his/her role in the equation: "I don't like that". The attribute in question may be fine and in fact preferred by others. But given 'who I am and what I value or prefer, I don't like X and instead prefer Z.'

Judgment is the opposite. It is a negative and often disdainful evaluation of the worth of something or someone. "You are a jerk" is very different from "I don't like that hat, or word, or way of behaving". "You are evil, or a rotten son, or a stupid person" puts the entire onus on the receiver, none on the sender. It communicates disdain from on high.

A judgment can also hurt because it is usually comes as a pronouncement, as an indisputable definition: "you are what I say you are and there is no disputing that fact."

Judgments also tend either to end a conversation with utter frustration or lead to a string of escalating recriminations: "Oh yeah, well YOU are a...."

The judger also does not take responsibility for his/her half of the equation. He/she fails to acknowledge that interactions are two-way streets. Usually judgments are activated when the incipient judger reacts to something he/she did not like. Rather than expressing an opinion or taking responsibility for his/her own feelings and point of view, a judgment literally evaluates the other person in negative terms and as if there could be no other point of view.

What about people who are not exactly judgmental but very opinionated? 'Opinionated' connotes a borderline fixation with one's own point of view and an unwillingness to consider other opinions. It is associated with being relatively closed and rigid...voicing an opinion so *strongly* that it feels and operates like the passing of judgment; in communicating the sense that 'there is no valid opinion but mine', a person can certainly insinuate that you are nothing but a dirty #&%^(@+#$%!

A suggestion: if you hear something you do not like, it is always wise to pause for a moment, withhold judgment or being opinionated, and realize that any impact you feel is in good part a commentary on your sensitivities and issues; given your background and values, you are responsible for things affecting you as they do. The best way to refrain from judging is to know yourself reasonably well, namely what pushes your buttons given your values, background and experience. You are then better able to take responsibility for things affecting you as they do. If you haven't a clue, then you run the risk of being seduced into instinctively rejecting whatever the world presents that is not tailored precisely to your conditioning and sensitivities.

To summarize: people who are judgmental and/or disdainful usually suffer from the *prickles* - which is a lot like walking onto a crowded bus with lots of chips on your shoulder. They tend to think everyone is like them – or should be. They are relatively unconscious and have a hard time acknowledging diversity and the differences of opinion that stem from different values and experiences. They assume people need to be sensitive to 'them' and their 'obvious' priorities. Communicating with a *prickly* person is a lot like walking through a minefield: their issues are everywhere and yet they fail to take responsibility for them. They are a particular problem at family reunions.

People who tend to begin and end with opinions, however, are more aware of their own stuff. They have come to accept their own histories and are conscious of – and thus in control of - their own visceral reactions. They know they have preferences but they are also willing to admit that most of them are conditioned by their own personal history. So they choose to live and let live, and thus tend to make very good friends.

"This entry is really stupid. It has nothing to do with the Soul", says the prickly one.

"I don't see it that way," opines the other. Certainly God has opinions but in being all loving does not attempt to make others feel less worthy – although some of the religions formed in His/Her name have done so with impunity. From the spiritual point of view, God is also never judgmental – of anyone or thing – under any circumstances. There is no sin to redeem, no devil to blame, no heaven as reward or hell as punishment, and no bad people – only folks who temporarily go astray.

Instead, the spiritual perspective accepts the fact that there are variations in how fast and fully each of us learns to exercise unconditional love. It asks only that we all take personal responsibility for our speed in getting there. At least, that's my opinion.

Focus and Energy

What is your focus today? To what do you wish to attend?

If you wish to achieve a specific goal, what kind of energy do you intend to use in order to achieve that goal?

Focus usually involves a content that is described with a verb and noun - something as specific as "writing another chapter of the book", "buying birthday presents", "helping the children with their homework", or "negotiating the new contract." It sets the theme of the hour, day or week. It is that which is sought. It is the goal.

Intention is the method you choose for achieving that focus or goal. It is the energy you bring to any project that activates it and brings it into being. And that energy could be almost anything - including loving, joyful, assertive or whatever set of energies you think will get you where you want to be.

Given all the things you have to do, and given all the additional things that could emerge, it may be helpful to actually choose a goal (your focus) and how you wish to attain it (your intentions) – lest the day, week or month go by with your only doing busy work.

It is not unusual for us to set goals for everyday and professional tasks and then allow those self-multiplying activities to out compete such issues as our spirituality. So if you haven't done so already, why not deliberately add an overtly spiritual goal to your agenda. It could be as specific as writing to a sick friend, greeting people with deliberate good cheer, sending a loving thought or healing energy to someone, or meeting someone's normal grumpiness with greater ease, understanding and love. A spiritual goal might also focus on praying for guidance, harmony and peace; learning to be a more empathetic listener; and setting time aside each day for meditation and prayer.

How about listening to your internal dialog over breakfast, and heeding the images of spirituality that arise spontaneously throughout the day. Those lovely thoughts will fade, however, unless they are formalized into conscious choices. It helps to write them down as they occur – increasing the possibility that they will not be pushed aside (again) by more immediate issues.

Now, how about achieving that goal or focus with some active *intending?*

What we actually do and what we attain in life is, of course, dependent on the quality and quantity of the energies we bring to them, on the means we use to activate and attain them. Intentions are the force fields that drive our actions toward achieving our goals.

In the spiritual realm, the options are enormous – and include such ways of operating as loving, playful, joyful, quiet, being present and attentive, speaking up, being appreciative, and displaying ease and general good will in tense situations.

There is great value in having at least one proactive spiritual focus per day, a goal that is then energized by equally spiritual intentions. Without such clarity, you run the risk of being sucked into purely mundane agendas or the energy patterns of others.

Everything

Everything offers an opportunity to extend love. Everything presents an opportunity to learn compassion. Everything you say, do and encounter contains the option to deepen your awareness of your identity as a divine being.

Everything - the big items on our to-do list as well its fragments, each hour of the day as well as each every one minute interval, every planned pursuit as well as the spontaneous happenings that unfold en route, every item and image and ticking of the clock - is loaded with potential for awareness and enlightenment.

Travel where you will. Accomplish what you wish. Think great thoughts and do great deeds. Yet learn as well to be receptive to the chance encounters that can affect you in strange and wondrous ways, when a momentary event opens your eyes to an obvious truth, when your sensitivity is suddenly pricked and the dynamics of love and life are revealed to you in some everyday yet momentous detail.

You cannot plan for such glimpses of enlightenment, and you cannot search them out - for they arrive without notice as gifts of grace. But you can always attend spontaneously to any and everything, not with expectation but with an easy and innocent openness. When the inner door is left ajar, the slightest breeze can swing it open – and in rushes people, events, happenings and insights you never noticed or celebrated before.

Something else is always stirring as we rush by the world in pursuit of outer concerns. But there is always the option to pause, to stop and observe - to pay attention to something that beckons to you: a sight, a sound, a touch, a sense a presence, an inner awareness, an energy you feel whirling around you. Suddenly, your brain is stimulated, your feelings aroused, your fingertips tingle, and there's a shivering along your spine. You smile in recognition, stop to breathe fully, and find yourself smiling and even crying – uttering such words as 'wow', 'oh my' and 'thank you'.

Habitual Movement

In our western, extroversive, externally driven culture, there is constant pressure – and desire - to DO something, anything but ponder and reflect, allow time for an intuitive insight to bubble to the surface or even consider slowing down in order to muse and commune with people or nature. The recommended behaviour: never stop - even momentarily - to see, hear, recognize, embrace or deal with the beauty and magnitude of what we discover en route to pursuing some outer goal.

Never stoop to smell the lilies or indulge in anything that is not concrete and immediately useful – even for the moment – because such things as accepting, letting or honoring don't produce any tangible results. Neither does schmoozing, meandering and just walking or strolling with a sense of ease. Such approaches are indulgent. They could even lead to contemplating the wonders of Life, or such do-nothing periods as silent meditation.

And you know where all that could lead: the ultimate slippery slope of laziness, confusion and sloth, wasting time and being unproductive. Unlike the introverts and mystics and those who spend precious time in prayer and reflection – we, society tells us – need to do stuff, accomplish things – anything as long as we are in active pursuit of something. Quietude and solitude is a waste…even if God allegedly did rest on the seventh day…which is irrelevant now because that was years ago before the invention of money, the watch, running shoes, corporate ladders, the Jones', multi-tasking, shops open 24/7, i-phones, tweeting, electronic games…and the need, man, the perpetual need for action!

Don't Get Sucked In

Someone cut you off, then gives you the finger. A relative at a family reunion turns surly and insulting. A man nudges in front of you on a long line at the supermarket. What to do?

Follow the offending driver. When he parks in his car, yell at him, or better yet, smash your car into his: that will show him! As to the relative, it is probably best that you hit 'em with the bowl of mashed potatoes, put gravy on his chair when he isn't looking, and then demand to speak to his mother! As to the line jumper, you grab him by the scruff of the neck and call the police.

Then again, why waste your time? Why pour good energy down the sink?

So you make the deliberate choice to stay calm - knowing that you are as vulnerable as anyone else to getting sucked into offensive behaviour. You check your impulses. You take a deep breath, count at least to five, choose a 'cool' mental approach over a 'hot' emotional one and deliberately decide to deactivate your pride. It's all a matter of assuming command over your instinctual desire to strike back, realizing that if you allow the behaviour of another to control the situation, then you diminish your own centeredness by getting embroiled in a senseless exchange of negative energy.

Besides, if you lose it and respond in kind, what happens to your commitment to love and joy? What happens to your desire to choose your own dramas and focus your energies on the things you hold dear?

Why collude in someone else's desire to be silly, obnoxious or egotistical? You have options to consider – including your belief in honouring all others, even under difficult circumstances. Otherwise, silliness has a way of begetting more silliness and off it goes – and with it the intention you affirmed just this morning to always cultivate your spiritual center.

Provocations can arise without warning: at a family reunion, in the coffee shop, while riding the bus. When they do – remember to step aside, smile, and excuse yourself, responding only when you can do so creatively and with positive intent.

You are responsible for yourself…and the state of your Soul. Don't give it or your loving nature away to anyone, under any circumstances.

Emulate

If you like and admire Angels, saints, sages and generally good people like Nelson Mandela - and the woman down the street who cares for her daughter and four grandchildren - then become like them, be like them, emulate their attitude and how they behave.

Do as 'the best' do: turn everyday incidents into opportunities to sow love and joy. Greet people at the coffee shop. Thank the woman at the check out counter and the elderly man who bags your groceries. Really listen to your neighbor, your son or daughter, and the person next to you on the train. The list of options is endless. If you would be angelic, then act like one. You don't have to give away money or do something dramatic. You need only notice people, stand witness to them and be present for them.

Everybody? Of course not. But choose to seize on those opportunities that present themselves. Nothing gooey or sentimental – please; that would be silly and borderline phony. Besides it may indicate that you really need to be needed. Simple and direct connection with whomever you are in contact will do fine: warm and gracious greetings, a look in the eye, stopping for minute to exchange greetings, sharing what is best in you with what is best in another – if for only a minute. All these little things, what Chesterton called "tremendous trifles',[34] can have an impact that is very uplifting.

---

34   G.K. Chesterton, *Tremendous Trifles* (Philadelphia: Dufour Editions, 1968).

Think of yourself as generating a giant chain of good will. Your greeting may cause someone to elevate their attitude and then instinctively pass on that good cheer to several others, who in turn communicate similar energy to all those with whom they come in contact.

Just think of the chain of responses created by just one thoughtful gesture: if you so honoured ten people in a day – which is certainly possible in just running errands or spending a day at the office – then look at the multiple impacts. The ten you motivated are likely to pass that energy onto ten others, each of who are likely do the same with ten more, and lo and behold you have stimulated a giant ripple effect of honouring and joy. Contact, contact, contact - express your Soulfulness and make loving contact every chance you get.

Summary – To Date

❖ You are a Soul and immortal.

❖ The body your Soul now inhabits is not immortal. It is very mortal and will pass sooner than you think. So use it well.

❖ Incarnation is the eternal process of the universe, the one by which we earn our stripes by applying the principles of Spirit in the domain of the material universe.

❖ So, please, please, please - accept the reality that your current body and placement are here for a little while only – and that during that elongated moment you have some spiritual work to do on yourself and for the sake of others.

❖ Ergo, the continual question: Before you let go of your current embodiment, ask yourself if you have – en route - contributed primarily to the care and protection of that which is bound to fade, or have you honored your mandate to dig deeper and fly higher?

❖ Remember: You are responsible – and answerable – for your choices. God and the spiritual hierarchies never fade and, like Santa, are always watching - and waiting to be asked to help.

- ❖ If you understand these realities, you understand everything.

- ❖ If you master these realities, you will master everything.

- ❖ Live according to these truths and you will stop hesitating to live and love fully. You will also stop protecting your ego from the reality that someday you will have to let it go so the real you can integrate the spiritual blessings it has earned.

- ❖ Adopt these truths and you will also stop senseless striving, worrying and fretting about your body, your looks, and your station in this temporary life.

- ❖ The Soul, the immortal Soul – is your center, your life energy, your true identity.

- ❖ The mission to spread love and joy, and enhance the presence of Spirit in the world, are your core concerns. It makes sense to align everything in life to these realities.

- ❖ And be assured that you – an immortal Soul - are an integral part of divinity. You will live forever, alternating between Pure Spirit and periodic incarnations, using your combined involvements to enhance the fullness of your Soul and the glory of the Totality.

- ❖ That's it. That's everything – or at least a solid introduction to everything.

SECTION FOUR

The Process of Incarnation

CHAPTER 14

REINCARNATION

Decisions

What happens when we die? What happens when the Soul decides to leave the embodiment we chose for this incarnation on the Earth - and resume its work as a Pure Soul in the realm of the Spirit?

We have first-hand testimony from those who have made those transitions – and returned to talk about it. Two books by Michael Newton, and Karen Cook's channeled information from Archangel Gabriel,[35] tell the tale. Newton, a psychologist has worked with hundreds of people, each of who told the same basic story. While under hypnosis, Newton took each of them far deeper than past life regressions and communicated directly with the Soul that lived those lives. And Gabriel has revealed the process by which we - when pure Souls in the spirit realm – chose the circumstances of our incarnation.

When the body had passed and the incarnation was complete, the Soul, as an energy field, returns to the realm of the Spirit. The work of the incarnation is then assessed with a group of tutors who do not judge what had transpired but help the Soul interpret the choices it made during its incarnation - including how it made those choices and what it learned relative to the framework it outlined in its original contract.

The assessment of the incarnation – by the individual Soul and its tutors - then leads to further study and reflection by the Soul as it contemplates the impact of its decisions. It reviews the opportunities it attracted, seized on, missed or neglected. It also begins to anticipate

---

[35] Michael Newton, *Journey of Souls,* and *Destiny of Souls* (St. Paul, MN: Llewellyn Publications, 2001-2); Karen Cook, Channel (see footnote 7).

what it might wish to do in the next incarnation, where and under what circumstances.

The implicit goal of the Soul - whether living in the state of Pure Spirit prior to or following an incarnation, or during any of its actual incarnations in the material realm - is to learn how to do four things in particular: how to love unconditionally, how to spiritualize or uplift whatever it encounters, how to make a creative contribution to the ongoing evolution of the universe, and how to attain greater awareness and understanding of the spiritual nature of the Kosmos.

Incarnating on Earth as a human being is among the most difficult assignments. Only the most courageous or determined Souls choose it. Other options include continuing one's studies and investigations in the state of Pure Soul, incarnating elsewhere in the universe, and training to be or serve as a guide, tutor, teacher or angel (if your cumulative experience warrants such an enlarged role).

The 'Death' of the Physical Embodiment

Let's say more then about *death* – of the physical body. The very term 'death' reeks of negativity: the dreadful, the horrible, the inevitable – and thus the theme that can stir the ultimate in denial. The prospect of death is so fearful that is has helped spawn (with the help of organized religion) the gigantic enterprises of funeral parlors and cemeteries. It was also provoked many to grant enough money to have a foundation or building bear their name.

Both cemeteries and monumental namesakes serve a societal purpose, of course, and are a source of solace and pride to the aggrieved. But both are also backdoor attempts to live beyond the grave and perpetuate one's persona beyond its natural limits. Never say 'no' in this case also means never say 'die'. If you can't fight death and taxes, then denial is at least a good try at ignoring their presence and inevitability.

Yet is physical death - the demise of the material housing of the Soul – really that bad? It may be downright tragic to the atheist (for then 'they' are really kaput), a little less so to the unsure agnostic, and puzzling to the person who tries never to think of such things. But to the religious who trumpet God-talk and promises of the eternal life, how can they possibly feel threatened unless they are fearful that they won't measure up to their adopted standards?

It is absolutely understandable that the family and friends of the deceased will miss them – and grieving such losses is a difficult part of the human drama. It is equally understandable for us – at the level of the ego or temporary persona - to want to hang on to our own bodies and the physical presence of family and close friends for as long at we can. The sense of potential loss, especially if it involves a loved one, can, of course, be incredibly painful.

And even if you are spiritually inclined, there is still so much unknown or in doubt at the moment of physical death that even the best of us hesitate to fully embrace its reality. Even if we accept death as involving only the outer casing of the Soul, there is the larger issue of grieving the loss of a beloved person and personality who for a while presented that Soul in material form. Perhaps it's only the mystics or others who are thoroughly enlightened, who do not instinctually fear their own or another's physical demise.

The physical passing of anyone thus needs to be put in context: the Soul rules, and the Soul is immortal, and the Soul - upon the death of its incarnated body – naturally chooses to move back home where It becomes a fully integrated and pure Soul once again.[36] It then evaluates its past life on Earth and anticipates where it wishes to learn next. This process holds true whether the Soul had just completed the life of a young child, a gifted surgeon, an average carpenter, an elderly person or someone suddenly caught in a tragic accident.

It is the Soul, the living Soul, the immortal Soul – the creative agent and essence of each of us – who decides when it arrives into incarnation, how it lives that temporary assignment, what experiences it wants and

---

36 Approximately ten per cent of the Soul resides within the body during an incarnation with the greater portion remaining in the Spirit world. Both portions are still integrally united, and as such help to guide and are responsible for the thoughts and actions of its embodiment. Its guidance is not self-executing, however, since the ego and the embodiment are also granted free will. Channelled information by Karen Cook: Archangel Gabriel or Benu, August 21, 2003.

needs to learn the lessons chosen, and when and how it chooses to leave its temporary embodiment behind, resume its immortal life on 'the Other Side', and what and where it wishes to learn next.

As noted earlier, there are exceptions to the dominant role of the Soul during an incarnation. The Soul employs and empowers the ego to coordinate the physical, mental and emotional activities of the embodiment. Thus the ego serves at the will of the Soul but also per force possesses free will – meaning it can become bloated, attempt in essence to dethrone the Soul or at least ignore its guidance, and potentially lead the embodiment in directions not intended by the Soul. This happens most often with a young and relatively undeveloped Soul – who still unsure of its true role, empowerments and potential - allows its ego to temporarily usurp It and thus undercut the kinds of behaviors the Soul most wants and needs for its continued development. Either way the Soul is responsible for the actions of its creation.[37]

So it is not only the alleged finality of the death of a person that instills at least a modicum of fear in all of us. If you believe in heaven and hell and reward and punishment, then death of the body could very well be a roll of the dice; your version of "being good" after-all may be different from that of your assumed Ultimate Assessor. And your assumptions could also be off the mark. As a cartoon in the *New Yorker* magazine suggested, a person may not have chosen the afterlife if he had known it was going to be such a schlep – and one that could be in an undesirable direction.

Despite our beliefs, life in physical form here on Earth has become synonymous with Life itself - at least for many. Even if you believe your Soul is immortal, and whether or not you believe it contracted for its current incarnation, physical life can involve a long haul on rocky and mountainous terrain. Besides, your Soul's memories of the eternal life are only faint memories. In the absence of an absolute guarantee, it seems only human to be a 'believer in God and eternal life' yet still suffer concern and heartbreak when faced with the finality of your physical form or that of a loved one.

---

37   See Chapter 9, *"What is Spirituality?"*, especially the material under the headings 'The Process of Affirming the Soul', and 'Trading Body for Soul.'

What's a Person to Do?

One of the foundations of the spiritual perspective is the dynamic of trust. It is not a belief in a structure or code. It is not faith in the truth of a book written long ago or modelling one's life on that of a master teacher. It is trust in what you absolutely *know to be true – a truth that has been validated as a living experience*. It stems from a deep knowingness of your identity as a immortal Soul, a knowing that is borne – in many cases – as a result of years of prayer, meditation and contemplation, experiential glimpses of the spiritual realm, and the experience of having had direct contact with at least facets of Prime Source Itself and/or His/Her angelic hosts.

Death thus is not an end to anything but the fleshy form that serves as your current vessel for learning while here on Earth. The life of the Soul, however, is continuous and immortal. You have gone through these transitions many times before. Each time you – the Big I, Self or the Soul – makes the decision to let go of its temporary ego, mind and body and end this particular phase of its endless learning cycle. Like E.T., you too have loved your time on Earth. But something in you also yearns to reclaim your full spiritual identity and return home.

Material death is merely a transition in form: sooner or later the material body relents and yields its remaining assets to the Earth. The Soul, however, returns to its 'place' of origin and is reunited with God and its Soul family. Such is the ultimate spiritual interpretation of Einstein's General Theory of the Relativity. Energy and form, spirit and matter, the 'E' and the 'M' of the equation, are interchangeable. The agent of each transformation is 'C^2', otherwise known as consciousness, light or enlightenment – which works its transformative wonders while the Soul has incarnated on Earth. The conversions are most evident, however, during the transitions from and to "the Other Side", when spiritual energy is transformed into a material body, and sooner or later is easily converted back again into pure Spirit.

Learning to Love: A Double Spiral

The underlying theme of all learning contracts is to learn how to be more loving - how to activate and realize one's capacity to be more and more understanding, compassionate, empathetic and helpful. How well we progress is gauged by how much insight we gain into the nature of love, and how well we are then able to express that awareness in a life intended to serve Spirit in any one of the gazillion ways.

Whatever the particulars of the learning contract, the goal of every Soul is to enhance its depth of character. It can do so, first, by expanding and deepening its *insight* into the reality of the loving consciousness (learning about unconditional love in all its depth, breadth and extensions). Second, it can include the themes of love overtly into one's overall learning contract – making a *commitment* to love unconditionally as a major aspect of one's role and commission in the material realm. Third, it can transform these commitments to be more loving into concrete *applications*, using the specifics of one's chosen placement and its situations to express and 'grow' one's love.

The three pillars of any effective learning experience - *insight, commitment and application* – also apply to whatever else we choose to include in our learning agreement, and whatever the venue. We could decide, for example, to:

1. stay a bit longer on the 'Other side', that is in a state of Pure Spirit, or

2. incarnate in one of many possible forms (human or other living form) - on Earth or anywhere else in the universe, or

3. accept a special assignment as offered – such as learning to be a guide (perhaps an assistant to a Guardian Angel), training to be a messenger (as in a Moses or John the Baptist), a Teacher (like a Gandhi), an Ascended Master (like a Serapis Bey), an Avatar (like a St. Francis), a Guardian Angel (like Amos of the Jewish Testament), or a Master Teacher (such as Abraham, Buddha, Brahma, Yeshua, Mohammed or many others).[38]

---

38 None of these categories are inferior or superior to each other. They simply play different roles

The sequence of the learning process is iterative, the completion of each cycle of insight, commitment and application leads to the next, and the next cycle - each one unfolding as part of an ever-expanding and deepening spiral of increased depth, height and thus maturity.

In fact, it may be helpful to visualize the process of spiritual development as a double spiral - the top portion going ever higher in a clockwise motion, and the lower portion going deeper in a counter-clockwise motion. Combined, the two would take on a diamond shape. In religious terms, the top portion might be analogous to spiralling upward toward God as one applies their spirituality in the world. The lower portion might thus be likened to digging ever deeper into the realities of one's Soul and the presence of Spirit.

In Jungian psychology, the upper spiral might be the world of materiality or the realm of material manifestation seeking spiritualization, with the lower or inward spiral being what Jung referred to as the Collective Unconscious. The conjunction of the two – likened here to both bases joining to form a diamond shape – would in turn be guided by a center visualized as a sphere (a cluster of radiant light at the center of the diamond). That center would be known here as the individual Soul, or in the total kosmic context as God or Prime Source. [39]

Whatever the image and metaphor, spiritual development means using each incarnation to live increasingly from one's soulful center – expanding the breadth of one's spiritual presence in the world as one cultivates the inner depths of love and understanding.

What Are You Learning?

The themes, challenges and particulars of your placement during your incarnation are totally up to you. You could, for example, choose a philosophical focus and wish to understand when and how a sense of

---

in the spiritual alignment or totality.
39 See the author's *Kindred Spirits* (Amazon.Com: Other Dimensions 2011), pp. 11-16. The image depicted on page 17 is also similar to the one described here. The three fictional stories of the book also contain serious yet witty accounts of the process of reincarnation.

beauty develops in yourself and others. You could choose to experience any of the gradations of spirituality in a series of settings and through various personalities and professions. You could choose to experience love as expressed between lovers, parent and child and/or colleagues and friends. You could choose to learn what it is like to be rich or poor, educated through books or working a farm, famous or abandoned, healthy or ill – and all the many combinations and gradations thereof.

You might now be thinking about your current life. Looking at your incarnation thus far, for example, you might ask yourself:

- What are my major themes in this incarnation?

- What do I seem to be learning – in content (what) and process (how)?

- Have there been any patterns regarding recurring issues and opportunities?

- How has the issue of love emerged during this incarnation?

- What have I learned about my ability to create and receive love?

- How have I handled issues of individuality versus community? Have I enabled myself to be unique and distinct, never giving my power away, asserting my individuality within groups and communities? Or have I wandered into one of two extremes, becoming an isolated person with hardened boundaries, or a slave to the will of others?

- Have I had an impact on others? If so, what was the source and means of my influence, and when and how did I use it?

- Do I still wish to accomplish something in particular during this current incarnation??

- Do I still wish to learn *something important*?

Can't answer yet? No clarity, yet? No problem. But you might want to begin thinking seriously about these issues. Keep some notes. Get out your old journals and pictures. At your own pace, let the clues, images and insights tumble into view. Take your time. Enjoy the process of re-discovering at least the general themes of your agenda, mission, priorities, learning and progress.

Hinduism and Reincarnation

Western Spirituality has been greatly influenced by the Hindu doctrine of reincarnation. There are however, some significant differences. Rather than karma – suffering in this lifetime for the transgressions of previous ones – being one's automatic inheritance, in Spirituality the Soul always chooses what it will do and experience in each of it's successive incarnations. Upon it's return to Pure Spirit, it is required to undergo a review of its last incarnation and to experience the impact of any earlier miscues. Then it is free to include what it wishes to learn and experience in its next learning agreement for its next incarnation.

According to Hinduism, each person also rotates through the wheel of reincarnation until such time as the Soul achieves unity with Brahma or Universal Consciousness. Incarnation is part of the great transmigration or movement of Souls from one living reality to another, each lifetime being an opportunity to overcome earlier difficulties, develop new depths of compassion and empathy, let go of one's illusion of separateness and finally be absorbed into the Godhead of Brahma.

As we will see,[40] Spirituality considers each Soul to be an indivisible aspect or cell in the universal body of Prime Source or God. You and I seek greater fulfilment with each incarnation, attempting to spiritualize our material encounters through love and compassion so we might more fully contribute to the Totality. Thus you and I as Souls are integral and distinct parts of the Totality. God has no desire or intention to absorb and eliminate our individuality. In fact, it appears She is expanding Her presence by creating more and more individual cells to the cosmic organism - or Souls in the Totality – in order to spiritualize what our scientists have verified is an ever-expanding universe.

---

40 See Chapter 26, 'Cells in the Kosmic Body'.

How Spiritual Reincarnation Works

The Soul decides to incarnate in material form after reviewing its last life with the help of angelic guides and counsellors. It examines what it has learned, assesses any and all gaps in its learning profile, notes its progress in learning to love unconditionally, reviews its options, and then decides if it wishes to continue learning in the realm of Pure Spirit or reincarnate again – on Earth of elsewhere in the universe.

If the Soul chooses to incarnate again – following a period of study, self-examination and reflection – it selects a placement and a set of traits, challenges and opportunities that are aligned with its learning objectives. As noted, rather than disappearing or being absorbed in the one identity of Brahma, each Soul continues to build on and solidify the contributions it may have made to the Whole during its earlier incarnations – much as a healthy cell continues to enhance the wellbeing of the organ and thus the entire organism of which it is a part.

As noted earlier, Michael Newton's two books and the teachings of Archangel Gabriel (via the channel, Karen Cook) shed a great deal of light on facets of the story normally hidden to us. Both reveal that the immortal Soul does indeed chose a series of successive placements in material reality in order to learn certain lessons, expand its repertoire and literally replicate the actions of Prime Creator by breathing life or infusing spirit into matter.

The Soul is constantly in school – both in the timeless state of Pure Spirit as well as when it chooses to incarnate in material form. When a given incarnation terminates and the Soul returns to the realm of Pure Spirit, it re-lives the life it just left behind. It thus experiences the pains and the joys it helped to generate, and is counselled on how it could have handled things with greater effectiveness, empathy and compassion. All that information, of course, becomes grist for the mill in selecting the learning lessons for the next learning cycle.

Each Soul also belongs to a Soul family of 50-200 Souls, all of whom serve as supportive classmates for one another. Within that larger group, each Soul works most intensely with a core group of 10-30 Souls - its closest and most immediate group of counsellors and the group from which it often solicits volunteers to play important roles in its new incarnation. Some may be cast as protagonists and others as helpers but all agree to play roles in one another's incarnations that help the others learn the lessons they seek.

Presiding over the entire learning process are the Master Teachers and Guides who help the individual Souls prepare their learning agreements. The guidance includes helping the Soul research the record of what it and others did or did not do in related circumstances and with what levels of effectiveness.

The Master Teachers also assist each Soul to evaluate their progress when the contract has been completed. The tone and quality of such evaluations are never accusatory or judgmental. The interchange goes something like this: what did you do, what were your options, how could you have chosen differently and with different or more loving results, what did you learn, and what would you like to study and research now in preparation for choosing the terms and objectives of your next learning agreement?

Dante and other medieval theorists to the contrary, there is no mention of hell and punishment, or heaven and rewards. There is a hint of something approximating purgatory, however, a period of cleansing in which the Soul, during its review, experiences the consequences of the choices it made during its last incarnation.

Another Variation

There is another variation on this theme of incarnation. Its emerges implicitly in the writings of such spiritual practitioners as Marianne Williamson, Western Buddhists like Alan Watts, enlightened process and depth psychologists like Carl Rogers and Carl Jung, writer-scholars on religion and mythology such as Joseph Campbell and psychologists of the Soul like Eckhart Tolle.

Rather than viewing incarnation as merely life-long, this variation of the spiritual theme understands that we are not the same person moment to moment: circumstances change, sub-personalities assert themselves, lessons are learned and goals are refigured, and new perspectives and actions are used that had not even been considered earlier.

Each moment contains the potential of a new incarnation, a new decision, a rebirthing, a redirection. It offers us the opportunity to liberate ourselves from any unwanted pattern of the past – even though that past is only yesterday or occurred just this morning. Right now, this instant, we are again given the option to be loving or oblivious, aware or blind, selfless or selfish. The opportunity to choose is constant and incessant, always giving us the option to alter, amplify, reverse or revolutionize our point of view and thus change our intention and choice of action in the flick of an incarnational second.

The past is never a millstone unless we choose it to be. And the future is not yet here. All that exists is now. So the new choice point – right now - need not be determined by old patterns or shaped by any preconceptions of the future. Trust must be given free flow or fear and habit paralyzes one's freedom to choose – now, and now, and again now. Rebirth or retreat, enlightenment or stagnation, flowing with or resisting an insight, intuition or dullness – selecting whatever you want - instantly and spontaneously – are always available options as each situation, nuance and moment demands that we again choose.

So: I am not the person I once was…a year, a week, a second ago. So be it! I have left - and will leave - no tracks in the sand. To paraphrase John Keats' living epitaph – true of all of us: "Here walks one whose name is writ on water." Brava! Bravo! I may not be able to change all the material circumstances around me but I can alter my consciousness, my state of awareness, my perspective and my approach to life…now… no matter what I said and did five minutes ago. Ahhhh! Every moment presents a new choice point, and each new point of decision-making presents another opportunity to relive, revive, reconstruct, revamp and uplift what was true only a minute ago.

The Soul Dost Travel

When you think about everything that is being said here, when you meditate on it and let it sink in, when you compare it to your inner awareness of your own identity, when you check it all out against your own experience, when you again or finally confirm what you have known for some time at your deepest level, you may begin to recall the experiences of your Soul traveling out of body each night as your incarnated body lays fast asleep. Do you ever awake in the morning with the distinct memory of having visited the sick, travelled to Darfur or Haiti to help the homeless, assisted someone in particular need, or even travelled beyond Earth's immediate boundaries? For example, have you ever recalled having an experience like the following?

> Earth is a dazzling spectacle as you glimpse it from outer space: it is tiny yet still glows, its glimmers of bright blue and vivid white are especially awesome in sharp contract to the surrounding darkness. It is truly awesome once it reappears as a sharp blue dot - after being shrouded by the presence of Jupiter and much later the shadow of its own moon. Finally, there it is in all its brilliance, first in ever-widening crescents…and finally in all its dazzling fullness.

> The closer you get to Earth, the more the dark frame of outer space gives way until finally all you see is the Earth: that once small differentiated object on a black background becomes an all-encompassing swirl of blue and white. Then the deep tans of whole continents appear followed by views of nothing but water. Mountain ranges soon appear, and in rapid succession, coastlines, large tracts of land and finally the flickering of city lights.

Your Soul not only travels as the body sleeps during this and all your previous incarnations. Given the constant cycles of re-incarnation, your Soul is actually in constant transition, alternating between particular personalities in various historical times and cultures. You may already be aware of some of your past embodiments – especially if your intuition is particularly well developed and you have allowed hints and memories of past lives to bleed through.

If not, you might consider working with a facilitator of past life regressions and/or an accomplished channel. Or you might just trust your own inner wisdom and enable yourself to investigate, mediate on or intuit your felt connections to a past culture, historical event or personality. It is quite possible that you lived during the past time that now fascinates you. You could also have been a member of that particular group that keeps finding its way into your references and readings. Or you literally may have been the personality with whom you persistently have felt a special affinity.

Earlier Identities

I sense, for example, that I've lived several lifetimes in India, a few as a beggar and then as a gardener - and several more as a Buddhist monk in Japan - one of them as a caretaker at the Zen garden at Kyoto's Sanbōin (I visited there twenty years ago and was stunned into tears – overwhelmed by the awareness of having lived there hundreds of years before).

I have also been aware since I was a small child - when drawn to read books about the journeys of Lewis and Clark - that I was with that expedition as a Shoshone Indian guide. I have been a close friend to both Michelangelo and Leonardo da Vinci. I lived the life of Assurnasirpal, II, the 9th century, B.C.E. warrior king of Assyria. As a former Roman soldier, I then served Yeshua, was a close friend and ally of Joseph of Arimathea, travelled with Mary and Yeshua to India and then escorted Mary back to Judea when Yeshua went to the Americas. (These connections, of course, continue to this day since the spirits or Souls of these beings – being immortal - are still very much alive despite the passing of their earlier and very mortal incarnations.)

I know I was a farmer in Sumer and later a philosopher and healer in Greece, a royal administrator in Babylon, a priest in Judea, a shaman in Brazil and writer and civil rights advocate in England. I played many other roles as well - as have you: a mixture of placements throughout the so-called high, middle and lower levels of many societies, in my case over 20,000 reincarnations in total so far, among them lives in which I was alternately old and young, male and female, a corrupt noble and loving farmer, a humble shopkeeper and popular writer, a warrior, a mystic and an artist or two.

I realize there's a lot of so-called accomplished personages mentioned here – but surely not all are wise, loving or high on the spiritual register. It fact, I have many a low-life in my veins and surely was a dedicated scoundrel on many occasions. But really, what could the value of any worldly title, alleged fame or position of power be if it was used to feed one's ego and thus neglect rather than help others? I suspect I may have fallen into that trap many times.

Your profile probably is no different. If you have been attracted to read this far you have undoubtedly incarnated thousands of times as well…and know that your Soul on occasion occupied the personhoods of many different people including some considered 'important' or 'famous' as well as those who were not exactly revered. One's spiritual attunement is not necessarily advanced while living as an historic figure – not unless your name at the time was Marcus Aurelius, Francis of Assisi, Julian of Norwich, the Dalai Lama or one of many other saintly people who have graced our planet.

So you think you were one of the Pharaohs. Not many of them rank among the best of God's servants. It probably would have served your Soul better if you had been a kindly and loving shopkeeper or peasant living in downtown Alexandria, beloved by their community because you worked with and healed the afflicted - while the local Pharaoh had millions of slaves building monuments to his alleged fame.

Gifts or Burdens

Actually, having been a famous person who achieved great things in the material realm may have been a burden for anyone simultaneously interested in attaining a deeper level of spiritual consciousness. Many of history's most famous people did some very bad things and were not very nice people. So suppose you were Louise 'Somebody' or Harold the

'Umpteenth' who attained notoriety - but for the wrong or self-centered reasons. If so, who cares about your title or allegedly famous lifestyle if you never moved beyond the first two rungs of Maslow's hierarchy (the fight for survival and power).

Unless you find out that Louise or Harold advanced their consciousness during their incarnations and helped others do the same, then there is not much to feel good about or honor in those particular identities - except that you may have learned something about the dangers of being merely famous. Knowing something about the lifestyle and energy patterns of any of your earlier incarnates is always instructive – for it is always possible that something from an earlier incarnate may bleed through occasionally to your current incarnation, affecting your intentions and behavior in ways you cannot otherwise explain.[41]

Besides, your most spiritually advanced incarnation may have been as an apprentice to a Knight in the 8th century, a mother of six in ancient Rome, or a farmer, soldier, juggler, teacher, cook or mason. You could have expressed – or suppressed - your love and compassion through any possible occupation or level of society. Like the rest of us, you undoubtedly struggled with the predictable set of life's transitions – during your many incarnations - but gradually learned a great deal about inner radiance, beauty and empathy in the process.

Signs of Other Dimensions

It is also quite possible that you have also experienced, during your current incarnation, brief glimpses into and momentary stays within other dimensions. In my own case, none of the specifics are clear but I do remember – on several occasions - feeling like I suddenly slid into a mirror at a 45-degree angle and flipped into another space, as if absorbed by a spinning glass door. In each case, the transit happened quickly: 'Zip' - I was on 'the Other Side', and 'zam', I was back. How much 'time' actually transpired I don't know.

---

41   See Jane Roberts, *The Seth Material* (New York: Bantam, 1972); and *The Education of Oversoul 7* (New York: Pocket Books, 1973).

Interactions with aspects of the 'other side' are reported by many - all the time. Many have experienced seeing tall angelic figures, sighted and even gone aboard space ships, talked with beings who looked like but were not human beings, or felt a loving presence that was different and beyond anything they had ever experienced before.

Admitted, some of the crop circles carved into the fields of England have been devised by locals in an attempt to debunk claims that they were formed by extra-terrestrials. But most of them are so huge and complex that they defy human imagination and skill - and suggest conclusively that they are the work of advanced spiritual beings from another dimension.

Funny: nobody ever spots flashlights or reports hearing any machines in an area suddenly marked the next morning by one more intricate crop circle. Many have seen lights in the sky but not along the ground. And how is it something so enormous, symmetrical, intricate and beautiful could be carved in a matter of minutes or hours by a handful of humans working in the dark without benefit of highly sophisticated and relatively noisy mechanical devises?

If they are not generated by something extra-terrestrial or other-dimensional, then what?[42] The data is in front of us. Why is it so difficult for many to realize that creative life does indeed exist beyond the immediate boundaries of the Earth? What a magnificent offering these crop circles are – created and presented to us as gifts by our advanced cousins from another dimension of our common uni-verse!

---

42 See, for example, *www.temporarytemples.co.uk* - for its postings of photos and studies.

CHAPTER 15

THE SOUL-GOD RELATIONSHIP

The Learning Agreement

When we signed on to incarnate – this time, obviously in bodily form *on Earth* (versus elsewhere in the universe) – we in essence signed an agreement or contract. It outlined what we chose to learn – which could have included any set of human experiences, intentions and attributes including the desire to learn how to be more patient, non-judgmental, accepting of diversity, artistic, become more forgiving, and perhaps even wanting to learn how to assert oneself in the face of group think or unjust authority. Our potential learning list could be as long or short, focused or varied as desired.

We then choose, not the details but the general outlines of the setting within which we wish to learn the desired characteristics. We may choose to learn empathy, for example, by selecting certain kinds of difficult experiences – thereby laying the foundation for commiserating with and helping others face similar circumstances in the future. Such frameworks would then serve to create and attract the specific circumstances needed to fulfil those wishes during one's incarnation.

This is all part and parcel of what we mean by 'creating our own reality'. We create and attract the experiences we need to attain our pre-selected learning objectives. Thus there are no coincidences. It is all a kosmic display of gazillions of Souls learning – and in some cases, later deciding to avoid learning - what they agreed to in their contract. Since the contract serves as a guide to our intended spiritual development, there are no punishments for not fulfilling all or parts of it. We are free to modify or void one or more of our good intentions and thus those portions of our development. That, of course, could mean having to 'Return to Go' when we return to the realm of Pure Spirit, and consider including the unfinished business of the last incarnation in the terms of the new one.

To facilitate our desired learning, we also choose the outline of our placement: the general characteristics of our parents, our own skill sets and vulnerabilities, our issues and dominant themes (like power or relationships), key marker events (major successes and disappointments), and the kinds of events and challenges that would activate those experiences.

The resultant learning contract, however, is set only in outline form; it does not specify what we will actually do, how we will handle particular circumstances or guarantee whether we will or will not complete, modify or avoid our desired lessons. Free choice is constant, and that means the freedom - while still in the Soul state - to choose the themes and general circumstances of the incarnation, and then – during the incarnation itself – the freedom to choose the specifics of how and when we complete (or modify or avoid) the framework of our intended experience on Earth.

Recalling Our True Identity

The decision to incarnate has its particular parameters. Our Soul, when it leaves its natural home and state, embeds only ten percent of its presence in the new incarnate, the great majority remaining in the realm of Pure Spirit. Even then it must contend with the laws of time and space and adjust to the realities of human development. During the time of the greatest growth in ego development - from adolescence to middle age - there is a corresponding further diminishment in the awareness of who we really. When the needs of the ego are predominant - rightfully concerned with establishing each of us as a secure, integrated and effective person within the material world – our primary attention is given over to developing our everyday mental and intuitive skills, and thereafter getting an education, establishing an identity and personality, and in most cases, finding a mate, founding a family and funding a mortgage.

Substantial glimpses into the nature of the spirit world – and gradually recalling aspects of our true identity – do occur, however. This is especially true (1) during infancy and early childhood (given their proximity to the pure Soul state), (2) when we experience severe need and endangerment ('fox hole' conversions being only one example), and (3) in the later years associated with mentorship and then retirement, when we are prone to receive many reminders of the body's mortality and the inevitability of completing the current round-trip.

Of course, some Souls re-enter the physical life as 'Old Souls' - having already achieved substantial cultivation of their spirituality through many, many earlier incarnations. Such souls are relatively attuned when they arrive and become increasingly adept throughout their incarnated life. This is as true for a given talent as well as one's overall profile. Look, for example, at all the child geniuses in music, art and science. They have all been many times before, attained great skill in some or many arenas and thus are very fast starts when they return.

As to the spiritual arena in particular - even if we have not earned the right to a fast start at the outset - all of us can and do receive clues, recalls, intuitions and images throughout life that help to remind us our true or spiritual identity. Some treat such glimpses as silly, or irrelevant or upsetting, while others learn to take them very seriously and accept them as invitations to cultivate their spiritual consciousness.

How the Interlocking Spiritual System Operates

Despite the lost of full memory of our Soul-essence during the many years in which we are simply trying to get established as full human beings in the material world, we still possess the inner capacities of the Soul, which include the ability to infuse spirit into our encounters with material reality. Whatever the progress of our human personalities, we all still harbour our divinely inspired inclinations to live according to the maxims of love and gratitude. Bringing that transformative attitude to our everyday encounters – that is, living by the golden rule – is the essence of the ensuing struggle to find a balance between serving God and our soulful identity while working within the material realities of Caesar.

Thus we deepen our spiritual consciousness as we work through our issues and challenges. The presence of God thus grows as we grow. And God His/Herself extends and deepens as our spiritual awareness extends and deepens, the health and fullness of each cell adding to the health and fullness of the Totality.

Aha! It is time to deal directly and emphatically with what many may consider the most Earth-shaking aspect of this entire dynamic. As we create, so does God. As we learn from experience, so does God. As we extend our spiritual presence in the world, so is the presence of God extended. As we create love and compassion, we add to the flow of love and compassion in the on-going and continuous creation of the Kosmos. It is all one big integrated system. As integral components of Divinity, what we do as cells impacts the entire Divine Organism.

Our divine status does not change when we make the trip from being a pure Soul to being a Soul temporarily embodied in a physical form. And the status of God does not change from the creator of Souls and the Kosmos to that of an absentee landlord. God continues to grow and create as the aspects of H/H universe continue to grow and create.

As we fulfil our contracts, within our chosen 'identities' and placements, God, being everywhere and in everything, is naturally at our side. As aspects of the Divine Organism, so are It's 'other components', such as our Guardian Angels and other members of the Divine Host (in particular, Angels and the Archangels). And since God is whole and united (in human terms, androgynous or an amalgam of the psychological traits of both masculine and feminine), God or Prime Source is quite capable of providing us with all the masculine rationality and assertiveness we need to complement and complete our innate feminine intuition and receptivity.

In Its creative pre-eminence, God enables all but does not personally create all experience. But God does get to know all by absorbing and learning from what Its Souls experience. All Souls - including you and me - whether incarnated or still living in the state of Pure Spirit, automatically communicate updates to God on what we are doing, how we are working through our roles and agreements and what we intend to do next. Our experience becomes God's experience; our learning is His/Her learning.

God did not set us adrift on a lifeboat with only an outline, a half bottle of water and a deck of Tarot cards. He is on the boat with us. She rides the same bus we ride. It walks the path we walk. He possesses the ultimate cell phone, e-mail, Facebook and texting capacity – instantly and constantly aware and apprised of our challenges, choices and requests. He is just like the ultimate Santa Claus who knows if we have been naughty or nice and adjusts His presents accordingly. Prime Source knows all because He knows us.

Our learning contracts are therefore part of a cosmic quid pro quo. God learns and expands as we learn and expand. It creates and re-creates the universe as we create and re-create ourselves spiritually and physically. As we experience our challenges, complete our lessons and exercise our creativity, we have the opportunity to increase the consciousness of the ever-expanding mind of God. As we learn and advance in attitude and behavior, so does God. As the cells grow, so does the entire Body.[43]

If we choose not to seize on such opportunities, or make decisions that negate the principles of love and joy, we create a temporary drag on the evolution of the universe. If enough of us do that, then it will inevitably be reflected in the quality of events that subsequently unfold. Individual, family, communal, political and planetary experiences are all part of a giant feedback system. God shapes and creates on the basis of what She receives. Look at what is happening in the world and assume some credit and responsibility for it – for you have helped to create its major dynamics, both the advances in loving consciousness

---

43 For an in depth exploration of this dynamic - with God learning from Job - see C.G. Jung, *Answer to Job* (Princeton: Princeton University Press, Reprinted 2002).

as well as the cumulative devastation, wars and suffering caused by the toxic impact of too many bloated egos bathing in their own greed and power.

Some Limits and Understandings

There is also a divine law that stipulates that God and His host of Angels cannot and will not do our work for us. Otherwise, choosing is neutralized, challenge is nullified, experience is voided and the learning contract becomes one big crib game. If God always moved our mountains it would undercut the meaning of our contracts and our contributions, both of which are significant precisely because they are freely chosen and personally completed (albeit with help as requested).

In other words, God will gladly help but He and His host needs to be asked - asked not to do our work for us, but to provide the occasional hints, insights, nudges and hunches that help us to see and pursue a creative alternative, including helping us to safety when on a physical or emotional cliff.

Michelangelo Buonarroti, *Creation of Adam*, 1510
The interchange of creative energy between God and the Soul accounts for the continuous creation of the Kosmos.

A spiritual contract with God is activated when we volunteer to extend our learning and choose a venue to attain it. We pledge our desire and intentions to learn - especially how to deepen our awareness and capacity to love. In return, God offers a helping hand as quid quo pro – proving again and again that we are all in this together. God is not out there – somewhere, or eternally beyond and above us. God made the playing field so He could be coach, umpire and groundskeeper – thus fulfilling His desire and commitment to be 'in the game' and participate along side us. God provides for and maintains a level field in which everyone is involved and has a role - including God, the Seraphim, Archangels, Angels Avatars, Ascended Masters, the couple down the street, your mother-in-law, the butcher, baker and candlestick maker – and, of course, you and I.

The energy is collaborative and moves in both directions. The Universal and the particular, The Spirit and the Soul are mutually interdependent and complementary. God the Whole, and all of us as Her divine particles, co-create the universe through our individual and cumulative intentions and experiences. The desire to spiritualize the Earth is a joint task. It is a cooperative and collaborative adventure. It is you and I and everyone else – working with God. *We are each and all partners with one another*, loving colleagues on the joint mission to create and spiritualize the Kosmos.

Inventory

Now let's be specific. Since you agreed to your life themes and patterns before you arrived on Earth, it may be a good time to clarify what you agreed to. One of the best ways of finding that out is to examine your current life and assess how it is unfolding. If you can spot the themes and patterns of your incarnated life, you will surely get a clearer sense of the terms of your contract.

Ask yourself the following sets of questions, and note any of the related issues they generate. Take some notes: single words, phrases, partial or whole sentences will do just fine. If you want, respond by drawing doodles, symbols, stick pictures and short headline phrases. You could even cut pictures from magazines to summarize the essence of an experience or your response to an issue or question. And you can take your time – doing some of it now, and returning to it as motivation and memory suggest.

You may not be able to respond with complete ease and clarity at first because some of the questions may cut deep, raising issues you may not have considered before. But your answers, no matter how partial or incomplete they may be at first - are still crucial inputs to helping you make sense of your current incarnation. Surely the questions will invite you to return again and again to its themes, each time filling in more information or detecting one more pattern - until you uncover the clarity you want. So read on and respond – perhaps silently at first - but soon and inevitably with pen and paper. This is a record you will want to keep – and add to as the weeks, and years unfold.

But please, for your own sake, get started today. Some may complete a quick overview in one sitting and come back later to add specifics. Others may prefer to think and reflect before answering anything. Either way, it is your life and gaining more insight into it should be both fun and revealing.

There are several categories. Not all of them may seem immediately relevant or crucial at first. If so, return to them later. But for every issue that does catch your attention, be sure to ask yourself three important questions:

1. What has been my experience in this area?

2. What have I learned so far? and

3. What do I still want – or need - to learn?

Start – and end – with the awareness that you are a powerful magnet, a force-field who has attracted into your life the people and issues needed to learn the lessons you chose in your life contract.

Here's the list of possible issues. The set of examples are examples only – intended to stimulate your thinking.

A. What major themes (topics, issues) have reoccurred, dominated and/or been central to your life story (personally and professionally)? In terms of content, for example, has it involved establishing your independence from or your unity within your family, bucking or cooperating with organizational systems, or perhaps learning how to partner and parent under both favorable or trying situations? Have the dominant themes been relationships, personal or professional identity, or developing a personal value system? What particular dynamics have characterized your life: losses, gains, confusion, hard work, gifts, sorrow, joy, sense of progress, feeling of adventure?

B. What energies have dominated your life? Have you, for example, displayed courage, acceptance, insight, poor or excellent decision-making? Have you learned or resisted learning how to give and receive empathy, compassion and love? Have you received unconditional love from others – episodically or ongoing? Have you learned to give unconditional love – to at least some people or in certain situations? Has your ability to love grown or diminished over the years?

Similarly, has any tendency to judge others increased or decreased over time? What character traits have pushed your buttons? Do you have any regrets, carry any grudges, resent any situations, ever felt demeaned or overlooked? What clues do you receive when you review your list of unfinished business – namely those issues or challenges you still experience as ongoing?

C. What have been your key decision points? List them on a separate piece of paper or use small post-its and then either reduce each to a marker word or two or create a ledger using letters next to each item. You could then plot the issues on a graph - using either the marker phrase or the letter designation. You could develop a time line of approximate years on the horizontal axis and your estimate of significance – low, medium or high - on the vertical one.

D. What key issues are now significant and what decisions are you now considering?

Consider whether any of your current patterns and anticipated issues relate to those of the past.

E. Who has helped and who has allegedly hindered you on your path: personally, professionally, in relationships, in the development of your spiritual life? You may have experienced some situations and people initially as blockages but on reflection now see them as making a contribution or having created a life-enhancing test that in retrospect you now see as a blessings in disguise.

F. What kinds of characters, personalities, or types of people have been dominant in your life? For example, have they been challenging, accepting, annoying or loving? What impact have they had on your spiritual development?

G. How would you characterize your relationship with God? And,

H. What keywords – verbs, adjectives, movie titles or symbols – best describe the essence of your story? Has your life, for example, been fascinating, eventful, filled with contradictions or opportunities, painful, challenging, joyful, loving – or whatever? What movie titles would you give to your life story? What might be the alternate subtitles? Could you summarize the essence of your story – or its main issues or learning – in a symbol (or two or three), a drawing (with crayons or markers), and/or some form you could mold with pieces of play dough or clay?

*   *   *

This is a lot, of course. Who said your life has been simple? And who would deny you have the capacity to make sense of what you designed? Who is better qualified? And who would gain more from gaining clarity on your life themes and patterns than you!

Please – for your own sake – begin to make some notes *now*. Do some more tomorrow. Don't fret. Enjoy. It is your opportunity to focus on you - for as long and as frequently as you wish. Please don't neglect or refuse this wondrous opportunity to inquire into - and both clarify and celebrate - YOUR life story!!

And as noted above, whenever you have accumulated a bunch of notes, apply the three essential questions to any of the issues, themes and patterns you uncover. Make it work of you. Call on your Guardian Angel for courage and persistence. Have fun. You are after all an immoral Soul here for a reason and with a set of very significant agendas. Here is your opportunity to sort through them and clarify what you wish to do next.

The three main questions, again:

1. What has been my experience in this area?

2. What have I learned thus far? And,

3. What do I still want – or need - to learn?

CHAPTER 16

MANIFESTING YOUR SPIRITUALITY

Not Limited

While on Earth, you, the immortal Soul, are asked – by the very nature of your incarnation – to form a mind and body that complete your earthly tasks, and a coordinating ego to supervise that work. While on Earth your ego becomes your or the Soul's designated coordinator of your mental, emotional and physical capacities. The ego, then, does not have a Soul. Rather, you - the Soul - forms and then informs your physical presence and its ego to implement its earthly involvements on your behalf.

Thus you *do not have a Soul*. You *are a Soul. It is your* ultimate and immortal identity. So remember: You are not limited. There is plenty of time. There is also plenty of space. How can that be? Well, the Soul, *your Soul*, is limitless and timeless. So relax. Trust. Have no fear – no matter what happens around you. And live from your focus: be conscious of what enlivens you. And be aware of what you wish to do, and how you wish to do it.

So – work hard, if you want. But be ever mindful that you have reason to 'be at ease' – at ease in the awareness of who you really are. It is a spiritual life you are creating – not just a set of earthly achievements. When your earthly deeds serve your eternal spiritual identity, they become the vehicles for your continued and unlimited development.

The Soul Directs, The Ego Coordinates

But you need to be ever mindful that the ego, if not overtly directed by your resident Soul and spiritual presence, can become egotistic and assume it is the director versus the coordinator of your affairs. If and when the ego is allowed to inflate itself, it means, you - the Soul - have not properly guided it to follow your spiritual directions.

A constant and firm hand is needed. That is why nurturing your inner life is so important. It is there that your spiritual identity is most evident, and your spiritual direction most needed. It is there that your intentions are clarified and selected. It is from such periodic grounding in the reality of your spiritual identity that you can most easily converse directly with God and your spiritual guides. It is from the base of quietude, prayer and meditation that you are reminded of your true identity and mission, and thus automatically recharged with the energy and direction needed to guide the ego in spiritual directions.

As you know - but tend to forget: you are here to learn deeper lessons than striving, achieving, becoming number one and driving yourself and everyone else crazy in the process of proving you're worthwhile. Remember the bumper sticker earned by the ego-bound: "Places to Go, Trinkets to Buy, Prizes to Win, People to Use and Nature to Subdue."

You may want to accumulate a strong and lengthy professional resume while on Earth - giving a positive twist to all the things you do. But there is also such a thing as a 'spiritual' resume. It does not contain lists of purely material achievements but it is capable of listing the many ways you have developed and applied your spiritual energies. Gandhi summed it up best: "I don't have a resume," he said. "My life is my resume."

God is likely to answer only two questions as you arrive at the pearly gates: One, what have you learned? And two, how much have you loved?

Fixed, Chaotic or Flowing?

How we behave has a lot to do with how we view the life process. Are the patterns of our individual lives and the outcome of life itself preordained? If so, why struggle, why even try to make the best decision or attempt to be loving if it involves sacrificing something that is of more immediate importance? Some theologians have preached that it makes no difference what you do since everything is already predetermined; only some will be saved and all the others are doomed to eternal hell. Lovely.

On the other hand, suppose there is no foundation at all, no less one prefaced on predestination: no underlying process, so system, no understandings, no conceivable chain of events that makes sense of 30 or 50 or even 100 years of living; its all unconnected and random. We might as well realize life is like a plate of marbles where everything collides and nothing really adheres. Comforting.

Now what could possibly exist between viewing life as fixed on the one hand, and totally chaotic on the other? How about something that has a basic form but flows? How about something analogous to Mother Nature carving the contours of a riverbed while enabling those who sail on it to select and outfit their own boats as well as chart their own course as their journeys unfold? Or how about the example of the artist who sketches out the basic pattern of a tapestry but enables each weaver to choose the specifics of their own design as well as the details of its colors, textures and sequence of threads?

To be more specific, would it not be wonderful to realize the roles of both the boatman and the weaver apply to you, and that you are after-all an incredibly empowered Soul dressed in human clothing here on Earth to sail and weave as you prefer. Building on such metaphors, you might then realize that you had the ability to do all of the following:

- First, design a framework – in consultation with your spiritual mentors - that outlined the dominant mission, major themes and key lessons of your current incarnation.

- Second, choose to incarnate in material or bodily form, and do so in a setting and under circumstances that enables you to live the kind of life and learn the lessons you sketched out in your learning agreement.

- Third, have the free will and power to choose how you will actually complete the general terms of your contract.

- Fourth, exercise the right, through your choice of particular attitudes and actions, to fulfil, in part or whole, the terms of your contract, and thus complete, modify or reject your stated mission and desired learning.

- Fifth, experiment - trying *this*, doing *that*, perhaps back paddling *here* while shooting the rapids *there* – discovering, as you proceed, what produces certain outcomes and why.

- Sixth, learn about Life from whomever and whatever you encounter, including how to handle difficulties, and how to convert challenges into opportunities.

- Seventh, literally create a spiritual life during your incarnation, transforming your challenges into spiritual lessons, developing your capacity to act on your loving intentions, and demonstrating your ability to infuse everything you encounter with love and compassion.

- Eighth, live your life fully, contributing – with conscious intention - to the co-creation of the ever-expanding Kosmos.

- Ninth, deepen and expand your level of consciousness - including your awareness of the connections between your mortal and the immortal aspects, your material incarnation and your immortality, the heights of your everyday consciousness and the depths of your divinity, and your individual soulfulness as an integral part of the universal Soul.

- Tenth, affirm and celebrate your everlasting identity as an immortal Soul who exists to serve Prime Source and manifest spirit whenever and wherever you choose.

Now doesn't that sound a bit more fulfilling than being a part of either a fixed or a chaotic universe? Let's face it: doesn't the combination of 'choice within a pattern' describe your life story!

Ambassador

You are an ambassador of a number of affiliations and values. Everywhere you go you represent something or someone: male-female, north-south, presumed citizen-presumed immigrant, rich person-poor, East side-West, Episcopal-Jewish, whoever-whatever.

Whatever you do and say, however you dress and behave, there will be somebody who will experience it as a commentary on your gender, age, ethnic affiliation, nationality or a host of other real or presumed identities. Your energy patterns and characteristics register with others – no matter what you do or don't do.

People in military dress, for example, are perceived as ambassadors of the armed forces. Men wearing a collar or women donned in a habit – despite their individual traits – are assessed to be representatives of a religious class or grouping. Carry a cane, wheel a baby carriage, wear a carpenter's belt, drive a Cadillac - and it is assumed you possess the traits or identities associated with such accoutrements or paraphernalia.

Try it: as you encounter others, be aware of the traits or identities you naturally associate with some external appearance. You may not know the person walking toward you but you probably make assumptions about him/her as you superimpose on them identities you associate with their appearance, demeanor, attitude or behavior. Note how many of your assessments, for example, are descriptive ('he is probably from the suburbs', 'a foreigner' or 'from down South'). Also note how many of your assessments can be judgmental ('he's probably a rich snob', 'a high school dropout', 'won't she make a lovely teenager') - despite your repeated desire not to participate in negative stereotyping.

Now, let's raise the stakes. What is it about others that leads you to believe they are 'Ambassadors of God'? Is it their dress, words, attitude or tone? If your conclusion rests heavily on appearances or activities associated with formal religion – like a praying figure or denominational dress or pendants - try eliminating those externals from your assessment, and see what happens.

Either way, do you assume religion and the overt signs of religious affiliation automatically qualify that person to be an 'Ambassador of God'? Conversely, do you assume that spirituality is an attribute, perspective or lifestyle that is independent of a person's outer activity, social class, accent, dress, profession or verbiage?

More pointedly, do you think there is something about you – your words and values, your activities and associations, the books you read, the things you honor and how you honor them – which if they were known would elicit from others the conclusion that you probably were an "Ambassador of God?"

Would that association bother you or would you be honored by it? Besides making you a bit self-conscious, would you act any differently - at least some of the time - simply because someone associated you with God? Would you be more careful? Would you be more aware of what you say and do, and how you say and do it? Would you become more conscious of how you present yourself and the associations your words and actions might activate?

By the way, what things, traits, perspective or activities do you associate with anyone rightfully perceived as an 'Ambassador of God'? Do you think Gandhi, Helen Keller, Black Elk, Martin Luther King – or any figure in modern or ancient history – was an Ambassador of God? Is there anybody in your community, family or neighborhood you think would qualify? If so, how do you know, or why do you feel that way? What do 'Ambassadors of God' do that indicates who they are? What is it about their perspectives, language or behavior that you associate with being a 'spokesperson for divinity'?

Among those associations of alleged godliness, are there any you personally would prefer not to exhibit? Are there any with which you would be pleased to be associated? Putting it bluntly, are you satisfied with your spiritual repertoire – if indeed you consider yourself, now or potentially, an ambassador of the Spirit?

Has any part of this 'question and answer' session been helpful to you? Or do you find it disturbing? Either way, do you know why?

What will you do now? Do you want to make some changes in your role, inner thoughts patterns, the images you cultivate, the words you use and/or how you behave – in order to become more representative of God and an effective ambassador for that which is loving and divine?

Page in a Book

Remember: this incarnational life, the life you are now leading, is but:

- an infinitesimal puff of smoke within an Indian kulpa of 432,000,000 years,
- a page in a very, very long and cyclical diary written by you over many, many incarnations and thousands if not millions of years,
- a flicker of light within a light-year (with light traveling at the speed of 186,000 miles a second),
- a subplot in a novel of 13.8 billion annual volumes (the current estimated age of the physical cosmos), and
- a fleeting but brilliant moment in Earth's four billion year history.

It is also like

- a speck, of a grain, of a particle, on a tiny star within the giant Milky Way,
- a remnant of chocolate in a Grand Canyon of chocolate sprinkles,
- a dot on a petal of a flower in the jungles of the Amazon.

Yet you also know

- micro inputs have vast and Kosmic impacts,
- everyday decisions have divine implications, and
- an infinite number of such units forms an integrated Whole.

Knowing all this, you have reason to honor everyday for its

- stability - yet cohesive flow
- fleeting glimpses - yet vision of the Essential
- beginnings - yet astounding capacity for fulfillment
- multiple segments - yet unifying completions, and
- meanderings - yet epic achievements.

So your current incarnation may only be a single page in a very ancient and enormous book:

But - oh what a page

And - oh what a book

Here to Learn

First, we are here to learn how to *trust* - every event, every happening, every choice we make; to trust that everything is part of our unfolding; to trust that we created or attracted everything that happens to and for us so that we might experience and learn from its lessons; and to trust that whatever we experience in our current embodiment and its particular circumstances are communicated directly to God – adding to His empathy for and awareness of every conceivable living circumstance.

Second, we are here to learn *awareness*, awareness that we are creators, that we create our own lives through our choice of thoughts and the actions that flow from them, that we attract the external circumstances that enable us to experience the consequences of our inner choices, and that none of it – even if it is temporally experienced as painful, joyful or something in between – is neither good or bad but simply part and parcel of our intended and desired awareness.

Third, we are here to learn how *to honor* ourselves, immediately as mortals learning how to be integrated human beings who can set limits and attain goals, and more deeply, as Souls capable of guiding the ego and infusing its material world with spiritual intent.

Fourth, we are here to learn how *to raise our consciousness*, to uplift the Soul and transform its incarnated encounters with matter into reflections of sacred energy.

Fifth, we are here to learn *wholeness*, completing a set of unique experiences of the material world, which when added to the lessons of umpteen earlier incarnations, enables us to acquire more of the experiential breadth and empathetic depth of Prime Source.

Varied Goals and Missions

If we monitor the themes and patterns of our lives – as we just did in Chapter 15 – we uncover the outlines of our learning contracts, and the purpose of our current stay on Earth. A review of one's life story may make it self-evident, for example, that we chose to experience certain challenges and sorrowful experiences on Earth so we might learn greater empathy and compassion. Others could have discovered that they are now using the traits of humility and forbearance that they learned from the illnesses experienced in a previous incarnation.

Still others may find out that they agreed to experience great disappointment in relationships in order to challenge themselves and others to love under the most trying circumstances. "Don't judge a book by its cover" is a spiritual truism. So is 'don't judge, lest you be judged' – for who but the spiritually attuned person really knows or figures out the patterns and purposes of their experience. Yet with reflection, we discover that different Souls play different roles to learn different things. Some even choose allegedly 'negative' traits deliberately in order to be catalysts, creating challenge and change so they and others can learn how to deal with and overcome disruption.

Over the long haul, through many incarnations - and perhaps a comparable number of placements in the realm of Pure Spirit - the Soul tries to experience everything it can, so it can empathize with every conceivable life experience – and thereby fulfil its desire to be more like God. So, like energetic children, all Souls seek its next, and then next experience - with the intent of the progressively expanding and deepening its state of consciousness. In each case, it seeks to be more and more like its Creator. The desire – and related opportunity – to learn never ceases, no matter what our role, mission, contract or 'success' rate. The attempt to approximate infinity is indeed an eternal task.

Names as False Labels

Be careful of the names you ascribe to yourself. They make a difference in what and how you actually manifest. There is a tendency, for example, in New Age and even Jungian circles to refer to the 'higher self' when a person operates according to their so-called 'higher' or spiritual sense of being. It suggests – rightfully so – that there is some extra-ordinary identity that enables that person to supersede the ordinary. But it inaccurately implies that a person is a 'lower self' when not a 'higher self' – an apparent variation on chopped liver, a lesser being or a corrupted individual.

Such labels inaccurately splits the 'Self' in two and undercuts the integrity of 'the person' who is the incarnated being. Yet the 'Self' or the incarnated Soul is here to learn how to broaden and deepen its experience so that it might better serve God. Based on what it images and how it behaves, the Self may 'ascend' to planes of spiritual consciousness not accessible to it when it is in an egocentric state of mind. It may also descend to denser planes of awareness, to true levels of darkness - as Jung did deliberately to learn more about the psyche,[44] and as others do when they lose their way and undermine their good intentions.

Thus the source of the misnomer: the Soul, the whole and continuously evolving person is an undivided spiritual being no matter where it is in its spiritual evolution. There is no 'higher' or 'lower' Self but only the whole and integrated Self who chooses levels of consciousness that will aid in its immediate and long range development. And there is no 'higher' of 'lower' level of consciousness – only that which may be more or less enlightened.

---

44 C.G. Jung, *Memories, Dreams, Reflections* (New York: Vintage, 1965), and *The Red Book* (New York: Norton, 2009).

When cultivated, the spiritual level of consciousness chosen by the Self or Soul can take many forms. You may, for example, be intensely motivated by compassion. You may become more receptive to the guidance of your Guardian Angel and other spiritual beings (such as earthly Avatars, and Ascended Masters). You may gain greater insight into how the mind operates when it is attuned to God and in the midst of raising its level of consciousness. Your meditations and dreams may also bring you first-hand validations of your status as an empowered cell in the universal organism of God.

At the so-called denser ends of consciousness, there may be a long-range reason for choosing and suffering through the experiences of greed, sloth, pride and the other forms of ego puffery. Wearing any of these 'negative' costumes will not make you a lower Soul any more than the consciousness of charity will make you a 'higher' one. Either way, you're an immortal Soul experiencing whatever consciousness you're chosen to further your education.

Venturing to Areas Below and Beyond

I went on an archaeological dig several years ago – to Israel. Our particular group dug at the foundations of the Western wall of the old Temple, built not by (as the history books say) but *at the behest* of Herod who was considered by some to be 'great' because he used the taxes he collected to mobilize millions of slaves to build a lot of buildings.

So there we were working with tiny shovels and whisk brooms – careful, c-a-r-e-f-u-l not to ruin anything we might uncover beneath the thousands of years of cumulate dirt that shrouded our potential view of ancient – and in many cases – sacred artifacts.

In another time and place, feeling the need to sake up my perspective and investigate beyond the boundaries of my everyday world, I started gazing at the heavens. Orion became a favorite and I began tracking the movements within and around it. M-52 or the Great Nebula of Orion - a continual birthplace for new stars, the second of the three points of light that form the hunter's sword - became my point of departure. From there I was able to observe the cluster of stars that help to outline the figure: Betelguese near the extended club, Rigel at his left knee, and Bellatrix on his left shoulder.

So my attention for a time was riveted on what was buried beneath the crust of the Earth and then on what was moving across its skies: below and beyond – symbols of the past and the future, the deeply cavernous and the far-flung celestial, the personal unconscious and the super or Collective Unconscious, the call to dig deep and the beckoning to fly high.

If I could dig in the sand and rock of Jerusalem, why could I not do the same for and within myself? And if I could scan the visions of the limitless sky, why could I not employ the same metaphor to explore my own visions? Not surprising – both perspectives took me where I wanted to go: deeper into the layers of my own landscape and beyond the purview of my reading glasses, both entrees into the universal and limitless.

So I tracked my own history more closely – not just my biological family – but the unfolding of my own perspectives. How did I proceed from being a devout, daily communicant in the Catholic Church raised under the auspices of Francis Cardinal Spellman of New York, one of the most conservative bishops of a then very conservative Church, to then admit the first glimmers of being spirituality freed from such institutionalized and enforced teachings? How did I become a freewheeling, system-independent, self-proclaimed transcendental Zen-Catholic (as in 'in the moment' plus universal) who now feels free to communicate daily and directly with my spirit teachers, guides and The Lord Itself?

I will not bore you with the details – that is until I write a book about my evolution as a spiritual devotee, although I did disclose significant parts of it in Chapter 5, above. But I am at the point of being very conscious of being thankful for my journey. Various twists and turns, have brought me to the point of not only feeling liberated from the inherited, codified and formalized restraints of my childhood. I also have embraced my freedom and learned to trust the integrity of my own experience. So I am now able to accept personal responsibility for affirming a belief system and spiritual practice that consolidates and honors my own experience rather than being confined to the catechism I inherited.

Tracking the implications of my vision of the Soul has also enabled me to investigate vistas and realities I was unable to see earlier - or out of fear, chose to denigrate and ignore. Now that I have surrendered many of the insecurities of the earlier inexperience, however, I can lift my gaze beyond the ordinary, step around the rules devised by others, reinstitute my journey with gusto - and acknowledge the presence of God everywhere.

The buried treasures of old Jerusalem, and the continuing star clusters of Orion, have been transformed from fixtures in a set universe to metaphors for the unbounded and ceaseless creativity I have come to know and revere as Prime Source.

CHAPTER 17

EVERYTHING CONVERGES

Columbus Did Not Discover America

The spiritual experience is not a matter of experiencing something that is above and beyond. It involves experiencing the usual, the ordinary and the everyday in a dynamically new way. "It", "God", or the entity or energy field we assume exists in some other, extraordinary realm actually *is here and now, over there, in that, ever present, always available - everywhere and in everything.*

When we allow ourselves to enter or 'tumble' into the spiritual realm, it is our lens or way of seeing that switches into a deeper, accelerated, more intensive level - like moving from ordinary speed to "warp speed" in the movies of space travel. Spiritual warp speed takes us into the beyond and allows us to see and experience that which always existed. Our ordinary perspective, however, normally is not perceptive or conscious enough for us to see beyond the end of our noses.

It is we who change in our spiritual evolution; it is our perception or way of 'seeing' that is transformed. The world we might experience tomorrow – say, from an airplane or mountaintop - have always been there: natural, full, and complete. Today, from our seat in our own living room, we simply are not in a position to witness those vistas. Just because our ordinary lens can only perceive a tiny slice of reality at any given time does not mean that everything that is part of the globe or the universe - is not already there - waiting, if you will, for our consciousness to expand.

In the same way, Christopher Columbus did not "discover" America. It was *here* all the time - waiting for European consciousness and cosmology to confirm that the Earth was round, that some gravitational force kept the oceans from spilling off the planet, that evil spirits did not inhabit the uncharted areas. "It is only in appearance that time is a river," writes Thornton Wilder in *The Eighth Day*. "It is rather a vast landscape, and it is the eye of the beholder that moves."

Growing Up and Out

When I was a kid, growing up in the Bronx, New York, going to another neighborhood was a big deal: different people, different stores, strange in many ways and certainly, for the first few times, anxiety inducing. After a while a few of us tackled the subway trains into Manhattan to see the Rovers play their hockey games at the old Madison Square Garden. Somewhere along the line I visited New Jersey and then Connecticut, which felt like visiting foreign countries – especially since getting there involved a trolley, two subway rides, a bus and long lines at each point of transfer.

Much later on, going to Wisconsin for graduate school was like going to the West Coast – and much, much later – my teaching and professional appointments took me to various places in Europe, then Asia, then Africa and South America. Add in visits to every art and historical museum I could find en route and you had the makings of a cosmopolitan kid. There certainly was life beyond the tenements, routines, scents and accents of ethnic New York.

"*Listen to me,*' I now say to myself – laughing at my current nonchalance in referring to such far away and famous places. But at the time, each increment in my experience, as I am sure is and was true for all of us, was eye-opening, thrilling and boundary breaking. Every new vista made me aware that I was evolving, growing, developing mentally and emotionally. If you still anticipate the arrival of National Geographic each month, no less travel domestically and internationally, you know how exciting it is to experience the sight of new places and thereby broaden your sense of reality and identity.

Today, of course, children and college students have physical and electronic contacts all over the state and nation, if not the world – while we 'older' citizens once associated 'new and expanding vistas' with going all the way to Brooklyn or having a pen pal in Staten Island. Now there are so many intercultural, international and global electronic connections to choose from that it's almost impossible not to feel that one's universe is indeed in constant flux and expansion.

International to Common Ancestry

Years ago, after traveling a great deal around the world and witnessing both the plight and joy that pervaded most cultures, I suddenly realized I wanted, no - I needed – to acclaim my 'international citizenship'. I was proud of my American (and Bronx, NY) heritage but realized that my place of birth and early experience this time around did not stop me from also embracing a larger sense of identity – one that reflected my own experience.

Suddenly, the Irish were not simply the forbearers of political dynasties in America but cheerful farmers and young students and a witty men and women who work in lovely buildings, tend community bars and herd sheep on the green-green hillsides that are constantly graced with a soothing drizzle. Moscow, U.S.S.R., soon to be 'Russia' again, was no longer a name on a map: it had a violent history, yes, but also a modern voice and a literature. But in 1991 – although it was in the process of embracing glasnost (free discussion of social issues) and perestroika (freer markets and the end of central planning), it had broken streets, heavy hearts, empty stores, and scores of loving, adventurous and vibrant people, many of whom were in the midst of unearthing the icons their families had hidden under the floorboards during the long and repressive Stalin era.

Tokyo was so fast, furious and busy that I could not wait to get away. But Kyoto – ah Kyoto: I went there for a week-long conference, left before the first speaker had finished, and thereafter immersed myself in its dazzling array of Zen gardens. Leaving modern and efficient Japan for ancient and laborious China was a culture shock in itself: both had super-highways but Japan had rapid transit and cars galore while the eight-lane roads of China – except for the tourist buses - were then (late 1980's) used almost exclusively for thousands of bicycles and horse drawn carts.

By the mid nineteen-nineties my awareness of the world was no longer confined to the myopic perspective of Steinberg's cartoon in *The New Yorker* – the one in which the view was confined to New York City with only hints of other states and countries in the distant haze. Suddenly, the strange and new became the delightful, stimulating the realization that the world was indeed a single community made up of slight variations on how people perceived the world, enjoyed its gifts, mastered its challenges and prayed for its continuance.

My growing awareness of a common humanity became a stunning reality when I visited Sterkfontein in South Africa, the place where Robert Dart had uncovered the bones of Australopithecus Africanus - literally the 'australo' or southern 'pithecus' or ape, our ancestor hominids that lived in Africa 2.7 million yeas ago.

It was then and there that I became intensely aware of the common roots of humankind's entire biological tree. There in Africa was 3.2 million year old Lucy in Kenya (afarensis). There were the humanoids (human-like) called homo habilis (the tool maker) who lived in the Near East 1.7 million years ago. And there were all those pre-historic peoples who ventured up the Rift Valley linking Africa to the Middle East, eventually producing the Neanderthals who roamed Europe beginning 250 thousand years ago, and then our most immediate forbearers, the homo sapiens. Suddenly the sense of connecting to moderns who lived internationally was transformed once again. Now I realized I was directly linked to all humanity through our common ancestry.

Cosmic

Some years later – while spending a lot of time reading about the pollution of the planet's waters, the devastation of its land and the disappearance of numerous living creatures - I passed a sign in the window of a restaurant in Portland, Maine, which summed up the process of synthesis in a witty and profound one liner: "Think cosmically," the sign read, "but eat locally."

The advertisement activated an awareness that had long been emerging within me, one that helped me to recognize and acknowledge (versus taking for granted) – a series of astronomical realities. We had a Sun – by golly - and it was our essential source of heat and light! I always wondered why people get so excited by neon lights and fireworks but fail to notice the crescents of the moon and how it waxes into a full face. There was also the perennial shine of the Milky Way - that band of hazy light that stretches over the night's sky and on which we, as residents of our solar system, are but the tiniest dot on one of its outer arms.

Then there was the vast array of moving planets, apparently stationary stars with their Greek and Arabic names, and the constellations that taunted us to remember their shapes and the stories they symbolized.

The term 'Polaris', for example, was not just derived from the Latin term for pole but was our north star. And Cassiopeia's five stars invariably looked back at Perseus and toward their daughter constellation of Andromeda. The Pleiades did indeed consist of seven sisters, and Arcturus, glorious and orange Arcturus, was both the name of an enormous single star as well as an entire star system. My perspective was expanding once again – but hardly at the rate of the distant stars - the farthest ones rushing away from us at 90 percent the speed of light.

With each opening, with each realization - my sense of identity expanded, deepened, became more inclusive. And each jump in awareness followed a similar pattern. First, I had a new experience. Then I was gifted with a word or phrase that crystallized the experience and made it 'pop' – thereby converting the initial glimpse into a genuine realization or 'Aha'. Thus the sense of expansion and inclusion I still associate with the such words and phases as the 'icons' of Russia, the 'greens of Ireland', the 'mosaics of the Moscow subway stations', the 'waterways of Leningrad', the 'jewel-like Zen Gardens of Kyoto', the actual bones of 'australopithecus' (it just rolls off the tongue), the stark reality of gigantic, red-orange 'Arcturus', the speed of light ('186,000 miles a second'), the invitation to 'think cosmically' and increasing lure of the word 'infinity'.

Expansive Sense of Identity

And so it is: we develop as we explore, we include what we notice, and our identity deepens and expands with each development. From the Bronx, to our common humanity, to the Earth, to our long human history, to the heavens above and around us, to the realization of being a creative part of an ever-expanding universe: all insights, all analogs of the infinitely expansive nature of consciousness itself.

Any rendering of our progressive insights, any sketch of the boundary-busting impact of our life experiences, demonstrates how our identities deepen and extend with awareness - how an expanding consciousness is both a tool and the outcome of being open to what the universe offers. And the consequences are cumulative, interactive and induce an exponential growth in awareness: adding one more experience to the vertical side of a life grid or matrix while also adding one more awareness along its base means new entries naturally intersect with each other but also interact with everything else on the grid. The progression is thus one, four, nine, sixteen, twenty-five, thirty-six and so on.

It's a commentary on the developmental process: new life experiences not only have the potential to spark an immediate and related growth in awareness but can ring the bell and thus transform the meaning and significance of each earlier experience and awareness as well. Each increment in identity thus expands and renders our consciousness ever more inclusive. Yet my experiences as a kid from New York City (or yours from 'wherever') - rather than being diminished by each successive experience — have been greatly enhanced because they are inevitably reinterpreted and re-synthesized in light of each new learning experience. Similarly, the next, and the next, and the next awareness will inevitably deepen and expand the continually emerging sense of Self, enabling us, in turn, to love an ever-widening set of things, people and experiences. We thus inch closer and closer to emulating the creative and reflective all-inclusiveness of God Herself.

Each addition merely absorbs and then expands upon the one before; each progressively subsuming the others into a cumulatively more inclusive, less ego bound and more soulful understanding of how our spiritual universe works. Everything interacts with and reflects the influence of everything else. You and I, our inner and outer experiences, the feelings and challenges of our youth as well as our mature years, are really all facets of an interactive and unified system.

And note the direction of the progression: from tight and restrictive boundaries to wide and open ones; from a localized sense of self to the realization of one's common roots and common ancestry; from hesitation in exploring the new to actually experiencing one's boundless capacity to develop, connect and include; from fight and survive to protect a boundary to flowing into new and elastic ones; from 'inner experiences' not being affirmed by others to the celebration of any and every feeling and intuition in resonance with others; from 'Johnny One Note' to the 'The Age of Aquarius'; from living in a bounded area to learning how to trust in the multiple aspects of Plastic Man and join in the joyful antics of Mr. Blue;[45] from the holder of a token on a local bus to a cosmic passport to everything and everywhere.

Ah: Zee Quality of Zee Wine

As a lover of wine, I can only reflect on how different this process of psychological identity is from the labelling of French wines. The more local and specific the area or chateau listed on a wine bottle, the more pure and revered the wine. 'Mis en bouteille au Château' means this local vintage has produced a wine that is far superior to that bearing the more generic or regional label of 'Appellation Bordeaux Contrôllée'.

---

45 *Plastic Man* - capable of multiple and ever expanding capacities and identities - was the character depicted in a famous comic strip written and drawn by Jack Cole in the 1940's and 50's. *Mr. Blue* - by Myles Connolly (New York: Doubleday, 1954) is the story of a joyful and uninhibited, man who lives in a large box atop a tall building in New York City. He spends his day in gratitude – living in the moment, celebrating with signs and balloons and giving away whatever he possesses to anyone in need.

In the summary words used to identify our spiritual-human qualities, however, the reverse is true. The more our local identity gives way to a generic one, the more open and inclusive our reality. The more expansive and deeper our consciousness, the more we *see*, the more we become, the more we realize the full quality of who we are.

"Appellation Universel Contrôlée". Ah: now that's a wine of the finest quality, a veritable nectar of the Gods: it has a delicate scent yet a full-bodied taste; pure, clean, easy to swallow…and blessed with a wonderful aftertaste that sustains as it lingers for a cosmic lifetime.

The Pièce de Résistance

Now add to this cumulative sense of a deep and inclusive identity - one highly significant and clinching factor: I, you, all of us - are immortal Souls having an Earthly experience! How broad and inclusive does our identity now become? Is there nothing with which we are unable to empathize if not identify? Is there no person, living entity, material manifestation or spiritual entity that can be rightfully excluded from the embrace of our love and compassion? Are we fundamentally not part and parcel of every person and thing? And can our integral connection to everything and the All ever be exhausted?

And given the dynamics of reincarnation, where each of us has been so many, many different people and living in so many different profiles and circumstances, is there anything that by its nature can be an exception to our all-inclusiveness? Mention anything at all and we invariably we have the right – with all humility – to say that "we've been there, done that, I can identity with and have first-hand empathy for that - for I have been that kind of person and had that kind of experience myself."

Male, female, black and white and Indian and Asian, tall and short, dark and light, red headed and blond, been divorced, had six kids, died young and at nearly every age, on and on. Name a trait, attribute, lifestyle, nationality, living circumstance, point of view, spiritual tradition, BCE or ACE (Before or After the Common Era) and anything in between, and it is likely that we have experienced much of it personally.

Only our refusal to admit the immortality of our Soul, our reluctance to accept the reality of reincarnation and the fact of having lived numerous lives over the millennia prevents us from fully embracing our universal connection to everyone and thing. We need only face the reality that we are so much more than the name of the moral person listed on the birth certificate of this particular incarnation – and, voilà, the sense of inclusiveness and universal identity is ours.

In each incarnation, we are each like individual flowers. But at our core we are part and parcel of one gynormous root-stem, one all-encompassing and uniting rhizome whose roots incessantly spread deeper and more extensively as it continues to produce what it has for millions of years (from humanoids to sapient humans) up to and including you and I as today's variation on the eternal substance.

What could be more inclusive in its impact than the process of reincarnation? What could be more inclusive in essence than being an immortal Soul? What could be more reflective of the multiple variations of the universal God than the continual reincarnation of your immortal Soul and mine?

So let's add to our awareness of being a member of a local community, a state or region, and a citizen of a particular nation. The reality is that we are also citizens of the same Earth, fellow travelers in the same universe, and most importantly, an immortal Soul intrinsically connected to the same God – and thus all other Souls throughout the entire Kosmos. Those who once were labeled as 'them', are now irrevocably greeted as 'us'. What used to be called 'other' and 'over there', really needs to be referred to as 'us' who are 'right here'. What used to be experienced only as additive and cumulative and part are really to be absorbed as simultaneous and always and All.

And here are the consequences: What we once may have excluded or dismissed, we now know we must greet and include. All others are us but with different noses and hairdos. That other who once was relegated to the sidelines is now rightfully eligible to center stage. And we are delighted for them – for we all have the same spiritual parent.

Whenever another person or aspect of the same Being succeeds, we all succeed. Where they do not, we are all the less for it.

Where we used to be anxious and hesitant we now have the best of reasons to feel confident and trusting. And where we used to be fearful of losing our life and being judged by some mysterious Overlord, we now know we cannot die and are eternally protected by a loving God. Where we used to be unsure, asleep, and perhaps lost, we now know we are part and parcel of a unified Totality – always challenged yet safeguarded, forever the explorer yet always at home.

The Psyche and The Soul

Carl Jung, the founder of Analytical or Depth Psychology, called 'consciousness' the agent of separation. He referred, of course, to what we know as 'everyday consciousness', the normal acts of cognition, the process of our being conscious of the discrete objects and flow of events in our environment. This consciousness is the agent of the ego identity and all its external persona of roles and personality traits. It is that which creates the bifurcated experience of dualities – hot and cold, good and bad, inner and outer, you and the other.

In spiritual terms, everyday consciousness is akin to the earthly, the particular, the material world of detail and differentiation. It should not to be confused with the impulse to increase our depth of *spiritual consciousness* during our stay in the material world, or that *state of consciousness* that awakens us to the mission of all Souls and their link to Prime Creator.

In fact, Jung refers to the ordinary consciousness of the ego as the agent of separation because it experiences the world as separate units – not as noted here, the unfolding aspects of the all-inclusive presence we call God or Spirit. Rather, the ego identity and its earth-bound consciousness encounters the world as fragmented, divided into discrete parts. The spiritual consciousness of the Soul described here, on the other hand, literally experiences a universe in which each element is a facet and reflection of a divine unity.

We become aware of the underlying unity of everything, Jung tells us, when we are able to access images of what he called the Collective Unconscious – that which supplies the major themes of such common experiences such as birthing, parenting, home, the hero/line, tricksters, the warrior and so on. The central and unifying core of the Collective Unconscious is the Self, common images of which are likened in spiritual language to images of God, Spirit, the Soul, and divinity in any form.

In other words, the more external the emphasis, the more mundane our concern, the more egotistical our values and ways of operating - the more separated and fractious our experiences become. This is the land of judgment, criticism, time and space, 'me and mine' versus 'us and ours'. Its energy tends to divide, to over analyze - akin to what Wordsworth referred to as "the meddling intellect misshapes the beauteous forms of things: we murder to dissect." [46]

Analogs of the uniting impact of what Jung called the Collective Unconscious, however, are unconditional love, acceptance, empathy and compassion – energies that bring people together because they honor and create a sense of oneness. These are the agents of community, synthesis and integration. To Jung, the Collective Unconscious is the archetype of the One similar to our references here to the Totality and our experiential images of the One.

And what we might call 'the center', 'the self' and the 'fully integrated person', Jung refers to as the 'individuated' person - the undivided and complete person who has developed sufficient depth and breadth of repertoire to tap into, and trust, the inner guidance of the Self (or what we call 'the divine and immortal Soul').

Depth Psychology's examination of the human psyche and the tenets of spirituality thus dovetail. The healthy, integrated, undivided and thus 'individuated' person is whole because he/she is linked to their images of the Self, the core of the Collective Unconscious – analogous to the Soul being connected to its center or God.

---

46 Quoted in William Barrett, *Irrational Man* (New York: Doubleday, 1958), p. 111.

The Open Door

Eckhart Toole, in his CD entitled "Though the Open Door", [47] sums up the definition of life in the following way (arrangement of lines added):

"Before life becomes a thing,

Before it becomes a form,

There is life,

There is consciousness."

In other words, before the Soul incarnated and took on a body,

And before that body comforts itself with blankets and toys,

Before it's incarnate uses the amusements of childhood

And tools of adolescence,

Before it acquires the things and materials of adulthood,

And the necessities of the ego life,

Before it thinks it needed one more chair, car,

salary increase or plaything,

Before it becomes consumed by the

desire for more titles and entitlements,

Before all that - there is Consciousness.

That Which Looks Out From the Body's Eyes,

Is the 'I Am That I Am'. [48]

It is also the immortal Soul that chooses the mortal body,

The spiritual wisdom that precedes and guides the ego,

And the reflection and partner of Pure Consciousness.

---

47 Tolle is also the author of *The Power of Now* (Novato, CA: New World Library, 1999).
48 Exodus 3:14. "I Am That I Am" is the Greek translation. 'I Am That I Will Be' is the Hebrew.

CHAPTER 18

THE CHALLENGE OF CHANGE

Change Within Unity

Change is a constant, everywhere, and in everything. It is the dynamic of the universe. Our cells are constantly in the process of regenerating every seven years. Our bodies grow older and sometimes larger. Our thoughts are incessantly awhirl, the events of the world are in constant turmoil, and even our personal and professional lives seem always to be evolving.

And the universe around us is one of constant movement and expansion – from the spinning of the electrons within each cell, to the incessant movement between the synapses of the brain, to the rotation of our planet on its axis, and in turn, its movement around the sun and within the whirl of the Milky Way as it moves through an intergalactic space which itself is constantly expanding.

In the midst of such endemic change, we tend to embrace whatever structures we can, while we can. We acquiesce to what already exists because it gives us something to hold onto, some sense of security that momentarily quiets our anxiety. Not wanting to invite more risk and change, we live in a bad marriage, concede to the strong opinions of others, follow religious codes long out of mind but practiced out of habit, stay with the tried and the true mainly because they're available and don't involve the work of finding replacements. In short, we often passively accede to the arrangements devised by others, following their patterns for mere convenience or our own fear of trying anything new.

Have No Fear

None of the tactics outlined above ever works very well or for very long. We raise the issue of how to work constructively with change because it is quite possible our world will soon experience a series of changes. As Gaia or the Earth cleanses itself from our cumulative neglect and misuse, it may challenge the physical and mental structures society now holds dear. Resisting or ignoring the need to change and evolve never really works. What does work in handling change – big and small, societal and individual – are two major realities.

The first is to reaffirm our confidence in our Self, that abiding center of the human psyche that insures – a la the mystics, Jungian psychology and history's great spiritual leaders – that we have the capacity to act calmly and wisely and with an integrity that sustains our sense of wholeness. Adopting calm, measured, wise and creative responses to change – of any kind and size - is also instinctual for the mature Soul. The approach is summed up in the book title used by philosopher Emmanuel Mounier years ago, namely "Be Not Afraid", as well as the emphasis on the world 'Trust" in the title of this book.[49]

The second factor, and most conclusive and controlling, is the affirmation of one's spiritual identity, one's immortal Soul and one's integral connection with the All-Knowing Maker and Adaptor of Creation Itself. That's a lot. Could there be another empowerment that could possibly exceed the combination of "Trust Your Immoral Soul"? Is it possible we could fear any change – no matter how global and allegedly devastating – and allow it to negate the reality of who we are?

The reference to 'global' change is deliberate. We usually associate change flowing basically from personal and organizational changes that affect us personally or those we know and love. Sure there are the changes affecting people and events reported on the evening news but

---

[49] I was inspired by Emmanuel Mounier's, *Be Not Afraid* (New York: Harper, 1954) when I read it initially in the 1960's, and am delighted now to transform his admonition into the more affirming "Trust".

they usually don't affect us directly. Well, that assumption may be about to change. Global changes are now definite possibilities. They are likely to affect everything and everyone on the planet.

The Challenges Ahead

Substantial changes have been occurring in the structure of the Earth since the year 2000 – including, most recently, the hurricanes that hit New Orleans and Haiti, the earthquakes and tsunamis in Indonesia and Japan, the flooding along the upper Mississippi and the northern Atlantic states, and the earthquakes in Washington, D.C., Indonesia and Chile, and flooding throughout the U.S., Europe and Asia. Such catastrophes have multiplied annually and will continue - if not worsen – until at least the year 2018.

Such changes are not caused by global warming and the depletion of the ozone layer (although they continue to be major problems). And they certainly do not come as punishment by God or signal the so-called end of the world as predicted by Mayan and fundamentalist interpretations of the Book of Revelations. Rather the Earth or Gaia, as a living being, is recreating itself by cleansing and purifying the many areas of her being that have been repeatedly devastated by war, physical and psychological aggression, greed, brutality and suppression.

These are the kinds of changes and disruptions that may challenge everything we do and believe in. Many will decide to pass back to "the Other Side". Some Souls may forget their empowerments and allow their incarnates to sink into despair. Most will stay, adjust, adopt the most creative strategies they can devise, and learn to live with and thrive despite the new and initially very destructive realities.

Please read on, remembering you are an immortal Soul – and so truly cannot die or be separated from God under any circumstance. Your friends and family and all the citizens of the globe are also immortal Souls and are encouraged to think and act as such, although it is understandable that many may lapse into only 'fight or flight' reactions as the changes unfold. Despite the massive losses of life and property there should be no reason to panic. Trusting in your self, your immortal identity and the love of Prime Source are the ultimate protections and cure-alls.

So what is likely to happen? Barring direct divine intervention - which is possible but not probable at this late juncture - here is a summary of some of the major events.

First, the consciousness of Earth, Gaia, will continue to cleanse herself, the current manifestations of climate change eventually evolving into devastating sets of volcanic earthquakes all along the Pacific Rim and on both sides of the Pacific - from southern East Asia north to Japan and along the Aleutians into Alaska and down the western coast of Canada, the United States, Mexico and South America.

Second, this ring of fire will in turn set off world wide catastrophes including tsunami and hurricanes of prodigious force – resulting in the world-wide flooding of many of the coastal areas, including unpredictable and prodigious wind storms on the seas and on each of the continents.

Third, the cumulative impact of such radical disruptions and earth changes could cause the axis of the Earth to tilt – and thus bring about substantial weather changes throughout the globe.

Fourth, the atmosphere will be affected by the impact of these cumulative disruptions, resulting in horrendous meteors falling on large parts of Europe and Asia Minor – especially on those parts ravished by the effects of past wars and thus in need of cleansing.

Fifth, many of us who remain to deal with these catastrophes will elevate to the fourth and fifth dimensions where the current veil (of third dimensional consciousness) between ourselves and Spirit will disappear: Angels will then walk among us, and beings that science fiction might consider alien will be revealed as loving and care giving. The structures and creeds of any localized, historical religions which have been ego-centric, judgmental and divisive or claimed exclusive entrée to God, will collapse as people return en masse to practicing spiritual amalgams based on the common ground of love and compassion.

Six, there will be great suffering and many incarnates will pass to 'the Other Side'. As usual, however, there will be no victims; the suffering and deaths that do occur will have been planned for and anticipated in the learning contracts of those affected.

Seven, the physical cleansing will introduce a renaissance in spiritual awareness emphasizing two core realizations:

- One, trust in God, knowing that even these revolutionary planetary changes are part of God's re-creation and subsequent elevation of life on Earth, and

- Two, trust in our capacity as divine beings to not only survive the dislocations but then help in reconstituting the structures and processes needed to sustain life on our planet.[50]

Preparation And Cooperation

What then can we do to prepare for this set of changes?

First, we need to condition ourselves to accept and flow with change. As noted above, evolutionary – and at times revolutionary - change has always governed the unfolding of our bodies, our emotions, our thoughts, our communities and societies; it is also the underlying dynamic of every aspect of the planetary and intergalactic universe. We are already the purveyors and reflectors of change, each aspect of our lives conveying the reality that we personally evolve constantly – as the 'Y' tells us, in 'Body, Mind and Spirit'.

As it is, nothing is stable, unchanging and secure. Nothing is the way it appears to be on the surface: the electrons in every cell are always moving, the space between the electrons and the protons is tantamount to the space between the Earth and the sun, our bodies and minds are evolving constantly, and as already noted, the Earth already spins on its axis as it revolves around a sun that is part of a planetary system that

---

[50] The difficulties outlined is channeled information, communicated by Archangel Gabriel to Karen Cook, www.benukcook@gmail.com, "Earth Changes: The Seven Unchangeable Ones", and "Earth Changes & The Changing Earth."

is swirling within one of the spiral arms of the Milky Way. And, of course, our galaxy is but a dot among the billions of galaxies distributed throughout a universe that spans the breadth of 40 billion light years.

And the cosmic universe is still expanding, with quasars, the most distant objects yet observed, emitting the "energy of hundreds of galaxies from a volume far smaller than our Milky Way" and receding from us at speeds that are ninety percent the speed of light into what apparently is limitless space.[51] We think we have stability and firm footing. The reality is anything but.

To prepare for these additional changes on our planet, we need – as emphasized throughout - to affirm our roles as immortal Souls, aspects of Spirit, here to manifest Spirit within matter. The purpose of our existence is to convert everyday earthly realities into spiritual realities, and to do so through our presence, our awareness, our intentions and our actions. We are not here to follow the structures of others in the hope of embracing 'heaven' in the hereafter. We are here as divine beings, capable of trusting in the counsel of our immortal Souls. When we act in accordance with that identity we not only survive the coming destruction but transform it into a spiritually motivated society. We will continue to be what we always have been: co-creators - not only of our inner universe of thoughts and emotions – but also of our outer world, which after all, is nothing but the manifestation of our cumulative thoughts and images.

We create according to our beliefs. If we approach and experience the coming changes with dred, fear and anxiety then that is exactly what we will manifest. If, however, we believe in a loving God, in joy, abundance, and the continuing evolution of the material world and its spiritual underpinning – then what we create on Earth will reflect those realities.

We human beings have been involved in change since Day One, constantly transforming ourselves through spiritual insight and recreating our world through one creative innovation after another. Now

---

51 "Journey into the Universe," Supplement to the *National Geographic*, June, 1983.

the time is coming for us to ride with and master a set of revolutionary changes that will at first be greater than anything we have faced before. Once the creative cleansing is complete, however, we will be the ones with the responsibility and capacity to reconstruct according to the norms of compassion, inclusion and the common good. To paraphrase Gandhi: "There is enough on our planet to meet everyone's need but not everyone's greed."

Will the spiritual transformation be preceded by substantial dislocation, Gaia cleansing herself of all the bloodshed shed on her soil, all the malice, all the hate and toxic thoughts and actions that have poisoned our air and debilitated our planet for centuries? Yes.

Will there be a set of events that signals the end of the current structures before a new Age of Revelation can be manifest? Yes.

Substantial destruction, then calm, then the grand awakening to the love and unity that is both abundant in God's grace and imprinted on our immortal Souls.

Taking Stock

What will life be like during and immediately after the coming of what can best be described as a global cleansing?

Life may very well be upended throughout the planet. Learning to survive, to do without, and to create new ways of living anew will be the fate of those who decided to stay and not transit back to the Other Side. These are the Souls that will see the changes through, and then rebuild. And the recreation will not reinvest in the old values of power and greed for the few and poverty and disadvantage for the many, but will be governed by the same spiritual values that insured their survival: cooperation, community, equality and sharing.

The great destruction will surely will not be the end of the world or spell the coming of doomsday for the planet - as predicted by the ancient Mayans and many current religious groups. Rather the cleansing will be the start of a new beginning – a Recreation - that ushers in a new era of love, peace and spiritual abundance.

This new, creative construct will not immediately transform everyone's state of consciousness. But avarice, greed, judgment, cutthroat competition, authoritarian and dictatorial leadership (political and economic) and the incessant urge to inflate the ego will no longer reign supreme. In the new Earth, the immortal Soul will be recognized, the sacred role of our incarnations will be honored, and the common good of our shared universe will become the standard by which humanity learns to express its divinity.

What If?

What would likely happen if we also – and suddenly received a discernible beep from outer space? We have had listening devises aimed at the skies for decades with the assumption that there is intelligible life out there. There are too many galaxies, and too many stars, and two many potential planets – billions and billions - for life not to exist somewhere else in the universe. Here we are tucked away at the end of an arm of a medium size galaxy – comfortable in our alleged isolation, our concerns riveted on the everyday and often the most mundane and inconsequential things - and suddenly one of our instruments registers a 'beep'.

Suppose that single beep is then followed by three beeps, which in turn is repeated three times. It sounds like the musical tone made by the craft from outer space that landed on Earth in the movie, "Close Encounters of a Third Kind."

The technician on duty instinctually gives a command to his computer to simulate the tone of the three beeps. He then quickly calls his supervisor but not wanting another second to go by, decides to send a return signal in the same cadence, three times, to the spot on the cosmic map from which the beeps were received. By the time the supervisor arrives, the beeps are received again. Out goes the same response.

Five minutes later there are ten scientists and senior managers in the room, each either leaning over the technician's shoulders or listening in on their own monitors. We are now sending short excerpts from Bach and in turn receiving strings of overlapping chords that sound like a majestic symphony.

By midnight the President is on the phone talking to the Secretary General of the United Nations. A special session of both the Security Council and the General Assembly is scheduled for the next day.

Headlines refer to the 'Big Beep" and "Music from the Heavens" while some politicians, of course, never missing an opportunity to spread fear, issue warnings of an interplanetary attack. Meanwhile, some preachers tell their congregation to protect themselves from the hordes of non-Christian demons who supposedly are about to descend on our major cities.

Impact of Encountering 'Aliens'

What would you do? What would you think? How would you react? If you haven't done so already, it would help to begin thinking about this very probable if not inevitable event. The impact is likely to be horrendous and everlasting. And there's little chance communication would be cut off given the nature of such an inter-planetary breakthrough and the predictable enthusiasm for continuing if not expanding the contact.

Suppose as well, that the Air Force then begins to release the data it has collected for the last fifty years regarding the appearance of space ships or 'Unidentified Flying Objects' in our skies. Releasing that documentation had always been suppressed for fear of generating a so-called 'general panic' – but no more. Now it is viewed as a public service that corroborates the fact that we earthlings do indeed live in a neighborhood of other beings, some of them apparently representing more advanced civilizations.

Landings occur, with permission of course. And lo and behold, these other beings look like us - except that are leaner, taller and have slightly larger eyes. They bring gifts of music, flowers, maps of Lemuria and Atlantis, and greetings from the star clusters of Arcturus, Cassiopeia and the Pleiades.

How did they and their craft cross the huge cosmic divides? Was it a super jet fuel, or some device obviously unknown on Earth? Rather the interplanetary beings tell us their travel and speed is propelled by non-material 'thought and intention'. No fuel is used except a little bit of CO_2 generated by the trees living in their 1,200 foot space ships! Rather than thinking of the issue in terms of the cosmic distances of light years, they urge us to cast their appearance on Earth in terms of their ability to slip through time and space – instantly – by exercising their powers to live in the fifth and sixth dimensions. In fact, they tell us they have been sending signals and even watching us and visiting us for hundreds of years. Fortunately, this time we had an instrument that enabled us to receive their signal.

Talk About Your Challenge and Change

A double whammy: a horrific devastation, cleansing and reconstruction, followed by the appearance of beings from outer space and other dimensions.

Amazing? Yes – it certainly would be. Hard to believe? For some, yes, but not everyone.

Planned and coordinated by God? Yes – but a more accurate explanation would be: facilitated by God and implicitly invited by the critical mass of advanced Souls now incarnated on Earth.

Would it be a time for fear and panic? Yes - for those congenitally fearful and judgmental, but definitely not for the spiritually attuned and adept. Would such events signal the dawn of a new era? Yes - without a doubt. And would it usher in a prolonged period of peace, unity and love? Yes - given the combined energies of the loving God, the cumulative spiritual empowerments of our immortal Souls and the willed dedication of our current incarnations.

So when the great spiritual re-creation comes to Earth, and the great extra-terrestrial encounter inevitably occurs, the additional consciousness they will generate will fit in perfectly with all other epic events and awesome realities that already form our universe. The 'recreation' and the 'encounter' will merely be the most recent and the most immediately experiential of the gazillions of life-giving miracles God has gifted to Life.

Immediate, experiential and 'in your face' events certainly are much more dramatic and attention getting. But if we had been attending to incredible and awe-inspiring events that have and continue to transpire throughout the history of our universe, we would greet the new changes with optimism and take them in stride. Consider that our universe was born in a horrific bang 14-16 billion years ago. It continues to expand through the million of stars, already millions of light years away, speeding away at the edge of a universe at 90 percent the speed of light. And four million years ago the Earth was formed and ever since life has evolved from single cell bacteria to the relatively complex bundle of billions of cells that now shape the human form.

Why then would it be so surprising that after all these years Gaia or Earth wants and needs to cleanse itself of all the devastation and neglect visited upon it by sets of insensitive, greedy and power-driven citizens? And why would it be so surprising if God simultaneously decided to enhance the spiritual powers of its incarnated Souls, and in so doing enable them to communicate – at last – with those beings in the universe who already live in the fifth and sixth dimensions? If you have had your head buried in sand, then all you expect to see is more sand – and are surprised when you lift it that your consciousness has been free all along to see and live in the light, to eat finally of the Tree of Life and participate fully in the spiritual transformation of our Earth.

Once we accept the incredible nature of the universe we live in, and credit God for being exactly that He/She is – a loving creator that wants us to spiritualize Its creations – then a cleansing, an upgrade and an expansion of empowerments and vistas seems downright logical, seemingly overdue and mighty adventurous, all of it in keeping with the miraculous nature of our immortal Souls and the spiritual nature of our Universe.

Look All Around

Don't just look up – as if "up" really means heaven, or 'higher" as if something was lodged in the sky, or even the 'higher self' as a place allegedly 'more highly attuned or elevated" than right here and now.

And don't just look 'down' either – as if the word or concept alone will automatically make you more grounded, humble, realistic, able to see into the grain of wood or peek at the electrons circling the nucleus of an atom.

Besides – in this age of Einstein's relativity and quantum physics - who could tell what is really 'up' or 'down' or predict that everything you see would not change the instant you altered your perspective. When you are whirling about space, and constantly in motion, who could possibly tell which node was where – given the fact that the Earth is constantly rotating on its axis, the planet is whirling around the sun, the planetary system moves ceaselessly within the Milky Way, and our home galaxy is itself in endless movement relative to the other galaxies. And those other galaxies - like points on yeasty bread in the oven – continue to grow apart from each other at dazzling speeds measured in thousands and millions of light years.

To be a bit more specific, do the math. Light travels at the speed of 186,000 miles a second, and that comes to six trillion miles a year (a 6 followed by 12 zeroes). Factor in the number of light years astronomical bodies are from the Earth, and the size of our ever-expanding cosmos is staggering. Consider, for example, that the star Deneb is 1600 lya (light years away) from Earth, the star Monoceros is 20,000 lya and the galaxy NGC 300, itself made up of millions of stars, is 7 million lya. There is not enough space on the average calculator to record all the zeroes involved in such distances.

So what could possibly be higher or lower, or stable and predictable in such a universe? And psychologically, what is 'up' or 'good' or even continuous for one person may be down and out and constantly changing for another. Such polarized terms are metaphors, convenient figures of speech used to express the dualities we experience in the world of material incarnation. Such polarities are instinctive to the senses but are meaningless to our interior lives and the awesome nature of our integrated physical-spiritual universe.

So why not choose the revolving, flowing, creative and spiritual point of view, and 'look all around' at what is supposedly 'in front' of you, 'around the corner', 'up there', 'to the right', then 'a smidge to the left or down under' – accepting all of it as present and true, facets of the constant unfolding that is true of every aspect of spirituality. None of it can be your reality, however, until you notice, pay attention, accept and then affirm it to be as real as the nose on your face.

Look for and at everything. Swivel, bob and weave, bend your neck and waist and knees, shift perspectives, clean your lens, lie on you back, tumble or spin, unfurl your hands from your eyes, wash away the cumulative crust – and let your enlightened self be dazzled by your mind, your heart and your spirit. Blow away the cob-webs, get rid of your blinders, open the shades, poke your head outdoors, and activate your capacity to envelop the entire universe with your innate capacity to see and understand everything. If so, you will be delighted, surprised and grateful for your ability to honor the incredible reality you've never allowed yourself to see and experience before.[52]

---

52 See a copy of the famed woodcut included in Claude Flammarion's book, *Astronomy* (New York: Simon and Shuster, 1964) as reprinted in my book *Kindred Spirits* [noted earlier], p. 13. The woodcut shows a "bedazzled pilgrim lifting a curtain on his everyday universe and discovering the huge cosmos that surrounds it. On the 'outer or [expanded] universe' are huge mountains, discs of light and even the wheels of God's throne as envisioned by Ezekiel."

SECTION FIVE

Nurturing the Soul

CHAPTER 19

CREATING SOUL CONSCIOUSNESS

Raising Your Consciousness

What does it mean to 'deepen or extend' your state of consciousness?

Consciousness is your perspective, the way you view yourself and the world within which you live. It answers such questions of *who am I, why am I here, what do I value and wish to attain, who do I seek to be, and what is my destiny.*

Most do not explore such questions overtly or explicitly – for most are too busy or action oriented to ponder the foundational issues of their lives. But our images, our words and our actions do reflect our dominant values – which in turn reveal underlying intentions and our state of consciousness. We all will – at least, on occasion – invoke and act on the principles of love on the one hand and then be tempted into thoughts of anger on the other. And we all move up and down Maslow's[53] hierarchy of values according to our immediate living circumstances.

But the key to understanding our own or another's state of consciousness lies in detecting the dominant themes of our imagery, words and actions – which reveal our underlying and relatively persistent values, independent of fluctuating need. Many rich people, for example, do not need more resources but the acquisition of more is always on their minds and agenda. And some people constantly have sex or food

---

53   As a reminder, Maslow's scale runs from survival-sex, safety-power, acceptance and belongingness, self-esteem, self-actualization (wanting to activate one's full potential in one and many areas), and then self-transcendence or spirituality.

or some other sensual gratification on their minds – even if they had just had sex, consumed a delightful meal or visited a spa only an hour before.

Others may persistently seek ego gratification or the need to be needed no matter how many compliments they had received. Others pursue achievement to fulfil a genuine wish to contribute while others do so to stuff one more thing into their resumes. The back pages of the newspaper or end of a broadcast may feature a story of a loving person doing what they always do, revealing a dominant state of consciousness very different from those who grab the headlines with efforts to project their egos or display their alleged power and fame. The same process also works for the spiritually adept and the mystics who manage to remain very loving and giving people despite the relatively 'poor' conditions of their outer lives.

It really does not take much to uncover one's own or another's dominant state of consciousness. Listen to what people consistently talk about, refer to and admire. Become aware of what they seemingly value and espouse above all else. What to they seek and value – so matter what, and how do they prefer and actually act in attaining it? Again, everyone bounces around Maslow's hierarchy on a daily if not hourly basis as living circumstances alternately motivate us to seek to survive, satisfy our hunger, and so on up and down the line.

The key is where do we cluster over the long haul – at the lower end of his hierarchy or to those things that relate to cultivating one's interior life and spirituality? Where do we and others gravitate or get stuck – most of the time even though one's basic needs have or have not been fulfilled – is the key to discovering one's dominant values or state of consciousness.

Obviously, the core of spirituality is in knowing you are an immortal Soul cloaked in human attire. Maslow's sixth level of transcendence is the state of consciousness most sought by the adept and would-be practitioner of spirituality. In fact, transcendence can be so dominant that some persistently seek prayer, meditation and the spiritual state of mind, and/or the spiritual practice of service to others, even though they have not sought or fulfilled the more basic needs concerned with survival, power, acceptance and belonging. Many spiritually attuned go without, ignore or reject such 'lower end' values and practices as being relatively important.

Such a constant preference for transcendence is not necessarily the norm or desired by many of the other 'full-bodied' exponents of spirituality, the spiritually attuned people who indulge in the entire range of Maslow's hierarchy but prefer to do so from a spiritual point of view. One can indulge in sex, seek security for themselves and others and delight in social gatherings through belongingness but do so with a spiritual lens and from a very loving point of view. To such robust and sensual adepts, it all depends on their intention as they tiptoe up the scale – never overstaying or stopping for the wrong reasons. Depending on one's motivation, participating in all the levels of human experience can be catalytic for contemplation, a means for expressing delight in their incarnation, and a way to honor their commitment to transform matter into spirit.

Pure Consciousness

We have read the words of Jane Roberts: "You create your own reality".[54] We have also witnessed the truths of Roberto Assagioli. To paraphrase: "I am not any of my roles or any of my past or present sub-personalities. Rather I am a center of pure consciousness".[55]

When we apply these insights to our own life, we come to realize that: "I may have been conditioned by my family dynamics and environment, but I am not an indelible imprint of those conditions. In other words, I can overcome and neutralize the impact of any past experience, and certainly any that I've allowed to delimit my true and full identity. I now realize I am a center of pure consciousness capable of attracting the conditions I want and need to create (and re-create) my life."

---

54 Jane Roberts, *The Nature of Personal Reality* (New York: Bantam, 1974 [2004]).
55 Roberto Assagioli, *Psychosynthesis* (New York: Penguin, 1971 [2005]).

In the same way, it is appropriate to say: "I am not a mechanical device hard wired at birth by my parents, family or social group. At my core, I am not any of my earlier personal roles or cluster of traits. I also am not an automatic extrapolation of my earlier interests, values, and lifestyle. And I surely am not anyone's version of who they thought I was or ought to be. I am able to choose and constantly create myself."

Having shed the peripheral and the historical, I affirm my true identity: "I am a person of free will. I choose the happenings and experiences I wish to encounter. Whatever I was, or am now in the eyes of others, does not define me. I realize that I create and recreate myself as my consciousness expands and deepens. I am naturally empowered to live in the moment, and am responsible for the realities I create through my images, intentions and actions."

And so I with confidence state: "I realize it is risky to claim the power to create my experience and thus my life. That makes me responsible for the realities I generated and attracted in the past – even when I was unaware of the innate and tremendous power of my consciousness. But I am no longer willing to allow any past identity or any possible cluster of limiting and debilitating traits to define who I am. As a center of unlimited consciousness, I am totally free to choose and develop my capacities, my abilities and my priorities - and create my own reality accordingly."

Now that I am on a roll, I also want to declare the following: "I have no one to blame for anything. Everything that has happened in my life is the result of the decisions I made or agreed to in order to learn the lessons I outlined in my learning agreement."

"So, I hereby declare that I am the creator of my life. I am a center of pure consciousness - unencumbered by the past, living in the now and trusting in the future. I choose to nurture images and take actions that express the immortality of my Soul, and my capacity to be a loving and deeply appreciative human being."

My final word (for now!) on the subject (another drum roll, please): "As I affirm my spiritual identity, I consciously choose to create a life of love and understanding, and attract everything I need to expand and deepen my spiritual awareness. By trusting in my innate divinity and the abiding presence of Prime Source, I consciously choose to image, intend and express that which is loving, creative and makes a contribution to my own spiritual development as well as others."

Fences and Open Fields

There comes a point in life where the bustle of day-to-day activities gives way to the yearning for quietude, an acceptance of what already exists, the realization that there really is no need to strive for or pursue anything else. Quietude and acceptance? That's right: a blissful sense of quietude accompanied by the realization that you already are everything you are ever going to be.

You come to know these truths not just as cognitive insights but as real, living experiences. They may dawn on you at fleeting moments throughout life but they seem to register more fully and consistently with age. If you are still in that state of consciousness that revels in achievements and visions of a still more glorious future, be aware that quietude and acceptance will inevitably beckon to you and joyfully await you a little further down the road. Whether embraced or allowed to happen, your openness to quietude and acceptance will inevitably enable you to live more fully and frequently 'in the now'. It will also engender in you a sense of empowerment that far exceeds your current image of your next professional advancement, exercise schedule and romantic involvement.

Let's see how this realization works by tracing the process of our inner development. Each of us is born into this world of materiality with an ego, the psychic capacity to establish one's sense of identity. Obtaining that identity is not easy. After being totally dependent on the nourishment and support provided within the womb, we are suddenly expelled into a whole new world – our first major experience of becoming a separate being and laying the foundation for developing our individuality. The old unity is still approximated, however, through the nurturing of and dependence on one's mother and family support.

Gradually we graduate to a care and feeding program that is supervised by our parents during infancy - our growing need for independence emerging around the at age of two when we yearn for and begin to declare our own boundaries. Saying 'no' to one's parents is gradually superseded in subsequent years by learning to say 'yes' to a desired set of friends and new experiences. These experiments in self-affirmation lead to a growing separation from our biological moorings and a growing dependence on the approval of friends, groups and selected societal norms.

Then competition ensues - for grades, schools, dates, colleges and employers. The arrival of marriage, children and the first mortgage certainly reinforces the feeling of being on one's own; for many it even creates a feeling of being hemmed in by both responsibility and ambition. In fact, each point of achievement creates the need to live according to a new set of rules, structures and constraints.

Time and energy are expandable but are not infinitely elastic. So choices need to be made en route: wanting and attaining some things is usually counterbalanced by the need to give up or let go of something else. Falling in love and getting that dream job may mean less freedom and time for other things. Marriage brings love and support as well as diapers and pressure to get a bigger house. A promotion means more money but also more work and responsibility. And bigger contracts and incomes always run the risk of creating a bloated ego - with the urge for more power and an allegedly position outcompeting the primacy of love and relationships.

Certainly many make great strides inwardly as well during the years of getting established outwardly. But it's difficult: the ego is finally getting to exert itself - claiming, fortifying and defending each new set of external successes. And with each notch in its belt, the ego becomes increasingly convinced that it must push on, gain more, and if necessary, fight to maintain what it has achieved.

If our inherent spiritual promptings are expressed during this period, it usually takes the form of adhering to an established religion – a selection process usually induced and sponsored by family practice and cultural tradition. The codes and rituals of a structured religion thus add solidity and predictability to one's growing definition of oneself. Joining a religious community also serves as a counterweight to the confusing sets of values that compete for our attention in what is often experienced as a very materialistic world.

As Carl Jung pointed out, the first half of life is concerned with affirming and building a personality and getting established in the world. The second half is concerned primarily with reversing field - learning how to first quiet and then gradually let go of the ambitions associated with youth, middle age and society's definition of 'success'. In short, it involves slowly shedding the bravado we spent so much time cultivating in the early years.

In psycho-spiritual parlance, the ego – once affirmed and solidified - finally learns to hear and heed the beckoning of the abiding Soul and move into a more balanced relationship with its inner Self. In societal terms, the person gravitates to viewpoints and projects that are less competitive and oriented to external achievements, and makes a conscious effort to become more collaborative, enjoy the 'little things', make peace – even friendships – with unexpected others and develop the deeper aspects of oneself.

At work, the 'softer' posture is reflected in the late middle years as a desire to mentor. In the family, the grandparent gives up the external job and seeks more love and joy within a larger sense of family and friendship. There is also an increased desire to 'give back' and serve others. Such diluting and then surrendering of the ego's need for a defined turf and another round of accomplishments involves substituting 'we-ness' for me ness', contributing to others versus trying to out-compete them, and broadening one's sense of community to include more than the immediate or biological family.

Ah - Yes: That Last Third of Life

The phenomenon – or benefits of the last half of life - has three dimensions, and each one reinforces the impact of the others. Notice now how quietude, acceptance and love become increasingly dominant.

First, with increasing age, and certainly by the time of full maturity and retirement, more time and energy becomes available for the non-egoist or Soulful aspects of life. The excitement - and related pressures and burdens - of 'making it' dissipates: mortgages are eventually paid, financial needs are reduced, children move into their own homes, big houses are traded for smaller ones. The need to survive and thus strive dissipates rapidly. Time and energy are freed up and we begin to feel liberated: we sign up for a course we wished we had taken in college, explore a new hobby, volunteer at one or more community agencies, and spend more 'quality' time [56] with family (especially grandchildren) and friends.

Second, with maturity, there is the growing acceptance of the reality of physical death. That awareness in itself stimulates an in-depth and concerted search for meaning.

Third, the mature years give us the time and energy to attend to such things as our spiritual interests. As the ego's needs are met, then reduced and eventually put into a relaxed context, there is a proportional increase in the desire to attend to the needs of the Soul. More and more, we are able to heed the inner voice we ignored or kept under control during the busier times dominated by egocentric and overcrowded schedules. Now we have the time and interest to cultivate the simpler energies, spend more time witnessing nature, commune with books we always hoped to read, express compassion, appreciate all the animate and inanimate things we had taken for granted for so long, and even participate more fully in the rewards of prayer, meditation, contemplation.[57]

We have more freedom and thus become liberated from earlier obligations, responsibilities and identities. Security attained or at least greater insight, our perspective changes to include everything that comparative freedom allows - letting go of the old need to extend and

---

56 Quality' here means unhurried interaction – in which we choose to share, attend to the other, look them in the eye, listen to their words, be sensitive to their body language, attune to their unvoiced messages and be fully present with another.
57 See Chapters 21, 22 and 22.

defend silly boundaries and attain long records of accomplishment – and learning to live fully in 'the now'.

Whatever the number of earthy years you have contracted for in this incarnation – fifty, seventy, eighty-five, whatever – you realize, again and again, that whatever lifespan you allotted to your body is really only a mille-second in the life of the Soul. You realize as well that your years of earthly trial and error contained hard work yet produced its own honor and integrity. It took fortitude and patience to learn the many lessons that dominated your early and middle periods of development. It also took enormous inner strength to keep your spiritual inclinations alive and not be (thoroughly) seduced by materialistic frame of mind. Now – finally – you no longer need to protect your spirituality but can actually and freely develop, extend and project it.

Then at the pinnacle of our internal 'success' – accompanied by an increasingly forgetful mind and the increasingly tilting torso - we are reminded repeatedly that it soon will be time to shed even the memory of fame, fortune and material living. Working from our spiritual core, we feel more aware, gifted and appreciative despite our increased physical frailty. We grow increasingly ready and able to transit once again – dropping our interest in striving, gaining and protecting in favor of giving, communing and letting.

Thank God, we proclaim, that we have at least a few years in which the energy patterns are reversed: pursuit becomes acceptance, *then* becomes *now*, willpower becomes trust, running after the future becomes living in the present, 'you must' and 'you should' become utterances that make us laugh, and the earlier and now structured enclosures of old fences give way to the depth and expanse of open fields.

Create Your Day

You don't have to plan your day to 'create' it. Scheduling a series of events is not the same as having clear intentions and then attracting the energies you desire. 'Planning' only indicates what you might do – if you are resolved and the world cooperates. 'Creating' determines what you want and, most importantly, how you will experience whatever you attract into your energy field.

First, determine what you want by imaging what you want to unfold. That fact alone attracts the energies needed to fulfil your image. You may not get all the specifics you want on the timetable desired, but you do create a force field that acts like a magnet and draws the desired energies to you.

By imaging your goals, you allow your mind's eye to see how your desired future will unfold. Finally going to Greece, offering a workshop on spirituality, building a sense of community - are all likely focal points for imaging. Obviously, it's good to reject any lingering images of 'the big dollar', power, 'winning' whatever - and other types of goals that may have periodically dominated your untutored and younger days.

Declare what you want, write it down, draw it, act it out, and imagine having already attained what you want. Affirm that image whenever you think of it. That image will become your magnet, your positive force-field that will – sooner or later - create and attract the energies needed for it to be realized. Again, you may not get exactly what you want – or is good for you – or on the timing you desire. But you will activate a creative field of energy that will, over time, bring you at least a good approximation of what you desire.

'Over time', did you say? Well, God and the energy clusters of the universe do not serve at your command. A million and one alternatives in the schedules of others may have to be rearranged and reconnoitered to honor your images. Besides, your current sense of need or relative deprivations may be the result of years of doubting yourself and sending out messages that you were not worthy. If so, that's a big boat to turn around in a short time. But it will – for now is a new time, featuring a more affirming and spiritual you.

How then do you live – or frame - your life? That brings us to the second aspect of creating.

Framing Your Experience

The most neglected part of creating a life is learning how to frame your experiences. This applies not just to a specific goal you want to enhance the quality of your life. It also involves all the big and little events and experiences that unfold in the course of everyday living.

If you choose, for example – preferably early in the day – a focus for the day (or some particular event or meeting), you create the lens through which you intend to experience the happenings of the day. You thereby help to 'create' your day – not only attracting to you the kinds of encounters that will fulfil the content of your intentions. Most importantly, it will also determine how you choose to interact with and thus experience those encounters.

Consciously creating your experience, the process of how you will interact with what unfolds, is likened to 'setting the tone', 'selecting your perspective' or 'choosing the frame' for how you choose to experience whatever happens. Both your content and your process are gist for the mill: you could, for example, deliberately chose 'joy' or 'trust' or 'non-judgmental acceptance' for how you will interact with whatever unfolds. You thus set the tone for fulfilling your own desired prophecy.

It is silly to assume that our experience is caused by external events. We bring ourselves – our values, goals, of ways of operating – to everything that happens in our lives. So external events do not determine how we choose to interpret or respond to them. Our experience, our frame, our emotional response, the value we place on any of our encounters, is determined by how we choose to engage it. We create reality through our process and perspective; the happenings of the external world merely prompt us to reveal our state of mind.

A number of people witness a parent berating a child. One person walks away, reasoning the issue has 'nothing' to do with them. Another condemns the parent - activating a judgmental frame of mind. Another jumps to protect the child – activating their 'protective' mode. Another talks with the parent and asks if there is anything they could do to help the situation – thereby choosing to experience the incident from a 'caring' frame of mind and displaying compassion for both the parent and the child.

Who is right – or wrong? Nobody is either. But each person experiences the event from a different perspective - a point of view often ingrained and thus expressed whenever anything triggers that frame of mind. And if the frame or complex is strong enough, practically everything will activate it. We all have many frames. The key is to choose deliberatively one (or two) at the beginning of the day, deliberate frames, perspectives or attitudes that reflect how you prefer to interact with the world. If you are intent and committed, you stand a good chance of activating that preferred frame 'no matter' happens'. So you could chose and commit to being caring, jovial, understanding, or whatever attitude you prefer and wish to develop. Without such deliberate setting of your antennae you could more easily lapse into some more negative, default or 'automatic' energy setting that was ingrained long ago, and which you may not have consciously updated since.

Our perspective and sensibilities – whether we are consciously aware of them or not – create our internal responses. Outer events provide the stimulus and cue, and we – based on our cumulative values and the depth of our past experiences - supply the means by which we 'see' and interpret what is going on in a situation. It is 'we' - not 'they' - who determines what transpires within us.

So why not set your desired frame early in the day – the one drawn from your repertoire of spiritual skills and perspectives, rather than allowing some unfinished business - still simmering beneath the surface – to become the continual filter through which you experience life. Accentuate the positive often enough and you have a good chance of re-wiring your circuits, insuring they do not make the same old connections to a less than admirable frame of mind that has the power to turn a positive (or even neutral) situation into a negative experience.

Framing the day with a loving, joyful, caring or some overtly 'spiritual' focus, in particular, helps us attend to what we want to notice in the world. It indicates what we are looking for and what we intend to see, hear, discover and feel. It pre-selects – from all the possible options – what we intend to experience, and predisposes us to find it in every situation – even those that on the surface initially seem to justify a negative reaction.

Suppose on any given day you had chosen to attend to 'beauty'. What might normally escape your attention on your walk home would then appear front and center; what had been there all along but not 'seen' before would suddenly be noticed because it is highlighted beforehand. A painted water pump you passed everyday might suddenly be appreciated. The colors in a magazine ad, the lovely look on the face of that elderly woman, the colors of the birds and those two Irish Setters, the design on your grandson's jersey, the vibrant picture in that window shop, the mahogany stain of your books shelves, the unique jackets of book covers, on and on, signs of beauty, unique, varied, everywhere. "Those things were not there yesterday," you might initially conclude. "What happened - to that street – or did something happen within me?"

Let us further suppose that you witness a car accident. You could choose to perceive it as something totally sad or tragic. But suppose you had deliberately chosen 'love' as your focus that day, and in remembering that frame, you immediately send love to everyone involved – both the person hurt and any others who may have been emotionally shaken. You don't rush in immediately with either a condemnation of the alleged guilty party or glorification of the alleged innocent. You let the police analyze the situation, the rescue workers to supply physical aid and you just 'instinctively' send love to everyone involved and thereafter assist in anyway needed or requested. Having set the frame of your experience, you enable your love to rule your agenda and thus dominate your reactions, responses and experience.

Without a pre-selected focus, you run the risk of being seduced by the negative connotations of a drama or tempted into creating a purely negative experience for yourself. When focused, however, you are able to give thanks that no one was killed and send healing energy to those involved. And rather than being paralyzed by the sight of the accident, berating an errant driver or walking away, you infuse love into the situation - reinforcing your own spiritual values and the flow of good will in the world.

In the same way, a developed and focused attitude of good cheer can neutralize a potentially toxic experience, in the same way an empathetic one can help anyone to minimize their 'normal' attitude of self-absorption and instead actually see and attend to the needs of another.

Set the thermostat on 78 and you get your normal steamy heat. Set it on 52 and it no wonder the atmosphere is cool if not downright cold. Set it on joy, or loving, or gratitude, and any of us can learn how to experience the guy on 'anger automatic' who 'flips us the bird': be calm, smile, take a deep breath, and respond with a wave of good cheer. Hey: who's in charge here?!

Clearing the Passages

When the passages are blocked, the water, the blood, the vitality of life does not flow. So we use roto-rooters and the plumber's snake to clear the house pipes of debris and unfreeze whatever is clogged. We take statins and blood thinners to keep the blood flowing unencumbered through our arteries and veins. Similarly, we invoke prayers and use meditations to keep the channel to Prime Source open and direct.

What then can we do to cleanse ourselves of the cumulative hesitations and doubts we might continue to carry in life? How do we rid ourselves of our recurrent spasms of guilt and the nagging fears that keep us from doing something new and innovative? How do we reactivate our sense of center after so many years of learning merely to avoid or outmaneuver difficult people and situations? What can we do to reclaim our capacity to love after allowing ourselves to be lured into the enveloping and negative energy of others? What can we do to clear out the self-perpetuating distrust that can compromise our physical, mental and emotional – and thus spiritual - health?

Regular massages will help clear out the toxins in our bodies. Eating healthy foods will give us greater energy and vigor. Writing in our journals, drawing, and working in clay can be cathartic as well as self-corrective mentally and emotionally. Psychotherapy surely can help unearth and eliminate the sources of self-defeating thoughts and behaviors.

But there is one more 'therapy' often neglected – because it is so simple. It is called 'dumping it" – willfully, deliberately, with clear intention – creating a simple ritual that enables you to personalize the act of shedding what is no longer wanted or needed - including those attitudes and behaviors that no longer serve you or undercut your integrity.

If the effects of slights, teasing, bullying, 'put-downs' or condemnations still linger in your mind from childhood or any part of adulthood, then summarize each one briefly in writing and then deliberately burn each one at a time. If a memory lingers beyond its instructive value, then draw the situation or cast of characters – in rough approximations, caricatures or stick figures - and then put it in the shredder.

Use whatever ritual or active demonstration you can think of – tossing old plates, tossing rocks, burying a piece of clothing, burning old letters, literally brushing your body down with brisk strokes over your face, arms, legs and torso to simulate letting go, literally chanting out loud as you release or brush away the past: "Let go, let go, let go," "no more, no more, no more," or "be gone, be gone, be gone."

In each case, name what it is you are dumping - using your voice, pencil, crayon or hands to demonstrate your freedom from whatever you wish to discard, whatever you think is hindering your free flow of energy and aspirations. Call upon your God-given capacity to be your own psychological plumber and roto-rooter technician – and apply those images to any area of your life that feels burdened or blocked or weighted down.

Then fill the empty spaces with energy that is nourishing: confident, affirming, grateful, loving, clean, flowing free. Energize not only one area of your life but every nook and channel. Become - once again - the creative being you were meant to be: alive, in love, an embodiment of ease, trust, gusto and good will.

Clearing Out

It is also good to periodically clear out the garage, attic, basement, pantry and the bathroom cabinet – in general getting rid of things that you no longer need or use.

Give things away to people who can make better use of them - like that table in the antic and the extra TV in the basement. It is also good to clear out the backyard, the front yard, even the address book, and make room for the new things and new connections.

While you are at it, it is also good to let go of ideas, structures and people that no longer fit your beliefs and values. Endless accumulation invites stagnation and psychological bloating. We all tend to save and repeatedly savor memoirs of the past, fearful of never having another good time or another love. If your inner space is already filled with memories, there is no room to create and attract new experiences – equally delightful, loving and invigorating.

Saving some stuff with its extra special memories - of course. It's good to affirm the past. But living in the past, or perpetuating loss with relatively empty attitudes about the future? It is no wonder you have barrels of stuff stashed in the back room, 'hope chests' (now there is a fascinating name for you!) brimming over with forgotten clothing and covered with attic dust, and boxes of memorabilia in the rooms the kids have long vacated: what's going on?

Getting stuck on saving stuff is like putting on too much weight. What's being avoided? What's being protected? Every extra box and every extra pound of insulation reflects a fear or vulnerability that only the heart can decipher. The process can be likened to how we use our hand to hold something. A flat hand will hold little but it is always open. A cupped hand – soft and flexible - will hold some things we value yet still have room for the new. A tight-fist only crushes what it wants to preserve and insures nothing new can be added.

Clearing out - letting go of *at least some* of the mementoes that symbolize old times, makes room for the creation of new joys. Dwelling on the past – no matter how loving and joyful - and grasping at those yesterdays eliminates the potential of today and tomorrow. This is no room for fresh coffee in a cup that is already filled with what once was grand but which is now tepid and stale. Besides, who wants a cupboard filled with cracked cups and saucers? Throw out or give away as many as you can, reawaken your receptivity to the continuing unfolding of your life. Then envision a new mug or two in your uncluttered cupboards, and free space all along your freshly painted counter tops.

Change Your Response

You cannot always change an event or circumstance. You can, however, change how you react or respond to it. 'Reaction' continues and reproduces the same energy you just received. It is visceral or instinctive and thus replicates the energy of the 'other'. Someone hurts you and you respond in kind - an instinctive tit for tat. Reactions do not involve a 'time out' to think of alternatives; if anything allegedly new enters into a reactive decision, it usually only involves variations in tactics, not a qualitative rethinking of the issue in a creative and constructive way. As a consequence, reactions usually are fast and immediate, producing only silly actions designed to protect oneself or punish and block the other.

Creating a "response", however, involves taking at least several moments (if hours or days) to evaluate the situation, think it over, consider the alternatives, and then choosing a constructive option that maximizes your potential benefits. In sports, it is called 'playing your game' and playing to your strengths. In life it is called momentum, pursuing a goal, feeling your energy, focus and thus 'not allowing yourself to be distracted or provoked into doing something stupid'. It also involves making a deliberate choice to choose a response that is creative and classy any time you are confronted by another's uninvited and negative pattern of energy.

Rather than choosing a reactive 'fight or flight', the creative response (based on experience, intuition or a naturally creative temperament) deliberately chooses a third and innovative alternative. A perceived offense, for example, need not provoke a counter reaction. A finger for a finger, an eye for an eye – only means that vengeance and degrading behavior wins the day: you follow another's lead and you also lose control of your center. Ignoring an insult at least stops the negativity. But waving a hand of peace in response transforms the situation because it affirms your integrity and values. The days of dueling over every slight and miscue are over.

Even an invitation, for example, to march or speak against this or that public policy could prompt you into preferring a third alternative - like praying for the cause. Distaste for the attitude of a public or religious official, for example, could provoke you to shout out or walkout during a public ceremony. Or you could choose to dampen such visceral reactions and choose a positive way to oppose whatever policy it is with which you disagree. Reactions tend to identify the baby with the bathwater. A response is more measured, mindful, innovative and self-enhancing. It is motivated by the desire to reposition an initial difficulty by handling it with a transforming and creative attitude.

Act and react immediately, of course, if survival or a serious injury is at stake. Usually that is not the case, however. If you react viscerally and become automatically defensive to an alleged provocation, if you allow the instinct of 'fight or flight' to take over and your emotions to run wild, you lose control and surrender your centeredness. Upon reflection you may discover you had no reason to feel threatened and nobody intentionally meant you any harm. Not everything needs to provoke the mindset of an emergency – that is if you are not 'touchy', are really in control of yourself and possess internal mo-jo. But if you love the sound of fire engines, you best be careful that you don't automatically transform a firecracker into a five-alarm fire.

So despite the provocation to do otherwise, please help yourself and the situation by resisting the temptation to strike back if provoked. Hesitate, calm yourself, and regain your balance – enhancing the possibility that your response will be measured, clear and creative. It also keeps your blood pressure low and literally gives you time to get 'a hold' on yourself. Your honor has not really been threatened so please do not get all excited, draw your sword, risk hurting another and inciting your own heart attack.

Whenever tension emerges, be sure to take a deep breath, count to seven (or seven million) and pause long enough to activate your creative center. Invoke the guidance of your Guardian Angel. Utter a simple prayer to stay calm. Remember you are an empowered Soul - capable of adopting the right combination of assurance, wisdom and creativity. [58]

Thoreau

"I went to the woods because I wished to live deliberately," Thoreau said in *Walden Pond*.

"Deliberately' is the key word: consciously making decisions - throughout the day – quietly alert, aware, attentive to life's constant flow

---

58 These are lovely and wise standards for sure - yet none of us can predetermine how we apply them to any given circumstance. For example, I still allow some silly things to push my buttons and instantly ignite the protective instincts of my limbic brain before my preference for calm, ease and reason even knows what is going on. I am getting better at living up to my own standards – noted here - but obviously am far from being 'perfect'.

On the other hand, not all situations are silly and not all immediate responses are unjustified or governed by a prickly ego. Sometimes I knowingly allow myself to blow off a bit of steam when faced with something really egregious - but then quickly try to activate my best intentions as soon as possible.

At other times, I also feel that someone's words or actions are so unjust (toward myself or another) that I don't hesitate to confront them head on, immediately, directly and with some heat. So when is an incident 'silly', making a visceral reaction by a bruised ego totally unwarranted? And when is it so egregious that it calls for blowing off a little stream (for one's own sanity), or involves something so unjust that confronting words and actions by an empowered Soul is the best and most appropriate response?

Obviously it is a case-by-case call. Whatever the circumstances, however, it is my hope always to initially calm my limbic brain and muster as much reason and creativity as I can before I react and do or say anything. If I can – in that initially highly charged mini-second or two - keep my composure and retain my center, then I am in a better position to discern the difference between situations that are silly, egregious or unjust and responding accordingly. That at least is my best intention – which is no guarantee of success but it does offer a way of monitoring my progress.

of moment to moment experiences. Thoreau retreated into a more simplified lifestyle in order to be more active internally. The absence of complexity and 'noise' in the woods of Concord, Massachusetts, enabled him to notice and commune with what E.K Chesterton subsequently called the 'Tremendous Trifles' of the everyday life. To Thoreau that meant the capacity to experience the warmth of the sun, hear the buzz of bees and the chatter of animals, watching the plants and flowers sprout and unfold, witness the changing colors in the fall and experiencing as many of Nature's affirmations as possible. Thoreau's attention was attuned to the immediate and the Soulful. His journal became a record of his dialogue with the eternal *now* - his encounters with each scent and sound evoking a deeper awareness of life's seamless web and its endless trail of fascinations.

Henry had three chairs in his cabin: one for solitude, a second for company, and a third for what he called "society". When he finally left Walden, he said it was because he had 'other lives to lead', other places to see and experience, other encounters to stimulate, and other ways to nurture the resonant perceptions of his Soul.

Atmospherics

What kind of emotional and psychological atmosphere do you wish to create as you anticipate your next encounter with Life? And, is the setting you are about to enter supportive of what you wish to do?

In approaching any situation, for example, be aware of what kind of atmospherics you want to create - such as witty, interactive, creative, conciliatory, celebratory, honesty, confronting, or some combination thereof. In other words, *attend* to what you want to create and receive.

Then, consciously imagine sending those energies with and before you. In other words, *intend* what you want.

Last, be aware of what actually happens. Did you activate the kind of energy you wanted? Did you renew it during the interaction? Did you also summon other desirable energies? Remember what happened and what worked. In other words, *retain* memory of what actually happened.

Attention, intention and retention.

We know people exude, emit or 'send off' one pattern of energy or another. But we're often unconscious of what energy we create and forget it can be chosen or regulated. Ah – but it can. We can choose to emit a desired energy, take it with us and thus re-create wherever we go. We can even choose particular energy force fields for particular encounters – and thus influence the way the transaction unfolds.

So you are encouraged to send *loving energy* before you if that is what you want to create and experience. Or you can choose to send *joy* down that corridor as you walk to a meeting. You could send and 'walk with' whatever energy you desire and choose to create - *mutual understanding, respect, empathy* or even *outrageous creativity*.

Pay more attention to the energy, the atmospherics or the process of an encounter and don't get caught up in just its formal content. If you know what you want to create, the content generally takes care of itself, even if there are factual differences to be resolved. The ability to attain simpatico is crucial: it influences the flow of events by enveloping them in desired field of energy.

Thus in entering any new situation, it helps to know and consciously image what you want to achieve in terms of content. But it is especially important to consciously choose the kind of energy or the process likely to support your goal. There is no guarantee you can override the disposition of another. Being consciously attentive to creating an energy field that supports your desired outcome will at least neutralize any countervailing blockages.

These dynamics are particularly important for spiritual matters – creating multiple opportunities for us to choose and create Soul consciousness. It means we can deliberately attend to the atmospherics of trust, service or peace - and intend them as we walk through the day - literally becoming a carrier and disseminator of our chosen energy fields. If we wish to create empathy and mutual respect, then it would be wise to personify those energies and send them down the corridor as we approach that important business meeting. Ditto for empathy and respect and creativity: consciously becoming and radiating whatever we wish to share and create.

Attach, Detach, Affirm

It's good to get attached to people and life's happenings, to feel a stake in the lives of others and the outcomes that affect them. We support our relatives, root for friends, take sides on political issues, even get emotionally involved in issues happening half way around the world. Being interested in and concerned for others is a loving trait.

But there is a point at which our list of attachments and concerns can grow too long, when we begin to feel over extended, when an issue or concern or desired outcome begins to 'own' us rather than our selecting it again as a freshly energized and conscious choice. Having velcro when you need it is wonderful. Being a matching piece of sticky-stuff for anyone or anything else makes for an entirely different dynamic.

Parental care and concern, for example, is surely to be encouraged. But hovering over a 35 year-old child and the details of his/her never-ending trials and tribulations is a bit much. Liking one's new car is also understandable but washing it everyday may be a sign of a fixation. Interest in the events of the day indicates good citizenship but yelling at the television over each segment of a newscast suggests the need for a little detachment.

How much attachment is too much attachment is a question of boundaries. Let's say each of us is like a circle of some two inches in diameter. The smaller circles that cluster around us would be our interests. Some are close, indicating our high interest; others are farther away, suggesting milder interest. A circle that touches the rim of our boundaries would suggest strong interest. One that overlaps with our boundary lines may indicate substantial involvement. One that has moved wholly within our circle may suggest it is consuming us – or we are consumed by it, raising the question as to where we begin and such an attachments ends.

How to attain a balance between attachment and detachment is an especially key issue for the spiritually inclined. In terms of eternity, a year on Earth – or elsewhere in the universe – may equate to a millisecond. But while we are here, time and involvement with the things and issues of the Earth is an essential part of our incarnation; we experience the passage of time on a daily basis as well as the periodic transitions from childhood to maturity to being elderly. And we're also expected to work at attaining the major objectives outlined in our learning contracts. Thus we are expected to engage with the people and events of our earthly tenure if we are to learn from of our incarnation.

On the other hand, it is essential to keep these attachments in balance, never forgetting that our primary mission is to further the development of our Soul and create more love and understanding. What we do in the physical world and how we behave toward others are always functions of our spiritual identity and development. We are here to empower our Soul qualities, not simply to get engrossed in the lives of others or get lost in the immediate trials and tribulations of the Earth.

The process of attachment-detachment is like an on and off switch on the thermostat. Our involvements heat up as we also attach ourselves to the comfort level of the world. But we need to set a point for cooling down as well and do things that help us detach from the mesmerizing effects of personal sentiments and worldly engagements. Reflection, self-assessment, meditation, prayer, contemplation, retreats, and taking 'time off' and 'time-outs' are all helpful ways to cool down and put our earthly involvements in spiritual perspective.

The more we learn about our responsibilities and empowerments as Souls, the more we can regulate our capacity to stay both engaged and yet slightly detached, never overdoing our concern for the events of the world at the expense of our Souls.

Ten Aspects of Learning

There are ten aspects to the learning apparatus of every human being.

First, there are the five most obvious and most used: the sense of seeing, hearing, tasting, smelling and touching. Add the sixth: the very important capacity of humans to think - to absorb, sort, coordinate and integrate the inputs of the senses.

The emotions would be the seventh component, the ability of the mind to generate a sense of worth and the heart to express value. The emotions enable us to evaluate and select – positively or negatively – and thereby determine our preferences, evaluate our experiences, assess the value (to us) of alternative courses of action, and most important, to like and love ourselves and others.

The eighth would be intuition, the capacity that builds on thinking and the emotions but goes beyond them. Intuition also takes into account (1) the larger context of creative possibilities - not accessible to sequential logic, and (2) the spontaneous insights and hunches that can bubble forth from the unconscious. Intuition does not try; it allows. It does not force; it confidently awaits that extra spark and insight. Intuition opens to a whole new and ever expanding set of ideas and impulses because it trusts itself to uncover a range of new possibilities – some of which are wild and crazy and exactly what staid logic needs to break out of its box.

By trusting our intuition, we are free to mix and match the past, present, daydreams and even the allegedly outlandish and thereby produce new extensions at an exponential rate. This new and enriched alphabet soup is then allowed to simmer and incubate and create new combinations - and even new questions. Where logic produces rational 'answers' that can resolve an issue, intuition enables and explores insights and can dazzle and motivate.

An intuitive decision includes the calculations of rationality and the value assessments of the emotions but then goes far beyond them. Reason alone will help you sort through the options which, unfortunately, are usually extensions of what already exists. Then our emotions assess their relative value. But somehow one's intuition excites wholly new ideas, validated by a supra and deeper sense of inner 'knowingness' – producing the sudden and spontaneous clarity of: "Aha! That's it. This is the way to go."

That brings us to number nine, the Soul. Soulful decisions are supra intuitive, beyond or greater than even the instinctual openness, trust and knowingness of intuition. Soulful insights come to us - not from our human or mind consciousness - but from the depths of our Soul consciousness. They are most accessible to us during and after periods of quiet, solitude, mediation and contemplation. A soulful choice or decision, then, is a composite awareness, one that arrives or arises from the fusing of both unconscious insights with the results of conscious awareness – a third or combined way of 'instantly' accessing and verifying the deepest facets or truths of the integrated Soul-mind.

Soul consciousness is the source of inspiration and direct knowing. It happens whenever we are attuned to the life force in one of a million ways, evoked perhaps by the sight of a baby or young child, a walk in the woods or along the seashore, the rediscovery of a old love letter, a playful romp with a dog, sighting the elegance of the elderly, hearing the wind in the trees. Soul consciousness can also be activated through regular prayer, meditation and contemplation: such is the awareness and testimony of the world's great mystics.

With Soul awareness, the pull toward the divine is very powerful indeed. It operates like a giant magnet: there can be on other way. Jump into a fire to save a child, risk life and limb to help another, take a stand for righteousness with utter disregard for the personal consequences – all spurred on by the awareness that 'the other is also me, that we are all bound together'. It is the ultimate 'walking your talk' and 'the rubber meeting the road' of instinctual soulfulness: the Soul can do no other for it is a integral member of the All.

The tenth and highest capacity of the human Soul is that of Mastery. The great Avatars that have come to Earth, for example, began like the rest of us: they were Souls living within a body and progressively guided by the bodily senses, rationality and the emotions. Trusting the insights of their intuition, the resident Souls of such Masters slowly assume direct guidance of their Souls; they both united with and detached from the mind and body of their incarnates and became living symbols of love, ready and able to use their embodiments to express the essence of their Souls.

At this tenth stage of Mastership, the Soul becomes a spiritual Presence - the fullness of the Soul not only guiding the body and mind but subsuming them as well. The result is the unfolding of the fullness of love: a unified and sacred spirit at one with God, able to emulate Its Presence in everyday life.

Surely we all know we have the five senses at our disposal. We also know we can make even better use of our innate rationality in making decisions, and hone our emotions to value those things that reflect love, empathy and compassion. Intuition – and its capacity for creative insight - is also a 'human' empowerment that many are learning to trust and perfect.

As to Soulfulness: it certainly is within our capacity as we learn to seize on the spiritual potential evident in each of us and each eternal moment. And since mystical union with God has been and continues to be attained by Souls just like us, it is wise to assume - with practice and intent - that each of us can approximate and attain similar depths of Soul integration.

All of which leads us to the tenth stage – the one of total integration and individuation. Having earned God's blessing to incarnate still one more time – the Soul is blessed as a Master Teacher, capable of living the ordinary life in the most extraordinary way, a true mystic in the marketplace.

CHAPTER 20

PRACTICAL SPIRITUALITY

Spiritual Practice #1: The Loving Relationship

Ah, the subject of all subjects, the focus of philosophic tomes, self-help books, sitcoms, mini lectures at Thanksgiving, painting after painting, song after song, greetings and partings between family and friends, last minute salutations at the airport, the compelling pulse beat of all teenagers, the source of whispers in darkened rooms, and the hope and aspiration of every betrothal, marriage and delivery.

Love is invoked universally on all occasions. Much of it emerges as a result of conscious and heartfelt intention, although some seem to use the word as a proverbial throwaway. Either way, we express it, we think it, we hope for it, we study it, and with hesitation and the occasional rush - act out our opportunities to experience it.

It is especially lovely to receive love – at least in the form or packaging what most pleases us. We also love to give it away to selected and significant others. As a concept, its role – and significance - is never denied but its presence can be. As a desired outcome, it is often sought but as a process it is often dismissed or avoided. And, of course, the immediate relevance of love is frequently questioned - especially in business, political, legal and military circles. Pay homage if you must but don't dare to act according to *it* if you care to be accepted in the boardroom or survive in any competitive arena. Witness the New Yorker cartoon of the grumpy old man at the post office who in placing his order says tersely: "Any thing but those love stamps."

Each of us hopes to feel both loved and loving - whether in a relationship, family, friendship, profession and/or community. If it emerges, momentarily or in relatively lasting doses, it is treasured, recalled and relived for a lifetime, even by the most prickly and resistant. When we love and are loved, we feel alive, joyous, supported and thankful - the radiance of love's force affecting everything we image, say and do.

It is when such connections are broken that we most yearn for its presence. We miss not only the formerly beloved but also – and perhaps most significantly – we miss participating in the exchange of love and its enlivening source of energy. The deep sense of connection and belonging that comes from giving and receiving love stems from the awareness that we are involved in a mutual exchange of goodness - exhibiting trust and honoring that is impossible to duplicate. Prestige, reputation, recognition, great wealth and influence - may help for a while but inevitably pale when compared to the joy of being involved in a loving interaction with another.

Ah, but now the rub. Different people mean different things when it comes to how they want love and operate within the different forms of relating. Whether it is as a parent, child, friend or colleague, some may give but only if they get. Some may be cautious and others wear their hearts on their sleeves. Some may operate from fear and thus want control. Some may want and need protection while others may be all too willing to wield it as a power. Most of us probably – and unconsciously - use all these approaches at one time or another – and most, I am sure, yearn to both give and get, not material things, but the honor and respect that comes with deep sharing and selfless caring.

Whatever the venture or venue, what we might call 'true love' for another actually begins with loving oneself – believing in the integrity of one's values, perspective and basic behavior. Loving another is grounded in the respect one has for one's own personhood. Only integrated personalities who have reason to respect their own identity can truly extend themselves in a loving interaction with another.

People lacking such a center or who are not aware of their capacity to develop their own wholeness, will tend to use any biological or situational context to advance their own personal needs first and foremost. Such non-connectedness, insecurity and anxiety accents the need to rely on mechanisms of control. Fear has many sources – everything from wanting to be with someone in a relationship for fear of being alone, to keeping a relationship at arms length for fear it will interfere with one's work or tightly controlled lifestyle.

This brings us to the vital question of whose needs are to be served in a loving relationship of any kind. If any one person assumes their needs and convenience are non-negotiable, then the relationship quickly becomes imbalanced with the other party feeling their integrity has been ignored or badly compromised.

Some people are more than willing to give up their sense of personhood just to be in an allegedly 'loving' relationship - failing to realize that needing is antithetical to loving. When one person is needy – and willing to attach their persona to the other – the other may like it because he/she gets their way and exercises control, or may hate it because they are suffocated by the weight of the reliance. Neediness can also be used to control another, a dynamic that can destroy any mutual exchange of equality and support.

But all relationships are meant to be supportive of both or all parties, activating, for example, the give and take called for in a marriage vow. It is not 'me' versus him/her' but 'us' that makes the process of relating so wondrous and yet so taxing and difficult. Love can only be created and exchanged by two (or more) self-affirming people (or groups). Being in perennial orbit around another (like the moon in orbit around Earth), obtaining light and gratification chiefly as a function of the other - denigrates the intended role of a relationship, namely to help each other attain greater degrees of wholeness and integrity.

The best or most effective mates – no less friends and team members - are those who bring their individuality, integrity and sense of un-dividedness to the relationship. Then and only then can they really be present for and open to the other. Entering into a relationship like marriage or parenting in order to find oneself has all the makings of a disaster.

Anything less than a conscious sharing of two different but compatible identities, who are supportive of each other's individual quest, and who desire to support each other's deepening sense of self – qualifies as a loving relationship. True love will flow from one to the other only in proportion to each other's sense of identity and self worth. It is not a loving relationship if the so-called loving energy is used to fill a vacuum, compensate for loneliness, serve as a bromide or fulfil a need to directly or subtly manage another.

If both or all parties are not clear on why they're in the relationship, and are not consciously working to develop their own identity within the relationship, then their presence in it is probably built on need, habit or convenience. If so, their attachment will wane and like the proverbial leaky bucket, slowly lose its meaning and its vitality.

One more thing: there are the 'two or more' parties to a relationship, of course. But there is also *the relationship* itself, and that needs as well to be nurtured and supported as a field of energy unto itself. Therefore it is wise - in the search for balance and mutuality - not to think just of acting on my and his/her behalf, but to think and act as well on behalf of the relationship itself. Sacrificing one's convenience and forgoing something desired is often the best thing one can do to preserve and strengthen the relationship.

Being sensitive to and serving the needs of this third or 'it' factor is what integrates the relationship. It involves depersonalizing the process of giving and receiving to doing something that simply serves that mysterious, sacred, creative and at times the magical *field of energy* that exists between you. There is 'you' and 'him or her', and then there is 'it' – and sometimes 'it' needs and deserves all your love and devotion.

Spiritual Practice # 2: Unconditional Love

Unconditional love is difficult at times but remains *the* standard espoused by mystics and parents and followed by most if not all grandparents. It is the foundation of trust and mutual giving and receiving. It accepts differences and honors individuality yet never makes the exchange of love and support conditional upon one party doing the bidding of the other. The nature of a relationship is changed dramatically if pre-conditions are placed on the love, or worse, if one party threatens to withdraw their love if the other does do certain things, in certain ways.

Conditional love is manipulative. "I'll love you only if you do as I want' includes a threat. The accent is on self-interest rather than love for the other – a situation that eventually corrupts the relationship. If the other succumbs to the threat, he/she inevitably feels angry toward the manipulator. If they don't give in, they feel guilty. Neither dynamic serves the mental health of the individuals involved or the integrity of their relationship.

The familiar and poisonous messages of conditional love – not always announced but clearly communicated – include such threatening messages as: "I will love you if you

- do what I say...."
- follow in my footsteps and become a...."
- honor me in the ways I need to be honored."
- behave like me."
- obey my rules and regulations."
- And the worst and most conditional of them all: "if you pay homage in one of several ways ...which I won't list because you ought to be able to guess what will make me happy."

Such conditions can be communicated directly in words – in sweet tones or harsh - but also indirectly through tone, gesture and body language such as 'that look' or an icy air of disapproval. And often the norms are not announced beforehand leaving the so-called offending party to discover the offending boundaries only when he/she crosses them.

But the message is clear and often cutting: 'there is a quid quo pro involved here, buster, and you better listen', 'read between the lines and you will realize this is a really a power play', and 'please understand one thing: we have the power to dangle the carrot and you should know by now what you have to do to obtain it'.

Either way, the threat is real. It means, "If you do (or don't do) what I wish, I will...

- never give you another dime."
- condemn you."
- be very, very angry."
- write you out of my will."
- hang up on you."
- abandon you."
- never speak to you again."
- act as if you no longer existed."
- simply not love you any more!"

The 'do's and don't' we communicate to children – for their own health and safety – are, of course, part of the parental responsibility. But the line is crossed when the boundary setting used to guide a child is laced with manipulation and veiled threats. Such approaches may serve the distorted needs and unfilled dreams of a parent but they hardly insure the psychological stability and interests of the child.

Unconditional love, on the other hand, is spiritual in nature and a concrete application of Soul energy. It is the kind of attitude and behavior we Souls are trying to learn and perfect while on Earth. Placing conditions on expenses, use of the car and curfews may be warranted as conditions suggest. But the withdrawal of love and psychological support is never justified. Placing conditions on one's love is a denigration of love. It dishonors the integrity of both parties, corrupts trust, undermines the relationship and degrades that which should always be treated as sacred.

Spiritual Practice 3: Creating Focus

Now that we have laid the foundation for spiritual practice by outlining the standard of love, let us proceed to some more specifics.

The following spiritual practices are cumulative in impact. They begin with the suggestion that you select a focus for each day or week, and culminates in an outline of the spiritual lifestyle – where the elements of spiritual living are no longer discrete units but become integral aspects of a natural and seamless web of behavior.

Many a mystic has reminded us, of course, that no matter what the level of consciousness we may have achieved the day before, the new one can be filled with so many challenges that we feel we need to start over again. Having to stop and 'Return to Go' – as in many a board game - is a jolting experience. Yet each alleged setback also offers us the opportunity to start each new beginning with greater humility, intent, wisdom and focus.

Please treat, then, the recommendations that follow as encouragements from a kindred Soul who has failed again and again but who keeps on trying. I am also summarizing the suggestions others have formulated and followed, over the centuries.

A word, then, about intentions and focus. Vague intentions – mini-invocations made as you rush out the door – have little lasting effect: they are easily forgotten, quickly out-competed by the rush of events, forgotten until days later when they may reappear only as vague memories. No, no, no: setting an intention that will guide your actions takes a little bit of time and some concentration.

Sit quietly, close your eyes, choose to let and allow, and patiently wait to receive a thought or image that captures the essence of the kind of energy you wish to attract and highlight that day (or week). You may or may not already have a theme in mind – like forgiveness, or living in the moment, or looking people in the eye when talking to them, or befriending others, or greeting strangers you meet at the market. If not, allow your intuition to receive an image of focus that is surely lurking just below the level of consciousness.

If your focus is not immediately apparent, then you could pay attention to any images, ideas or symbols you recall from a magazine article, a newspaper headline, a line in a book or something you heard on television. Either way, reduce the theme of the focus to a word or two, a simple phrase, and/or a drawing, picture or symbol.

I, for example, write down words or phases on post-ins as they occur to me and make a special impression. I then reflect on them and/or use them to select a focus for the day or a particular meditation. I also tend to be highly visual so I collect a lot of post cards, mostly of paintings, and cut out a lot of images from magazines - giving me a backlog of stimulants from which I can select the one that 'speaks to me' on any given day.

Whatever the word, image or symbol that captures the essence of your desired focus, choose the one that energizes you, that vibrates within you, that beckons to you like a child enthusiastically raising his/her hand at school.

There you have it. Give yourself a little extra support by making sure your word or symbol is transposed into a format that can serve as an effective reminder. You could, for example, write your focus word on a post-it or take the picture or postcard you already have in hand and tack in onto your refrigerator, dashboard and/or desk. You could reproduce a smaller version for whatever word-symbols you've selected and place it in your wallet or purse. You could also make a banner to hang over the kitchen door or garage! Whatever your reminder, place it (or multiple copies of it) in a conspicuous place – and keep it (them) there for as long you wish to express and attract that experience.

Spiritual Practice 4: Let In Love and Then Let Go

Once you have registered your intended focus, do not allow yourself to become distracted by the events of the day. For example, be aware of the world's current events but do not get drawn into them – fuming, raving, writing an endless number of letters to the editor, kicking the cat, inadvertently dumping your annoyance over some political event onto the innocents in your home or who you just happen to meet at the supermarket. If you do find yourself chronically distraught about the state of the world then it is time to reframe - and regain perspective.

So continue to feel and express your concern for the silly actions of others. But also take time to pray and meditate. Refocus your attention from what is 'wrong' in the world to what is 'right' - expressing gratitude for the blessings of life and all the things that are also working so well. Give money to various charities as you wish. Communicate news of really 'good' and heart-warming developments to friends and family. Mentally send energies of joy and abundance to the unfortunate, intended healing energies to the infirm, and cards and personal visits to those who are ill or who you sense are lonely.

There is also both a personal and a cosmic reason for adopting a less militant response to the perceived injustices of the world. The personal one relates to humility, and the cosmic one to context. We are each entitled to our opinions but we still may not 'be right', right that is in the larger or cosmic context. The spiritual nature of the universe suggests that down deep, everything – but everything - is as it should be, whether we happen, at the moment, to perceive it differently.

We also need to accept the fact that those who are now involved in unfortunate and tragic events have cooperated in creating or attracting those situations. They may have done so for any number of reasons – including the fulfillment of a contract, the desire to learn patience through difficulty, the desire to learn a particular skill or nurture a specific perspective, the clearing or balancing of a past regret, or even the desire to experience an emotional or physical pain in order to gain the empathy needed subsequently to help others in similar predicaments in the future.

So bless a given situation – especially if it involves difficulties – and send wishes of love and healing to those involved. Then let it go. When in doubt, take a deep breath, affirm your center and remind yourself of your God-given capacity for ease, love and non-judgment. Trust that the world's unfolding – and your attentiveness to it – is part of the constant challenge to let news in but not get paralyzed by it.

Even in tragic circumstances, those involved know at the Soul level what best serves their learning and overall spiritual progress. So the best thing we can do is honor that reality no matter how positive or negative a situation seems to be. Send loving and enabling energy to those involved, of course, and if possible, follow up with material aid or resources. But allow those involved to assume responsibility for what happens to them, and then work through the situations they helped to create or attract. With God's help and guidance from their Guardian Angel, those involved or affected by various situations are fully empowered to extract from it the experience and learning they want and need for their spiritual progress.

Spiritual Practice 5: Quiet Time

Spend some time each day in reflection and reception.

Many use their quiet time in meditation or prayer. Others write in their journals. Joseph Campbell, author of marvelous books on the world's mythologies (that is, tales of a group's origin and destiny), used to underline in books. Some meander and others walk at a brisk pace. Some sit and pray in structured ways while others simply sit and commune in ways that are spontaneous and free flowing.

The power is in the commitment – devoting time and energy to your receptive and reflective self. No planning is needed and no evaluations are encouraged. Quiet time does not entail 'doing' anything but being quiet and allowing your inner spirit to admit and honor its stream of consciousness - all those wondrous images and messages that bubble up from the unconscious, free from the editing we normally impose on our conscious activities.

If you are so inclined, you can pose an issue beforehand. But then do not devote your attention simply to attaining specific outcomes. Simply allow your intuition to receive impressions from your unconscious mind. Trust whatever clues you receive no matter how fragmentary or mysterious. You can jot down brief notes as you proceed or when you are finished if that helps you honor and retain what you have received. There are no rules except the commitment to spend some concentrated time alone with your Self - just breathing, relaxing, awakening your inner counsel - enjoying some uninterrupted time, honoring whatever you experience (no matter how fragmentary, strange or seemingly unrelated). When your meditative time is over (ten – twenty minutes, perhaps), be sure to follow the clues you've received. Embellish and play with them, and then heed whatever insights and advice they present.

Spiritual Practice # 6: The Importance of Context

Look at everything from an ever larger and more inclusive context, what the Greeks called a set of progressive 'holons'.

The finger is part of the hand, which in turn is a component of the arm, which is connected to the entire side of the body, and so on. By analogy, no image, thought or action is isolated unto itself: it is both a temporal composite of smaller parts and, in turn, a part of some wider or more inclusive holon. This progression is as true for quarks, atoms and molecules as it is for individuals, families and communities. It is true of a stairway, a house and a housing complex. It is also applies to an insight and a story and a mythology – each of which are made up of a series of smaller or antecedent parts, and all of which are in turn capable of becoming a part of an ever-widening evolution of holons.

When reflecting on an experience, for example, see it as an emanation from something smaller and deeper as well as the seed for something wider or bigger, as both a holon made up of a set of cumulative parts as well as an aspect of something larger and more complex. Understanding events in context allows us to experience life in a way that is less immediate and personal and more long-range and spiritual.

Want to see something in context - first its parts and the role it plays it being itself part of a larger holon? Get out two sheets of paper – the regular size of 8.5 by 11 inches (line or unlined). On the first sheet, make believe you just threw a rock into the middle of the pond (or paper) and will now draw the resultant ripples in that pond. Draw a set of approximately six to eight ever-expanding concentric circles on the page – beginning with a small circle of about an inch in the center (enough space to write in a word or two), and enough space between each subsequent circle to insert another word or two onto the spaces created between each circle. Use a compass if you want but jagged or approximate circles drawn in freehand works just as well; in fact it might be helpful if you are playful and spontaneous.

Now think of an issue you are dealing with in your life. It could be personal or professional, positive, negative or unclear (which is why you wish to explore its implications). Place a one or two word descriptor of your issue in the center circle, then work outward - noting something that expands the scope of the feeling or thought that preceded it. I, for example, might choose to write 'ease of writing' in the central circle, and then 'energized by release of new book' which might lead me to list 'new computer,' then 'free schedule', 'joy of retirement', 'affirmation as published writer,' 'open-ended lifestyle', and then 'a way of nurturing Spirit' – each rung encompassing a larger context, each smaller holon progressively becoming part of a larger one.

On the second piece of paper, again draw six to eight circles. But this time fill your responses in by beginning on the outer rim and work toward the center of the paper, as if you stood on the outer shoreline looking at a set of ripples flowing toward the horizon. If you started, for example, with a larger issue of "not feeling well' in the outermost circle, then each subsequent circle will give you an opportunity to explore its component parts. Thus 'falling yesterday' might be next, then 'lower back pain', 'lumbar region', 'L 4 and 5', 'swollen sacrum', then "out of joint" and then perhaps 'lonely'. (Hmm: yes – lonely: the body, mind, and emotions do interweave to reveal what is going on in and for the total organism).

The first set of circles listed the holons becoming wider and thus more inclusive fields of energy. The second set explored a given issue in terms of its smaller or deeper parts.

This exercise is also fun to do with children, for it helps them to see any immediate issue in context - in terms of both its larger reality as well as its deeper parts and possible causes.

We are both generators of our future situations and carrier-composites of our own histories. Investigate both by throwing a stone into your mental pond and tracing the ripples that flow out or away from your immediate situation or feeling to their larger context as well as those that go deeper into the possible component parts or causes of a given issue. Context – larger and smaller – evokes and involves everything.

Spiritual Practice # 7: Being Aware of Life

It is helps to be reminded periodically that Life – the living, pulsating, evolving energy of Spirit – exists everywhere and never stops churning and creating.

It is at our feet in the form of emerging stems and leaves, manifest in tulip bulbs and insects, reflected in the capacity of seeds to send roots into the Earth and blossoms into the air. We see and hear Life as the wind gives undulating forms to the trees. In the air, we again witness seeds shaped like helicopters, parachutes and parasols floating with the currents, traversing fields and lakes and even oceans. And surely the constant generation of life is evident in the continual birthing of human and animal children and the incessant emergence of one generation after another.

It is also overhead and all around us, evidenced by the star incubators called nebulae which continually birth new stars within the billions of galaxies. Images dance on the synapses of our brain nerves – exciting never-ending sets of flares and connections. Life streams forth from the faces of everyone we greet – each person a carrier of an incessant beat that seeks understanding and acceptance. It is all around us: listen to that bird, hear the bark of that dog, the whining of that horse, the deep grunts of the pig, the purr of the kitten in your lap.

Be aware of life unfolding whenever you hear the rumble of a passing car, clank of the delivery truck, shout of a merchant, hum of your own breath, rhythmic stops of the mail truck and chatter on the school bus. Be aware of it when you see the smile of the druggist, the moving eyes of the grocer, the hand waving from the delivery van, the greeting from a neighbor and the laughter from the next room.

Realize how our senses are enlivened as we hear the sounds of breakfast, and inhale the aromas emerging from each restaurant and shop. And 'ah': the delicacy of that perfume, the bouquet of this wine, the touch that hand. Our lungs swell with the scent of spring, then falling leaves, then whirling snowflakes. And how incredible it is to taste our favorite foods, linger with certain sounds, sidle closer to what and who you love, luxuriate in the giggling of children.

Life everywhere, inside and out, e-v-e-r-y-where, every sec-ond, every MO-ment, in every Sit-u-a-tion and EX-PERI-ENCE, never stopping, ever popping, always exuding, right now - in front of you, within you, life meeting life, big tweets and little murmurs, all embracing LIFE, here-there and around every corner, under every rock, within every cloud, on every lip, with every image: tumultuous, bubbling and cascading life, vibrant and continuous, ever present, ever peaking, ever watching, ever dancing, ever vibrant, incessant, joyful, always expressing and always creating…one more sign of Life.

Spiritual Practice # 8: Being Mindful of the Eternal *Now*

Each moment has significance. Each thought has repercussions. Each gesture has an impact. We need be very mindful of each – choosing, deliberately choosing to be conscious of what we do and how we do it, moment to moment, choice point by choice point.

In terms of time, the digital watch is instructive. Unlike the analog watch with the dial and the moving hands, the digital has no hint of past or future: the 'time' is always 'now' – this minute, this second. The earlier countdowns are past, gone - and the so-called future has not yet emerged as a new 'now'. The mechanism seems to suggest: why focus on either the past or the future when your point of choosing is always in the eternal present.

Think of the airwaves that instantly communicate our telephone messages: we call and someone answers – a dramatic demonstration that there is always a new *now, then another, then another*, each one creating a string of new interactions like new ripples on a newly discovered pond. When a new message – whether carried by carrier pigeon, telegram, fax, e-mail, i-phone or text – is 'opened' and attended to, it immediately brings the recipient into the experience of being 'present'. Hot mustard or tamales have the same effect: no past, no future, only the zow of 'now.'

But suppose we decide not to depend on incoming e-mails or the surprise zing of a pickle or grapefruit to interrupt our reverie and bring us into the moment. Suppose we deliberately choose the open hand versus the closed fist, the smile to the frown, the slight bow at the waist rather than the glance down the side of our nose. We know that certain gestures invite and create: ah, the embrace of grandma's hug, the hearty hug of old friend.

Yet rather than embracing the moment with our best, we often allow the disappointment of an earlier moment to affect the current one – and thus project the memory of that undesired experience onto the current moment. Getting over whatever 'it' was - and getting on with a fresh view of life is not easy. But we can train ourselves to bless and let go of disturbing memories by reminding ourselves that we know how to breathe fully, invoke the potential of the new moment, image the positive, and experience the delight of trusting in our own spontaneity.

The trick is not to do a lot with time but to be so *immersed* moment to moment in what you consider to be worthwhile that you forget about time. Compare the tone and agenda of a busy adult and that of child flying a kite. We adults can't 'afford' to play children's games all our lives for we now have responsibilities and tasks to complete. But why can't we retrain ourselves — at least part of the time - and regain the ability to joyfully choose to be at one with whatever we do. The adult or busy-busy way is comparatively fecklessly and unaware. The childlike, on the other hand, flows with intention into an being immersed in what is here, present, now.

We tend to remember the choice of epoch events: selecting a school, profession, mate, home, the names of our children, and other so-called marker events at home and work. Yet we forget that we also have the opportunity to consciously choose at the foundational level, at the deep strata that effects everything else: deliberately choosing to nurture *this* image and not *that*, attending to one intuition rather than another, selecting one intention and not those others, deciding to approach a situation with joy versus suspicion, to choose — at the depths of our Souls — to let go into this instance, this situation and this *immediate experience*.

In a spiritual sense, choosing to live in the *now* is the experience of mystical bliss. It is the point of entrée for the contemplative experience of oneness with God. Time is the dominant reality of the incarnated or material state of mind. And 'no time' or timelessness - aka 'eternity' or nowness - is the essence of the divine.

Admittedly, the Soul is born into the eternal yet agrees periodically to surrender that awareness by taking on the challenge of regaining it in and through — and thus despite the distractions of - incarnate life. We agree to slog through time and the density of matter with the intentions of gradually reawakening to our true identity, and thus reinstituting our natural capacity to live in the eternal *moment*. And when our embodiment dies and we return it to the Earth, so does time come to an end, and we are free, once again, to live totally as Pure Spirit in the state of divine timelessness.

In the 'meantime', however, we must learn to keep that eternal light burning. Taking time outs — through creative imagery, literally doing what we love and energizes us, getting lost in giving and receiving love, hanging around with children, nourishing the direct link to God through prayer, meditation and contemplation - these are the 'time-outs' we need within the realm of time in order to transform our material involvements into moments of timeless grace.

Spiritual Practice # 9: It's Good to Be Alive

On waking in the morning, it's nice to know the fingers are still working and the eyelids still open. It's also wonderful to realize that our hearts pumped and our lungs bellowed perfectly throughout the night – and did so without our direct supervision.

Every aspect of the living process is indeed a gift. And most of it is on automatic - with no need for us to issue minute-by-minute commands – as in 'beat heart, beat', or "I now command that enzymes be released in my stomach to aid in digestion,' or "okay, synapses: it's time to transfer your information along the cerebral network.'

The fact that the system works – all 100 billion cells in the brain alone making their contribution without conscious reminders from us - is reason enough to offer thanks for the priceless blessings we receive every moment of every day. It seems only right that we note our gratitude - now and then - in recognition of the continuous support that Life offers life. And it is non-stop 24/7/365 support - to be exact. To paraphrase Mel Brooks: it is indeed "good *to be alive*".

Spiritual Practice # 10: Sending Energy, Creating Energy

First, if you want joy, then send joy. If you want to receive love, then consciously send and give love. If you wish to be part of a festivity, then enter a situation in a festive mood.

Remember you are a magnetic field: a charged, vibrant center that naturally creates an electrical field of energy, a pulsating dynamo capable of setting off vibrations that affects everyone and thing you experience. You are like a tuning fork: if intentionally tuned, you send out a loving and joyful resonance. If chipped, dulled or brittle then those are the vibrations you create – and others sense – as soon as you enter the room.

Whatever you want, first *be* it by personifying and displaying it. And, of course, our personal force field always attracts more of whatever we create and give away. As noted earlier, if you want to experience certain energies, then consciously send those energies before you as you enter a situation. Creating your desired energy as you proceed is like sending a courier or a chorus ahead of you: you announce your intention, set the tone, and invite and attract others to join in. You vibrate all the time anyway: you might as well go forth with the tuning and tone you both prefer and wish to attract.

Thus the revealed truisms:

- Plant discord: harvest discord.

- Plant hardy potatoes: unearth hardy potatoes.

- Sow some really good stuff: reap some wonderful stuff.

- Sow love and joy: attract more of the same.

CHAPTER 21

PRAYER

Making Time

It seems we make time for everything but communing with God. Tasks and responsibilities dominate the day: phone calls, errands, business meetings, the continual care and feeding of children. There always seems to be something: the television screen is blurry, the car is making some strange noise, there is 'no food' in the house, the dog needs disciplining, the school bus is coming, the boss wants this by 8 a.m., I need to fly to LA tomorrow, and where oh where are my black shoes!

Finding the time to take a deep breath – no less talking with God during an easy walk – always seems to get out competed by the latest 'hot' news and our sense of needing to handle an immediate 'problem'. It is, of course, a matter of priorities. The day will not get any longer and our energy reserves are not likely to expand dramatically. The only thing to do is reframe what we consider to be essential.

The teeth need brushing: we find time for that - for we deem it essential. Three meals a day: what could be more important! Sleep 6-9 hours: a physical and mental necessity. On the other hand, it takes but fifteen minutes to sit or walk in mediation, ten minutes for a stop at a sanctuary or park bench and only a few seconds to spontaneously give thanks.

Admittedly, there is considerable momentum each day for the immediate and the worldly to out compete the desired and the spiritual. But we also know that we won't make it – today, or in the long run – without also taking time to honor our Souls and our connection to the divine. We could take a moment or two to give thanks, ask for guidance, listen to the silence, smell the roses, say grace, watch children at play, enter a house of worship, read an inspiring passage from a book, listen to music that stirs our highest motivations, write in our journal, go to an art museum, allow ourselves to dwell in *this wondrous moment*, stop *to* experience *something* that catches our eye and *beckons us to commune with God…for just a moment.*

Think of these tremendous opportunities as chores, and they become chores. Think of them as invitations to attend to the care and feeding of your Soul – experienced in mere minutes at a time – and they become portals, entry points to that which is energizing, timeless and yes - essential.

The First Thing We Should Do

Prayer is without a doubt the most effective tool we have for changing a negative situation to the positive. Usually, however, it is the last thing we think of doing. There are millions of incarnate Souls who have tried everything to relieve a difficulty, only to say: "So I finally decided to pray." Finally? It should be the first thing we do.

Why? We are talking here of the Soul reaching out to the One who is most disposed to listen – and help. It does not need an intermediary for it goes directly to the Source. Human strategies certainly are helpful in handling the material aspects of an issue: to think, strategize, build a support group, be careful, clever and unemotional. It is different with God and prayer. This is the time be direct, clear as you can be and as heartfelt as you want. Seeking God's guidance is the wisest thing to do – even with everyday personal and professional situations since they all inevitably involve some spiritual issue like love, fairness, honesty, emotional pain, justice, or compassion.

And let's face it. Difficult situations can also bring out the worst in us. Suddenly we can feel threatened and on the verge of saying or doing something we know we will regret: an eye for an eye and all of that. Best stop for a moment and consult with God – or at least your Guardian Angel (see Chapter 24, "Angelic Beings"). So protect and project your self if you must – but fairly and with spiritual guidance for what you do and how you do it. Prayer – reaching out to God immediately and then continuously – is the most effective and enduring way to resolve both immediate and protracted difficulties. And with God's support, we are able to reach solutions that also preserve – if not increase – everyone's moral integrity.

Diego Rivera, *Flower Day*, 1925 *The archetypical urge to pray, to request guidance, and to give thanks.*

True Gifts

There is a woman working at a local coffee shop whose mere presence radiates light and good will. She greets everyone with a gentle smile, stops to chat, waves goodbye, is always cheerful if not quietly ebullient. She is difficult to encounter if you are in a bad mood; her gracious manner will soften you within seconds. Any signs of the doldrums simply do not last in her presence. It is not that she is 'in your face'. Her energies simply create an easy-going and upbeat mood that is hard – no, impossible - to resist.

Things were different yesterday, however. She looked strained and pale. I asked if everything was okay.

"It's probably stress," she said with a slight stutter. "The doc's running a series of tests."

"Can you take some time off?"

"No - I am afraid not. My mother-in-law is coming to live with us - she's been very ill. I am saving what time I have to be with her - at least during this initial transition."

As I said goodbye, I raised my right hand with conscious intent of sending her healing energy. I will think of her today - especially during my meditation. I keep forgetting that prayer is the most powerful thing we can do to help another. So I silently sent her loving energy - not with the intention of making her 'better' or her circumstances lighter but simply sending an unspecified gift of loving or healing energy - to be used as she sees fit in meeting her challenges.

The Focus of Prayer

I have often prayed for something in particular – hoping to obtain relief from my distress over a personal situation or what I assumed was a difficult experience for another. I prayed to resolve difficulties, cure pains, heal ailments, and forestall death.

I have realized since, however, that praying to relieve my own physical or emotional pain, for example, was inappropriate and misplaced. I, like everyone, was only experiencing something I contracted for or had attracted in order to learn from the experience. Besides, praying to be relived of a certain distress is too specifically egotistical. But praying for an increase in the capacity to deal with my pain - such as strength, forbearance or insight – would help me acquire the generic character traits needed to deal with both the causes and the symptoms of my pain.

Prayers to relieve the difficulties of others can also be in part self-centered if the person praying is motivated by a need to feel better about their own pain or loss: if that other was not suffering, then I wouldn't be anxious or feel threatened. Certainly I wish them full health and a long life. But praying with the hope of neutralizing their experience - however painful – may be contrary to their contracted desire to undergo a so-called negative experience in order to raise their level of consciousness. Who am I to pray that they avoid what could be significant learning – something they may have agreed to prior to incarnation? Even well intentioned prayers do not give any of us the right to substitute our sense of what another person needs for their own insight and development.

So in praying for another, we need to keep our needs out of the picture. Feeling the pain of another can be a sign of true love. But we have no right to interfere with another person's implicit desire to learn whatever lessons are inherent in their particular situation. There is a larger spiritual purpose behind every earthly condition. Our prayers are most effective when they are given as pure energy packets for others to use as they wish - rather than as we designate in order to relieve our own anxieties.

I wish my friend at the coffee shop well, and hope her mother-in-law's condition will be healed. I also wish both of them an end to their suffering, of course. But I wish to offer my prayers within a deeper spiritual context, sending both of them pure love for them to use as they wish – which could include their desire to heal, experience a difficulty with honor and integrity or embrace their own transition back to the Spirit world.

Once we get rid of this notion that we have but one life to live, and that suffering and especially death is the worst thing that could happen, then everything falls into place. We have all lived here before and will be back again – each time hopefully learning what we desired when we designed the terms of our incarnation. Sending and receiving prayers that help us fulfil our mission are among the most significant and effective things we can do.

Ask, Search, Knock

Ask, and it shall be given you.

   Search [seek] and you will find.

      Knock and the door shall be opened for you.

         For everyone who asks, receives,

            And everyone who searches [seeks], finds,

               And for everyone who knocks, the door will be open.

This passage is, of course, from the New or Christian Testament, Matthew: 7: 7, part of the much longer 'Sermon on the Mount'. It epitomizes the gospel of love. It summarizes the sacred partnership. It emphasizes the power we have to activate God's assistance.[59] How can we possibly ignore or refuse such an invitation?

If you need balance in life, then you are free – in fact, invited - to ask for 'divine balance'. If you need healing – of mind or body - then you are encouraged to ask for the strength or the humility to do that which will 'heal' you. If you need guidance in any area of your life, then ask for 'guidance.' Whatever you need, ask for it and it will be given to you. It is essential, however, to ask only for the kind of energy you need, not for a particular outcome and certainly not on the timetable you assume is best.

Simply, and with humility, request the type of energy you desire, and then get out of the way. Let God determine what is in your best

---

59 Also see the essay 'Knocking on Doors' in Chapter 11, "Affirming Our Spiritual Core".

overall interest. Then work with the forces and circumstances sent to you - for what unfolds may not be what you hoped for originally but which may actually be a more useful, effective, deeper and/or longer-range resolution of the issue.

Everything has a context, so your request will be viewed and evaluated by God - and the angelic Spirits attending to you - within the total context of your life, your life mission and your learning needs. It will also be viewed and responded to within a greater social context, considering, for example, how granting your request may impact on the many others involved or affected.

We are each particles of God and thus His/Her representatives within our chosen placements on Earth. We are invited to file our requests with trust and confidence, realizing, however, that millions of others are doing the same. Some of those other requests, if granted, may affect us directly, and some may initially neutralize or postpone a response to the request we filed just this morning.

So stir the pot by sending God your desired recipes. But let God prepare and serve the meal. Which ladleful of what goes to whom and when, is God's decision. To ask is not to command or specify; requests are not meant to be self-executing. A door, perhaps not the door you had in mind - undoubtedly will open. Trusting in whatever you do receive is a crucial part of requesting.

Requesting Assistance

When in doubt, when troubled and in need, when frustrated with how life is progressing: ask for assistance. There are all sorts of options.

You can, for example, petition the guidance and intervention of God directly (who is never too 'busy'), or call on your Guardian Angel (who is always by your side).

You could also call upon your favorite Archangel – for example, Gabriel for inner awareness, to be awakened or nudged into activating your next contribution; Raphael for healing of mind, body and Soul plus general companionship; Michael for wisdom and protection; Uriel for perspective and structure; and Ariel to receive an infusion of 'libido' or enlivening animal energy.

There's also a long list of Ascended Masters, Souls who have learned - over multiple incarnations - to live exemplary lives, thereby elevating their consciousness to the status of revered teachers (the list is a very long one and includes such notables as Serapis Bey, Osiris, Moses, St. Germain, Djwhal Khul, Kuthumi and Paul the Venetian).

And, of course, there are the Avatars or Holy Ones – like Yeshua (Jesus), Mary, Socrates, Sophia, Abraham, Lao Tzu, Confucius, Zarathustra, Mohammed, Buddha and Krishnamurti – all sent by God as divine messengers.

You could also invoke the guidance of any Soul who has since rejoined the realm of Pure Spirit – with particular attention to the teachers and mystics of all the spiritual traditions such as St. Francis, Maimonides, Leibnitz, Rumi, Basho, Hildegaard von Bingen, Plotinus, Mary Magdalene, St. Catherine of Genoa, Rudolf Steiner, Joseph Campbell and William Blake. Given the process of incarnation, the Soul of every person who ever lived is still alive and well and living somewhere in the universe. Their Soul qualities thus are always available - even though their essence may no longer be embodied or has since taken on a new persona in a new incarnation. When called on, all Soul essences – including those of our acknowledged luminar are sure to respond and share their insights and talents with you.

Open Yourself to Receive

Taking time out for a meditative moment is not the same as meditation per se. We will say much more about that in the next chapter.

Meditative moments involve deliberatively withdrawing from the busy-ness of day-to-day activities by reserving a few minutes – or even seconds - for a literal and spiritual 'time out.' Find a quiet stop and just relax. Let go of the steady stream of thoughts, sensations and emotions.

Simply concentrate on your breath. Choose a state of 'relaxed alertness'. Let your breathing become slower and fuller. Image something or someone you love. Relax, unwind, re-energize, allow.

Invoke the Kind of Energy You Wish

Imaging is to your Spirit what eating is to your body. If you need vitamin C, you consume something like orange juice. Need more iron, reach for the spinach. In the spiritual realm, the analog of vitamins is energy. And you can create energy fields as you need and desire. All you need do is ask for the qualities you want, be it trust, joy, insight, confidence, courage, compassion or any other spiritual nutrient you desire. Invoke your power to attract that energy and feel it grow in and around you — especially around your head and in your heart.

You can invoke the energy you sense you need — with a gentle request, or you could image that energy arriving in a particular form: as a light and airy cloud, a golden halo, a fluttering sets of wings, an array of sparkles or as a lovely tune.

You can even request and receive such energies in the form of colors. If you find yourself attracted to a color in particular, then include it in your dress, stop to absorb it as it comes into view during the day, purchase it as a colored pen, and buy a few sheets of paper in that color - putting a patch of it on your refrigerator, dashboard and in your purse or wallet. Let the color naturally present itself to you — symbolically delivering the kind of energy you want or need.

Imaging and invoking energy are among your natural empowerments: you are able to create energy fields and thus be nourished by them. You do it implicitly all the time as you select the clothing, music, programs, activities and foods that make you feel good. You are encouraged now to be more conscious of these choices — and creations — and become more deliberate in choosing the energy you need, whenever you need it. You name it, you image it, you invoke it - and then you attract, create and receive it in a way that energizes you.

How Does Prayer Work?

Prayer is a petition to God. An appropriate and effective request is for energy rather than a specific outcome, and a prayer for peace or harmony versus wanting the war in Iraq to cease tomorrow or your grandmother to be cancer free (although you could effectively help to surround Iraq with prayerful energy, and send prayerful energy to your grandmother to help her deal with her illness as she sees fit).

Petitions for energy give God plenty of options, allowing divine energy to weigh each request in light of:

1. The person's learning contract, the experiences they desire and the lessons they wish to learn as they face the challenges chosen for the incarnation.

2. The history of the person or situation, the overall context, namely what preceded and what could possibly unfold if the latest request is granted or supported.

3. The general social impact, namely how the other people or factors involved or affected would fare if your prayers were answered.

4. Whether the petition supports the unfolding of a primary energy such as love versus one that intentionally or unwittingly serves a form of egotism or a destructive energy such as greed, vengeance and pride.

5. The key is the intention: Is the petition generated by love? Does it send love and/or wish for loving energies to prevail?

6. And does it support the spiritual welfare and integrity of the person or situation for who it is intended?

It is possible, then, to anticipate the kinds of petitions likely to gain the support of God and the angelic hosts - whether the intended beneficiary is oneself, another, or a situation.

- Generic *healing energies* to another - conveyed by intention (with/without open hands) - to be used by them in any way their Soul determines (without specifications, or attempts to tell another what you think he/she needs to do). A person who is dying, for example, may not want their ailment to be 'healed' but rather may need loving energy to help them let go or learn the lessons of dealing with their transition. Receiving 'discretionary energy' rather than specified energy would be in the best interests of the recipient; he or she is then free to determine how to use it, not the petitioner.

- *Generic loving* energy of any kind – confidence, trust, belief in self, perseverance, understanding, any of the positive energies – again conveyed by simple intention (with/without open hands) as intended as a gift to be used by the recipient as they wish.

Prayers are most effective when we do not attempt to take charge of another's situation. Prayers and loving petitions are not intended to *save* others from experiencing what may be to them crucial learning lessons in their over-all development. It is best to send general support and then get out of the way. Resist the well-meaning temptation to so wish another well that you inadvertently try to substitute your desires for their needs and inner knowing.

Prayers That Are Likely to Go Nowhere

There are kinds of prayers that are likely to be ignored or that could – if overly egotistic - boomerang on the petitioner. Examples include:

- When the intention seems skewed to self-interest: anything that focuses primarily or purely on one's own or another's selfish or materialistic means or goals.

- Winning a competitive match, getting a better grade, scoring a touchdown, winning the affections of a particular person or support from some other - all appropriate and desirably outcomes at various stages of life but not the appropriate focus of prayer unless it is linked to the energy of love and the desired learning and mission of the targeted Soul.

- Very specific material outcomes - like obtaining a particular cure, job, apartment or some such self-centered wish, again unless the desired outcome is part of a larger spiritual intention that supports what a given Soul is here to do, experience and learn.

Praying for a specific outcome also puts God on the spot – for S/he might be faced with the unwelcome task of favoring one person over another. Specificity invites a domino effect. To work things out for you, or a loved one, may involve changing something important in the lives of other people. The repercussions are potentially endless and not all of them are likely to be fun-filled.

As noted earlier, it helps to remind ourselves that there is a huge network of interactive forces out there. The cumulative ripple effect of granting your request could involve God altering a million-and-one other situations for millions of other people. And praying for a beneficiary or 'winner' makes it all the more probable that there will be an unintended 'loser'. So pray, perhaps, that the outcome of some basketball game will enhance the esteem of all the players but not that one team win and the other loses. What kind of spirituality would that be? Root and cheer for your team if that pleases you but it is best not to attempt to invoke God's support for any one-sided, win-lose material outcome.

Prayer is not a game of arithmetic or a 51/49 proposition that shifts the outcome to one side or another. If your intention is loving and supportive of another Soul's learning contract and commission, then it is likely your prayers will convey loving support and make a difference.

God loves to hear from us. In fact, it is our responsibility to pray: it is one of the most significant ways we have to let God know what helps and what hinders our work here on Earth. So supportive adjustments are best honored when they are overtly requested; God is indeed powerful but there is an expanding universe out there. So rather than waiting for God to notice you and your needs on the cosmic radar screen, let H/H know emphatically that you need divine counsel and support.

Of course, we must also be patient. Communicating with God through prayer is not a guarantee that our requests will be self-executing - presuming to tell God when and how He should respond. It is our right to propose but God's right to dispose.

And neither God, our Guardian Angel, or an Ascended Master can do our work for us: they will guide us but we bear the responsibility for choosing our intentions and implementing our actions.

Set prayers may be helpful if entered into with awareness of what is being said – versus repeated mindlessly. When in doubt, it is best to pray spontaneously and from the heart.

Prayers of thanksgiving are especially powerful and invoke God's presence and love. Father John Giuliani of the Benedictine Grange in West Redding, CT, has composed one of the loveliest: *"Bless our hearts to hear, in the breaking of bread, the song of the universe"*. [60]

The Impact of Prayer

The New York Times reported on March 31, 2006 – in a front-page story - that a large and long-awaited study found "prayers offered by strangers had no effect on the recovery of people" who had coronary by-pass surgery. The patients who knew they were being prayed for, however, did experience a higher rate of post-operative complications like abnormal heart rhythms - perhaps due to the expectation of change their participation created. The study was reported to be the most scientifically rigorous investigation to date on whether prayer can heal illness; it took ten years to gather the data from more than 1,800 patients.

The patients were broken into three groups. Two were prayed for; the third was not. Half the patients who received the prayers were told that they were being prayed for; half were told that they might or might not receive prayers. Members of three congregations — St. Paul's Monastery in St. Paul; the Community of Teresian Carmelites in Worcester, MA; and Silent Unity, a Missouri prayer ministry near Kansas City -

---

60 Marcia and Jack Kelly (eds.), *One Hundred Graces* (New York: Bell Tower, 1992), p. 22.

delivered the prayers using the patients' first names and the first initials of their last names. The congregations were told that they could pray in their own ways but they were instructed to include the phrase, "for a successful surgery with a quick, healthy recovery and no complications."

The problem? The study investigated the wrong end of the communication process, and presupposed the desired outcomes. The key inputs of the study were the bone fides of the praying groups: they believed in prayer and intentionally directed their prayers to those receiving heart surgery. But the study said nothing about the general disposition to healing of the 1800 people who had the heart surgeries. Did they believe in the efficacy of prayer? The belief systems of the patients was never tested or monitored; the study simply assumed the intentions of those praying could of themselves have the intended impact. It does not work that way.

Without knowing more about the mindset of each patient, the study could not determine who wanted to let the prayers in, who was doubtful and who may have blocked them – in short, who was and was not disposed to receive such non-medicinal assistance. We each control and create our own reality, and receive and absorb according to our general belief system. It is our emotional dispositions and attitudes that facilitate, filter or block the kinds of energies we allow into our hearts and bodies.

Impact and effectiveness are not one-way streets. You can send telephone and e-mail messages to someone all year long but if they do not pick up the phone or have the software (intent) that enables them to receive your message, then little if anything will get through. A wall is a wall is a wall. An open mind, heart and body are quite another thing. Any study on any aspect of spirituality must begin and end with the belief system and receptivity of the intended receivers.

The Purpose of Prayer

There is another significant factor: the purpose of prayer. Prayer is not necessarily intended to produce specific results that science can measure. It often it is not based on achieving some specific outcome. And it is not self-fulfilling, as if we were obliged to follow or obey the intentions of any outsider. If we trust in the life process, in the contractual nature of our incarnation, and in the presence of the divine in all things and situations, then the most helpful prayer is not one that attempts to change or override our own conscious and unconscious choices, that delivers 'physical healing' whether we want it or not.

Recovery from a heart condition may not be what a given patient desires; their desired experience could be quite different from some 'outsider's' disposition to allegedly 'save' or 'cure' them or have them live longer. The study did not determine the intentions of the patients beforehand; it was not asked and thus not known what they wanted to do with or learn from their heart conditions.

Again, as emphasized earlier: whether our prayers are intended for our selves or another, we had best pray not for a specific cure but for the strength, insight or courage needed to walk through and learn from whatever is in our, or another's, best interests spiritually. Prayers are most effective when they are directed to and for the person's Soul, to be used by the Soul to guide their incarnate toward spiritual not merely physical progress.

For all we know, heart surgery may be the best thing that ever happened to a particular person – for any number of possible reasons. A person, for example, may want to undergo the experience as a way of learning how to be empathetic to others in similar situations or as input to a future incarnation when they might be a heart surgeon or caregiver of some sort.

A heart condition, and choice or necessity of surgery, could also be embraced by the receiving Soul as a way of bringing a family together in a common cause, possibly gaining access to and sharing one's own healing energy (despite their own condition) with someone they encounter during the hospital stay, learning how to be proactive and stave off a massive heart attack, or unconsciously using the pre-op screening to discover a more severe problem with another portion of their body.

On the other hand, some may choose to use the surgery as the means to exit the planet as planned and desired. A successful outcome is one that supports the intentions of the patient's Soul, not their immediate physical needs, the wishes of their relatives, the procedures of the medical profession or the good intentions of a researcher and selected prayer groups.

The best kind of prayer is not for outcomes but energies, something like "I send to X loving energy to be used by them in any way they choose", or "to strengthen their ability to complete their mission", or "have the experience they desire", or "learn the lessons they seek" or "serve their spiritual intentions".

To be effective, prayer needs to empower the other, not seek to control their destiny or do their goal setting for them. There should be no contest of wills between what you wish for them and what they as Souls wish for themselves. Sending generic love, joy, energy, courage or whatever energy you think might be helpful - supports the other in attaining what they want and need - given their lights, their contract, their learning needs, their choices and their Soul wisdom.

So create and convey your best wishes and prayers for others with the intent that your love will heighten their spiritual awareness and support their inner guidance. Honor them fully by praying for their empowerment, receptivity, responsibility, learning and trust in their own mission, insights and wishes.

Letters

Variations on these themes were expressed in a series of letters to the editor printed in *The New York Times* during the first week of April, 2006 - following its March 31 story on how the prayers of others affected a group of heart patients. Selective quotes are both informative and insightful.

"Prayer is simply talking to God," said one writer. "We pray because it deepens our relationship with God and reminds us in our distress both that a loving God is always with us and that regardless of what happens in any crisis we are part of something that is larger than ourselves."

Another wrote: "I checked my Bible today for prayers petitioning God for 'a successful surgery, with a quick, healthy recovery and no complications.' I found no instructions on prayer by committee or how to test the results afterward. I did, however, find simple instructions on praying in secret, the importance of seeking and offering forgiveness and expressing gratitude for what God has already done. No wonder the prayer teams in this study weren't successful in aiding in the recovery of patients: they ignored the most basic guidelines, as any Sunday school student would know."

Still another person said: "One significant flaw in the study of the effect of intercessory prayer on patients undergoing heart surgery is the assumption that the 'proper' answer to prayer is always healing. There is nothing in the Bible, in Jewish or in Christian prayer, that teaches that God always gives petitioners what they ask for. He answers our petitions according to his will. Sometimes his will is to teach us about suffering, patience, and perseverance. Sometimes his will is to take us out of this world. Sometimes his will is to humble the proud who think they can manipulate him like an idol."

And one letter emphasized the possible benefit the act of praying has on those who pray: "Perhaps the value of prayer is not to the sick who are prayed for, but rather to those who pray for them. Medical research increasingly demonstrates the health benefits of being in caring, connected relationships."

Four Approaches to Prayer

It is important to phrase your prayers and petitions in a way that reflects reality. Here are a few suggestions regarding how to approach prayer, and a few more regarding the words you might choose and how they are phrased.

First, be affirming of yourself in your approach to prayer. You are a son or daughter of God and have a right to request aid. As a Soul you are also empowered to create your reality in partnership with Divine Source and Its angelic hosts. Since giving and receiving is a cooperative and mutually supportive venture, you are encouraged – and expected - to request God's assistance.

You may have made what you consider a mistake in handling a certain situation, or in creating your reality in general. If so, they does not make you 'a sinner' – for there really is no such thing. Your nature is still whole and certainly has not been diminished by the alleged 'original sin' of Adam and Eve [61] or your latest diversion from what you consider the standards of morality and justice.

You always stand before God as an essential component of Its Being – untarnished and certainly not depraved. You are and always will be a member of the royal family despite your occasional lapses. There is never a need to grovel or to diminish yourself. Your divine status does not excuse any false bravado either. Even if you have been unloving or unjust, you are still an integral component of God and are as naturally entitled to seek guidance and solace from your Godhead today as you were yesterday.

Second, in praying it is helpful to begin with a note of appreciation for the gifts already received. It sets a realistic and loving tone. We may be integral parts of the Divine but each of us is still a created speck - of a speck, of a grain, of a dot of sand. Giving thanks for the many bless-

---

[61] See the author's psychological analysis of the Book of Genesis: *The Creative Impulse: Celebrating Adam and Eve, Jung and EveryOne* (Melbourne Beach, FL: Helicon Publishing, 1998). Eve is the heroine for she is the feminine aspect of humankind that evokes individual consciousness. Eating from the symbolic tree of 'good and evil' and then leaving the 'Garden of Eden', are metaphors for the reality of material incarnation and the creation of individual Souls – who remain part of the Totality but are now also differentiated as distinct cells within the Total Organism of God. The myth thus signals symbolically the creation of the individual Soul and the process of incarnating in the physical realm. It is a triumph of epic proportions – not an indelible stain or sin (as if sin exists at all) - for it celebrates the birth and creation of human consciousness and the sending forth of incarnate Souls to spiritualize the material realm of the Earth. Genesis needs to be read as an extended metaphor that reveals the development of deep psychological realities and should not in any way be interpreted literally as the explanation of a concrete or specific historic truth.

The concept of Original Sin in which Adam and Eve allegedly degraded the human nature of all persons for eternity, as propagated by Augustine and adopted as doctrine by the Catholic Church, is one of the silliest, most degrading and nonsensical falsehoods ever perpetrated on humankind. To revert the normal theological interpretation: the species has never needed a Savior for there never was anything to redeem. The subsequent appearance of such avatars as Yeshua has always been God's way of affirming the integrity of human nature and guiding it to deeper levels of spiritual fulfillment.

ings already bestowed is both an affirmation and a humble acknowledgment of reality.

Third, it is also wise and appropriate to include a note of appreciation for the blessings about to be received – from God or whomever you are petitioning for guidance (such as your Guardian Angel or some other angelic force).

Fourth, regarding the wording of our requests. The repetition of standard formulas can be very meaningful but only if mindful. The mere recitation of set phrases is not likely to be any more meaningful to God then they are to us. So always speak from the heart and use whatever words seems best to you. We are not recommending a precise formula or set wordings but are only giving examples as to how you might express the intention involved. The most important thing is that you be genuine and authentic, communicating your prayerfulness in ways that are consciously chosen and heart-felt.

Put all three approaches together and you have a request that could sound like - and include the themes – of the example that follows. Obviously, this is only an illustration. If you use it, you are encouraged, obviously, to adapt, reword and change the wording as you see fit.

"I hereby ask for the guidance of God (my Guardian Angel, or whoever you are speaking to)."

"I give thanks for the many blessings already received, for the gift of life as an immortal Soul and for the opportunity to serve Prime Source in my incarnated state."

"I now express my openness to receive X energy (loving, insightful, joyful, guidance, whatever on…), and/or to send Y energy (identify the kind of energy) to… (and name the person, group or situation)."

"I am confident of your loving support. It is my intention to support the continued development of all involved and affected. I ask only that the energies requested (for myself or another) serve (my or another's) best spiritual interests."

Blessings on the Food

Before the evening meal, the leader of the conference would always invoke the phrase, "Blessings on the food." It is a meeting of the Anthroposophists, the lovely group of joyful and fascinating people who sponsor the Waldorf Schools and gather each summer (most recently at Stonehill College in Easton, MA) to celebrate and apply the insights of Rudolf Steiner, the German mystic and teacher.

The practice of 'grace' or giving thanks for our food is heard only intermittently in most homes – depending on the inclinations of the household and the composition of the gathering. Of course, the advent of Thanksgiving increases the number of participants and usually simulates many to note their personal reasons for expressing gratitude.

So like the Anthroposophists, let's assume there is reason for giving thanks every day, and that gratitude is more a state of mind than a single point on the calendar. We could, for example, at any time or day:

- Give thanks for the wondrous ways in which our foods sprout from the Earth.

- Give thanks to God for enabling us to share in the world's bounty.

- Thank the universe for the sowers, pickers, cooks, packers, shippers, distributors, managers, clerks and servers who help to deliver the food to our tables.

- Bestow personal blessings on our food in to maximize its nourishing qualities, and eliminate the effects of any physical and/or psychological pesticides.

- Give thanks to God, the Earth, and the animal and vegetable kingdoms for their glorious gifts of nourishment.

Give Thanks

Your knee hurts, we know. But the rest of you, all those billions of cells and hundreds of parts are still working very well and efficiently. So let us give thanks.

And there are all those difficulties at work. But you're very good at what you do and are very well liked and even have seniority. So be thankful.

As to the loose shingles on the roof - nothing is leaking, you have a friend who can fix anything, and the rainy season is over. So, again, you have good reason to give thanks.

Money is in short supply, we realize, the furniture is worn and the kids are home this week with the flu. Yet your marriage is solid and before too long it will be time to work in the garden. Let's be frank: there is plenty for which to be thankful.

So your bank called and so did you car mechanic and plumber. But you are almost finished with your degree and that means an immediate and substantial increase in pay. Besides: Mr. (Ms.) Right also called - twice - and you are going out this weekend, so why not see the most gifted side of life...and give thanks.

Admittedly, there are many reasons to feel down, all justified. And there are so many other reasons to feel good, all equally justified. So while there are a few things that are less than perfect, think of all the gazillion things that are going well.

Good, bad, and in between. We all have at least a little of each in our lives – all the time. But it is what we choose to attend to that makes all the difference. It is what we focus on that determines our mood and perspective. Some things do weigh on us more heavily than others, and if any of them is not going well, nothing else seems right. For many the problems usually have something to do with relationships or money.

But when put in context, and viewed over time, you know the dips in the fortunes of your life do even out and in general have been on the uptake over time. Still it takes patience, a lot of trust, and constantly reminding yourself that you are talented and well liked - and so have ample reason not only to endure but insure your attitude remains loving and joyful. So it makes sense to count your blessings, realize your heart is still pumping, your legs move – even foxtrot and rumba on command - and from what you can tell a majority of the synapses in your brain still fire automatically.

So – please - take a few deep breaths, maybe as many as three. That's one, now a second, and ah - finally the third. Just attending to your breathing, you realize how good it feels. So do yourself a favor and take one more deeeeeeeeeeeep breath. As you do, you give thanks for your breath and your lungs - and all the blessings we all tend to take for granted.

Some things are not perfect, we know, but most things – including the 'biggies' – are doing quite well. Let's face it – despite the occasional upheavals, disappointments and reasons to worry - you consistently have many, MANY reasons...to give thanks.

Give Thanks and Receive

I am reminded of the story of the person complaining that God had apparently deserted him. Why? The tracks of two people walking side by side were intermittently replaced by only one set of footprints. 'Obviously' those were the times God had allegedly abandoned him.

"Au contraire," says God with a hearty laugh. "There was only a single set of tracks during the many times I not only counseled and guided you - but carried you as well."

Being open to receive continuous guidance and counsel is one of the options of being alive. We are divine beings who despite now being incarnates in the three-dimensional world, are still eternal Souls in continual contact with the Prime Source. So requesting help periodically is not only normal: it is expected. This is after-all a cooperative venture between God, and all of us who are It's cells or components. The Total Organism can expand, deepen and create only to the extent that It's parts are healthy and themselves capable of continuous development (see Chapter 26: "Cells in a Cosmic Body").

As immortal Souls, we are always empowered to request additional assistance, and granted the grace to grow in consciousness. If we occasionally feel limited or get a little lost – or fail to nurture that inkling of who we really are - it makes sense to ask for clarity, a reminder, a boost, a reaffirmation so we can continue to receive whatever 'upgrades' are warranted.

It also helps to constantly reaffirm the foundation, all the sacred preliminaries that make praying for enhancements and adjustments such a remarkable testimony to the eternal giving and loving nature of God. Our prayers and petitions can surely invoke the sacred structures of Life:

- ❖ "I give thanks for the immortality of my Soul."

- ❖ 'I give thanks for my capacity to deepen and expand my loving consciousness."

- ❖ "I give thanks for my continued ability to manifest - in word and action - each new awareness, hunch, beckoning and intuitive insight that I attract or is gifted to me."

- ❖ "I give thanks for Your Presence, your availability 24/7/365, and the constant flow of your guidance, support and assistance."

Opening our prayers with such notes of appreciation changes any implied sense of lack, or deficiency into acts of thanksgiving for the Soul-Spirit connection. God does not necessarily need to hear such affirmations. But we need to express them - lest we grow complaisant and presumptuous.

Dealing with Difficult People

One last thing: how to deal with people who are instinctually resistant to mending their ways – even though everybody in the family and at the office has been praying for them.

God is as aware of these folks as you are. But there could be something going on that accounts for their record of chronically negative behavior: something in their learning contract perhaps, or their need to experience difficulty this lifetime as a possible précis to being empathetic in a future one, or the fact that they - as a Soul and thus incarnate — are still very young and immature. Whatever it is, it could really help if the chronically troublesome were able to alter their behavior — even a little — so you and your loved ones can get some relief from their toxic attitudes and behaviors.

If a person has been repeatedly resistant to change and has ignored or blocked the impact of your prayers and requests, then you have the right to bypass the physical person, and in a quiet moment of prayer or meditation, ask to speak directly his/her Soul. Don't argue or plead. Just explain to their Soul that their incarnate is having a negative impact and you are requesting certain changes for the good of everyone involved.

Second, when you speak directly to the Soul, ask his/her Guardian Angel to attend and speak directly to the Guardian as well.

Third, you can ask your Guardian Angel to also speak directly to the offending Soul and his/her incarnate.

The intent, of course, is to create a win-win situation: if the incarnate and its sponsoring Soul and Guardian Angel are all involved and your requests are wrapped in as much loving energy as possible, then you stand a good chance of convincing the person to amend his/her ways and embrace a more loving and spiritual state of consciousness.

CHAPTER 22

MEDITATION

Dealing With Reality

Life is busy; there is always another thing to do, a deadline to make, a bed to be made, a list of chores to be completed. The 'to do' list never seems to end. E-mail and cell phones are wonderful but now you can be reached everywhere and at any time. And given the speed of transmission, everyone seems to expect a thorough response - immediately.

What's a person to do with these constant invitations and enticements to speed up and attend to one external thing after another – especially if cultivating one's spirituality seems to require the opposite, namely slowing down and finding time to reflect and meditate.

Meditate – me – for more than two minutes? A quick prayer now and then – is certainly possible. But becoming prayerful or meditating for some length of time? That is a different story. You think about it, your intentions are pure - and so you promise yourself to do something about it later in the day when things calm down. Unfortunately your vagueness gets out-competed by the demanding realities of work, interacting with friends and life's inevitable assortment of tempting involvements.

So – today - you are invited to begin again, now – and in earnest. During these entries on meditation, you will be prompted to convert your earlier good intentions into action – and actually do something you consider to be meditative. Okay? Okay! You smile, thinking, 'we shall see'.

Priming Yourself for Spirituality

Priming yourself is the apt metaphor – as in priming the water pump by pumping the handle several times to bring the well water up to ground level, or putting on that sustaining first coat of paint which ensures the outer or top coat adheres and endures.

Priming is a way of prepping your inners for inner spiritual activity. Such prepping could include occasionally – and then frequently - taking time-out to walk in the park, stroll along the promenade, saunter along the woods, peruse and smell the flowers, catch snowflakes with you tongue, or suddenly stopping all your activity and just sitting in your favorite chair and breathing deeply.

You could also find some alone time in the back room at the office, or enter a place of worship after lunch – anything to trans-locate mentally and emotionally to an environment that encourages calm and being at one with your self. Once there, you sigh – and realize how essential it is to create a psychological oasis for yourself, a time and place where you can nurture your inners.

Once you stop responding to the incessant demands of the outer world, you also realize that you are responsible for creating your own life. You can either create it proactively, or you can allow it to happen. Whether you like it or not, your life - in all its glories and fragmentations - is your creation. If you now want more time and space to cultivate your spirituality, then you know you must assume overt responsibility for making that happen. You are the creator and the magnet that attracts your life situations. As Lincoln once observed, you are even responsible for your own face – more so every year.

So you begin by sneaking in a quiet moment or two during a coffee break. But you also want to use such moments to nurture more than your body. So the mini-breaks start to include deliberate deep breathing, then drawing an image of what you call 'your emerging spirit', then progressively praying for a sick friend or world peace, reading a short passage from an inspiring book, and escaping the maelstrom totally with a stroll around the block to the chapel on the corner.

Eventually you go to a series of 'break away areas' to contemplate the glory of your family, the veins of a leaf, the wondrous insistence of your own heartbeat. And you realize you don't need any of the old formulas or stances; nothing beyond your desire to re-connect with the deeper part of you - the part that honors your inners and your connection to God.

In responding to the inquires as to 'where you go each day', you tell folks you are deliberately tuning into yourself spiritually - and that involves slowing down and getting away occasionally from the splintering effects of external activity. You are priming yourself, you reply - priming yourself to go a bit further and deeper.

Different Styles

As you can guess, the extroverts seem to have the hardest time slowing down, eliminating external business given their almost compulsive desire to be interactive with as many people in a day as possible. These are exciting and positive traits, to be sure, but if they accumulate into a lifestyle, they tend to minimize if not destroy that otherwise vague intention to also cultivate one's inner life.

For introverts, it is much easier to slow down since they instinctively prefer more alone time anyway. While the extrovert may be tearing about town in search of one more external stimulus, the introvert is quite content to sit, think, schmooze or participate in an activity more internally focused. While the extroverts never turn down an invitation to a party, the introverts are often no-shows because they prefer to finish reading some 'great' book.

Even the initial steps of priming, then – on a regularly or instinctive basis – is not easy or natural for the extravert. Formalized prayers at the agreed time are just fine but it takes near catastrophes to bring them to their knees and admit anything is wrong, or get them to reach out by going in. As to mediation – devoting time to sitting or walking alone with spiritual intent for many minutes at a time – is really pushing it. Spontaneous flowing into prayer and meditation is so much easier for the introvert; their instinct is to be reflective and inward as soon as they get out of bed.

Ah – there is a saving grace: most of us are at least a bit of each psychological style, and even the extroverts eventually tilt with age and learn to love the lure of being a grandparent – an active one, of course, but who is increasingly more willing to live in the moment.

Whatever one's psychological bent, prayer does involve the choice to slow down one's outer activity in order to focus one's inner energies. One must deliberately invoke their spiritual center when requesting God's aid and counsel. Now, prayer can amount to quick invocations for guidance, and prayers completed as part of a devotional practice are usually standardized and repetitive. And many members of religious organizations spend much if not all of their prayer time in designated and formalized group activities.

As to meditation – what we might call 'sustained prayerfulness' – it involves deliberately taking time to communicate freely and at length with God. It is even more dependent on priming then prayer because it is in essence solitary (even when mediating in a group) and involves a deliberate decision to be quiet, let go and be receptive. Unlike prayer - which is a reaching out to God - meditation invites God to enter and communicate directly with the Soul.

Meditation also tends to reverse the proportional time devoted to normal praying. There certainly are as many meditative moments as there are prayerful ones. But most devote at least 15-20 minutes to such 'full' meditations. Anyone who meditates regularly is also predisposed to welcome as many shorter, spontaneous ones as possible. Prayer can surely be spontaneous but is often encouraged by some issue that is already on your mind, the religious calendar or a pre-planned devotional activity. Both, of course, play highly significant roles in the development of one's spiritual life, and both are important preludes to entering into contemplation (the next chapter).

Note the Progression and Deepening

Note how one spiritual practice leads to and builds on the others. First, priming-prepping-enjoying the moment and nurturing one's inner life – not as something in which you had to participate but which is embraced as a welcome approach to life. Priming then tends to facilitate prayer – both the formalized and the spontaneous kinds, and can lead to a lifestyle of prayerfulness. In so cultivating one's spirituality, one is often drawn to go further – into the practice of meditative moments and then into the fervent practice of 'full' 15-20-30 minute meditations. And if it all melds together it often excites the desire - and capacity - to become more fully immersed in one's spirituality and embrace the many avenues to contemplation.

Most important: where prayer can lead to a lifestyle of prayerfulness, so does a sustained attitude of reverence lead to mediation and a meditative approach to life. In each case, they become perspectives or ways of living that eventually lead to a spiritual lifestyle.

Entering into Meditation

Initially, meditation offers a prolonged and relaxing break from the routine. If you like the way praying creates a mini-respite from the demands of the outer world and provides solace and even insight, then you are sure to love the slightly longer and deeper devotions of meditation. In meditation you communicate with God as you also intentionally commune with your inner self – becoming receptive to both the Totality and your Soul essence. It is like prepping-and prayerfulness combined. If you have enjoyed slowing down and accessing your inner thoughts and images, and if you participate willingly and naturally in the various forms of prayer, then you certainly are a good candidate for 'sliding' into 'full' meditations with relatively ease and enthusiasm.

Realize, first, that you can meditate initially for two or five minutes, and then progressively devote fifteen to twenty minutes to a given mediation. You can also complete it in any way that is comfortable and effective for you: sitting or standing, walking or strolling, at your home or while on break at the office. When asked how he meditated, Joseph Campbell, the famed ethno-psychologist, replied: "I underline in books."[62]

There are many ways to enter into the process. No specific way is better than another; it all depends on your situation and what you find works best for you. You can sit in silence with eyes closed or gaze at a lovely picture or a mountain stream. You can sit on a chair or with crossed legs on the floor – with or without a supportive pillow. You can walk in the park or in your back yard. You can initially repeat a word or phase (like love or gratitude), envision the image of a maple leaf streaked in autumn red or chant the ancient rhythm of 'AUM'. You could also recall and be delighted by the sound of a child's voice, or the face of a person dear to you. Whatever the facilitating link, flow with in and be at one with it; let it encourage you to be calm, trusting and receptive.

As to how you mediate, you are free to mix and match any of your natural body postures: sit, walk, allow your body to move, sway or dance – as long as you keep your concentration, sustain your quietude and nurture your receptivity to Spirit. You may also select a theme or essence-energy beforehand or allow it to unfold spontaneously.

Remember: meditation time is designed to facilitate focus and centeredness in order to minimize the sense of separateness from nature or Spirit that we often experience during our normal, waking hours. As we trust ourselves, relax, and focus on an essence of spirituality, we slowly become aware of our inner world, our Soul essence and the presence of God. It is like taking the first step onto the 'down' escalator. Once on,

---

[62] Devotees of Eastern religions – such as Buddhism and Hinduism – and practitioners of Yoga in the Western world, tend to sit in prescribed ways, and spend many hours learning to perfect their posture and methods of concentration. That is all wonderful, of course, but only if those approaches support your particular meditative practice. But if they are not right for you, if they are not comfortable or conducive to your attaining the concentration and receptivity you want, then adopt a way – an approach, posture and setting – that *is* right for you. The mechanics should help not hinder or obstruct the ease and fullness of your meditation. Whatever works for you is the right approach for you – as long, as we shall see – your posture is designed to keep you alert and centered.

the process takes care of itself, and you naturally flow deeper and deeper into a natural conversation with your Soul and Divine Source.

Initially, you may find it difficult to quiet yourself and shut off the stream of competitive ideas and images that continue to race through your mind. Nevertheless, sit or walk quietly, attending either to the silence or the sound and sensation of your breathing. If your mind does wander – similar to what it does during the normal 'waking' day – don't try to halt the flow of images. Allow them to rotate until you discover one that is spiritually inspiring and attractive and which invites you to be ever more receptive to the glorious yet nondescript cosmos within.

The goal in the meditative state is to attain relative quietude - as if you literally were beside a pond: calm, totally at ease. As you become one with your breathing or image, you become increasingly receptive to the deep underlying silence, to the sensation of being unhurried, at peace with an enveloping sense of nothingness. Emptying yourself of all your normal chatter and entering into a sense of nothingness is therapeutic in itself. Yet it also deeply spiritual - for the quietude is the place of your inner abode, a state of mind that enables you to honor your Soul as you open to the influence and experience of the divine.

What's Next?

Perhaps that is enough for now. You don't have to measure up to some quality standard or meet some minimal time scale. And surely do not try to assess the so-called value of your experience, although you may find it helpful to make note of the image or sound that facilitated your entry and/or those you discovered en route which helped you attain whatever level of centeredness you experienced. The purpose of meditation is simple: it invites you to trust the process of relative mindlessness, to turn off the blare and incessantly noisy frequencies of the outer world and allow you to be receptive to your inner sense of joy, quietude and inner peace.

As you renew the process, realize that it is possible for images to bubble up from the your personal unconscious – all the unfinished business you have stored in a lifetime. If so, acknowledge them and then let them go. More importantly, however, messages, assurances and insights may also cross the threshold of your consciousness from the Collective Unconscious, that reservoir of archetypal images that deals with such generic themes of human life as mother/father, the trickster, hero/line, lover, explorer, warrior, nurturer, child, and wise man or woman. Such images of the great archetypes of life, although reflected in our everyday life, derive not from our personal experience, but from the ongoing and collective experience of all humankind.

You could thus receive guidance and assistance during meditation – whether you consciously asked for it or not. Whenever you slow down and go inside, what was earlier 'unseen', not noticed or recognized may begin to become more evident. Once the ego has been quieted, the mind turned off, and body put on active rest, your immortal Soul is able more easily to make direct contact with Itself, and become ever so receptive to the counsel of the angelic realm and God Herself.

Anything from a vivid dream, to the glimpse of a scene, a remnant of a person's face, the partial recall of a place or sound could then 'pop' into mind. Whatever it is, 'save it" (write it down later as insurance against poor memory), treat it as a clue, then leave it alone until something happens in life or in a future meditation that suggests it is important.

Occasionally there will be difficulties. Sometimes images and emotions come to you during mediation that trigger linkages to everyday concerns, your worries, even the 'to do' list you recently posted on the refrigerator door. Your ego or normal state-of-mind, is like a well-intended but frisky dog that can easily interrupt a mediation as it continues to fight for attention. If this happens, don't scold yourself or deliberately try to suppress such images. It is normal that your everyday concerns would continue to press upon you. Turning them off after spending so much time intensely engaged in them is not easy; entering into the universe of quietude and inner receptivity is a new experience or venture that has yet to be perfected. It is only with practice and persistence and patience that the meditative state becomes easier to access, enter and sustain.

Sometimes the meditative state will also evoke a sensual experience like the tingling of the skin, or tears coming to your eyes. Sometimes it may create a mysterious and overwhelming sense of thanksgiving and love. Whatever transpires is not a sign of a 'better' or worse meditation. No specific happening or 'product' makes a meditation 'effective' – only the choice to be at one with one's Soul and thus receptive to God. Each meditative experience may be and feel different. So be it. Are you not a wondrously complex and diverse being!

Entering the Land of Your Origins

Let's review the basics again – this time adding a little more information and outlining the aspects of meditation in a bit more detail.

Meditation does not involve asking for assistance: that's the work of prayer. Meditation is act of receptivity to divine guidance, an opening of your self to receive a glimmer, an insight, a message, a realization - some form of intuitive guidance. It is a way for you - as a Soul - to commune directly with God, and in opening that channel be in a position to receive gifts of awareness and guidance you might not access otherwise. Such communication occurs most easily and forcefully when you deliberately stop participating in the busyness of everyday life, attain quietude and then dwell in the realm of Spirit.

Meditation involves removing yourself from the hurried pace of ordinary life. It involves detaching from the concerns and tribulations of everyday in order to rest for a while within the land of your origins – directly in the timeless realm of Pure Spirit, where the main portion of your Soul still resides, and which was the launching point for your current incarnation.

How Do You Do It?

How do you nurture the meditative state?

First, you quiet yourself, as noted above. Initially, that is a means to an end. Quieting yourself is a way of getting ready. Eventually, prepping and praying and meditating will so affect your life that your lifestyle shifts: you slow down as a matter of course. Prepping or priming no longer becomes a distinct set of acts but a natural part of how you interact with the world; it is not what you do but who you become. Once you have cultivated a meditative lifestyle, you don't need to prep to attain quietude, you merely glide into it seamlessly.

In completing the meditation, you can choose to sit anywhere you wish, stroll along some quiet path or simply 'go into yourself' in a focused way during the long bus ride home. If you sit, be sure your body is naturally aligned. If sitting on the floor, assume a position that is comfortable and upright - such that your spine is relatively straight and your head and shoulders are aligned with your hips. As noted earlier, most Eastern traditions have strict prescriptions on how to sit with your legs tucked and hands affixed in certain positions. Such postures may be fine for the Eastern culture and religions; it is hardly necessary – certainly not in the West. The best rule of thumb: be comfortable; it is very difficult to relax and focus the mind if you are struggling with a set of painful sitting prescriptions. Again: how you position your body should facilitate your mediation, not obstruct it or render it painful.

If you choose a chair, sit upright with both feet on the floor in front of you, your hands in you lap, your head and shoulders loosely aligned with your hips and the small of your back firmly supported by the chair. This general alignment seems best for remaining attentive and alert. If you choose to walk, then find a setting that allows you to commune naturally with your surroundings. Try to keep a steady but modulated pace, your head and shoulders and hips aligned. Then silently relax into your inner Self.

If on occasion, you find your body is tense or simply not relaxed, then breathe naturally for a few seconds before raising your shoulders a few inches, hold them and then let them drop as you exhale fully. Repeat a few times. You could also swivel your neck slightly and slowly each way before stretching it up toward the sky, letting it go with one more full exhalation. Feel your spine align with the top of your head. Deep and slow breathing also helps the body unwind. Inhale slowly and fully (to an approximate count of seven), hold your breath for a few seconds (for a similar count of seven), and then release the breath slowly (again for an approximate count of seven). You will undoubtedly feel your entire body sigh as the kinks and tensions wash away.

To consolidate that emerging state of *being in the moment*, you could strike a brass bowl or ring a small bell: follow the sound until it disappears, and repeat as desired until you feel your shoulders are totally relaxed, your spine aligned, your tensions released and your mind letting go of the day's ordinary chatter. *Quiet, relaxed but alert* – in mind and body – you are ready to proceed or slide into your meditation. As noted, invoke a word, image or sound if so desired, or attend to your breathing – whatever helps to make you aware of God's presence and guidance.

Benefits and Extra Gifts

When you meditate, you are choosing to be at one with God and to listen. You could be totally non-directive and just experience it as restful and nourishing. You could also, on occasion, include a request for information – asking perhaps to know the name of your Guardian Angel or for guidance on a particular issue. You could also pose a specific question regarding your spiritual life. Then let it go. What you seek may 'pop' into mind during your meditation or you may receive what turns out to be an important clue shortly thereafter or in the next few days. The clue or clues could arrive as a word you see or hear, a shape you feel compelled to draw, a color that literally 'calls' to you or a sound that stirs your memory or focuses your attention. Whatever happens – or does not happen - is right and fulfilling, and is significant as an experience unto itself. If 'nothing' happens, then you might follow that experience in the next meditation by focusing initially on 'emptiness'. Any and everything is grist for the mill.

And one meditation may be likened to consuming a nourishing meal. It may please and energize you immediately, and that alone would be wonderful. But repeated doses of nourishing foods helps to build a strong mind and body – the results of which may not be noticeable immediately but are experienced over time. The meditative process is such an investment in both your immediate wellbeing and your long-range spiritual health and welfare.

So don't push any expectations or desired outcomes. Allow or 'let' whatever wants to unfold - unfold. It is all you and from you, including the many times you struggle to attain quietude, receive no particular insights and only feel more relaxed or energized. Remember: meditation is a time to quiet the ego and the will. It is the time for letting, and that means honoring your Soul and communing with God. Surely that is enough on any given day!

Any identifiable benefits you receive – pieces of information, intuitions, insights – are extra gifts. Take notes if you want once the meditation is over. Amplify any clues received by freely associating them with related words and images. Include your discoveries in your next mediation if so desired. Once the meditation is over, follow up on the leads you receive - no matter how clear or fragmentary a clue may be. An image or intuition may appear that evening, or it may not bubble across the threshold of consciousness until days or weeks later. Insights and clues to the issue you may have posed may also reappear in your dreams. Something serendipitous may also occur in your life that suddenly clarifies that mysterious clue from last month's meditation.

A relaxed state of mind and sense of calm is, however, a gift unto itself that will effect how you approach everything for the rest of the day - if not your life. Besides, too many messages, received too often, could disturb your meditative practice and lifestyle. The main purpose of meditation is to honor your connection to God. Like everything else, the best guide is ease, moderation and balance.

How Long and Frequently Should I Meditate?

How long should a meditation last and how frequently should I meditate - for it to be helpful and meaningful?

Well, as noted, if you are a beginner, you might start by sitting or walking quietly in meditation for approximately five minutes – more if you can. Increase the amount of time spent naturally to approximately ten minutes, and within a week or more you should feel comfortable setting your internal clock for fifteen to twenty minutes.

If it helps, keep a watch nearby or clock within sight. Initially, it can be difficult to tell how much time has gone by; after a while, you will just know. Whatever the precise or approximate time you spend in meditation is fine; whatever it is - is. No judgments, please. You may want and need twelve minutes on a given day and then twenty the next. Trust yourself and allow the process to evolve naturally. Fifteen minutes is usually about right for most people. Once a day, a few times a week is lovely. Morning and evening, every day is like nirvana – but only if that feels like nirvana to you. Listen to your Soul and you will know what to do and when.

Whatever you do – is perfect. Whatever feels right to you is right for you. Scale up and down as your inners suggest and your outer involvements allow. No shoulds. No judgments. Relax and allow the process to work for you. If sitting and not focused on a specific item or image, then it is best to close your eyes to avoid any distractions.

Remember meditation time is not an Earth-time exercise, ruled by the calendar or the ticking of a clock; nor is it a sort of fast food concession in which service is delivered on demand. Meditation time is eternal, immeasurable and flows on timelessness. It is an approach of *not trying* to make something happen. It simply *invites* and *allows* something to *unfold – in its own way and on its own timing.* The inner gifts received – immediately and over the long run - are directly proportional to your sense of trust, ease and receptivity.

There is 'an experience' that many Westerners undergo when visiting Africa for the first time. They are in a totally new culture and at first can't quite identify the mysterious and endemic change in mood. The newness is the sense of slowing down – especially once you leave the Western-influenced urban areas and travel into the heart of Africa. Then its vast deserts, plains, forests and savannahs invite your shoulders to drop, your mind to relax, and your entire sensorium to slow down and enter the glorious ease of "African time."

The key to meditation - especially at first – is not to try to cultivate some discernible product but to enter into its Soulful way of being. It is a powerful way of nurturing your connection to your Soul and insuring that it in turn nurtures its connection to Prime Source. Like any spiritual exercise, mediation is not a destination but a way of traveling. Its purpose is to remind you of your primary identity. Its most significant reward is experiencing a return to the land from which you came and will one day return.

Resting in the Presence of God

The experience of *flow, honoring, trust and love* are also among the ultimate rewards of the meditative lifestyle. The process of getting there is usually cumulative although a given instance can be experienced as sudden and direct - like an immersion in deep but calm waters or the glory of a wrap-around hug. Such experiences emerge not from the hope of an adult anxiously groping for guidance. It is more like the playful flow of a child naturally becoming at one with the focus of the moment.

As receptivity and commitment grows so does the experience of communing directly with oneself. It also slowly replicates the inclusive relationship the Soul-cell has to Totality of Prime Source. The individuality of your Soul is not lost in meditation – but it can provide a vivid reminder of how bonded we all are to Spirit and the spiritual universe. You and I, immersed in matter and decked out in human clothing, are – through meditation – given an opportunity to re-affirm and experience the awesome nature of our connection to Unity. If that is not a good reason to at least try meditating, I do not know what is.

CHAPTER 23

CONTEMPLATION

The Everyday Buddha

It takes
a long time
for each Buddha
to realize that it lives
within the outer branches
of the Tree of Life. It takes longer
still for it to realize the many branches
of the Tree all lead to the same center. It takes
a lifetime to traverse the many thickets that grow
under the tree and even more to journey to the center
of the Tree's trunk. But it takes but an instant to awaken
to the practice of sitting quietly at the eternal vortex, where
tree top,
you, and
and the
ground
converge [63]

Lovers of the World and the Word

Lovers of the world glory in the myriad details, nuances, subtleties and shades of the known world. The umpteen variations in form, color, sound, taste and texture are not only noticed — a triumph in itself —

---

63 An earlier version of this Bodhi tree design and layout was included in the author's *AHA! Creating Each Day With Insight and Daring* (Melbourne, FL: Helicon Publishing, 2000), p. 66.

but they are also celebrated by those who seek to be more fully aware of themselves and their environment. These are the folks who always need a thesaurus on hand so they might pull from its compendium of synonyms that which describes *this* and *that* gradation of experience.

In a similar way, lovers of the Spirit glory in the 'substance' of things, in their *thingness* as well as their incidental and fleeting attributes. But they use a much thinner reference book for their encounters - for they seek to uncover synonyms for how the world and the Word intertwine.

The view of the world is broad, varied and multiple while that of the Word or Spirit is focused on uncovering the underlying the essence of things or their points of unity. Contemplation uses one to seek the other, the world being its point of entry into the realm of Spirit.

The two views – and experiences – converge and magnify each other. They are the two covers of the same book, the opposite but complementary sides of the same manuscript. Those who attend to life's proliferation, eventually - if not simultaneously – also want to discover its center. Those who begin at the core are also fascinated by its manifestations. Diversity and unity imply one another.

Unity amidst multiplicity is the message of the Mandala. Everything that streams out from the convergence at the center are but reflections and elongations of the core. Simultaneously, the outer particulars and complexities of a painting or tapestry are designed to bring the eye toward the center and thus to its midpoint. The inner eye of the mystic looks outward – delighting in the world of people and things that the center has spawned. The outer eye of the mystic sees the world's variations as proceeding to their Source at the center.

The Word and the World. The sacred and the profane. The Source and the Cosmos. The One and the Many. The mystic and the marketplace. The inner and the outer. Consolidation and dissemination. Creator and Creation. Essence and proliferation. The loving expressiveness of the One and the unending exuberance of the Kosmos.

What is Contemplation?

Contemplation is a sort of advanced meditation – involving the choice to attend to and give thanks for any and everything as a reflection of God's Creative Energy. If praying is 'requesting', and meditating is 'receiving', then contemplating is 'being'. The first focuses on the 'I', the second on the 'Soul' and the third on 'God'. The first 'reaches out', the second 'invites in', and the third 'simply is'. And where prayers 'add and alter', and mediation 'deepens and extends', contemplation simply invites you to 'enter and dwell - in unity and timelessness'. Obviously all three intersect, interweave and dovetail.

As is also true for prayer and meditation, contemplation is facilitated by a consciousness of ease and quietude. So prepping or priming is an essential route to attaining the contemplative perspective as well. Everything you do to enter into a prayerful and meditative state is thus equally true for contemplation.

Yet contemplation - which really is the culmination of the prayerful and the meditative consciousness - can also catch you unawares. Suddenly, before you are conscious of slowing down and going in, you can be drawn instantaneously into a contemplative state of mind and become as if one with an object or image. The contemplative experience is one of immersion and unity. It may last only seconds or minutes but it is profound and seemingly endless – as if transported to the realm of eternity. Whether fleeting or prolonged, it enables you to glimpse into the essence of Life: timeless, loving and unified – where everything is an aspect of everything else.

You could be pondering the beauty and vitality in that flower, face or social interaction and be suddenly transported mentally and emotionally. Propelled as if by warp speed, you can – in an instant - enter into the underlying reality that is the unifying essence of Life. Some liken the experience to being fully immersed in an extraordinary and mysterious field of energy – in a totally different world or dimension, one that is enveloped by a spiritual sense of total serenity and love.

God seems to know if and when you are ready. The induction can happen after many minutes or years of prayer or meditation, or during a simple walk down a street you have travelled many times before. It can be provoked by something as innocent as the sighting a rose petal or a raindrop at a leaf's edge. The feel of a gentle breeze, the sight of a tree, or the sound of a new-born could also instantly trigger the sense of having been transported to the realm of Pure Spirit. Suddenly you are drawn into a vastly different universe, where you are transported to eternity, where you are ushered into a profound encounter with Life, where the loving essence of everything is revealed.

Obviously, the contemplative experience cannot be sought, but it can be cultivated. Then suddenly, without warning, it is granted by the grace of God or unfolds as the natural consequence of one's growing attunement to the depths of their spiritual reality. Those who have entered into such a state of consciousness have included the naturally innocent, the humble and unassuming as well as those who have developed that devotional state of mind through regular priming, prayer and meditation. Mystics and the spiritually adept, of course, live contemplative lifestyles. Many ordinary citizens obviously have contemplative experiences but tend to dismiss them as silly because they are unexplainable. They continue to be gifted, however - perhaps as God's way of awakening the naysayer, jolting the fence sitter and sending confirmation to the doubting Thomas.

The Experience

Imagine seeing a particularly lovely flower or a long raindrop at the tip of a leaf, or perhaps feeling that breeze or hearing the first cry of a new-born - and suddenly feel that you are witnessing - and understanding - the vitality that underlies the universe. Any such encounter can lead to a contemplative experience – a pinecone or a simple rock, for example, evoking such an intense experience that you are awed, overwhelmed, dazzled by its presence. Perhaps you have experienced such events thousands of times before but may have passed over them, never 'seeing' or experiencing that one object as you do now. It comes as a pure gift or maybe because you have been cultivating your spiritual practice and perspective, or both. In a flash, everything changes: you have new eyes and a new consciousness, and so you see through the veil of everyday life to "the Other Side".

The contemplative experience can be so transformative that a mystic – having already accumulated or developed a contemplative lifestyle – can become so absorbed in that eternal moment that they become one with the object of their 'gaze' - mentally and emotionally.[64] In other words, what they first encounter as merely an external object, is suddenly experienced with spiritual consciousness. What was initially only physical and shrouded from the contemplative insight, is transformed into a living testimony of the One and our integral connection to It.

The contemplative moment is like being transported to a universe you just know exists but have never really entered or experienced. But now it may be calling to you, beckoning to you – inviting you to witness it and be awed by its obvious splendor. With sufficient build up in quality prayer and meditation, time will suddenly stop for you one day when you pause to honor one of God's myriad reflections – and zoom, you enter into the realm of the timeless.

That moment becomes everything. The object before you suddenly 'offers' you its entrée into the depths of the spiritual realm. Any earlier need to rush on to some anticipated event suddenly seems unimportant. All of life's busy stuff becomes irrelevant as you lose your sense of outer boundaries and become absorbed in experiencing an unexplainable but intense sense of oneness with some random aspect of the universe. The message is: 'this is it,' 'this is what awes the mystics,' 'this is the kind of experience that transforms, shatters the obstructions, allows a person to glide into another space,' 'here is the sacred dimension, the all-encompassing place where everything is part of everything else,' and 'you and it are part of the All, and All is One.'

---

64   See Evelyn Underhill, *Mysticism* (New York: Harper, 1947), especially Chapters 3 and 4, for an examination of the experiences of such mystics as Teresa of Avila, John of the Cross, Francis of Assisi, Jacob Boehme, Plotinus, Eckhart, Ruysbroeck, Richard Rolle, and Al Ghazzali.

And so the internal chatter fades instantly. You let go of the thought of this morning's spelt milk and your concerns about your afternoon agenda. You surrender to the moment, allowing the Big Self – appearing now in the form of rain, or a puppy, or a pinecone, a symbol, a face, or a wondrous insight into an everyday event that simply makes the universe stand still. Suddenly, your senses are focused, your intuition alert, your Third Eye radiant - as you penetrate the outer coating of the material and instantly witness the glorious presence of the Divine.

Chirp

The bird just 'chirped'
Hear it: it's a crisp sound, yet almost two tone –
   in between a 'too-eet' and 'tw-eet'
There it is again …
Notice the quick bobbing of its head - as it pecks at the seed –
   looking around, proud of its catch,
   always hopping to a new spot
   on that small wooden platform
Ah … there's that 'chirp' again …and again…and again

In the Flow

There is nothing to attain. There is only to witness.
   Zen
I don't sculpt anything. I only uncover the form embedded in the stone.
   Michelangelo

He writ his name on water.
   Epitaph for John Keats

People say that what we're seeking is a meaning for life.
I don't think that's what we're really seeking.

I think that what we're seeking is an experience of being alive,
So that we actually feel the rapture of being alive.
Joseph Campbell

Just to be is a blessing. Just to live is holy.
Abraham Joshua Heschel

The Knower looks through Her eyes, And knows that it is known.
The known listens with his ears, And knows that he is heard.
Knower, known – According to what is sown.
Anonymous

Advice from a RIVER
Go with the flow. Immerse yourself in nature.
Slow down and meander. Go around the obstacles.
Be thoughtful of those downstream. Stay with the current.
The beauty is in the journey.
Inscription on a T-Shirt

So much depends,
   Upon a red wheel barrow
Glazed with rain water,
   Beside the white chickens
William Carlos Williams

A Radiant Field of Energy

o Imagine yourself to be a pulsating field of energy.

o See your inner essence as a radiant core - beams of light spreading in every direction.

o Envision yourself in the fullest of your spiritual identity.

o See yourself leaving your home and entering the marketplace of your town or city.

- o As you enter, image sending forth Christed energy.[65]

- o How do you feel? What do you see? Hear? Sense?

- o Who is present? What do you do and say? What do others do or say?

- o What happens thereafter? What is your impact? What has an impact on you?

- o What happens to the environment – as you enter, interact then leave?

- o Who are you when you return home?

- o Who do you wish to be tomorrow, when you awaken and venture back into the marketplace?

That's It

Once we've accessed this capacity to experience God in and through one of Her reflections, we never again consider ourselves to be just another material being living on a planetary rock sometime in the so-called twenty-first century. We are a living and thriving aspect of 'It" - and "It" is everywhere and in everything.

Amazing. Dazzling. Truly mind blowing and awesome.

Once 'there', you return to material reality 'here' where it is shrouded by your normal eyes. Yet you know 'It' really is everywhere – just on the other side of a very thin veil.

Dazed and delighted. Numbed - but oh so alive.

Riveted to the core - as if struck by divine lightning.

---

[65] In many spiritual circles, Jesus or Yeshua is not considered to be the one and only 'Christ', a historical messiah or savior. Rather he epitomizes the 'Christed' energy that is in - and of the essence of - all of us. We are all "Christed". We are all divine beings who possess a potentially transformative role in whatever settings we encounter. Like the 'Christed' Yeshua, we are also children of God and of the same divine essence - with the capacity to bring our innate divinity with us wherever we go. We are who we are - and always have the option to express and activate the primary 'Christed' energies of insight, understanding, empathy and compassion.

You stretch your arms out - and overhead, unable to do anything but cry in tribute and thanksgiving.

Inner Knowing

Once you've had a contemplative experience, it changes everything. What you once believed could be true, you now know is true. The grand review begins. The affirmation of the Soul begins to emerge with intent and awareness.

So you review what you believe and compare it to what you now know experientially. And you realize your lists of beliefs may be longer and more complicated for they are mostly inherited mental constructs or acquired primarily through reading. The ones attained through your experience and your inner knowing - cultivated through prayer and meditation - are clearer, simpler, cut much deeper. You also know that such experiential encounters are totally independent of heritage, habit or logic.

Despite the frowns and glances of the traditionalists, the contemplative experience is impossible to deny. Despite your inability to explain rationally exactly what happened, you know the 'cosmic' view revealed to you needs to be trusted. Yet you still need to live and act in 'the everyday' world - although having 'tasted' a bit of eternity radically changes your approach to what is honored by the ordinary calendar and your kitchen clock.

Increasingly, your preferences and decisions depend on longer-range values and how a given decision might help or hinder attaining your now expanded view of reality. The perspectives of the 'answer man' and the ordained intermediaries are no longer relevant or persuasive. You now know you must re-double your efforts to live a spiritual life and seek the company of those who can help you nourish your spirituality. Your life is now informed by your experience of "the Other Side" and its irrefutable affirmation of your soulful identity.

Inspired, you may think of retreating from material reality. But that would only undercut your realization that you incarnated on Earth to complete an earthly mission and ministry. What good would be served if you became so spiritual that you were of no earthly good? The challenge and the opportunity now is to unite the two realms of your reality – with your spiritual identity taking the lead in informing - and as necessary transforming - your material lifestyle, preferences and decisions.

Transcendent

A contemplative experience is the direct experience of that which is transcendent. It:

- is beyond the immediate, material world but emerges from an extra-sensory encounter with the material world.

- reintroduces us to the wider, deeper and inclusive spiritual dimension.

- involves the ability to see, touch and be enveloped by that which is embedded in the material world but which also provides access to that which lies beyond it.

- bypasses the material boundaries of people and things, and experiences their essence as reflections of the divine.

- involves a true 'Namaste' – an immortal Soul, incarnated in a physical body, honoring each and all 'other things' as facets of the One.

- testifies to a Soul's capacity to transport experientially from the physical 'realm' to the domain of Pure Spirit, and back again.

- is an experience of the Holy.

- invokes the 'sense' of being in the presence of God.

- is an awareness, an intense awareness, of communicating directly with Prime Source.

- indicates the temporary nature of alleged boundaries and the reality of interconnectedness.

- absorbs us into a loving state of ecstasy.

- is a means of being at one with God, not in thought or just emotionally, but literally being *at one with God* by experiencing unity with one of His/Her material expressions. And

- is founded on being aware, experientially *aware* of being immersed in and surrounded by a sacred universe.

What If You Are Unsure?

If one or more of the above definitions or connotations of the transcendent 'fits' your experience, then give thanks and run with it. Transcendent experiences are more common than we think. If you are not sure, however, if you have had such an experience but don't know what to make of it, then the following questions may jog your memory and help you clarify what you wish to do with the experience.

❖ *Where* were you, *what* were you doing at the time, and what preceded and possibly evoked your contemplative experience?

❖ If you see any pattern in your experiences - regarding *where* you were, what you were doing, and *what* preceded the experience?

❖ What is most likely to facilitate or evoke your next 'glimpse' into the realm of Pure Spirit? Where are you likely to be, what might you be doing and what could possibly trigger the experience?

Warm-Up Exercises for the Contemplative Wannabe

1. You can choose to see beauty everywhere, or you can wait until someone tells you what is beautiful.

2. How do you think it feels to be angelic?

3. Are you happy to be alive or are you putting life on hold until you find something to be happy about?

4. Is it possible to become better or worst when you are already divine?

5. Are you living your truth? Not spouting it - but living it?

6. Are you becoming a better person or merely uncovering who you already are?

7. What is your unique expression? What is your special contribution? What do you sense is your particular mission?

8. Take time out occasionally from your usual routine and go to that physical, mental and emotional space where you can be genuine, true to the deepest part of you.

9. God made everything simple. We make it complicated. Try returning to simplicity.

10. When you remember who you really are, everything begins to make sense.

11. If you attend to the process of experiencing everything in the moment, you suddenly realize that you and your experience are the same.

12. Holding onto beliefs, attitudes or behaviors that are negative and self-defeating is like holding your breath. Perhaps it is time to blow out the negatives, let them go, get on with the joy of taking chances and actively create your life by fully experiencing it.

CHAPTER 24

ANGELIC BEINGS

Ah, thank God, there are so many ways to ask for and receive assistance and guidance. First, there are Angels who, unbeknownst to most, are literally everywhere, all the time. And that includes the glorious and famous set of Archangels called Gabriel, Raphael and Michael – not to mention Uriel and Ariel. More on each of this five-some in a page or two.

Once God created Life, He/She created the spiritual hierarchy to assist in the administration of the universe and guide the emergence of the created world. It was also God's will that Archangels supervise the legions of Angels as they in turn provided wise counsel and loving guidance to the millions of immortal Souls (like us) – especially during the times when we assumed physical embodiments in the material world.

The Range and Variety of Angelic Roles

The word 'hierarchy' is often used to describe the various tiers of angelic beings. But this is not like a military hierarchy where there is literally higher and lower, where one tier either commands the others or is beholden to them. The angelic hierarchy is really a community of beings who in attending to God assume various roles. The roles are different but they are mutually supportive and interdependent. All are members of God's "Supporting Group", and all share a common commitment to help God administer the varied aspects of the Kosmos.

Each so-called type assumes a different set of responsibilities. The Archangels, for example, carry out the decrees of God, attend to the overall well being of the universe's inhabitants or Souls, and supervise the hosts of Angels. And each being within the type - for example, Gabriel – assumes a set of primary roles; in Gabriel's case that means being a teacher, guide and messenger.

As to the Angels, folklore has always associated Angels with conveyors of love, purity and selfless service. According to Christian Science, Angels are God's thoughts passing to man, while the history of Western art has usually portrayed Angels anthropomorphically with human bodies, haloes, of course wings, and symbols of their main attribute or reason for renown.[66] Thus Gabriel is consistently depicted in the West with a flower (symbolizing the purity of his message) or horn (based on a false myth – which has no basis in either the Old or New Testaments - that he will blow the horn at the end of time). The paintings of Michael, on the other hand, usually include some kind of sword or pronged spear (to symbolize his role in discerning truth from falsehood).

Medieval angelology records nine orders of angelic beings.[67] The broadest realms of authority and responsibility belong to the Seraphim, Cherubim and Thrones. Being 'closest' to God and in God's immediate presence, these three orders regulate substantial structural portions of the spiritual world. The Seraphim are revered as the Angels of love and light – the very essence of divinity – and help to propagate both these energies throughout the universe. The Cherubim are threshold guardians – like those mentioned in Genesis guarding the gates of the Garden of Eden. They also design and administer the coordinating links between the divine structures and processes used to maintain them (such as the special grids determining relative placement in space

---

[66] The one exception to such depictions - known to this author - is a painting by Henry Ossa Tanner (1898). In a rendering of the Annunciation to Mary, Tanner depicts Gabriel as an elongated cluster of shimmering white light within a field or halo of golden light. The composite is about the same size as any angel depicted in human form. The painting now hangs in the Philadelphia Museum of Art.

[67] See James E. Lewis and Evelyn Dorothy Oliver, Angels A to Z (Canton. MI: Visible Ink Press, 2002); and Rudolf Steiner, *The Spiritual Hierarchies and the Physical World* (Hudson, NY: The Anthroposophic Press, 1996).

and the electromagnetic fields that sustain them). The Thrones, on the other hand, serve as Angels of justice and monitor and enforce the rise and evolution of the galaxies and planetary systems.

Then there are the Dominions, Virtues and Powers who maintain balance among the basic physical and social structures supporting life throughout the Kosmos. The Principalities serve as guardians of the material world of nations and individuals. And, as noted, the Archangels are preeminent among the Angels as their guides and supervisors.

Finally, there is the corps de ballet – the millions of Angels who assist in helping, counseling and carrying messages to all of us during our tenures in both the material world and the realm of Pure Spirit. It is from the Angels that we select our personal Guardian Angel, although God will occasionally appoint 'someone' from among any of the nine orders of the hierarchy to serve as Guardian as well, especially when a given Soul is on special assignment or is receiving advanced training. Guardian Angels, of course, play significant roles in our lives; they are the wise and loving tutors who guide us on a daily basis and are always available for counsel and support.

Small wonder then that the angelic influence is everywhere. Consider the Angels of the Apocalypse in the Book of Revelation; the appearance of Angels to Yeshua's disciples and later to Peter, John and Philip (Acts 5, 10 and 23); Isaiah's detailed description of his interaction with the six-winged Seraphs (Isa.6); and the hundreds of angelic appearances referred to throughout the Jewish and Christian testaments.[68]

Guidance and Assistance

Any and all of these spiritual beings could be responsible for activating an insight, intuition or poignant inner image that guides us at a given moment. Any one or two or of these wondrous beings could have encouraged the 'aha' you received in the middle of the night, stimulated

---

[68] See the hundreds of references to various 'Angels' listed, for example, by John R. Kohlenberger, III, in *The Concordance to the New Revised Standard Version* [of the Jewish and Christian Testaments of the Bible], (New York: Oxford University Press, 1993).

that creative understanding that suddenly passed over the threshold of your consciousness, been physically present to offer you that cup of hot tea when you were alone and frightened at a train station, appeared at your side as a very large man in order to scare off someone who was about to threaten you physically, eased your fall on a slick of ice, and instilled your impulse to wait as that car suddenly caromed around the bend.

Messages, nudges, pokes and encouragements of all sorts constantly arrive from such hidden dimensions. Consider the overt assistance we receive from people we never met before, the loving words and encouragements that just occur to us as if someone had whispered them directly into our ears, the polite gestures and loving vibrations of strangers, the chance meetings with an old friend, the serendipitous convergence of helpful events and experiences, and the gifts of guidance and insight that arrive daily.

Often we are puzzled by the suddenness and timing of an inspiration or chance meeting; having no immediate explanation, we tend to slough them off and forget them. It is only when something particularly powerful happens, or jogs our memory of earlier and similar occurrences – that we stop to think and realize: there is something extraordinary going on. The source of these spontaneous gifts is difficult to detect, of course, for our physical senses cannot easily trace their source. But the third eye and ear of the resident Soul can. It is to this inner counsel that we increasingly turn - and learn to trust.

And then it dawns on us: we are not only - not alone; we are constantly surrounded by seen and unseen forces that aid, abet, guide, protect and support us. The supportive angelic apparatus that envelops us is similar to the one depicted in the television ad featuring the huge cast of characters who support the man promising instant connection to a vast communications network. It is symbolic of all of us: as spiritual beings we each have an enormous team on hand, all the time: spiritual workers, technicians, surveyors, engineers and builders whose jobs are to aid and support us - anytime and anywhere.

Call, ask, invoke their presence, meditate, pray, contemplate or just dial 'g' for guidance. If you wish, you might complement your mental and emotional requests with a physical gesture. Become physically what you are spiritually - a receptive funnel: legs slightly apart with both hands up, palms open, arms raised over your head - like the figure X or an hourglass. It is one way of demonstrating your appreciation for the aid you've already received as well indicating your receptivity to continued guidance.

Archangel Gabriel

Let's say a few more words about some of the angelic figures who have been especially honored and recognized by the writers and artists of the Earth for their special roles and contributions as Archangels. We note only five of them here although the Book of Revelation suggests there are seven Archangels who are always present with God.

First, appropriately, there is Gabriel who was the first of the Archangels created by God. Gabriel's role has been recognized in the Jewish Testament, the Christian Testament and the Koran. For example, it was Gabriel – at God's request - who stopped Abraham from slaying his son Jacob (according to the Jewish Testament, Yahweh had previously ordered Abraham to slay his son as a test of his allegiance). The Bible also tells us Gabriel's duties included interceding on behalf of oppressed people (1 Enoch, 9:1-11; 40:6) and bringing Enoch to God's presence (2 Enoch 21:3-6). He also explains the mysteries of certain visions (Dan 8:16-22; 9:20-27).

But it is in the New Testament that his role as messenger and intermediary is most pronounced: Gabriel appears to the aging Zechariah to announce that his elderly wife, Elizabeth, would give birth to John the Baptist (Luke 1:11-20), and later appears to Mary to announce she was pregnant and would give birth to Yeshua (Luke 1:26-38).[69] Later, Mohammed revealed that Gabriel had dictated the Koran to him. [70]

---

69 James R. Lewis and Evelyn Dorothy Oliver, *Angels: A to Z*, cited earlier: p. 170.
70 Moslems believe Gabriel, as a 'Holy Spirit' dictated the Koran directly to Mohammed over a 23-year period. Sura II: 97 reads: "Who is an enemy to Gabriel! For he it is who hath revealed [this

It is Gabriel, then, who in general loves to encourage new visions, births and discoveries and encourage a person to fulfil a chosen or designated mission. He is the ultimate in a personal coach, facilitator and teacher. In current times, when he speaks through the channel, Karen Cook of Albuquerque, New Mexico [71] – he counsels each communicant on the issues confronting them, reviews – as requested – their personal history of incarnations, and shares his wisdom on the nature and history of the universe. He is also well known for uttering a series of pithy statements with profound implications:

- "There is no spot where God is not."

- "Some people are so spiritual they are of no earthly good."

- "You are a spiritual being having an earthly experience."

- "Ninety percent of joy is attitude."

- "God made everything simple. It is humans who make it complicated."

- "God is Love. They are one and the same. You don't need to know anything else."

And...

Gabriel's most immediate companion is Raphael. Raphael is also always present – in his case, to heal, console and advise. Raphael is the spirit that is most likely to appear as the joyful and insightful person sitting next to you on the bus or join you while walking along the street - chatting away while offering tangible and subliminal aid and comfort. His most pronounced appearance is found in the Book of Tobit of the Apocrypha[72] which describes Raphael traveling with

---

scripture] to thy heart by God's leave, confirming that which was [revealed] before it, and a guidance and glad tidings to believers."

71   Karen Cook channels Archangel Gabriel – also known as Benu - during her workshops and personal readings (BenuToo.Com). Her and thus Gabriel's weekly lectures and monthly workshops are incredibly loving, dazzling, witty, insightful and empowering. Benu is Egyptian, an honorary title meaning 'gateway' or 'opening'.

72   Biblical literature not found in the Jewish canon of scriptures but included in early Christian

Tobit's son, Tobias, facilitating his marriage to Sarah, his rediscovery of family funds and his ability to restore his father's sight upon his return home (Tobit 5:4-11:8).

Then there are the episodes of Archangel Michael – who appears as the so-called captain or leader of the heavenly host [Dan. 10:13, 10:21, 12:1]. Michael's main role is to protect us from harm – physical and emotional - his sword symbolizing the need to discriminate between what is serving us well and what is not. He is not to be called upon lightly for his stance, stare and sword are very mighty indeed. He appears stern yet enthusiastically befriends all children and both men and woman in distress.

Archangel Uriel is the very wise one (I imagine him as reflecting a cheerful face, broad smile and rosy cheeks – much like a Santa Claus); he works with Gaia and her earth systems - adjusting the mental and atmospheric climate, and helping each of us create positive mental and emotional environments and attitudes. His presence is particularly powerful now given the Earth changes in process and about to unfold. [73]

If the Earth is to cleanse itself of the scars of past wars and the effects of all the hatreds, repressed shadows and poisonous emotional states that have contaminated the physical and mental atmospheres of the Earth, then Uriel is the angelic force which will coordinate those adjustments. He will simultaneously, along with the other Archangels, work to temper the disruptive force of such cleansings in order to minimize their impact on human and animal life.

And Archangel Ariel, one of many psychologically 'female' Archangels,[74] is the guardian of animals and so-called wildlife. As

---

versions of the Old Testament. They were then excluded in Jerome's Vulgate translation (ca. 331-420) but subsequently gathered together as the Apocrypha by the Protestants during the Reformation.

73 See Chapter 18, "The Challenge of Change."

74 The entire Angelic Alignment or divine administration, is, like God, trans-gender in the physical, mental and emotional sense. Individual members, however, are referred to psychologically as 'female' or 'male' given their dominant traits. Someone like Michael, for example, usually personifies the 'male' traits of assertiveness, thinking and planning, while Ariel possesses the more female traits of receptivity and nurturing. Gabriel seems a blend of both, while God is the perfect amalgam of both.

such, she also promotes - within all beings, including we humans - the particular type of animal or libido energy we might need to fulfil our missions. Ariel is thus synonymous with the life force within all beings – the particular field of energy that enables each us to be who we are – expressing, as needed, the archetypal forcefulness of a Polar Bear, the gentleness of a Teddy Bear, the cleverness of a Squirrel, the vitality of a Sparrow or the loving joy of a Golden Retriever.

Archangels have extensive responsibilities including the care and development of the kosmic energies associated with their names: that would mean 'creativity' and 'commitment' for Gabriel, 'camaraderie' and 'healing' for Raphael, 'justice' and 'protection' for Michael, 'structural balance and stability within change' for Uriel, and the expression of one's particular kind of 'animal libido' for Ariel.

Guardian Angels

We all have at least one Guardian Angel, an angelic being who protects and guides us as we face our challenges and seek to complete our learning contracts. They are always on duty and always offer wise counsel when asked. One's Guardian Angel is one of our most powerful and potentially most influential resources we have. Unfortunately, many don't acknowledge, honor or ever call upon the loving wisdom of their personal guide.

If you want to know the name of your Guardian Angel, then ask during a meditation. The name may appear to you instantly or may jump out at you from a book or e-mail later in the day. For some, it may take a week, month or more for the name to float into consciousness. Then suddenly one day you'll see a name on a sign, notice one scrawled in the dust of a truck, or overhear a name while passing through a crowd – and you'll know that's 'it'.

Our Guardian Angel also automatically guides us through the traffic of life without asking for our permission in advance - as in protecting us from ourselves in moments of near crisis (if indeed such guidance is in our best interests and does not negate a desired development or essential learning). But if you want guidance on anything in particular - however earth shattering or mundane - then it is best that you ask. Angels are forbidden to make our choices for us – otherwise they would end up living our lives for us. They are also forbidden to do our work for us – although they are more than willing to work with us when honored and asked.

Then There Are the Cherubs

When you are down and out, or just a little sad - who do you call? A cherub!

Cherubs are depicted in medieval and renaissance paintings and sculptures. They are all smiles and have tiny wings. They are always pictured as babies or infants, with fleshy bellies and very rosy cheeks (upper and lower). They love to flutter around people and scurry in and out of situations. Choices and outcomes are illuminated when they appear, and their laughter, constant flutter and continual jostling inevitably creates an air of lightness and joy.

They are not only children but totally childlike: they laugh, stare at you, stand on one leg, do cartwheels, defy gravity by tumbling spontaneously into all sorts of funny positions, and bounce about constantly with curiosity and exuberance. And they are strong, very strong, capable of supporting people, and pillars, and ceilings, and even careening chariots.

Nothing can repress or neutralize them. They are like a gaggle of geese in the early a.m. They dart back and forth like chickadees at mid-day. And they personify the self-empowered arrival of cardinals at dusk. Invoke their presence and it is impossible to remain gloomy, doubtful, pessimistic or anything less than gleeful and buoyant. Want to transmute your worries and experience the lighter side of life? Call on a cherub - or group of them. In a wink and a whirl, you will not only smile and feel better - but also become contagiously playful.

Signs of Angels in Our Midst

The waitress asked a customer what he was reading.

"A book on Angels," he replied. He in turn asked if she had seen any Angels that day. "Not that I was aware of," she said with a smile.

Let's make it even more mysterious by linking that interaction with what is being revealed by our physicists – those inquisitive folks well trained in the science of materiality and who love devising experiments for and explanations of what is going on in our universe.

The first so-called 'reality' – the one that describes the workings of the macro aspects of the universe (like the formation and movement of stars, planets and black holes) – is best represented by Newton and the workings of gravity, and then by Einstein and the laws of relativity. This is the kind of universe that is predictable, measurable and about which you can trace the cause of any change to its source.

The other reality is represented by a set of physicists who are proponents of 'Quantum Mechanics' who are interested in the mini-mini world: the sub-atomic, micro universe of neutrinos and quarks. Their experiments suggest that these basic units of material existence themselves consist of unpredictable waves and/or particles. Such scientists cannot, however, trace exactly where any particular wave or particle comes from, what caused them to be where they are, or what accounts for their linking serendipitous with other 'units' that are not even in their local area.

Then there is a set of physicists who have proposed what is called 'String Theory'. This approach attempts to couple the two 'realities' – the macro and the micro, the movement of planets and the movement of quarks – into a unified theory. It proposes the building blocks of the universe - at its most basic level – are not waves or particles but strings of matter. And these strings allegedly support both the predictable workings of the macro cosmos and the unpredictable micro stuff of the sub-atomic universe. A mouthful, eh?

In addition to the 'string theorists' there are now physicists who propose there are ten to twelve additional dimensions to the universe[75] – or at least seven more than we experience in the current batch of height, width and depth.

The earlier work of Jane Roberts and her many channelled books with the spirit entity called Seth, also pointed to other extra-ordinary aspects of our identity - extensions of ourselves in other dimensions, times and places. Moreover those extensions cross over and extend into all historical periods; still 'alive', the experiences of such extensions could and do occasionally bleed through to 'us' – our main identity or OverSoul - as an awareness, feeling or recollection experienced in our current timeframe and incarnation.[76] Time and life thus are not linear and progressive but cyclical and repetitive, not projected forward on a straight line but revolving as a series of overlays. It is thus like a giant two edged spiral, the top part growing in expanse - up, out and clockwise – while the bottom half simultaneously grows downward, deeper in a counter clockwise motion. Such a spiritual view of life has us living not once in a given incarnation followed by a conclusive death, but a series of re-incarnational lives in which the issues, unfinished business and wisdom of any 'previous' life cycle could bled-through to any of its so-called past or future extensions or incarnations. Past, present and future thus all exist simultaneously.

Now which is the stranger proposition: the one proposed by the passerby to the waitress regarding the sighting of an angel (the story with which we opened this exploration) – which in itself defies the so-called traditional laws of Newtonian science - or those posed by the most modern physicists and such channels as Jane Roberts? All of them – the sighting of Angels, Newtonian physics, quantum mechan-

---

75   Dale Glabach, "Do We Know How Many Dimensions There Are?", *Astronomy,* May 1, 2006; "Superstring Symphony", *Astronomy,* January 10, 2007; and "Do Hidden Dimensions Exist?", *Astronomy*, February 8, 2007.
76   See, for example, both *The Education of OverSoul 7* (New York: Pocket Books, 1973); and *The Further Education of OverSoul 7* (New York: Pocket Books, 1979).

ics, string theory, the scientific proponents of multiple dimensions and the perspectives of such spiritual writers as Jane Roberts - defy our average, everyday experience and what the average person accepts as the laws of 'nature'.

It is difficult to offer conclusive evidence either way – that is if you are not aware as yet of having bumped into an Angel, or if you don't allow your self to flow with any of the afore mentioned scientists and writers. Stories of the Angels have, of course, been around a lot longer. But when a set of scientists propose the existence of multiple dimensions, it at least makes the presence of Angels seem as possible and realistic to the non-believer as oxygen is to the gazillions who have never seen it but are living testimonies to its existence.

The sacred literature of the world has instilled the existence of Angels in religious thought and practice, and the art of the Western world in particular has solidified their place in both the religious and public imagination. As noted, there are repeated references to the many types of Angels throughout the Jewish Scriptures, the Christian Testaments and the many books of the apocrypha. Such writing and the many commentaries on those stories also emphasize the roles the various types of Angels play in everyday life.

Do the many historical references to Angels in the Western biblical literature equate to the sum total of angelic appearances? Certainly not. There are frequent references to and stories about Angels in the literature of every historical age, and the many personal tributes to their existence testify to the fact that Angels have been part and parcel of human lore for centuries.[77]

Given their alleged powers, it is not difficult to imagine any number of Angels suddenly slipping into our time and space from places unknown. They arrive totally unexpected, assume a series of invisible forms and very visible-human forms, sing a few choruses from the texts of quantum Mechanics, String Theory and the proponents of a

---

77 Among the most popular are Lorna Byrne's *Angels in My Hair* (New York: Harmony, 2009); and Joan Wester Anderson, *Guardian Angels* (Chicago: Loyola Press, 2006).

multi-dimensional reality, and then intermingle with various scientific and spiritual groups as they effortlessly share their wisdom and spontaneously respond to a range of needs and requests.

Fast forward to a conversation you might have tomorrow.

"Seen any Angels lately, an actual Angel with wings - up close and in personal?"

"No - not really."

"Have you ever encountered a person who seemed holy, sacred or angelic?"

"Now – yes! That has happened to me – several times. In fact, let me tell you what happened just the other day. I met this woman who…"

"And what about encountering a mysterious field of energy, or your being in a situation where you know you were being helped by an invisible hand?"

"Oh yes: that too. Last year, it was unbelievable. I am sure I was being guided when…"

Surprise!

Would it change your life if you knew you were an Angel in training? Would it make any difference when you go to work or shop at the market if you knew you were not only an immortal Soul but also an Angel disguised in human clothing? Would it make any difference to you if you realized that many of the people you'll meet today are (also) angelic beings – here to observe, here to learn, here to help, here to radiate a loving presence?

Would it shock you to know there is but a very thin veil that separates you from a series of other dimensions and realities? Would you be surprised to know that some of the characters you have been attracted to in history (good and not so good) actually were you in other incarnations? Would you be amazed to realize that many of the people in your current life were also among the cast of characters from other or 'earlier' incarnations – and even dimensions?

Would you be astounded to learn that some of those repeat characters from 'earlier' and other incarnations were cast in very different if not reversed roles, that one of your children, for example, could once have been your parent, and a good friend now was once an honorable foe? Would you be blown away to recognize that there are extensions of you – other aspects and offshoots – that exist in other time frames and which are playing very different personal and professional roles from the ones you are playing on Earth? Would you be stunned to know the thoughts and actions of these other incarnations and aspects sometimes bleed through to you and in your current embodiment and placement, such that you find yourself having vague memories of things you don't recall doing during this lifetime?

Wouldn't it be stunning to accept the fact that the universe not only includes Angels but consists of multiple dimensions - more mysterious and fantastic than anyone ever imagined? And wouldn't it be a joy to affirm - and celebrate – the awareness that you really are a divine being, an immortal Soul, maybe even an Angel in Training - here to help Prime Source raise the vibratory consciousness of the Earth, working with your human and angelic colleagues to recreate our universe with a strong and steady infusion of insight and love?

CHAPTER 25

ASKING FOR GUIDANCE

How to Proceed

Although God, our Guardian Angel and other angelic figures are working in the background all the time – aiding us in big and little ways, helping us to learn our lessons, activate our empowerments and fulfil our learning agreements – both the so-called heavenly forces and you profit by your being very clear on what you need. As noted throughout – the receiving process basically begins and ends with your asking.

This is as true for responses to longer devotional prayers as it is for spontaneous requests for on-the-spot guidance. And although meditation puts the premium on simply being receptive to whatever happens, you may find it helpful on occasion to focus your meditations on obtaining insight and guidance of a certain type or on a particular theme.

Either way, when asking for angelic guidance, be quiet for a moment, breathe into and then out from your center, be prayerful in tone - and then mentally express your need for assistance. That alone will marshal the angelic forces - since they often cannot act in specific ways and certainly not answer questions - unless you ask and focus their attention. And they will respond when requested - for service is their job description - although they do reserve the right to help in ways you may not have anticipated.

If you want to become more patient, then ask for angelic assistance in becoming more patient. If you need more clarity in a given situation, then ask for it. If you need help finding a job, or protecting your family, or learning to be more playful or confident or helpful to others, then say so. You might even by more specific: "Is it in my best interest to do x or persist in seeking y? Either way, please send me guidance". Or, "I would really appreciate guidance on…"

Whatever happens, don't evaluate, belittle or grumble about the results or the timing of what unfolds. Just accept and give thanks for the gifts offered, trusting always that the loving spirits did hear you even if no discernible answer arrives immediately. The angelic forces will not do our work for us but the fragmentary hints and clues they supply are meant to nudge us in the right direction. That assumes, however, that we follow up on the clues, hunches and intuitions they activate. Don't try to force the guidance; it is best activated and received when we are relaxed – even playful.

Don't Wait

Never assume you are bothering your particular Guardian Angel, especially if you are raising an important spiritual issue. While other angels may not be in a position to respond - because they are on assignment with someone else - your Guardian Angel will respond fairly quickly: they have agreed to 'guard' you in general and thus guide you as you face particular challenges. So don't wait for a difficulty to grow into catastrophic proportions, or threaten the core of your sanity. Request the assistance of your Guardian Angel as soon as a need genuine arises. Ask for courage if that is what you need. Ask for counsel on how to approach someone. Ask for whatever you need – making sure, however, the issue is important and not a reflection of your every passing anxiety.

Sometimes your Guardian will enlist the aid of another Angel if your issue falls within their specialty. Either way, please realize that none of the Angels put your requests on a scale and weigh them in terms of their alleged significance to them. If something is really important to you, it is really important to them. Of course, the person who is hanging off the side of a cliff, or whose request would serve a larger community, may be aided seconds before you get a response on your 'need' to sell your house. And although there are thousands if not millions of Angels, there could very well be a billion requests emerging worldwide at any given moment. So you may need to be patient. If so, it probably means you included the intention to 'learn how to be patient' - in your original learning contract.

Delete the Self-Serving Trivia

Your Guardian Angel will not give advice on the outcome of a sporting event, the future of the stock market, how to win the lottery, anything shady and potentially harmful to others or silly requests that are purely self-centered, superficial and egotistic. Winning whatever is not likely to draw much support but learning and loving and contributing surely will. So its best to focus your requests on the deeper issues of life, which could include, of course, your general financial stability, your professional development and how you can best express your talents and creativity.

As immortal Souls with a spiritual identity and heritage, it is also assumed that you are empowered to handle the details and all the mundane stuff on our own. Lest you become dependent and lapse into posing requests on trivia or every millimeter of life, it is best to focus your requests on the more significant issues that can enhance your capacity to be loving, effective and a creative and contributing member of your community.

Range of Possible Responses

Realize that you may not receive what you request. Getting what you want — on your preferred timetable - is not always in your best interest. Delays and modified versions of what you think you now need - although initially disappointing - could in the long run work in your favor especially when viewed from the vantage point of your overall learning contract. Who knows: it is probably best that the response or intuition you do receive nudges you in a direction that is different from what you initially assumed was best. Serendipity is known to align complex events into positive outcomes. So ask with humility and trust — and let the universe work for you.

It is also useful to know that sometimes the clarity you requested simply will not be honored — indicating perhaps that you are either intended to wait, rephrase, work it out on you own, improve or expand your modes of receptivity, realize that what your request really is not in your best interest, or a clue that your Guardian Angel had better things to do than respond to such a silly question or ego-enhancing request.

Realize as well that sometimes your receptors may not be fully attuned and you fail to recognize or decipher a given message. As to delays, realize that time does not exist in the eternal realm, and our impatience is not likely to speed things up. A response could also arrive in the form of an unclear clue or hint – inviting you to continue the search and complete the discovery on our own. Those hints and clues accumulate, however, with the designed angelic counsel finally dawning on you with the sudden awareness of - 'Aha'.

It certainly is not a good idea to quit your day job and devote full time to trying to communicate with your Guardian Angel or get so self-absorbed that you try to monitor every little thing that happens to you – as if posting requests on some electronic kiosk or viewing everything the happens to you as 'a sign'. We are expected to take responsibility for our choices and to work through our decisions - with the advise of our guardians as needed – not the other way around.

Even with angelic guidance, we are still expected to row the boat, master the waves, bail as necessary, improvise if the oars break, remember to bring a sandwich and some water, know how to read a compass, and instinctively pack a sun hat and a rain coat. But drown – probably not – not with your Guardian sitting at the bow steadying the winds and helping you remember there's a flashlight in your knapsack or something you can use for handling the current difficulty – thus putting you back on track to completing the next set of wondrous activities included in your life contract.

Align Your Boundaries

Until you feel assured that you are communicating with a loving spirit, it is wise to note emphatically that you "are requesting the assistance of a loving spirit, one who has your best interests are heart," and that "your boundaries are closed to all who cannot meet those standards" - or words to that effect. This will protect you from any sinister influences since not all entities in the spirit world are loving or interested in being your ally.

If you know the name of the spiritual entity you wish to invoke, then be specific: "I would appreciate the loving counsel of…" It is also helpful to note at the out-set that "I give thanks in advance for the wise and loving counsel received." Then pose your request for guidance.

And then - you wait as you go about your life. Remember that clues can arrive in so many different ways: an intuition, hunch, even an impulse. It can 'come to you' during prayer or meditation, in a dream, as something that 'pops' out at you from a book or billboard, appears as a repetitive image, dawns on you as you walk down the street or during a spontaneous event or meeting, as you smell a flower, act on an urge to investigate X, read Y or visit Z. It can arrive as a feeling, an internal whisper, an urge to draw or write 'something' or even a jolt – something like a metaphoric knock on the side of your head or a kick in the seat of your pants.

Cranking It Up and Slowing It Down

Sometimes the guidance you receive from God or your Guardian Angel (or other angelic presence) is so muted and subtle they are difficult to discern. The glimpses are too shrouded, the messages too faint. You need more. If so, ask for the volume to be turned up and the channels of communication realigned and adjusted.

Realize, of course, that you have the responsibility to insure that you are being receptive to the guidance you *do* receive - not judging it (as silly or irrelevant), not dismissing it (as too fragmentary or elusive), or refusing it (because we don't agree with or want what is offered). Receptivity means being thankful with whatever you receive and working with it by following its invitations and leads.

So God and the angelic beings will crank it up if you ask them – but you can't expect them to use a megaphone to reach a mind that refuses to focus, a personality that wishes to avoid risk and change, a mind and body that can't meditate for more than a minute, and a Soul that does not trust its own intuitions. So make sure you are doing your part, namely aligning yourself to the basic requirements of effective communications: slow down, concentrate, relax, be clear, be confident, be open, be loving, be thankful - and to be at ease with yourself and your divine helpers.

Above all, trust. Live your life with deep abiding trust in the powers of your immortal Soul, your ever-present Guardian Angel, and your divine connection to God Herself. No fear: CONFIDENCE. No anxiety: TRUST. No misgivings, guilt or anger: LOVE.

SECTION SIX

Extensions of the Soul

CHAPTER 26

CELLS IN THE KOSMIC BODY

We Are Talking "Significant"

So we are back to where we started. You and I, as immortal Souls, are part and parcel of everything, for nothing is - except Spirit. As we trust ourselves as immortal Souls, we express and transfer our nurturing energy to every other particle (wave, string and dimension!) of the kosmic and universal God.

You and I - and all the incarnations of all the Souls that have preceded and will follow our current embodiments – are integral portions of Prime Source. Together with the Divine Hierarchy, we are the cells that compose the universal organism known as God. We thus participate in the eternal becoming and extensions of Divinity. And through our ideas, intentions and decisions, we contribute to the inputs used by God to constantly update and recreate the Kosmos.

Haw! And there you thought you were just some relatively insignificant speck living a very challenging but short life somewhere on a tiny planet at the edge of a disparate arm of the Milky Way. I don't think so! And if you have come this far – you don't think so either! In fact, we are each so significant – with all our empowerments and divine status - that rather than regretting our alleged unimportance in the great scheme of things, we need to make sure we don't get spiritually haughty or presumptuous.

Given the immortality of our Souls, we each play a highly significant if not crucial role - not just in the development of our family, community, organization, or country - but in the spiritualization of everything we encounter. We possess and continue to create the kind of loving energy our Godhead needs to nourish and extend the Kosmos. Zow, wow, and holy mackerel!! ? Could we be any more gifted and blessed? Could we be any more central to the universal Life process itself!

Nothing But Spirit

According to philosopher Alfred North Whitehead, the best way to describe the universe is *panentheist*.[78] It is a new composite word but when you break its parts down it makes perfect sense.

The prefix 'pan' means *all* or *whole* (as in panorama). The other prefix, 'en', means *to cause to be* (as in endear). And 'theistic' obviously refers to *God*. Translation: everything in the universe is of the Spirit of God yet God is also its creator. God is a universal Being - both transcendent or *supreme, beyond our ordinary perception* – as well as immanent or *inherently present in* everything throughout the entire *Kosmos*.

God created everything and abides in everything. God is the Prime Mover as well as the all-inclusive creative expression of Itself known as the unfolding Kosmos.[79] To help Him/Her administer and spiritualize the Kosmos, God created the hierarchy and angelic hosts. S/He also created each Soul or cell of Its all-encompassing and inclusive 'body' of spiritual and material Reality.

---

78 See Chapter 2, "Outrageous", footnote 5; and Chapter 5, "The Spiritual Experience", footnote 18. Whitehead wrote dozens of books. See in particular: *Process and Reality* (New York, The Free Press, 1978); *Modes of Thought* (New York: Macmillan, 1938); and *Religion in the Making* (New York: Macmillan, 1926).

79 The term 'Kosmos' was referred to in footnote 1. It was adapted from the Greek by philosopher-author Ken Wilbur as their/his reference to the Everything: the universe of physical entities, buildings, and galaxies as well as the cosmos of living things (the *biosphere*), our mental and emotional constructs or *noosphere* (our images, thoughts and intuitions) and the entire domain and workings of the *theosphere* or Divinity. Kosmos, in short, is everything, 'all domains of existence'. We as immortal Souls are cells in that sacred Wholeness. See Ken Wilbur, *Sex, Ecology and Spirituality: The Spring of Evolution* (Boston: Shambhala, 1995), page 35 in particular; and *A Brief History of Everything* (Boston: Shambhala, 1996).

The growth and development of each cell contributes to the energy and development of the total organism. Our individual Souls contribute to God's continuous creation as we communicate our intentions and experiences to Prime Source – directly and through the angelic hosts. God (or Prime Source) in turn uses that information to manifest Itself throughout the Kosmos in a never-ending set of creations and recreations. The result is one big, unending, integrated and universal partnership.

How exactly do we - as incarnated Souls - contribute to the process of continuous creation? As embodiments of the Soul, our incarnated personhoods combine physical attributes with a series of cognitive, emotional and intuitive abilities. Together these physical and mental capacities constitute the housing within which the incarnated Soul resides. As the Soul's container, our material-mental composites serve as each Soul's local agent in fulfilling its physical mission on Earth.

The Embodiment: Body and Mind

First, a few more words about the body that houses the Soul. Then some comments on the mind of the person the Soul inhabits.

The body mirrors the creative process of the Kosmos. It is activated by a mixing of the generative and receptive capacities of the Earth – in this case, the mating of a male sperm with a female egg. As the fertilized egg replicates, the process of mitosis or the splitting and multiplying of cells emulates the original act of birthing, the result being the development of a whole new organism. The original donors nourish the new or third entity until it comes of age and repeats the process of partnering – producing in turn a new body to house a newly incarnated Soul.

No small accomplishment, this - a microscopic sperm and egg uniting to form a new human being with a heart beat, lungs, big toe, elbows, brain cells, genitalia and all. It is miraculous that life emerges, that it grows, that it differentiates into parts and organs and systems, that it is designed to know exactly when to emerge from the womb, how to continue and perfect its instinctive growth patterns, and when to complete or round off the total form and each of its aspects (two elbows, please, not three).

The emerging organism knows instinctually when and how to care for the maintenance and healing of its parts, and when and how to generate all aspects of the supportive brain and its complex network of nerves that are spread throughout the body. The result is a unified entity able of creating a lifetime of experiences - including the equally miraculous capacity of knowing when and how to let go of its physical accouterments so the abiding Soul may eventually return to its purely spiritual state, integrate its learning and get ready for its next assignment.

Now, a few more words about the development of the incarnate mind. The generation, growth and cultivation of the mind is as complex and mysterious as the material unfolding of blood, muscle and bone. As the body develops from infancy to maturity, so does the mind – a complex network of capacities, preferences and intentions. The basic structures of the mind in turn create the images and select the visions which when nurtured by emotional desires or preferences, crystallize into mental thoughts and intuitive insights. The conglomerate becomes the continuing generator of experience - constructing and attracting the circumstances needed to project a person's ideas and desires into activities and the creation of material forms in the outer world.

The mind's sense of me-ness is referred to as the 'ego' – a unified command post that coordinates the decisions and actions of this 'personality', this mighty cluster of intentions-images-thoughts-and-intuitions. This integrated body and mind house the Soul, and thus becomes Its medium for interacting with the physical world. Together the mind-body-and-Soul learns to set boundaries and aspirations, experiments, develops and adapts as it implements its choices and interacts with the other clusters of ego-Soul identities.

Gustave Doré, *The Empyrean*, Illustrations for Dante's *Divine Comedy*, 1855
It all unites, it all converges, and everything is and always
has been an aspect of the One.

The Soul

The body and mind of the potential incarnate – and its coordinator, the ego or personality – initially exists only in potential. It is actualized, however, when the Soul selects its particular conglomerate of attributes, skills and characteristics. The body, mind and ego then materialize through the normal earthly processes of conception, growth and development - becoming the Soul's residence as it incarnates in the material realm. The total or integrated incarnate – body, mind and Soul – is then the Soul's selected instrument for fulfilling Its learning contract and attaining Its spiritual mission while on Earth.

Unfortunately, the subsequent choices and decisions of the Soul's incarnation do not always translate into the decisions the Soul desires. The ego or personality has free well and thus can and will develop a 'mind' of its own, capable of fulfilling, resisting, modifying and even undermining the original contractual preferences of the Soul.

Besides, there are Souls and there are Souls. Not all are highly enlightened either because they may still be very 'young' or relatively underdeveloped spiritually – indicating that they may not have used their previous incarnations to develop and express their spiritual potential more fully. Obviously, such Souls would still not be in a position to guide their current incarnations appropriately. On the other hand, there are 'old Souls' or more developed Souls who have not only incarnated umpteen times but used their many incarnations to develop a clear record of increased spiritual depth.

Thus some Souls are ever intent and vigilant, providing their incarnates the guidance they need for spiritual advancement, while others may be unfocused, lazy or poorly motivated and do not provide the guidance any ego-personality needs to fulfil a mature spiritual mission. Some Souls, no matter how mature, may even allow their incarnates to go astray because they literally want to experience an ego-inflated existence and learn the lessons associated with losing one's way spiritually.

Either way, the Soul is the core identity, the central coordinator, the essence of life, the agent of choices and decision-making, the free 'spirit' endowed with free will and embodied temporarily in material form, the immortal being responsible for creating and integrating Its experience so It might expand and deepen its level of consciousness.

You and I – as Souls – were created and thus not eternal. But once created, we are immortal and cannot die or even fade away (as does the body). Whether we incarnate periodically in the material realm or choose to work and serve mostly in the realm of Pure Spirit, each of us is the director, selector, depository and integrator of its own placement, intentions and development. As part of Prime Source, as cells in the divine organism, we are divine - yet still need processes like incarnation to learn how to love unconditionally and thus inch toward the wholeness and perfection of Prime Source.

Whatever the specifics of its contract, the Soul's continuing assignment is to grow and develop in love and understanding. It uses its specific placements or incarnations to fill in the holes or gaps of its cumulative experience - like sewing patches into a wondrous garment that, although it is following a divinely inspired designed, is still a work in progress.

'Young and old,' immature and experienced, flaky and dedicated, advancing and advanced: there are as many kinds of Soul states as there are personalities. And each Soul proceeds at its own pace. All are on the path, however, for that is the universal DNA. And all are constantly encouraged by God to choose greater degrees of consciousness with each incarnation, and thus be drawn ever onward, rung-by-rung, from resistant and inexperienced to the realms of the dedicated and the adept.

Builders and Residents

In summary, one might say the ego-mind is our day-to-day personality while the Self or Soul is the person looking out from your body's eyes. The Soul is the depository and generator of the mind's expanding level of awareness, the 'It' that knows *It* exists, the psyche that wis through intention - to develop and expand Its level of consciousness and manifest Its awareness in the material world through an ego-led mind-body incarnate.

One might think of the Soul as the architect who designs and creates the house, and then selects the incarnate who will help him to occupy it. The Soul becomes the embodiment who rents the house for a given lifetime. It acquires the furnishings but the incarnate is at liberty to paint, repair, remodel and redesign as desired. Sooner or later the mind and body winds down and the physical or incarnate aspect dies and vacates. It is then that the Soul evaluates what It did and did not learn spiritually during its time in that residence in that neighborhood. It also gets ready to design a new house complete with a new décor and furnishings, selecting a new community into which it will introduce its new incarnation with his/her own set of skills, motivations, and learning objectives - all designed to help the Soul attain the next level of spiritual awareness.

The Soul-God Connection

You and I - your Soul, my Soul and all Souls - communicate our experiences as incarnated beings - as they occur - directly to God. Informed by these experiences, God creates and recreates the Kosmos accordingly – responding to our cumulative experience, needs and patterns, tinkering here and transforming there, making whatever adjustments in land, flora and fauna that both reflect our progress and entice us to go on the next step in our spiritual evolution.

God will even amend or amplify decisions it made eons ago if that is the will, the message and need of its evolving community of Souls and their incarnates. In other words, the composite incarnational experiences of groups of Souls can have a substantial impact, so much so that the Godhead uses the patterns in our intentions, experiences, preferences and advancements as bases for changes made in the successive unfolding of humankind, life and the Kosmos. Thus it is we, as Souls who in essence propose. And it is God, in Her/His wisdom, who in addition to Its ultimate power to initiate on Its own, also possesses the power to 'dispose' – namely dispose of any requests for continued evolution suggested by, or implicit in, the patterns of human experience.

Cleansing the Negative

Anything can happen over night or in the course of a century (which is not very long given the infinite nature of the universe). Catastrophes can happen as easily as God, angelic energy or cumulative Soul energy can intervene 'miraculously' to stop or temper an impending disaster. The agenda, the issues that emerge, the events that unfold on Earth are based – over the long run - on the cumulative pressures – for good of ill - that emerge from its citizenry, namely its incarnate Souls.

The process works the same for the system, in this case called the Earth', as it does of any of its individual Soul-citizens. If the emotional intentions and spiritual actions warrant an upgrade, then the individual, or the Earth and its species, advance as a group. If they cumulatively create stresses that can be peacefully transformed or vented, then all is well. If not, there are all sorts of physical and psychological disruptions and dislocations. Thus the need for individuals and societies to neutralize any cumulative increases in total toxicity with a countervailing amount of loving and healing energy. If the ratios don't equalize, problems and disruptions are bound to happen – that is, if not countermanded by God or the suffering minimized through focused human prayer and compassion.

Since we as cells in the Spiritual Organism play such a major role in influencing what happens to us, our communities, planet and universe, it is important to insure that we and our local 'houses' are in order. Our intentions and actions have profound impacts – positive and negative. The toxicity created by selfishness, hatred, greed and avarice can and does take its toll on both the physical and emotional planes – individually and planetary. The antidote, of course, is the intention of love and action of empathy. Our families and communities, and the peoples and nations of the globe - individually and collectively - simply need to generate a constant supply of loving thoughts and actions to outweigh and dissipate the negative energies that frequently spew forth from our individual and thus cumulative minds, mouths, policies and technologies. In the long run, individuals, communities, societies and entire planets gain when the cumulative loving energies dilute, counteract and undo the impact of those that are ego-centric and/or hateful. Similarly, any and all of these aspects of human society can and do suffer when the balance of energies becomes toxic.

Of course, we are not exactly aware when and how our thoughts and activities add to the eruption of potential difficulties or help to forestall them. Perhaps God has a fever chart and scoreboard that monitors all the shifting currents and comparative ratios, but it is a rare individual psychic or mystic who does. No one can dispute the fact, however, that the average person generates millions of thoughts, images, words, intentions and actions a day. Multiply those totals by the number of people in your family, community and nation. And think of the global implications: billions of people creating billions upon billions of energy packets – positive and negative – every minute of every day, year after year.

Factor in all the fine - and the destructive - things done by the world's industries and technologies, and you have an enormous amount of both loving and potentially toxic stuff being produced that can either help or hinder the fate of individuals, peoples and the planet itself.

Perhaps it's amazing that the planet is doing as well as it is – indicating perhaps that we are blessed with a sufficient number of devoted followers of the Golden Rule and the Sermon on the Mount. But it is sad to realize that many who end up suffering (and their loved ones with them) may have had little part in creating the negative imbalances that inevitably affected them and their psychic and physical environments. They lived loving lives in local communities and leveled no mountaintops to mine their coal, polluted no streams or oceans, released no poisons into the air, and did not contaminate any fields and crops. They did not foul the psychic airwaves with any poisonous intentions of greed, avarice or the desire to control and manipulate others. In fact, they may have and undoubtedly did live a stellar life yet have been or may now be in the process of being affected by an avalanche of toxicity that has the same immediate effect as an overdose of second-hand smoke.

Some Soul-incarnates, although motivated in general by love – may also have agreed in their learning contract to undergo certain sufferings in order to protect others. Either way, negative intentions and actions poison both our individual and societal atmospheres - with all the physical and psychological consequences. Such a dynamic can certainly add to the phenomenon that bad things also happen to good people.

On the other had, divine interventions happen all the time with individuals and communities: the 'instinctual' application of the car brakes just in time, a *hidden hand* that turns a potentially disastrous fall into a gentle one, and the many times an angelic force keeps us from turning into an oncoming car, getting electrocuted while fixing a set of home alarms, or being harmed by a potential attacker. And the residents of many communities annually have good reason to give thanks to both Mother Nature - and other indefinable forces - which at the last minute helped them avoid a flood, stave off an epidemic or help them survive the effects of an earthquake or tsunami. Many others may have volunteered to die or be injured under similar conditions – perhaps fulfilling a sacrifice promised in a life contract or motivated instinctively by the desire to save others.

On the cosmic level, look at all the outcomes of evolution – where dinosaurs overtime became lizards, where mountains and rivers replaced deserts and swamps, and where changes in the weather supported the movement of hominoids out of Africa, the peopling of all the continents and the spread of homo sapiens-sapiens around the globe. Unfortunately, the emergence of humankind has been a mixed blessing - releasing the human ingenuity that has created our cultures, technologies and civilizations, but simultaneously being unable to prevent the physical devastation and psychological pollution generated by human insensitivity, hatred and greed. It has been a constant battle of love and community versus greed and power, many advanced Souls trying to convert the actions of a minority of powerful and bloated egos. One naturally enriches the ground with compassion and infuses the atmosphere with harmony while a few but influential others use disdain and aggression to push aside, buy up or control everyone and thing they can.

Yet it may be that sooner or later God will have had enough. It is not unlikely, for example, that He will soon call on Archangel Michael and a band of Angels to cleanse the human psyche in general and the hearts and minds of the major offenders in particular. So don't be surprised to see Angels walking among us. It also appears that Prime Source is ready to give the go-ahead to Gaia and her desire to cleanse her waterways, airwaves, cities and forests of the toxins that have accumulated over the centuries. And third, it is then possible that most of the psychic, spiritual and physical polluters will then be escorted off Earth and transported to some far off, hermitically sealed non-environment where they can enjoy - at least for a while - exclusive access to the fruits of their labor.[80]

Dynamic Change Within Unity

What we are describing then is a highly dynamic system of change. Nothing is static – not God, not Souls, not the physical universe of expanding galaxies, not the universe of quarks and strings, and not the constantly developing Kosmos with its ceaseless urge to create and recreate. Rather, everything is in constant flux – including the human body and every aspect of the incarnational process. Everything is being made and modified via a process of continuous creation – supervised and implemented by God who is also changing given the continuous stream of inputs from the likes of you and I and all the other cells and spiritual components of Its Kosmic Being.

The role and responsibility of the average human being, then, is as enormous as it is sacred. As Souls or embodiments of immortal beings, our wishes, needs, actions, experiences, prayers and meditations help to co-create the universe. As Souls, each of us is an integral partner of the continuous unfolding of God as It adjusts, deepens and expands It's creative and loving consciousness. There are gazillions of inputs, constant two and three and billion-way communications, mini and cosmic components, an infinite variety of aspects – yet all of it is unified, parts of the All, guided by the One.

We are each a part of a momentous process - to be sure. And there you thought you were significant simply because you were the parent of two fine children, or the vice president of Eastern Sales, or the best player on your team, or the one who was musically gifted, or that magnetic personality who finally got that crotchety bunch to work together,

---

80 See Chapter 18, "The Challenge of Change".

or the writer of that great new book, or the person who really knows how to grow turnips and eggplant - no less being Mom of the Year, the kid who made it out of the tenements, the lucky devil who survived that car crash, or the one who spreads love and good cheer wherever you go.

Well, all those accolades are surely true and well justified. Yet the next time you get a tee shirt, realize you now have a more profound reason to feel connected and empowered. You might, for example, order a shirt emblazoned with such wording as: "Soul-in-Training" or "Co-Creating the Universe". You could even choose, "Expanding Consciousness", "I Create Love and Understanding", "God and I Talk Everyday", "Prime Source and I Are Best Friends", "You-Me-God", "The Trinity = You-Me-God", "i-God-you", or "We Are All One". Feel free to use of these or invent your own: they are all true. If you do and are also feeling generous, please order an extra t-shirt and send it to me (Large, please). Thank you - in advance!

Separate Entities or Aspects of a Unified Whole

We need to be concerned about the entire kingdom - because it is ours. We need to send love to our neighbors, for they are us and we are them...all parts of the same unity...all divine cells of a divine being. We are *it* and it is us.

If your pancreas is disturbed, do you reject it and fail to nurture it? If your eye is unable to see clearly, do you withhold care from it, refuse it healing, block its return to full health? If your leg is bothering you, do you discard it? If your head is confused, do you cut it off? If your heart skips a beat, do you berate it, argue with it, ignore it, tell it is should stop misbehaving, threaten to desert it and never use it again?

Would one cell knowingly tell another cell to go to hell - without hurting itself? Would a nucleus condemn the antics of its rotating electrons, demand they stop their unconventional behavior without setting itself up for disaster? Would a vein stop conveying blood because a nearby artery was larger or smaller, closer to a bundle of nerves, or momentarily more in sync with the central heartbeat?

Would your mammalian brain be in a snit because the cerebral cortex had more complex wiring and possessed the power to redirect, charm and even neutralize the mammalian instinct to fight or flight? Would your shoulders stop giving their support, your lower vertebrae refuse to absorb the weight of the spinal column, and your legs go on strike – because your neck, ear or index finger had comparatively little to do on any given day?

Where do *I* and 'it' or *we* - begin and end? Or is not 'it' and 'them'... also *me* and *us*? Are the parts separate from the whole or are we all essential aspects of one integrated body or being?

Should the people living on either coast care if the Mississippi overflows its banks and devastates millions? Is a tsunami in Asia any of Europe's concern or business? Does the wound of any assumed *other* do any harm to the unified body of humankind? Would the lost of art or mathematics have an impact on human civilization? Is the Earth alone or is it an integral part of a planetary system? Why should anyone care if Mars veers off its regular orbit, or parts of the Milky Way collide with another galaxy?

Is the injury, harm and destruction - or the healing, security and well-being - of any cell in our body, any person in our neighborhood, any state in our nation, any people on our globe, any activity in our solar system - of any real consequence to us?

Where do we draw the line? Do we need bounded definitions of 'mine and theirs'? Or perhaps there really are no valid moral distinctions. Maybe our ancestors invented and we sustained such divisive boundaries during moments of fear, anger, insecurity and greed, when egos aligned with greed and power, overwhelmed a short supply of Soul-consciousness, and convinced humankind that it was motivated primarily by egoistical needs as expressed in the formation of separate, competitive and warring units.

Maybe the inflated ego of one cell stimulated many others to react in the same way, and slowly it seeped into human consciousness that it was fun trying to be number one – even if it involved trampling on the many who were not interested in touting the ego, defeating others or hording money and power. Maybe that is how walls and barriers and boundaries got started and undercut our deeper sense of connection and mutual support. Maybe all divisions based on 'me and mine alone' are silly - helpful perhaps in completing some real estate deal yet hardly useful on a crowded planet facing exponential growth and greater and greater disparities in wealth, assess and opportunity.

Yet the core of spirituality means everything is one and everyone is 'us'. Maybe 'it' and 'I' really are part and parcel of the same field of energy. Maybe 'each' of us has a slightly different role to play, different assignment or particular way of contributing to the nourishment of a central theme and its common core. Maybe what all of us want is to experience a central and unifying identity, to be part of something larger than ourselves.

Maybe when we reject, degrade, exclude or harm any other, we become our own worst enemy – for we hurt ourselves by undercutting the foundational system of interlocking identities. Maybe we are all aspects of one big entity, one pervasive being, one united, inseparable and indivisible Oneness: from the One in process, for the One in contribution, and of the One in essence. If so, each of us must ask ourselves: "Do my – and our - daily intentions and actions support or deny such a spiritual reality?"

Facets of The One

I have a friend who is really good at fixing things: motors, door hinges, the roof of a house. You name, he can do it. Then there is the mother of three who organizes life for herself and her three very active sons with enormous zest and ease while still working everyday. There is another woman – another mother of three – who while coordinating a learning environment for her autistic child and an agenda of community involvements, also has the ability to make anyone laugh over the most innocent of happenings.

Then there is the friend from South Africa who sings and plays the guitar, has raised three children, coordinates a set of programs for the disadvantaged, and is working on her doctorate. Another friend brings enormous innovation to his job as he and his wife devote much of their energy and earnings to support their six grandchildren.

I, on the other hand, am at that stage of life where I no longer have to run to catch a bus or make a meeting. I now have the time to cultivate my love of nature, the DVDs produced by the Learning Company, watch the World Series, read everything I can - and write books.

Who among all these is the better citizen? Who is the more involved with the Soul? Is one contributing more to the greater good than another? Or is there equality within diversity?

At the Soul level we all possess the same energy potential. At the incarnated level, we obviously decide to contribute in different ways. The jewel of life does not have just one facet, just one Number one - the rest of us being losers or of no particular consequence. Each variation, cut or slant in the divine jewel is of the essence of that same precious stone, and as such, makes a unique contribution to the whole. Each facet is intended not to duplicate or imitate the uniqueness of the others but to be its special self - and in so doing complement the light of the others.

We each have a right to bask in the awareness of how our individual ways express the essence of the Divine. Each of us is good – and potentially superb – at what we do. As such, we need not be or try to be like any other aspect of the core identity. Given our unique role and skill base, we also do not need to worry about getting somewhere, no less somewhere other that where we are. Our focus is on contributing to the universe by putting our particular skills to work – here and now, where we are. Given our unique expressions of one or more of the infinite attributes of God, we have reason to be daily celebrants, delighting in our role as distinct, equal and indispensable aspects of the Whole.

Who Lives in Your House?

Your body may be likened to your house.

Your Soul is the one who lives in that house.

Your body is the residence.

Your Soul is the resident.

Your eyes are like the two windows on the top floor.

Your mouth could be the front door.

There are all sorts of analogies.

It is just another play on the theme of 'Inner and Outer':

The inner creates. The outer radiates.

Whatever you call the shell

- the body, house, the abode -

Reflects the wishes

of the occupant, custodian, person.

The one inside: the one who resides,

commissions and builds the house

Then paints it, furnishes it

and makes it into a home.

And that's you ...

the presiding spirit,

The resident Soul,

the divine energy

Able to infuse your special brand of spirit

into your unique embodiment.

One More Reminder

You are not alone. You are not a castoff. You are not forgotten. You are not inconsequential. Rather...you are a child of God. Even more, you are intrinsically divine. Just like that person sitting across from you on the bus, or the person who just waited on you at the grocery - you are an integral part of God, a living, breathing essential cell in the vast body of the Divine. As such, you are a manifestation of the Creator in material form.

You are divine energy temporarily merged within a little bit of matter. You are here on Earth - at this time - in order to manifest your divinity in your particular setting, and transform your chosen circumstances according to your desired style and personality. You have a distinctive role to play in the continuing creation of the Kosmos: no one else is exactly like you, has your distinctive perspective or skills, or is primed to handle your selected challenges.

You are also here to learn how to love and to do so unconditionally, versus loving only certain people (like your family or countrymen) and only under certain conditions.

Your earthly contract is all about learning, learning how to handle the placement and responsibilities you chose, learning how to utilize your circumstances to heighten your spiritual awareness. It is also all about teaching, teaching others how to love, and teaching others, through your example, how to become conscious agents of the divine, co-creating the universe in It's loving image.

Your situation, your capabilities, your challenges, your life experiences are not random or meaningless. You are on divine assignment, here to be who you are, a representative of God, commissioned and empowered to manifest Spirit on Earth.

Birds of a Feather

If you are interested in observing different human types, then watch birds. They are as varied and distinct as their human counterparts. Surely we are spiritual beings but often our humanity dominates – giving us an idea of how much our cooing and loving our inner dove must do in order to quiet our loud, 'its-all-about-me', inner hawk.

Which one of the following descriptions sounds most like you? The Great Heron, for example, will stand for many minutes, often on only one leg, patiently waiting for its prey to swim by in the shallow waters. How different is that from the sandpiper that scurries in and out with the tide, always going to the water's edge, never really getting wet but and always retreating in time to catch the tiny crabs that surface in between.

Backyard birds offer the same variety. The doves will flutter in and sit, burrowing slightly into the grass as if to make a gentle cradle of their temporary nest. They do not feel agile or small enough to fit on the bar of most feeders. So they eat what drops to the ground as other, smaller birds scatter the seeds (birds are notoriously sloppy eaters). And where the doves will walk around the area bobbing their heads, and the chickadees and sparrows hop from spot to spot, the blue jays bound about as if on a wiry bongo sticks.

The blue jay always announces itself with a loud squawk when it lands in the feeding area. Perhaps its squawk is designed to temporarily scatter the competing birds — and usually it does - but at least they are alerted that is it is only Mr. Blue Jay and not Mr. Menacing Hawk. The cry could also be the blue jay's way of expressing their happiness in finding another trough.

The male cardinal — the very red one in all seasons - arrives first as the female waits in the nearby tree. Once it seems safe — no cats or hawks in sight — down swoops the female. Like her mate, she too prefers the black sunflower seeds. They usually fly together and he loves to feed her what he finds.

The cowbirds, red-tipped black birds, and grackles, on the other hand, arrive in pacts, eat with great excitement and devour everything in sight, while the woodpeckers tend to dine alone, and invariably prefer to concentrate on the suet while hanging from the grates of its wire holder at every conceivable angle. Not many birds like the pieces of bread. The crows, however, eat just about everything, and so will collect three or four pieces in their bills before staggering aloft and carrying their treasure to the nest.

The view is turned up side down at most open-air restaurants. The chippies, finches, sparrows and the pigeons constantly scamper under the tables for any crumb dropped or left unattended…retreating occasionally to a nearby bush before resuming the search. Meanwhile the black bird sits none too patiently in a nearby tree waiting attentively for a particularly choice morsel to be left unattended by an unsuspecting diner.

You could almost hear the birds chatting as they observe *we* humans at our dinner table.

"Look at the one with the big gaping mouth."

"And over there: watch them run to get that empty table. Their swirling elbows make them look like they want to fly."

"Haw – see the human hawk leering at that roast beef. And that twosome, two peacocks in full plumage with their entourage in tow, using their loud voices and bodily swagger to announce their arrival and call for immediate service."

The birds sitting up high also spot some humans acting like chickadees – food falling out of the side of their mouth as they scurry to and from the buffet table. They also conclude that the large, patient one in the corner, the owner – the one watching and waiting – must have a cousin in the vulture family.

"But the doves," says the mother cardinal. "The doves: the humans don't seem to have many who behave like our doves."

"They would never survive," say the grackles, the leading exponents of "Number One". "It's like one of our frenzies down there. Who could keep their loving nature in tact in the midst of that competitive maelstrom? No one seems willing to wait their turn, everyone's talking with their mouths open and it's eat or be shoved aside."

"No: there's not much room for a dove and its meditative lifestyle," the grackles conclude, "at least not when we and our featured cousins are in town."

"We hear, however," says the owl, blotting the corners of its mouth with its napkin, "there's a new kind of humanoid coming, one who's intended to act like a dove – but it is still in the design stage. It's intended to be spiritually endowed, patient, at ease with itself and others, and – get this – willing and able to share" – at which all the birds laughed 'til they were cock-eyed.

"Surely this new and improved kind of human will slip now and then and act like a bald eagle," said the blue bird. "Or maybe that trait will be bred out of 'em. If so, its relatively loving and unassuming ways will put it much higher on the scale of evolution - than anything we see down there."

The Context of Life Changes

If we remind ourselves - that we are aspects of God,

    that we are all by nature divine,

    Souls embedded in a physical body

Then we can choose to activate our dovelike features

    And have them temper our occasional tendency

    to act like a grackle, blue jay, hawk or peacock.

When we reaffirm that our Soul is embedded in our body

    like the Hindu 'Atman',

    or the Self of Depth Psychology,

We'll be able to see with inner vision,

    Use Buddha's Third Eye,

    See All Through our Sixth Chakra

> Then we can allow the 'Big I' to guide the ego
>
> Enabling Presence to return
>
> And then reign within the retina.

Then, THEN – the entire context of life changes. The cosmic context is affirmed when we realize we are aspects of the kosmic divine. The meso (or middle) context is also radically altered as we honor our commission to infuse Spirit into our physical incarnations. The micro or personal level is also transformed as we cheerfully and offer our experiences to God as the building blocks of continuous creation.

And the everyday encounter is flipped on its head. The old, ego-oriented pursuit of power and emphasis on purely outer achievement seems silly. Development becomes spiritual rather than personal, with any desire for power over 'Z' or amassing quantities of 'Q' being replaced by the commitment to provide 'service' to 'all' and love to 'everyone'.

Our concrete involvements would still be linked to the major transitions of earthly life – from childhood, to mating and finally letting to go of the body. But any dominating drives to strive, thrive and accumulate would slowly give way – learning by learning - to the deeper impulse to accept, honor, enjoy and love one another.

CHAPTER 27

RELIGION AND SPIRITUALITY

Each, Every and All

A very insightful bumper sticker: "God is Too Big for Any One Religion"

Let us give thanks for the contributions of all religions. Each seeks to praise, worship and serve God in its own special way. Whatever you want and need, there is a religious expression to suit you. Love to kneel and pray? Well, come right over here. Sing and clap your hands? Ah, you have several alternatives just over there. How about speaking in tongues, or not speaking at all? Of course there are several options on each side of the aisle to choose from. Ornaments and statues galore, or a clean and clear décor – its all available – with one group or another, in one type of abode or another.

The multiplicity of religious expressions and spiritual practice mirrors the multiplicity of personality types; there is an option for every preference. And that is as it should be since such variety reflects the unending number of divine attributes and the infinite number of ways in which God's presence is spread upon the Earth.

Could it also be that each approach corresponds to a particular aspect or interest of God? Could it be that God might feel the loss of any one of the multiple ways the various traditions and practices honor their experience of Godliness?

Could it be that Prime Creator's potential extensions are so numerous and ubiquitous that not even the thousands of historical variations on religion and spirituality could possibly fill more than one tiny room on the fourth floor of one of His mansions? (John 14:2)

Combines

Your spirituality need not be a given or deposited at birth. It certainly need not be catechistic, highly structured or filled with prescriptive 'do's' and 'don'ts'. And it need not be either 'old' and traditional or all relatively new and recently renovated.

Is it not possible for one's core spiritual beliefs and practices to be gathered together in the course of one's entire life, a set of experiences that becomes a personalized amalgam of those various rituals and perspectives you have learned to revere en route?

Surely spirituality means more than choosing a codified religion, on the one hand, or nothing at all on the other. A New Yorker cartoon years ago quoted an alleged speaker who followed Patrick Henry to the podium of the Virginia House of Burgesses. "Surely", said this wise one, "there must be some creative alternatives between liberty on the one hand and death on the other".

If your brand of spirituality is a creative combination of religious practices - insights perhaps from both Oriental and Western philosophy and a mixture of 'traditional' and 'new age' perspectives yet honors love and compassion as its central core, then why not! If you wish to add, delete or expand some aspect of it tomorrow in order to further your connection to the divine, then why not do so. It is your incarnation, your contract, your choice, your learning and your relationship with the divine that is yours and no one else's to form and express.

Many of the paintings of Robert Rauschenberg are referred to as 'combines' – because they are neither just a painting nor just an assemblage of three-dimensional materials. They include bits and pieces of paint, drawings and objects, all on one canvass, forming one 'combine'.

The farm implement, the combine, is both a reaping and a threshing machine. A combine in business is a combination of different firms acting together to achieve a common goal.

Carl Jung advised his clients to reclaim their religious roots if that is what they wanted, encouraging them to embrace a faith or church - in whole or part – depending on what remained 'true' or meaningful, adding to it whatever beliefs and rituals helped them on their path to individuation.

Tapestry

The process of living may be likened to the weaving of a tapestry. Following a set design and working within a fixed pattern may be fine for some. Such approaches are offered by the established religions to those who want and need them. But that is not true for all – which is where the flexibility of spirituality comes it.

Spirituality offers the opportunity to align with God in one's own way by weaving a collage of practices into one's own – and often unique – synthesis. To many, no one set of ideas, perspectives, ceremonies, happenings or philosophies can occupy or fully express the whole of a their lifetime. Life's experiences and learnings are too varied and complex to be governed by any one approach. No one strand or section of life's tapestry can capture the essence of it all.

True meaning to such folks is achieved only by mixing the varied lines, curves and colors one has accumulated in life and combining them into a unifying collage of their own. As long as one's beliefs and practices express love and compassion, honor God and service, who cares if a thread or two are out of place and some of the colors clash? Who could possibly judge it to be anything other than a set of personal preferences, based on personal experience - influenced, of course, by a particular mission and one's learning agreement.

Such tapestries are woven over a lifetime, and often are still works in progress. They include references to the weaver's varied experiential choices, with the remnants of the textures, colors and patterns from an entire lifetime of adventures: childhood and adulthood, one's individual and communal life, the imprints of early religious structures and both the questions and affirmations that energized one's perennial search and discovery.

So, reaffirm the faith of your upbringing if that's your inclination. If not, then be as proud to claim your freedom - and power - to combine any set of spiritual beliefs and practices that have proven, in your context, to be useful and valid. Any aspect of the old and the new that reflects your cumulative values, meets your emerging needs, integrates your total experience, and nurtures your continuing conversation with the divine is worthy of being honored as your spiritual amalgam.

Beyond Three Dimensions

Place your pen on the paper and make a dot: one dimension. This, of course, is the very beginning, something like the universe before the Big Bang. Then make another dot horizontally across from the first one, a few inches away, and connect the two with a straight line.

Then draw a second line of the same length, but this time a vertical one that connects to one edge of your first or horizontal line, thus forming an approximate right angle – something that looks like an elongated 'L'. Aha: we have pictured two dimensions – the basic assumption behind the maps around the time of Christopher Columbus: a mass of flat land flowing on a flat ocean with the masthead of the Santa Maria pointing to the starry sky.

Now the next step: draw an additional straight line of the same length as the other two. But this time draw it as a diagonal line within the elongated 'L' shape, beginning where the two current lines meet and extending out – as a diagonal line – in between those two and equidistant from the elongated edges of the 'L'. You now have three dimensions: width and height have been supplemented by depth. (Perhaps the three dimensions are best revealed when each line is extended appropriately to form a square or rectangle.)

But how do you draw a fourth, and fifth dimension? We know as incarnated forms that we are three-dimensional beings. Yet we have intuitions - even experiences - of dimensions that exceed those that govern our normal or everyday life.

Einstein, for example, revealed that space curves when it goes around an object or mass. He also told us that energy equals mass in certain proportions. Specifically, he discovered that energy equals the square of the mass of an object, times the speed of light (which travels at 186,000 miles a second). The equation is the familiar: $E=MC^2$.

Then came along the physicists of quantum mechanics who discovered that the sub-atomic materials within the atom of each cell sometimes act like particles and sometimes like waves. Those materials are in turn composed of such entities as quarks and neutrinos that also change their characteristics and location according to what a given experiment is looking for. [81]

The materials that make up the atom and its nucleus thus operate in ways that contradict our three-dimensional notion of cause and effect; it is not 'the pool stick hitting the cue ball into the eight ball causing it to go into the corner pocket', like a sequential 'bing-badda-bam'. Instead, quantum mechanics - similar to the Buddhist notion of 'simultaneous awakening' - tells us that the allegedly separate parts of a progressive sequence actually happen, occur or 'appear' - all at once. And they continue to evolve into a variety of random structures, behaving like a continuously evolving kaleidoscope – constantly capable of producing or appearing in a new and different configuration.

The experiences of the mystics also confirm the existence of a realm beyond our three dimensional world. They actually 'see' and 'hear' the presence of God – accessing dimensions the traditional three-dimensional mind only dreams of. And the sacred traditions and literatures tell us that the likes of Zoroaster, Buddha, Jesus, Moses and Mohammed experienced bodily and mental transformations, and performed miracles that literally superseded the laws covering the rest of the physical universe.

---

[81] See the essay, "Signs of Angels in Our Midst", above in Chapter 24, "Angelic Beings".

Many everyday people also know there is a successor to the dot, the line and the diagonal. Their own glimpses of 'the sacred', although facilitated by their senses, go far beyond their sensory indicators and reveal extra-ordinary levels of consciousness that totally break the bounds of the three-dimensional box.

The stuff of religion – and certainly spirituality - is also the stuff of other dimensions. Its sacred books and literature abound with stories of other-worldly phenomena like the appearances of Angels, the blissful realms of 'heaven' or so-called 'higher' or deeper consciousness, and the appearance of God in various human forms – all suggesting that our normal three dimensions can and often are pierced and exceeded by spiritual experience.

Each of us can learn to trust in the reality of a more extensive and deeper reality. There is the testimony of our avatars and mystics. There are the clues offered by science and the glimpses created by our own experience. There does indeed seem to be a quantum-sacred universe in which the ordinary and the extraordinary intertwine and become evident in various ways and at the same time.

We all can go beyond the dot, the line and the diagonal. We can break through our self-imposed blinders and accept the reality that as incarnated Souls we not only came from another dimension. We are also empowered to evoke it at any time, witness the sacred in the ordinary, experience the presence of Spirit within the everyday, and both create and participate in the multiple dimensions of sacred space.

Particular Options

Organized religions have made, and continue to make, enormous contributions to human spirituality: they offer individuals a series of alternative paths, which in content and process, appeal to different needs, dependencies and personalities. If you want and need high structure, a codified format, a set of doctrines and clearly defined rituals, there are several to chose from - including the Roman Catholic, Episcopal and Lutheran churches. If you prefer some structure, less hierarchy and the governance vested in community elders, then you might be comfortable with the Methodist and Congregational churches.[82]

Today's United Churches of Christ, Methodist, Baptist and Presbyterian churches express great interest in societal issues. Most Unitarian-Universalist congregations pay particular attention to projects serving the larger community – which is also true for many of the Evangelical, Jewish, Muslim congregations and Buddhist assemblies throughout the world.

The Quakers have a very simple approach, devoting themselves to love, service and an open-ended guidance of spirit. And it is small wonder the evangelical churches are popular in South America and Africa since their appeals to God are rooted in emotive expression through song and music. Similarly, the Roman Catholic Mass is highly dramatic, predictable and solemn; but it is highly structured and the priest is still the intermediary for the congregation. Because of the Church's theology, the ritual gives a great deal of attention to sin, death and resurrection versus the joyful, exuberant and celebratory approaches of the services in most Black, Latin, and evangelical churches.

While the Mass for Catholics and Episcopalians is somber and has a fixed focal point, the Unity congregations tend to sidestep the dark side of life with a series of almost informal exchanges tilted to the positive and emphasizing individual and societal progress through self-fulfillment. Those who seek enlightenment through direct communication with the Holy Spirit have an outlet within the Pentecostal churches. And if you want 'big' and your gospel supported by entertainment and an atmosphere of a theatrical production, then head for one of the mega churches with their plush seating for thousands, their snack bars and state-of-the-art gymnasiums for the kids. Certainly there are variations in governance, doctrine, ritual and the intellectual-emotive tone among the many divisions of Islam and Judaism - but perhaps not as extreme as those who advocate the various forms of Christianity. But whoever you are, whatever your needs or wants, whatever makes you feel comfortable, whatever your preference in content and process, there

---

82   Also see Chapter 2, "Outrageous".

is a church or branch of a religion that is seemingly designed especially for you.

There are, of course, many others who do not want or need any intermediary or organizer: no priest, minister, elder, congregation or special building. They don't even want or need to meet on a regular basis. They tend not to abide by any governing structures - no less any that are set, rigid or hierarchical. As to ceremonies and group meetings, they prefer to join in those that are informal, relatively unstructured, and gatherings that unfold spontaneously around spiritual themes and issues: prayer groups, gatherings for healing and mutual honoring, commemorations, meetings for peace and social justice, and any community gathering that celebrates such particulars as a wedding, anniversary, home-coming, day of thanksgiving and gratitude, and even the advent of a solstice or a full moon.

The spiritually oriented thus are not without their rituals and communities. They simply prefer to honor Spirit - in any of Its umpteen manifestations - in any way that fits the need and the moment: spontaneously or according to some general format, regularly or on some special occasion, alone or together with a small groups of kindred spirits.

Spiritual individualists wince at the thought of established intermediaries or creeds but share a common belief in the spiritual Being who invented and personifies love and compassion. These folks hold their personal beliefs and practices dear but are quick to share in communal gatherings that are sacred in purpose and celebratory in nature. Spirituality to them is an inner experience approached mostly through meditation, prayer, contemplation, friendship and the loving and joyful interactions of daily living – supplemented, as noted, by honoring Spirit in and through various kinds of soulful gatherings.

Variety – the recognition of the diversity manifest in organized and spontaneous gatherings - is an apt description of the world of religion and spirituality. Whatever your need and preference, whatever your personality, whatever your inclination for extroversion or introversion, whatever type of creed, structure and ritual you may desire, there are ways to honor Spirit that fit your needs and perspective. And if your emerging style of religion and spirituality is not yet available, then you are free to seek and create your own.

So let us thank God for being so ubiquitous and all encompassing, and for enabling our diverse and creative ways of honoring Him. Viva God. Viva Her diversity. Viva all religions and forms of spirituality. And Viva the many paths around, into, and up the sacred mountain of love, light and joy.

Gifts

o   From the Roman Catholics, I take your love of rituals and pageantry.

o   From the Muslims, I take your devotion to prayer throughout the day.

o   From the Jews, I take your honoring of tradition, love of learning, sense of humor.

o   From the Native American Indian, I take your living in Oneness with nature, the animals and the Great Spirit.

o   From the Buddhists, I take your deep respect for all living things.

o   From the Zen Buddhists, I take your ease, spontaneity and flow.

o   From the Hindu, I take your wondrous pantheon of Godly traits and attributes.

o   From the Gnostics, I take your respect for inner knowing.

o   From the Protestants, I take your audacity, challenge of corruption, and re-claiming the individual's direct linkage to God.

- From the Unitarians, I take your desire to explore the full reach of God's Oneness in the direct service to humankind.

- From the Theosophists, I take your affirmation of re-incarnation, the wondrous aspects of ancient wisdom, and your blending of Eastern and Western perspectives.

- From the Anthroposophists, I take your ability to bring insight to the spiritual history of the universe, and your ability to produce so many edifying and practical expressions of Spirit.

- From the Agnostics, I take your doubt and all the learning it generates.

- From the Atheists, I take your vigor and iconoclastic confrontation of hypocrisy.

- From the Free Thinkers, I take your capacity to live without codes or fences.

- From the Civil Libertarians, I take your love of individuality, equality and freedom.

- From all those who embrace a religious or spiritual practice, I take your sense of commitment, service to others, trust in your self and the presence of God, and your ceaseless contributions to the advance of learning, peace, empathy and social justice.

Institutionalized Religion

Some religious institutions, despite their many contributions throughout history, have also propagated their beliefs and protected their structures in ways that are in opposition to the norms of love and equality. Many, for example, cite 'sacred scriptures' that allegedly offer conclusive proof for their adopted beliefs, when there are other passages that contradict those conclusions. And much of what has been adopted as 'articles of faith' stems from interpretations made by the hierarchical clergy. But the reward structure is circular: the interpretations and doctrines invariably seal the role and authority of the same clerical class that made the interpretations.

For Catholics, for example, this includes the issues of confession, the central role of the Church, the pre-eminence of the Pope, the exclusion of woman from the clergy, the hierarchy's preoccupation with sex, and the incessant intermediary role of the clergy in administering every aspect of Church doctrine, ritual and ceremony. But the faithful, conceding the right of their theological betters to reach such conclusions and their governing bodies to propagate such findings, are then enveloped in a set of self-effacing incongruities. Parishioners are asked to profess 'faith' in a set of beliefs but are not included in the adopting mechanisms. And they are asked to profess but do not necessarily understand or accept many findings (like Original Sin, the Immaculate Conception and the many issues noted above regarding woman and married clergy). Many Catholics simply take it upon themselves to ignore many such doctrines – and even such prescriptions as attending Mass, going to confession and not using birth control.

So many question or do not follow Church doctrine yet say they are 'Catholics' (although they hardly ever attend Mass). They appear to remain Catholics in name only - out of habit and tradition, fear of risking a family feud, being rejected by the tribe or, if they confront authorities with their doubts, risk being accused of blasphemy and potentially excommunicated. Yet when anyone adheres to beliefs they do not understand or agree with, or begrudgingly goes along with them to keep the peace, they not only end up kidding themselves but are being untruthful to themselves as well. So they hide from their own reality, reasoning that the discrepancies between their 'beliefs' and their actual behaviors don't matter. They never really rejoin and become practicing members of their childhood church or congregation. And they never really leave it either.

True, many clergy and the institutional leaders of many different churches and assemblies encourage their congregations to study and explore the depths of their religion. But the reactions for many are: 'It is easier to go along; lip service is so much more effective and consoling than raising doubts or being shunned; and who has the time?' Many are persuaded – and perhaps rightfully so - that 'nobody really knows or cares what the belief system is, and if they do, most don't believe half of it anyway. So why bother. Go to church or the temple once in a while; keep the peace. Besides: what's an hour a week, and a little extra time at the holidays? It is mostly social anyway.'

Unfortunately, such rationales negate the opportunity for involvement and consent that is the hallmark of most body politics. In other words, many adherents to institutional faiths embrace their respective doctrines because of their lukewarm 'belief' in the structure that produced it, not because they are aware of and believe in the soundness of the reasoning or the integrity of the process that created the official doctrines. To put it bluntly, many adherents to religious doctrines have compounded their own passivity and lack of real interest by acquiescing to a set of clerics who admittedly are more knowledgeable in biblical interpretation and church tradition. But then one's partial faith ends up being totally deposited rather than acquired, mouthed rather than embraced, inherited from one's family when a child rather than embraced for its integrity as an adult.

In short, many of the faithful of institutional religions embrace a product they don't understand, that was adopted according to a process in which they had and continue to have no role, was approved by a body from which they were excluded, and which is now administered by a structure in which they have little say. Such complete, automatic and seemingly casual and irrevocable nods to authority would be astonishing in any secular arena.

There is no doubt that many are convinced of the veracity of their adopted creeds and articles of faith, and thus worship according to a set of rituals and ceremonies they deem both true and worthy. It is only when such behavior is uninformed, unthinking and perfunctory that problems for the individual and the institution arise.

Trust, Love and Life

What would happen, however, if we valued 'trust' in a generic God to 'faith' in a specific set of propositions regarding a particular version of God? Suppose we reaffirmed love as the bottom line of all religious beliefs – and therefore assumed there was good reason to jettison any belief or practice that undercut, neutralized or did not in some way derive from or support the principles of love and compassion? And what do you think would happen if the world agreed to substitute the principles of 'love and tolerance' in place of any particular doctrine that excluded, criticized or condemned another purely on what they believed?

'Trust' attests to a clear belief in Divinity and the sanctity of the individual Soul. It implicitly champions all beliefs and practices derived from the perception of God as love. And it trusts in the constant presence of God, the direct I-Thou dialogue with God, the affirmation of all life and the pre-eminence of acceptance and compassion in all human interactions. It champions the power of intention, prayer, meditation and contemplation as the most effective ways of cultivating one's inner life and commitment to God. It is most exquisitely exemplified in the mystical traditions within all major, organized religions.

Beyond that, 'trust, love and life' may go many ways - according to the wishes of the particular assemblage, group or personal approach. Besides, who really cares what people formally profess beyond 'trust and love' as long as they use compassion to guide their actions. Believe what you will; it is what you actually do that is the one true article of faith that really matters.

Beyond that - there appears to be no doctrine or practice more important to our common spiritual development than the one that affirms each and all of us to be – at our core identity - immortal Souls and thus representatives of the loving God. Once we affirm a divine presence everywhere and in everyone, once we affirm ourselves as children of Divinity made in the image and singular likeness of our Creator - once we have affirmed our abiding mission to infuse love and understanding into everything we profess and do, then what else could we possibly want or need?

Combo Spirit Words

It is fun combining words to form new and creative meanings. It is also a worthy project for anyone creating their own amalgam of beliefs and practices - since most of the relevant words have already been co-opted by the traditional religious systems. All you have to do is combine the stems of existing words to new endings.

Collaboration, for example, is a good word; it means working together. As noted earlier, when we replace the suffix and transmute it into 'collaboratory' we create a new combo that describes what happens when we focus various people, perspectives and practices on a common goal.

Then there is the phrase, 'Zen Catholic', that combines two traditions long assumed to be separate and contradictory: the 'in the moment' stance of Zen Buddhism with some of the pageantry and rituals used by Catholics to honor the various stages of life.

There is also 'love' and the best of 'telethon', to create 'loveathon' – a setting or happening that celebrates the expression of love.

Spiritual messages sent via e-mail could very well be 's' or 'spirit mail'.

We send food and medicines to troubled areas. Why not use the combo word 'carepathy' (pronounced car-REP-athy) or 'careprayer' to express our compassion for others through the combination of material aid and empathetic prayer.

There are terrorists and marketers. So why can't we acclaim the work of Lightists who spread light and understanding; Joyists who exude celebration and appreciation; and Medicoms who wish to cultivate an inner knowing of meditation with the attitude of compassion.

We can also uplift and extend the influence of the noun 'insight' by turning it into the active or transitional process of 'insighting'.

There are mechanical and scientific systems as well as anatomical patterns and spiritual designs. Why not 'sacred systems' and the 'hallowed sciences'; 'celestial structures' and 'supernatural operating procedures' (SOPs)' as well as 'divine patterns' and 'blessed designs'?

And could not the names of spiritual teachers and mediators – such as minister, priest, imam, rabbi and shaman - be appropriately supplemented with the more generic 'spiritor'?

Where there is Presbyterian, Jew and Catholic – there could also be a name for those who revere the essential tenets of all religions under the canopy of 'Perennial Wisdom' who could be affirmed as 'Perennians' or 'Perennialists'.[83]

In addition to pointing to the grace of 'light' or 'enlightenment' and cultivating one's 'inner light', those with a spiritual bent could also refer to the equally poignant 'theolight' and ''Soulsight'.

Other conjunctions or combinations of two whole words include 'Soulradiant' (which is what the Soul is and does), 'BeingLoved', 'LoveBeing' and 'BeLoved'.

Do you have any other candidates – any word-combos that describe your particular set of spiritual beliefs and practices?

Sayings

If you believe in biblical sayings, then see if the following set don't jog your memory and peck at your conscience. Rumor has it that you have honored each of these invocations and admonitions - many times, perhaps without realizing it. Rumor also has it that you would appreciate reading them again now: it always helps to have a spiritual Burma Shave sign greet you as you round another bend in the mountain.

- "The kingdom of God will not come with signs that can be checked beforehand; nor will they say, 'Here it is!' or 'There!' because the kingdom of God is already among you."

- "You are the light of the world!"

- "Be wise as serpents and innocent as doves."

---

83 See Aldous Huxley, *The Perennial Philosophy* (New York: Harper, 1945 [2004]), and René Guénon, *The Crisis of the Modern World* (New York: Sophia Perennis, 1984 [2004]).

- "Do not be anxious about your life, what you shall eat, nor about your body, what you shall put on. Consider the ravens: they neither sow nor reap, they have neither storehouse nor barn, and yet God feeds them. Consider the lilies, how they grow; they neither toil nor spin' yet I tell you, even Solomon in all his glory was not arrayed like one of these. Instead, seek his kingdom, and these things shall be yours as well."

- "The scribes, elders and priests were angry because he reclined at table with sinners."

- "Beware of the scribes, who love to go about in long robes, have salutations in the marketplaces and the best seats in the synagogues and the places of honor at feasts."

- "Where your treasure is, there will your heart be also."

- "Love your neighbor like your self; guard your neighbor like the pupil of your eye."

- "Split a piece of wood and I am there. Lift up the stone and you will find me there."

- "Exalt yourself and you will be humbled; humble yourself and you will be exalted."

- "His disciples said to him, 'When will the kingdom come?' It will not come [he said] by looking for it. Nor will it do to say, 'Behold, over here!' or 'Behold, over there!' Rather, the kingdom of the Father is spread out on the Earth, but people do not see it."

Now the follow-up: has your interest been stimulated? Are you willing - even anxious - to spend a few minutes checking out the source of each quote? You might consult you memory, check the lead word or thought in a Concordance, or let your mind and finger do the walking through the Jewish, Christian and Gnostic Gospels.

Projecting Our Preferences

Where do our images of God come from?

We seem to create or prefer images of God that reflect our personal preferences for authority, protection, strength, lovingness, joy or any other set of attributes – and then worship those valued-images as being divine. In essence, we – as individuals and groups – have historically formed our images of God around our immediate needs and long range desires, projected those attributes onto our 'desired' kind of divinity and then worshipped that 'God' because It met our projections so perfectly.

And given the dominance of authority figures in our early lives, it is not unusual for our labels and descriptors to project our experience of the family. We are, for example - like the biological family - "made in the image and likeness of God". (Gen. 1:26-27) Want an authority figure – then 'Father' and 'Mother' (Superior), 'Brother' and 'Sister' - are perfect. Need a leader – then borrow from political life with the designation of 'a mighty king'. Want and need protection and forgiveness? Easy: 'savior' is the word to use. Whatever your style, characteristics and needs, you can describe – or mold - your God accordingly and then complete the process by venerating your own projections.

As we develop, we continue to describe God – or rather continue to project onto to Him or Her - those characteristics that coincide with and support our style, values and needs. Thus God is described as male by the male-dominated Christian, Jewish and Moslem faiths - a superior being who lords it over the inhabitants, whose judgments are to be obeyed and whose armies of Angels and earthly armies are to be feared. Reflecting historical conditions, God also becomes an avenger, savior, a warrior, a judge, a king, a father and even an innocent child – whatever reflects and meets the needs of the adopting agency.

It is very easy to project onto the image of God. The very concept of God as 'the All' almost invites and justifies selecting any set of desired traits one desires or already possesses. God has the capacity to be any or all of 360 degrees. The fact that we 'understand' God to personify certain traits versus others is a function of our not-so-secret set of individual and group needs and preferences. God can thus become a ready-made, a convenient target for and recipient of our deepest longings.

So the descriptions we have of God reveals more about us than it does about the objective Being of God. Obviously, our God would be like us – a strong parent perhaps 'if we need protection', an avenging God 'if we seek retribution over our enemies', a judgmental God who 'like us would justify the firm actions that need to taken', a loving God to complement 'our need for comfort and acceptance', an angry God 'capable settling all grievances', a forgiving God 'if we have erred', or a redeeming God 'if we feel burdened with sin and guilt'.

As revealed throughout the human history, the psychological function of projecting our wants and fears onto others can also be outright sexist, patriarchal and homophobic. Descriptions of God as male, virile, master and straight are direct reflections of personal and social preferences and prejudices. As a consequence of how they prefer to see God, many religious assemblies separate the allegedly lowly and inferior woman from the males, insist on a priesthood that is exclusively male, unmarried and straight (except when priestly child molesters are protected by the official church hierarchy), and elevate the husband to prime leadership while his wife is assigned the role of submissive and obedient follower.

The only image of God that survives all the historical projections is the one of unconditional love. It seeks nothing for oneself, is centered on service to others, deals with the essence of life and not any of its passing particulars, is transcendent to any of the six earthly needs described in Maslow's hierarchy, honors no particular group, individual, doctrine or ritual over another, extols the most basic and giving inclination of humankind, and holds in the highest esteem anything that emanates from and supports the experience of unconditional love.

Just Like Us

Thus we revere those who we consider extraordinarily loving human beings: Gandhi, Helen Keller, Mother Theresa, Dietrich Bonhoeffer, John of the Cross, Basho (the Zen haiku poet), Moses, Nelson Mandela, Elijah, Simone Weil – and the long list of other mystical persons from all cultural and religious backgrounds. We honor their courage and integrity and enshrine them in salutations, placing them in a separate and thus 'higher' category than we ordinary beings.

But this tendency to revere those of extraordinary talents and high spiritual lifestyles can - if taken to extremes, cause us – as it has through the centuries - to deify and then worship the so-called 'best of the best', the most loving of the loving, among them Osirus, Krishna, Buddha, Yeshua and Mohammed, and the many others who have been proclaimed saintly, holy or a sacred luminary. Surely it is a tribute to the human race to have so many of its kind recognized as sacred - despite the reputation of each for having upset their status quo and been condemned by those then in power. But what is most extra-ordinary is not our elevation of their status but our recognition that they were once not only 'ordinary' like us but always were and still are basically very much like us.

Our Gods, spiritual leaders, avatars, Master Teachers, saints and mystics were not necessarily born that way. They activated the divine essence of their Souls in the process of living. The successive waves of humans not only baptized their godlike attitudes and actions but also transformed some of them into Gods, falsely suggesting that our common divinity was really the exclusive property of the historically few.

Such a limited delegation of Soul properties to only some of our colleagues has for centuries inadvertently promulgated a sense of false humility by the average human being, and, indirectly, perpetrated a grievous disempowerment of the Soul of humankind. But 'they' (the anointed ones) and 'we' (the average others) are in essence the same. The only difference is our comparative failure to honor the divine nature of our own Souls, simultaneously projecting that special identity onto a selected few. History suggests that the revered have earned their status. But in the process of acknowledging the divinity of others, we have neglected to affirm our own status as immortal Souls and divine beings. Of course, many who tried were condemned and/or burned at the stake – such as the martyred saints of the Reformation and such mystics as Giordano Bruno.

The innate divinity that our Master Teachers have activated and fulfilled, are identities and empowerments available to the rest of us as well. They did not take a 'special' pill somewhere en route; they worked at 'it', slipped and fell and tried some more, transmuting the basic metal of the human psyche and its innate divinity into pure gold and manifest divinity. By work, determination and persistence, our saints, mystics and godlike teachers choose to exhibit what lies at the heart of our common humanity, namely their capacity to quiet the ego and master its bloated desires for power and greed. Instead, they cultivated their mission to love and serve Life (God, the Earth, humankind and all living beings) - not just in a material way but by adopting a joyful, loving and transcendent lifestyle.

All of our sacred heroes and heroines have experienced moments of doubt, all of them have expressed anger and sorrow, all of them – at one time of another – have experienced every weakness and foible in the human behavioral repertoire. All of them have also felt the need to jump-start their loving engines again and gain - each morning and every night. And all of them have learned to let go of that which did not serve the pre-eminence of their Souls.

We are no different. Their empowerments are our empowerments. Our Souls and their Souls have a common source and destiny. Their spiritual DNA is our spiritual DNA.

Like our enshrined heroes and heroines, we too are equipped to attain wholeness, to become full human beings, and to use our incarnations as opportunities to express our individualized take on what it means to be divinely human.

Jesus or Yeshua ben Yoseph of Nazareth

Take all the books written about Yeshua ben Yoseph or Jesus of Nazareth – the Gospels, the Epistles, and all the commentaries since – and boil them down to their essence and we are left with testimony of a life dedicated to loving and accepting everyone, including village women, merchants, military personnel and the most humble of the fisherman and farmers. Yeshua displays anger only toward the hypocritical, the power seekers, the moneylenders, the wealthy, the pretentious members of the hierarchy, and even a person like Peter who temporarily sought to use force in order to protect Yeshua.

Whether you consider the historical figure of Yeshua to be a good Jew living a holy life, a master teacher, a political or spiritual messiah, or the only or exclusive Son of God, the essence of his life as described in the Christian Testament is predominantly one of love, tolerance, understanding and assisting others. If anything he has all the trappings of a Buddhist monk: he lives a frugal life, travels on foot, wears simple sandals, dresses like his fishermen colleagues and tends to deal with concrete realities rather than theological theses. And rather than ornate philosophies he tells simple stories and parables.

Simplicity, frugality, honoring others, humility and full participation in the everyday activities of the earth are the hallmarks of his brief life. Yeshua ben Yoseph, since known as Jesus, surely was a Master Teacher, a personification of the best of human virtues and the epitome of a divinely inspired Soul.

He associates with people of humble origin. And many of the words attributed to him in the Christian Bible invoke metaphors of nature (the sea, trees, fish, vines, wine). He spends a good deal of time in prayer, meditation and contemplation. He is man of the spirit living fully in this world. He walks, he preaches, he bleeds, he suffers, he gets angry, but mostly he accepts, invites and blesses whatever he encounters.

It is no wonder people world-round relate to him. Unlike the more ethereal conceptions of God the Father and the mysterious if not wily nature of the Holy Ghost, Yeshua is real, alive, concrete. He is not only among us but one of us, and therein lays his power of attraction. He is not a theory but a human being. He leads by example rather than pontification. He epitomizes the person who 'walks his talk'.

Yeshua wears no fancy garments, writes no treatises or books, has no particular home, declares no codes or creeds, accepts men and woman equally, takes no titles, forms no structures or institutions, and never even considers no less propagates a creed. There is no tiara, throne, vestment or church structure in sight. His communication with God is always clean, clear and direct. He proposes no theology, collects no dues, builds no churches, creates no ornate altars and hierarchies, hears no confessions, and never fences off or hinders direct contact with the people.

This exemplar of an incarnated Soul is mystical at his core. He lives simply and leads with clear actions and loving words. He epitomizes the meditative lifestyle. He sustains his innocence and compassionate ways despite the doubts, suspicions and jibes of others. He constantly speaks from and aligns with his Soul center, and frequently reaffirms his direct connection to the Divine Source. He lives fully and trusts completely in the moment. He is person of inner grace - focused on service, honesty and wholeness. He cares little for the things of the outer world - showing disdain for the world of external pomp, power and structure.

Is the spirit of Jesus smiling or crying? Perhaps he found reason to do both during his stay on Earth but principally he appeared content to just be: contemplative, alive within each moment, shunning 'shoulds' and catechisms, possessing the radiance of a mystic in the marketplace, an extraordinary and enlightened being, quick to bless and welcome and soothe - always ready with a caring eye, a loving hand and an open heart.

Surnames and Essence

The original first and family name of Jesus was Yeshua Ben Yoseph (Hebrew for Jesus son of Joseph). The essence of the name of Jesus or Yeshua became and is 'Christ' (Greek) - meaning the anointed one, the bearer of divine love. According to Christian tradition, Jesus is 'the Christ', but according to the spiritual perspective, Jesus as well as the rest of us are each "Christ' - as in each of us being 'Christed', carriers of the 'christed' energy, blessed and endowed to represent and express the love and majesty of God.

During our incarnation, we are each given a first name and a family name. Yet as immortal Souls, we carry our status as divine children of God into our incarnations; we were made in the likeness of the Divine, as Souls and as carried into our embodiments. We share in the essence energy of 'Christ' for we are aspects of divine love. We are also co-creating partners with Prime Source, capable of expressing the Christed energy in our lives as did our brotherly exemplar, Yeshua. Mary was not the mother of the one and only 'God' but the mother of a divine being - as has been the case with your mother and mine.

Siddhartha Gautama (or Gotama) was the name given to Buddha by his parents in approximately 563 BCE (Before the Common or Christian Era). Gautama became a Buddha or 'awakened one" when he devoted his life to expressing his divine nature. The person history calls 'Buddha' is the person "who woke up [and] discovered who he really was". All of us share in this Buddha nature, and can activate our "Buddha" or 'Christed' energy by 'awakening' to the realities of our identity and the nature of our spiritual universe. [83]

The various Avatars – Souls who attained blessedness in the course of their incarnations – were sent by God to Earth on special assignment: Confucius, Socrates, Moses, Mary - mother of Yeshua, Mary Magdalene, Mohammed, Maimonides, Rumi, Aurobindo, Spinoza, Meister Eckhart, Azriel ben Menahem, Black Elk, John of the Cross, Francis of Assisi, Hildegard of Bingen, Plotinus, Chuang Tzu, Dio-

---

83 Alan Watts, *Buddhism: The Religion of No Religion* (Boston: Charles B. Tuttle, Inc., 1996), page 6.

nysius the Areopagite, Thomas Traherne, Theresa of Avila and thousands of other 'Christed' or 'Buddha-like' figures. Each graced the Earth as messengers of God, serving in different historic times and in different cultural contexts. Yet each incarnated to express the same loving essence. Their shared message has always had a common core: one, love is the quintessential energy of Life, and two, Prime Source encourages us to claim and express our individual reflections of the 'Christed' energy.

Each of us is gifted with the power to express divine love in his/her circumstances and in his/her particular way. Like the masters who have preceded us, each of us has a specific first name and a family affiliation. And like them, each of us shares the same divine identity and has the same capacity to 'awaken' and incarnate the same divine presence.

The Varied Images of the Archetypes

Many of the claims made by religious institutions are indeed puzzling. Why? Church officials have often translated the poetic or metaphoric language of various testaments into concrete descriptions of what they allege are unique historic events.

To Roman Catholics, for example, the Immaculate Conception describes the physical conception of Mary, mother of Yeshua, within the womb of her mother, as freed from the so-called 'original sin' committed by Adam and Eve. Mary is also known as the Virgin Mary for having herself conceived a child through the intervention of the Holy Spirit. Metaphoric descriptions of these events, however, points not to a special metaphysical reality for Mary and her mother - but to the immaculate and unblemished nature of any soul at the time of birth.

The essence of the allusions to 'immaculate' and 'virgin' are images of the archetypes of conception and birth – whether the initiation and outcome is of a new child, book, idea, organization, relationship or technology. A literal reading (in this case, the Catholic Church's desire to erase 'original sin' for Mary) converts the metaphoric reference ('as if') into a concrete reality ('the one and only'). It is the difference between the generic 'e.g.' - meaning an example, versus 'i.e.', the example.[84] But once adopted, such references continue to be interpreted concretely and exclusively rather than as approximate reflections of the related archetype – in this case the archetypal or generic human experience of motherhood, creativity and birthing.

Carl Jung refers to archetypes as "irrepressible, unconscious [and] pre-existent form[s]" and as aspects of "the inherited structure of the psyche." We naturally invoke such deep-seated structures whenever we express our 'take' on or image of such generic experiences as birth, death, marriage, childhood, the trickster, warrior, hero/ine, creativity, God, divinity, and tens of other generic human experiences. But our concrete, historic images of such archetypes (such as the image or historical appearance of Yeshua for a metaphor of the Divine, or Mary for the archetype of Mother), do not contain the depth and expanse of a given archetype itself. Our examples, words and symbols do evoke the unconscious power of the archetype and thus generate "strong feeling tones" within us which, according to Jung, definitely "impress, influence and fascinate us." [84]

As noted earlier, the theological concept of "Original Sin" is a case in point: it may be the first sin allegedly committed by a metaphoric Adam and Eve. In psychological terms, however, the act of eating the fruit of the ground was really a declaration of the birth of human consciousness - by our metaphoric parents – signaling the freedom claimed by human consciousness and ending its envelopment in the Unconscious (the Garden of Eden).

To suggest that this metaphoric description of the act of attaining psychological independence from the great Unconscious (God) actually created an indelible stain on human nature, which in turn denigrated all of humankind and necessitated redemption by the sacrifice of the only Son of God – is an example of an incredibly negative overreach.

---

84 Joseph Campbell expounds this viewpoint beautifully in almost all his books. See in particular, *Transformations of Myth Through Time* (New York: Harper & Row, 1990); *The Inner Reaches of Outer Space* (New York: Alfred Van Der March Editions, 1986; his four volume series on *The Masks of God* (New York: Viking, 1956-1964); and *The Power of Myth* [with Bill Moyers], (New York: Doubleday, 1984).

The sets of metaphors about the psychological evolution of human consciousness are thereby falsely translated into specific and extremely negative historic events. [85]

The same false interpretation and conversion of an metaphoric image of an archetype into a singular historic event is also true for such metaphors as the Incarnation, the Parting of the Seas, the Death and Resurrection, the Ascension into Heaven, and all the other supposedly concrete, historic appearances of divinity in the historical process. The descriptors use concrete images in order to point to or give an example of what an experience is like. But the selected and propagated image is only one of thousands of ways to possibly describe an encounter with an archetype. Thus the thousands of religions and their varied images of God – all perhaps true in part but none of which can in themselves approximate the Totality Itself.

The breadth and depth of God precedes and trumps sectarianism, and any attempt to enshrine one specific example of God as the one and only manifestation of the archetype of Divinity is both misguided and silly. Yeshua, for example, was an example of 'christed' energy. He is not the archetype of Divinity or its only example. He walked among us as a (and not 'The') Master Teacher. And he was not the only child of God. That inheritance belongs to all of us.

Likewise, the metaphoric energy of the archetype of incarnation is manifest every time a Soul is infused into matter. It is not limited to the historic incarnation of one person, in this case Yeshua. Similarly, 'ascension" alludes to elevation in spiritual consciousness, not the movement of any one body into a concrete heaven. Even 'heaven' is not a physical place but a figure of speech pointing to the archetypal energy of being at one with God.

These metaphoric references to spiritually generic processes are found throughout sacred literature because sacred literature seeks to understand and record our epiphanies or encounters with the divine.

---

85 C. G. Jung, *Memories, Dreams Reflections* (New York, Vintage, 1965), p.392. Also see footnote 61, on page 309 above, and the author's Jungian interpretation of Genesis, *The Creative Impulse: Celebrating Adam and Eve, Jung and EveryOne* (Melbourne Beach, FL: Helicon Publishing, 1998).

But the assumption that such indescribable energies can be reduced to singular historic events only serves the theological needs of the overly enthused, the naïve and those bent on falsely institutionalizing archetypal energies and building gated communities around them.

There also have been and continue to be gazillions of manifestations of 'immaculate conception' and all of the other signposts of the generic 'spiritual' processes. The images and activities we fashion as reflections of the archetypes are manifest in millions of different ways every second of every day and are not confined to the historic markers claimed by the hierarchy of any organized religion.

Literal interpretations of archetypal energies are attempts to contain what cannot be reduced or precisely interpreted within any concrete descriptor. Pour your concrete or exclusively historic version of archetypal energy into any mold or vessel you choose and you can feel justified in knowing it is manifest there. But it is not limited to your format, your interpretation or your particular concretization of that ineffable occurrence or experience.

Archetypal energies are infinitely free and indefinable for they relate to the levels of human awareness and realms of divine consciousness that go far beyond any specific, material inflection. Archetypes belong to the realm of what Jung called the Objective Psyche and the Collective Unconscious, and what spirituality refers to as Pure Spirit. They can be expressed here on Earth through a million and one metaphoric images, beliefs, customs and rituals. No one form is The Form. No one incarnation is The Incarnation of The Immortal Soul. Rather, every incarnation reflects the Incarnation of an immortal Soul.

Connecting With Spirit

Spirituality, given its dedication to the perennial philosophy of love and compassion as the essence of all spiritual paths, does not necessarily encourage us - as most institutionalized religions do - to follow a predetermined path of any one organization. Rather it encourages us to practice a religion with full force if that is what we wish. But it also encourages us to think beyond the boundaries of one institutionalized approach - to forge our own creation or supplemental amalgam, one that best reflects one's particular needs and varied encounters with Spirit.

Spirituality – like the archetype of 'the Divine' – precedes and supersedes any specific set of religious beliefs and practices – however useful, in whole or part, they may be to others. Spirituality is the foundation of all religions. It is grounded in the nature of the immortality of Souls and our God-given right to choose beliefs and practices that help us deepen our spiritual consciousness and reflect our personal experiences of the divine.

Every religious practice then is grist for the mill. Every religious practice needs to be viewed as fitting or not fitting our commission to create our own path to enlightenment. Spirituality does not stop at what formal religion has to offer but honors and anything that helps spiritual development. The Soul does not serve religion. Religions and religious practice are intended to serve the spiritual purposes and commissions of the Soul. Adopting – or modifying - any or everything, including the practices of organized religion, are among the options available to anyone seeking to maximize their spirituality. And membership in an institutionalized religion does not limit or forbid the searching Soul from exploring - and adapting whatever speaks to them from a wider range of religious and spiritual practices. Spirituality is that spiritual quest and amalgam.

Being aware that there is divine spark embedded in human nature, and that we human-Souls are empowered to create our own reality in and through our own experiences - are not theoretical propositions derived from standardized belief systems. Spiritual consciousness does not emerge from just thinking about the stories of any sacred book and then following the interpretations mandated by others. Spirituality is an experience of one's own making – a conscious choosing of beliefs and practices that may emulate the likes of an Abraham, Yeshua or Buddha but which are primarily personal, forged by the individual Soul in and through its own life mission and experiences.

The emergence of spiritual awareness is thus deeply intuitive and experiential. It is not contained in literal interpretations of allegedly historic events – which are then encoded by and deposited for others. One's spiritual life is earned and discovered. It is not dependent on worshipping the spiritual life of another but in having one's own mystical experiences and contemplative epiphanies. It does not consist of certain set prayers, forms of worship or belief systems but is a set of in-depth spiritual experiences that both precede and supersede the structures of any organized religion.

Spirituality is the process our Souls use to communicate who we are and do so directly to God. The depth of that dialogue consists of much, much more than the logical exchange of information between two or more brains. It goes much deeper than the seven layers of the skin. It penetrates far beyond the repetitive external ceremonies endorsed by others.

The spiritually inspired person, and his/her penetrations into the deeper realities of the universe, is certainly akin to the 'religious' personality (who may or may not belong to an institutional 'religion') and his/her experiential grappling with the challenges and opportunities of a lifetime. The spiritual or 'religious' experience is meta-physical in nature – concerned with what is deeper than the concern for the outer trappings of the material world. True to the reality of its incarnation, however, the Soul does use the concrete particulars of the material world to gain increased insight into how Spirit can be embedded in matter and how everyday involvements can become the means for expressing one's spiritual identity.

Sacred literature is filled with wonderful examples of how to interact with God once we are here or incarnated – as long as we remember that the stories of historic figures chronicle their approximate way, not the only way. The words and actions of historic personalities are worth emulating but not worshipping – for their way may or may not be our particular way given our placement and learning contract.

Again, the words of the great Spanish poet, Manuel Machado, speak volumes: "Pilgrim, there are no roads. Roads are made by walking."[86] No 'one way' or single path, no particular and certainly no designated set of activities, rituals, codes, belief systems, metaphors, literal interpretations or doctrines could possibly contain the unfathomable depth and extent of the Divine energy. Actually, God is the force that never ceases to invite the creation of one more way of honoring His/Her Presence.

Any specific reference to an everyday reality to describe an aspect or operation of Spirit only makes sense if we realize that our words are merely attempts to understand that which is trans-personal, something that is beyond us yet still involves the immediate; infinite yet infused into the concrete; indescribable yet mirrored in the logical and the intuitive; emanating from the realm of Pure Spirit yet reflected in our everyday thoughts and actions. The reality toward which we grope our way is transcendent by nature yet its presence is still reflected in the here and now, by you and me, in any and all activities which come from the heart.

All epiphanies, all new awakenings and the actions they generate - no matter how varied — make perfect sense if our perspective is wide enough and deep enough to realize that the numinous is in you and me — in that which inspires our fingers to trace its imprint on our tiny corner of the cosmic sands.

Who Cares

Who cares what a person's formal beliefs are as long as they do good things, work with others, treat them with respect, are caring and loving, go out of their way to help, are not narcissistic or self-assumed, don't hurt anyone, are exciting and energizing to be around, always have something good to say about whatever they have experienced, love to pet dogs and hug little children, don't hog the pretzels or the pizza, share their favorite food with others, make you feel at home anywhere you meet them, have a sparkle in their eye, are easy to laugh and love, emphasize the little joys of life, are not obsessed with bringing attention to themselves but are skilled at quieting their egos so they can

---

86   See footnote 14, in Chapter 5, The Spiritual Experience."

better attend to others, excuse themselves and go outside if their cell phone rings in a crowded restaurant, like to read the funnies in the Sunday papers, appreciate good jokes and wise humor, love to dance 'like nobody is watching' and enjoy downing a beer or two - the kind of folks who will watch your home when you're away, and who are always there when you need them - usually five minutes before.

Beliefs do influence behaviors, for sure, but formal theology - not necessarily. It must be that the 'wonderful people' from every sect and persuasion have fundamentally wonderful beliefs about themselves, others and God - and have simply learned to ignore anything silly or negative that's peddled from the head of the table, the podium or the pulpit. Either way, who cares how they got to be as decent and joyful and interesting - and as loving - as they are. As long as they are in our lives, and they act as they do – then who cares how they demonstrate their love of God and godliness.

Walk Away

- If someone tries to sell you a religious doctrine, walk away.
- If they tell you that you must do X or confess Y in order to talk to God, walk away.
- If they ask you to kneel before them, walk away.
- If they hound, badger or pursue you, continue to walk away.
- If they say you must surrender your free will to them, run away.
- If they suggest anything as a *must* or *have to*, sake your head and slowly walk away.
- If they encourage you to do anything that compromises your integrity, get away.
- If they do not honor you as an eternal Soul, an integral aspect of God, stay away.
- If they want you to give your power to them, insist that they remain far away.

- If they speak to you of sin and your blemished Soul, ask them politely to go away.

- If they tell you God is angry and vengeful, then ask them… please to walk away.

- If they suggest anything that diminishes your loving state of mind, gently glide away.

- If they say or do anything that encourages strict obedience to authority, pull away.

- If they present a preordained code or compulsory ritual - of course, slide away.

- If their manner does not enhance your deep respect for yourself, then stay away.

- If they say you need an intermediary to communicate with God, rush away.

- If whatever they do or say does not honor your right and capacity to serve God in your own way, definitely but definitely keep away.

- If they communicate a fear of the world or God, ask them please to go away.

- If they communicate anything but trust in self and a loving God, slip away.

- And walk – if not run - away from any person or group that does not honor you as a Soul, encourage you as a person, and enhance your trust in the loving God.[87]

---

[87] Personally, I greatly enjoy and feel perfectly comfortable participating in any and all religious and spiritual ceremonies. I do not seek them out but participate fully as an invitation or occasion arises. I particularly love High Masses, Gospel music, a great sermon by a first-rate speaker, the scent of candles, the sound of an organ and a mixed choir, prayer and mediation meetings, the grandeur and the simplicity of church architecture and interiors, Sufi dances, full moon celebrations, creativity and spirituality conferences and, or course, family gatherings.

CHAPTER 28

THE SOULFULNESS OF ART

God's Spirit Revealed in Art

If you really want to know about the workings of the Spirit, then turn to and reflect on the wonders produced in painting and sculpture. Everything but everything is there: every style, every approach, and every perspective on every situation and archetype.

The Medieval lens focused on the sacraments of the Church and the life of the Holy Family. It's two-dimensional images do not recede into the canvass but face you straight on – reminding you the sacred is here and now.

The Renaissance broadened the horizon with views of land, water and vegetation, stressed the ideal persona and setting, and drew the viewer into the vanishing center of its three dimensional space. It also included the pagan myths within the great religious archetypes of God, holy, sacred, celebrant and the enlightened. They also offered the pagan, Jewish and Christian stories and motifs in realistic detail as they focused more on the person and communicated a sense of movement within and among the characters depicted.

The Mannerists like Pontormo and Parmigianino elongated the figures of people and greatly expanded the range of intense color to challenge what they considered the staid, controlled and overly subdued 'perfections' of the Renaissance. The Baroque in turn dramatized everything, artists such as Rubens completing huge paintings of dramatic action and dazzling color – all of it moving across the canvass on the diagonal. Then the artists of the Rococo – Watteau, Fragonard and Tiepolo in particular - turned in another direction and replaced the dramas of the Baroque with feathery and pastel-pretty renderings of country gatherings, flirtations, mythic romances – with angels and cherubs fluttering everywhere and on every ceiling.

On and over and under and beyond, the extensions of the artistic eye have covered the spectrum - at one juncture being rational and orderly like the Neoclassicists David and Ingres, then flamboyant and dramatic like Delacroix, Friedrich and the Romantics, and then simple, commonplace and homespun like the Realists Millet and Daumier. Art like God is everywhere, expressing, expanding, deepening and re-creating everything.

The Impressionists, of course, were dazzled by the gradations of changing light, so they tried to capture the fleeting shades of the ephemeral with mere touches of the brush. The Symbolists like Moreau and Redon sort to go beyond appearances and explored the images of the inner world where dreams, the unconscious and imagination reign. The post-Impressionist van Gogh returned to the immediate and material, carving his layers of paint to depict vivid movement and transmit his deeply engaged interaction with a room, a chair, and row of trees and a starry night. Gauguin, on the other hand, adopted a primitive symbolism to explore the mystical themes of identity and the meaning of life.

Notice how seemingly every possible combination of content, archetypal theme, gradient, color, medium and process is painted, constructed or presented by one artist or another. Through art we obtain a full displays of all the aspects, particulars and reflections of ubiquitous humanity-nature-divinity, each era filling in the gaps left by their predecessors. Put them together and we have a rendering of the full story of our incarnational universe – that is until the newest artist on the scene 'sees', intuits or experiences what had not been rendered before – some new and emerging vista which 'needs' to be depicted from still one more vantage point.

So the Fauvists, for example – Derain, Matisse, Vlaminck – in essence noticed something was missing in the Impressionists and Post-Impressionists, so they quickly moved to complete the ever-expanding set of possibilities, outraging the critics with blue trees, green faces and stark juxtapositions of primary colors. Ah – but there was still one more way of viewing reality so the Cubists like Picasso and Braque dissected and reconstructed everyday objects into moving time frames experienced from multiple perspectives.

Still creation is not over; it is constant and continuing. So up come the Surrealists – de Chiroco and Dali among them – to dramatize the irrational pictures of the dream state while the Futurists make their contribution to universality by unfurling their fascination with speed and movement. Meanwhile Kandinsky, Mondrian and then Pollock add to the ever-deepening and uplifting reach of the spiral by growing increasingly abstract - blatantly declaring the superior role of the artist's inner eye over anything that merely reproduced any outer image of Nature.

On and on, change upon change, one approach amplified by another, the brash and the nuanced, basic life situations, grand archetypes and the endless pursuit of Spirit depicted in every style, context and perspective imaginable. And look at the range of approaches: a dab here, a dot there, a brush of paint then a layer over it. There is canvass, marble, plaster, plastic, bicycle parts – and even videos, mirrors and sound machines. That which is captured, arranged and celebrated by one of the senses is quickly supplemented by another perspective. Realistic scenes, concocted faces, found and purchased bits and pieces arranged – and sometimes flung together at random. Everything, everything: every degree of an expanding spiral of possibilities – artistic incarnations constantly released into the world at every conceivable pace and angle.

If the Spirit of God is everywhere and in all things, revealed in every texture, color and vantage point, then Its presence has been celebrated in art from gold leaf and pastel, posters and metal constructs, mere words arranged on a canvass and linens adorning Central Park. If you prefer anything in particular - from the rich, detailed and ornate flowerings of the International Gothic Style to the austere and simple renderings of the Minimalists - you can and will find it reflected in one artistic temperament or another. It is as if each artist and style – like each variation in spiritual practice – perceived a particular aspect of God and gloried in reflecting that slice of Its reality back to its Source. Together, spirituality and art reflect both sides of the spiritual coin: a story of God constructing the next layer of the infinitely expanding Kosmos, and the story of the resident artists documenting that creative evolution.

If you wish to understand humankind and its creative spirit, indeed its Godliness, then visit its studios, museums and galleries. These are the cathedrals and temples of artistic inspiration. It is within their rooms and corridors, on their canvasses and in their sculptures, that we constantly rediscover the essence of both That Which Is and That Which Will Be: immanence unbounded, transcendence in flight, from pigeon to peacock, all the attributes and expressions of God – all in full array, all simultaneously front and center.

Depicting the Luminous

What is so fascinating about viewing art is that you get to experience mystical depictions of life's archetypal moments. Among others, there is birth, death, a calling, celebration, sadness, courtship, friendship, the thrill of a sunrise or sunset, children, playfulness, mentoring, as well as joy, sadness and reflection. Attuned people like artists are able to depict such poignant moments as luminous distillations of reality. Viewing them is like experiencing a succession 'eurekas'.

Caravaggio used his trademark of stark lighting and shadows to capture the startled look of Matthew as the outstretched hand of Yeshua summoned him to the next phase of his life (Contarelli Chapel, Church of San Luigi dei Francesi, Rome). The scene, of course, is from the New or Christian Testament yet it invokes a deeper, older, generic, universal or archetypal experience of anyone called to respond to a 'higher' vision, and who thereafter embraces a mission that supercedes the current or ordinary one, that encourages a commitment to that which is bigger than oneself and more significant than anything they had undertaken before.

Michelangelo, who was driven to understand, invigorate and express Life, depicted the tips of two fingers – each reaching out to each other – to portray the momentous occasion of creativity, when God activates the incarnation of Adam on the ceiling of the Sistine Chapel. The scene is content specific - of course - but the theme is universal: the Creator Spirit inspires the incarnated Soul or Earth-bound identity to awaken to the truth of its identity.

Of all the paintings of the Annunciation - the story of Archangel Gabriel announcing to Mary that she was pregnant with the Master Teacher, Yeshua - the canvass produced by Fra Filippo Lippi is among the most dramatic (The National Gallery, London). A hushed Gabriel is adorned in a red robe, His wings are adorned with the spotted-eye feathers of a peacock. He leans forward slightly, one knee bent, his eyes lowered yet fixed on Mary, two fingers of his right hand extended in a blessing. Mary is seated, her red dress covered by a deep blue robe with gold trim. Her face is serene yet it also suggests full awareness. Bowing slightly at the waist, she seems to cradle the dove that hovers at her belly - the winged symbol of the Holy Spirit, sent by God the Father whose hand pierces the curtain above.

Caravaggio, Michelangelo and Fra Filippo Lippi - each in their own way expressed a variation on the archetype of creativity – that innate spirit yearning to give birth to a new form of reality.

The Inspiration

Who of us has not felt blessed by the call to create, the urge to give birth to something new and luminous, something of special merit, something that feels like an expression of a deeper and life-long mission. It could be symbolized - and epitomized - in the birth of a child and the rearing of a family. A new idea or a spiritual 'aha' could also lead to the inception of a new invention, book, organization or perspective. The next, and then the next portion of our life contracts and missions are always being activated by one more image, hunch or inner beckoning — and we are incessantly urged to give outer expression to such inspirations.

What is fascinating — as we attend closely to the process — is that the inspiration to create obviously comes before the expression of that 'inner calling'. The creative impulse is felt inwardly, motivating us to express it outwardly - or in the case of an artist, translating an inner awareness into a piece of art. The outer expression — of any sort - always reflects the energy of the inner vision. The impulse to create is thus likened to the unfolding of a physical pregnancy: conception is an internal creation and delivery is its external form or expression.

Artists seem especially attuned to their personal 'annunciations', calling them to embrace some new aspect of themselves and then revealing that expanded consciousness in a new piece of art. They trust the images and energies that emerge in their intuitions, daytime reveries and night dreams, and then pour the life force into their next form and contribution.

Michelangelo's depiction of the God-Adam dialogue, for example - symbolic of God first creating and thereafter always reaching out to us — was undoubtedly sparked by an internal infusion of insight from the Soul to the material self of Michelangelo. In the same way, the depiction of the outer events of 'The Annunciation' by Fra Filippo Lippi was a product that reflected his inner annunciation, just as the 'Calling of Matthew' also projected Caravaggio's personal calling onto a canvass.

Laughter

There is nothing like laughter - that natural response to a joke, someone's clever wit, an unpredictable outcome, a string of exaggerated reactions or an unusual twist on one of life's many comic situations. Those who create laughter — witty people, mischievous people, professional comics, pets and their antics — they are all among the world's great artists.

No brushes, no paints – just a way of seeing the human drama in all its comical potential. With a word or two, a look, the nod of a head, an array of gestures, a visual composition drawn in the air by a set of active hands – the comic makes us laugh. What artistry. What could be more spiritual than the capacity to make people laugh and create all the camaraderie it generates. Of course there are characters like the dour and aged cleric Jorge, featured in the *Name of the Rose*,[88] who wish to extinguish humor and anyone who enjoys it. But for most, what's funny about the human drama not only keeps *us* smiling; our silly habits and insecurities undoubtedly keep our Guardian Angels laughing. And rumor has it that God often laughs with us as well giving Him one more reason to be delighted in what He has created.

You can even make yourself laugh without even trying: you tilt an ordinary experience to the comical, or you see or do something unexpected – and you cannot help but laugh at yourself. The creation of laughter is also the glue of friendships and festive parties. Anyone's recreation of the habits of adults, children, dogs, certainly politicians - always stimulates a round or two of giggling. Friends, family members, lovers, even passersby – tease each other with both gentle and trenchant wit. The options to imitate others or mimic their habits are everywhere. Surely it is always a joy to be around perceptive, witty, iconoclastic and jolly people who are quick to perceive life's contradictions, ironies and juxtapositions.

Laughing not only releases pressure; it quickly brings us into the 'now' for it has the power to totally neutralize the mind's tendency to put things in rational order. A good joke is like a good jalapeño; it gets your attention and it keeps your attention. Being around funny people is particularly appreciated during times of stress and difficulty. People may complain there is too much violence and tragedy on television. No one ever complains there is too much good humor and joy.

The option and inclination to laugh has been with us since the dawn of time. The widening of the humanoid's jaw, for example, unfolded with the expansion of the human brain – giving us the means to express

---

88 Umberto Ecco, *The Name of the Rose* (New York: Harcourt Brace Javanovich, 1980).

the kinds of joyful laughter that once was not noticed by the smaller brain and not possible for the constricted jawbone.

If there is anything missing in much of early art and sculpture, it is the absence of laughter. There are a few statutes of Buddha laughing, and fewer still of a smiling Mary.[89] Plato, Moses, Yeshua, Mohammed and even Socrates and Confucius were either solemn all the time or they were depicted by artists who either had sour dispositions or worked for patrons who idealized suffering. But the Egyptians, for all their austere poses and mighty gestures, did produce a hymn to the Sun God Ra that revered the joyful side as well. "The priests go forth at dawn," it reads, and "they wash their hearts with laughter'.[90]

Ah – then there's the best of television and movies. We all have out favorites. Peter Sellers as Inspector Clouseau, anything by Mel Brooks, the old reels of Jackie Gleeson and Cheers, you could go on and on. One of most joyful scenes ever filmed, however, emerged not as a joke but as a commentary on life. It featured Anthony Quinn as Bombolini and Anna Magnani as his wife Rosa in the film, "The Secret of Santa Victoria."

Throughout the film Bombolini can't do anything right, and he earns his wife's judgment as 'the stupidest of the stupid'. But he cleverly outwits the Germans by coordinating the efforts of the townspeople to hide millions of bottles of wine in the nearby caves. Slowly his wife begins to see him in a new light: still stupid, yes – but also clever like a fox.

In the closing scene, Bombolini, a hero at last, turns to his wife for a look of reprieve. Slowly her dark scowl relents. A hint of a smile emerges as she picks up the hem of her skirt. The Germans have given up trying to discover the wine and have just departed. As their last truck exits the village square, Bombolini takes off his hat, wipes his

---

[89] There is a sign in the corner coffee shop of Bennington, VT that reads: "Buddha Died Laughing," and the Medieval Collection on the first floor of the Metropolitan Museum of Art in New York does have one sculpture of Mary sporting a definite smile. There is also another at The Cloisters: Mary is standing and holding the child Jesus, and both are smiling.

[90] Faith Javanne, *Numerology and The Divine Triangle* (Atglen, PA: Whitford Press, 1979), p.161.

brow, stares at his wife, and grins. Magnani's face softens: her austere snarl slowly gives way to a look of appreciation. She raises her eyebrows, then her chin and begins to smile. Strong glances are exchanged, and they both burst out laughing. Then they dance with abandonment – in sheer joy and celebration.

Looking Over Our Shoulder

There is a painting by Hovsep Pushman of an itinerant man with a walking stick in his hand and a bundle of belongings at his side. Behind the man is the shrouded but definable figure of Buddha.

There are similar pictures by many artists, from many periods of art, each depicting the same phenomenon in various ways. One may feature a single person, another a couple, while still others depict small grouping and even large gatherings. Yet always the human figures share the canvass with a representative of the spirit world, muted but clearly present, just to the side or the rear.

An angel – or group of them - might hover nearby, unbeknown to the main character or characters. Cherubs or putti might line the borders of a Renaissance painting. Hindu art often includes representations of Vishnu and Shiva or one of their many earthly incarnations: an aid, counselor, even a trickster. And in the depictions of the stories from Jewish and Christian scriptures, it is not uncommon to see angels hovering, walking, talking and even dining with villagers and kings.

There are several ways to interpret such paintings. Perhaps the artist is assuring us that where the material body goes so goes its invisible counterpart, the Soul. Or maybe the pictures are asserting the truism that the universe is filled with spiritual entities, which although invisible to the earthly eye, really are everywhere - all the time: assisting humans, delivering messages from God, and standing by to help distressed colleagues deal with some aspect of their incarnation.

Paintings like the one by Pushman seem to tell us that our Guardian Angel – if not God Himself - is always available for guidance and protection. Pushman may also be telling us that the itinerant man, and the Buddha, are one and the same.

Although the spiritual figure may different from artist to artist, they all convey a central message. The earth and the spirit world are linked. Whether the spirit figure is our guide, a freelance protector, a special representative sent by God, our own Soul, or God Itself, each depiction reflects the presence of Spirit in one form or another. Artists simply delete the veils that ordinarily shield such realities from view.

The character in a painting may not be aware of the angel or deity at his/her side but certainly the artist is. It is the artist who testifies to the fact that the two worlds are really one. Matter and spirit are intertwined if not the same. Spiritual energies are evident to those with the consciousness and inner artistry to sense, detect and honor them.

Inner Eye

The setting is filled with mystery: there is but one individual depicted amidst an awesome panorama of sky and land. The mood is contemplative. The effect is dramatic. The 'one' is juxtaposed to the One. Such is the drama created by the German Romantic artist, Caspar David Friedrich. *Mountain Sanctuary* (1804) - to be more descriptive - depicts a tiny pilgrim meditating at the base of a statue of a Madonna which is set on a snow-covered mountainside. A commentator refers to it as a "quest, a search for meaning in a natural world that reveals the sacred." [91]

"The artist," said Friedrich, conveys "not only what we sees before him but also what he sees within him." Thus an external site can activate the process of in-sighting as well as an inner awareness evoking the desire to express it in an external form. Either way, the two are inseparable.

---

91 *The Essential Guide: The Art Institute of Chicago* (Chicago: 1997), pages 212 (Friedrich), and 160 (Van Gogh). Selected by James N. Wood and Teri J. Edelstein, with entries written and compiled by Sally Ruth May.

At the other end of the artistic spectrum, but with similar intent, is the work of Vincent van Gogh. Rather than placing tiny figures in vast landscapes, van Gogh "prefer[red] to paint people's eyes [versus]... cathedrals [not to mention landscapes!]." It was a preference and way of seeing he displayed in his many portraits, including those of himself. "However solemn and imposing the latter may be – a human Soul...is more interesting to me," he wrote.

Similarly, artists throughout history have chosen their focus within this seemingly infinite band of possibilities. Big canvases and small; an individual, a group or the vista of the sea or land; three dimensions and the flatness of two; broad strokes, flickers and splashes; multi colors and monochrome; mere impressions to realistic details; paint, pastels, sculptured forms in stone – every approach, texture, tone, subject, technique and medium has been used by centuries of artists as they project their inner visions into outer expressions or use external stimuli to evoke and clarify what has been simmering within.

Universal Creativity

The artist is obviously able to dramatize what he or she sees, feels or intuits. But formal artistry is not the only or the predominant way we humans can project our inner values onto our external creations. We all create, all the time, and in great flourish and variety: families come into being, businesses are founded, gardens are planted and farms harvested, friendships are formed, backyards are shaped, birdhouses built and filled with nature's remnants, lives are chosen and buildings constructed. Meanwhile everyone's eyes and ears capture the light and create an incessant array of images, which when recognized by the mind, activates into an incredible array of related images, one act of creativity stimulating a series of others.

The creative mind overflows with constant creations - whether wired to the brush of an artist or the innovative senses of poets, lovers, parents, musicians, business people, engineers, writers and checkout clerks. The ubiquitous nature of creativity also provokes a series of questions on topics and processes we tend to take for granted:

- What does your eye and ear tend to notice and create?

- What particular intuitions and creative insights do you remember? Where were you and what were you doing?

- What image – or calling or creative idea – is stirring within you now?

- What excites your imagination? What activities generate ideas, insights and intuitions?

- Are you ever aware of actually being the chooser, the selector or the creator of your inner images, values and assessments? Or are you only aware of your creativity once it has been manifest in a tangible form like a painting, business decision or friendship?

- Are there any particular inner moods or outer circumstances that encourage you to think about and express the incredible power of your creative consciousness?

- Where do you go, and how do you stimulate your creative spirit?

- Under what circumstances does 'the profane' meet – and become – 'the sacred'?

- In short, what is the state of your inner eye, and what do you wish to create - and contribute – next?

What Are You Creating?

Imagine that you are an artist and your life is a painting.

Imagine as well that the various paints and brushes are the tools of your composition. Now imagine you are looking at what you have painted-created-composed to date.

There probably are some dark spots, unconnected lines or blotches. Surely there are also a lot of light and colorful areas, with a good showing of primary colors - red, yellow and blue. There may also be blends of those combinations – some orange, purple and rose perhaps, all presented in any number of hues, gradations and overlays.

Undoubtedly, your life canvass is as focused or fuzzy, integrated or fragmented, uniform or diverse – in whole or part - as your life itself. Step away from your canvass for a minute and realize how much it reveals: your major energies and patterns as well as your assumed triumphs and disappointments.

What dominant and passing themes you have painted or created? Can you now give them a name? What colors have you used for each theme, emotion or happening? And what are their approximate configurations – their shape, size and composition?

Now – please stop reading a minute - and think about - then actually draw an outline or overview of your life. Simply reach for a blank sheet of paper and a pencil, a set of colored pens or crayons, or a brush and paints. Then draw an outline of your life down on that paper – not with words – but with shapes and contours and colors. A quick sketch is all that is needed. Trust yourself.

Don't fret over it: just express whatever is on your mind – now. You could approach it like Jackson Pollock - changing it as you go by adding colors and contours. You could be meticulous or spontaneous. Big lines, little dots or geometric shapes: whatever you wish. Have fun. See what happens. You can always return to it later to add a detail, change something, elaborate or begin anew.

Step Back and Assess

Whenever you have finished your depiction of your life, please consider the following.

(1) On a separate sheet of paper - make a list that summarizes your dominant or recurring issues and themes. Chose only a word or two or three – to capture the essence of the issue. For example, you could note the general themes of family, parenting, getting that degree, fighting the glass ceiling, expressing spirituality or asserting your self. You might also note how you have tended to handle yourself: angry, loving, carefree, creative, too giving, controlling, needing to assert, or whatever energies you have displayed or yearned for. Make the list as long as

possible. If you think of something, just write it down. You can always edit or ignore an item later.

(2) Review your entire list and choose no more than approximately four to five items by underlining or circling them. Be sure to reduce each item you select to a label or header phrase of a word or two, and write each one on a piece of Post-In (an inch or so high and long).

(3) Now place each of the labels next to the portion of your drawing that you think best represents that theme or issue. Move your labels around as you see fit. Do you see any natural connections or combinations of items?

(4) What does your drawing tell you? Note the obvious as well as any new clarities and discoveries.

(5) Now change, elaborate or minimize anything in the drawing that you now think makes it an even better expression of your life.

Ah: Now for Your Desired Future

A. What creative and artistic choices do you *now* wish to make regarding your future? On a new and blank sheet of paper, draw your desired depiction of your future. Again: use any basic lines, squiggles and shapes you want, and then embellish it any way you wish with color and markings.

B. Whatever you do, please realize any drawing of your life will have an assured value at six gazillion pieces of gold. Please note as well that the prize money henceforth will double each time you choose to be completely honest, and it will triple if any of your drawing makes you smile.

C. On a separate piece of paper, list any of the themes, issues, roles and/or traits you wish to attract into your life. Choose four or five of them by underlining or circling them.

D. Then label each issue with a simple word or two, or a short catch phrase. Copy each label onto the appropriate part of your drawing. You could also list your labels off to the side, placing only the designated numbers on your diagram. Pointers can also help you designate which label goes where.

E. As you proceed, feel free to add, delete, enhance or change whatever you want in both your drawing and your labels.

F. Then assess what you've created. Be particularly aware of the following:

- What are your dominant themes? What delights you? Compare the drawing of your current life to this one of the future. What have you continued, enhanced, added, de-emphasized or dropped from your listing? Which of your current issues do you now consider complete? Are there any new starts, changes additions or innovations?

- How will any of the new items or emphases impact your life?

- Where is your Soul in all this? Where is Spirit?

- What is - or is likely to be - your next creation and contribution?

CHAPTER 29

CHOOSING AND CREATING

Not Theory But Practice

Our spiritual capacity is not dependent on any external catechism. They are too cerebral, tainted by phobias and fears, and filled with requirements and threats. Our capacity to be at one with and emulate the loving Spirit has nothing to do with theological systems, codifications, beliefs, worshipping historical heroes or heroines, or adhering to specified structures and culturally defined rituals.

Rather, everything depends on what we do, on the choices we make in the concrete world of everyday living. Believe what you want – but spiritual behavior means choosing deliberatively to act with love and compassion: simple, helpful, responsive, affirming. Our spiritual endowment is thus activated by our own choices, beginning with our affirmation of unity with Prime Spirit. Then we can naturally choose to create a spiritual practice that manifests who we are and how we can best fulfil our mission on Earth – given our unique circumstances, traits and challenges.

Our practice might include whatever symbols reinforce our image of Soulfulness. It could also include a set of invocations, prayers and ways of meditating. Similarly, we might participate in an array of rituals and ceremonies, perhaps blending childhood practices with those we've acquired or created along the way. Gestures, stances, ways of greeting and honoring others and the Earth, drawing on the world's sacred literature and emulating the behaviors of those we consider exemplary are also among the ways we each can nurture Spirit in our tiny but oh-so significant parts of the universe.

If we like last year's amalgam, we can decide to renew it. It not, we add this and delete that – allowing ourselves to tinker if not transform parts of our practice any time such modifications seem necessary to insure full consciousness and vitality.

The choice is always ours. Choosing our own way of expressing our spirituality is the best way to affirm our immortal Souls, nurture and update our development and pay homage to the trust the creator God has placed in us.

Be Aware

Awareness holds the key to everything. It opens the door to conscious choice, and then to consciousness itself.

Awareness of what we do and why enables us to be free – free of unthinking and habitual behavior that is locked into the patterns of the past or somebody else's images of tomorrow. Awareness means we are able to choose freely now, and now, and now - and thus always live in the present – able to reorganize any behaviors and structures in order to retain vivid contact with the creative Soul. Remember: it is always our Soul that we seek to express, that sacred identity which – with each decision - chooses *who we are, what we attend to, and what we want to become.*

Without the Soul's awareness of Itself, we surrender our power and risk being enslaved by the ego. The ego makes its contribution by coordinating the implementation of our external choices; it is not, however, the source of our inner power. And the source of that inner power, the Soul, can become shrouded unless we continually reactivate our *awareness* of it and affirm our trust in its instincts, impulses, decisions and empowerments.

Without awareness, the immediacy of the present is avoided, denied, never experienced – and the personality gets stuck in rehearsing its memories and regrets of the past, or lapses into fear and anxiety as it approaches its unknown future. With awareness, however, we stop the ego-incarnate from constantly checking its thoughts and actions against those limited views of past and future. In the hands of the Soul, the might-have-been and concerns for the future are transformed in favor of this instant and the potential of this immediate situation.

Awareness dissolves calcification, and the slow accumulation of walls and presumed limitations. It insures that we never become a slave to ego fashion or someone else's concept of who we were, are or ought to be. To be aware is to be awake - now - to all the creative options only the Soul can truly recognize and utilize.[92]

Awareness is scary because it affirms and utilizes our freedom. It is mostly sail and little anchor, yet invites us to moor our ship wherever we wish and then invite on board any packets of energy that supports our unfolding journey.

We know how we operate: that's awareness. We trust our intentions to create our experience: that is awareness. We live in the moment and thus create our continuing evolution: that is awareness.

When we deliberatively choose to get out of our own way and give up old, dysfunctional goals and perspectives – then we are in the flow of awareness. When we let go of old habits, outmoded ways of operating, egotistic goal-setting, and career and community ties that no longer support our spiritual journey - then we know we are ready, able and willing to embrace the next phrase of our ministry.

The Choice to Recreate

When you stop to think about it – really pause and reflect – you become conscious of the fact that you make hundreds if not thousands of decisions a day.

And each decision has the power to perpetuate the status quo. It also has the power to create a new platform - a new approach, a new adventure, a new way of behaving, a creative way of honoring and

---

[92] For further commentary of these points, see Robert Sardello, *Facing the World With Soul* (Hudson, NY: Lindsfarne Press, 1992); Gary Zukav, *The Mind of the Soul* (New York, Free Press, 2003); and Eckhart Tolle, *A New Earth* (New York: Dutton, 2005), and *The Power of Now* (Novato, CA: New World Library, 1999).

expressing yourself that probably was yearning to emerge - for who knows how long.

As I drive to town each morning, I realize I can stop for a cup of coffee at one of five different places, and within each shop I have several options for the type of coffee and bread I might order. En route, I may also begin canvassing the possibilities for the day: what to write today; what books, music and DVD programs I might tune into; and where and how I might take my exercise breaks. Then there are the choices that arise on the spot all through the day: what present to buy for an up-coming birthday, what to say to X when I see her, what to buy for dinner, and on and on – a string of innocent but at times important decisions affecting me and others.

Now for the difficult – or adventurous – stuff. I may have been annoyed with someone last week. What is my feeling and thus intention this week when we inevitably meet? I can choose to be loving or still annoyed, deliberately choose the higher road and let go of the lower. Such processes, images and inner chatter go on all day. No one decision on any one issue may be monumental in itself but cumulatively they create or reinforce a way of looking at, approaching and experiencing the world.

For example, let us assume that I was testy for much of the past week. Tomorrow opens a new page on the calendar. As it begins and unfolds, I may create - or simply recognize - ample reason to feel differently and create a new beginning – if only I allow myself to choose a new path versus repeating the one I already know so well. I realize I can choose to image my mind and my life as flypaper (as I often do) - allowing every silly and allegedly negative thing to stick to me. Or I can image my mind – and my life as 'writing on water' to paraphrase the epitaph of John Keats – and allow me the freedom to compose each new moment as it unfolds.

Not wanting anything to be incised in stone, or stick like gum to my shoe - I decide not only to let last week go but to nurture images that are loving and positive. With such a clean and upbeat lens, I realize that I no longer have to act consistently with former decisions but can enter into each aspect of each day with freedom and spontaneity. I keep the invitation to be compassionate in my frontal lobe, I just might optimize my ability to do so.

Choice point, choice point, choice point. Still – for another few seconds, I teeter back and forth. Choosing to tilt my lens to the positive could alter the direction of my life. But my earlier week of negativity has its own grooves and built-in excuses: I will miss my opportunity to be negative and self-pitying. They enable me to feel superior. It's hard to give up such rewards – even though I know they are self-defeating.

Whatever image, vision, energy or outcome you or I hold in mind quickly becomes a magnet for attracting the series of memories that allegedly prove its validity. What you sow, you grow – and must now mow. What you plant, you nurture and harvest. Garbage ordered, garbage delivered, garbage consumed. And being on 'automatic' is so much easier than catching yourself, taking a leap of faith and making a new start. The old way, mood or memory can only be destructed in the same way in which it was constructed - little by little, choice by choice. The new mindset can only be constructed by this next choice and then the next.

Realizing that everything presents a choice point is my saving grace. When I glide along on any track – and surrender my awareness and responsibility to choose – I go on automatic, become more of a machine than a person, no less a spiritual one. It is an enormous act of the will to reverse direction and reach for a larger, more loving and more likeable image of myself.

It really is that profound and that simple. After a while, you become so aware of your power to choose the big and the little frames of reference that it is a lot like turning the dial on the washing machine. Do I want 'cold'? Then push the 'angry-because-hurt' button. Or would 'warm' be best, suggesting you are - 'softening but-still-unsure'. Of course, there is always 'hot' - signaling your decision to drop the 'cold' and 'warm' - and go for the 'loving-and-joyful'.

You can even choose the speed at which you wish to wash away the old and make a clean start: 'slowly', 'with moderation' or 'now, presto and with gusto'?

Your next - and your last - set of washing choices is also important: how much love and joy – or whatever you want this time - can you handle: just a 'small' amount, something that is 'medium' or do your really want to 'fill it to the top'?

Your choice. Your set of little and big decisions. Your wash. Your laundry. Your wardrobe. Your life.

It's That Easy

Stay awake and be aware.

Be gentle with yourself.

Enjoy the process of living.

Revel in the joy of creating – images, ideas, actions.

Give thanks.

Choose.

Bow.

And

Walk on.

Paradise

When I moved to Maine years ago, I thought it was paradise: open spaces, trees, L.L. Bean, with both the ocean and the mountains nearby. Then I discovered people were people: there was politics, jealousies and the same percentage of shirkers, braggarts and litterbugs as anywhere else.

When I moved to Florida, I thought it was paradise: warm weather, scandals, a relaxed atmosphere dominated by ocean waves and palm trees. Then I discovered the condo cops monitoring every alleged violation of the rules, very hot and humid weather for six months of the year, and a lot of people who thought Wal-Mart and Elvis impersonators were quality entertainment.

Now I recall that I experienced the same mixture of great expectations - neutralized by the normal imperfections - during my stays in Madison, Wisconsin and then New York City as a graduate student. Ditto for my working stints in Washington, D.C.; Detroit and Oakland, Michigan; Buffalo, New York, and the north towns of Boston. And to my even greater surprise, I ran into the same mix of the wonderful and the awful during my extended stays in Ireland, Spain, and the old Soviet Union.

I have loved everywhere I have lived and travelled but have never discovered a location that offered sustained paradise. Aspects of the grand and the silly, the loving and the egocentric are evident everywhere. Could it be there are bits of both lodged in my cranium and living in my luggage?

No more fantasizing, I pledged at each juncture. Yet great expectations continued to be followed by periodic bouts of shaking my fist at the heavens. The indiscretions of people are universal, the weather keeps changing and our own demons are a constant companion. Where-o-where is that illusive paradise? Everywhere I go I need to purchase a new pair of transitional lenses to replace the rose tinted ones I brought with me.

I settle now for realism, an attitude that knows happiness is both a creation and a projection. The world mirrors us. Why not have fun with it and learn to scamper joyfully between the raindrops? In the meantime, what is silly can be avoided, what is unwanted can be neutralized, and what is nourishing can be cultivated. What unfolds around the bend involves recalibrating the fit between our evolving interests and the setting in which we choose to negotiate the next phase of our drama.

In the final analysis, it seems we are all capable of creating whatever bit of heaven, hell or limbo we choose - as long as we realize there's usually a gap between expectation and experience. Our hopes for *this and that* do not eliminate the appearance of their opposites since we, and the people, locales and situations we choose, are always churning and alternating between what is pristine clear and what can be downright muddy. Since it is we who choose our internal dispositions as well as our destinations, however, it seems only right that we assume prime responsibility for how we experience the situations we attract, interpret and thus play the major role in creating.

Once we realize what we choose to minimize, and what we want to multiply, then we are free to create the experience we want in any setting we enter. Learning to experience reality as loving and joyful – albeit varied and occasionally challenging - is a test of the inner self, not of others or the environment. Happy people are most often happy any and everywhere. And sad ones can convert the best of circumstances into a litany of complaints. Let's face it - we really are like turtles: we basically grow our own homesteads and carry them with us.

Authenticity and Compassion

Questions: How do you stay informed of the horrors experienced by many around the world without becoming jaded and negative? How do you also extend help and compassion to those within reach, yet not get overwhelmed and consumed by the cumulative grief you cannot reach?

A Possible Response: Such issues are at the center of living in the world with awareness and compassion. It is a cop-out to seal off our emotions when confronted by reports of tragedy. We also lose perspective if we allow ourselves to become emotionally paralyzed by our own egocentric and sentimental assumptions that we need to take care of everyone. The heart need not be buried beneath layers of denial or worn on one's sleeve. A middle ground does exist – which includes giving:

1. direct support to those in your immediate area (family, friends and neighbors), and which could take the form of listening, helping, and the gift of time and attention.

2. indirect material support in the form of financial contributions to organizations that help the needy all over the world, and

3. intentional energetic and prayerful support for anyone or situation you sense needs it – including those you hear or read about in the news.

Wanting to be at or go to the scene of a difficulty in order to attend directly to others is instinctual to most: you listen, you counsel, you bring chicken soup, assist in running errands, you even help financially: you do what you can. That is as it should be since we chose our earthly placements in part so we can provide direct service to those within our immediate community of family and friends.

Providing indirect support, however, can be the most difficult to accomplish: the people and situations we hear about in the news are usually hundreds if not thousands of miles away. We would prefer to meet those affected, hold their hand, listen to their story, provide some concrete support and in some way help to relieve their suffering. Cut off from direct contact, however, we do what we can: we give money, food and clothing to organizations like the Red Cross and the Salvation Army.

The third kind of outreach, sending healing energies and prayerful thoughts to others, is probably the most important and transformative of all the strategies. People – both those in need and those who wish to help those in need – often use the expression, "So finally I decided to pray." Hmm. Actually, prayer is the first thing any of us should do. It sets the foundation for attracting and delivering what is needed. And it reminds us of our common heritage: we are all spiritual beings here to help each other deal with the experiences and issues of the Earth.

So begin with prayer and continue to pray for those in need. And this applies to anyone and any issue that catches your attention: your family and friends, the folks you read about in the press, those hurt in local tragedies as well as those injured half way around the world.

Remember, however, the advice given in Chapter 21 on "Prayer". Do not be specific regarding the precise kind of energy you send to another. Intending love and sending a loving intention is about as fine as you can get. And do not wish for a certain outcome. Simply 'send' - or mentally communicate - the energy to the other as an unspecified gift, to be used by them as they see fit. Unbeknown to us, someone may want to stop a physical pain or simply learn to live with the situation, find a creative solution for a difficult situation or use your loving energies to obtain the courage to accept their own transition. It is their life, their contract and their commission. So send your prayers and loving thoughts and intentions, wish them the best, and then get out of the way.

The impact of such giving - through both intended prayer and meditation - also rebounds on the sender. As we include more people and situations in our spiritual concern – gifting both loving prayers and, where possible, a personal appearance and a material contribution - we naturally uplift and perfect our own state of consciousness. We not only help others but in so doing create a positive outlet for our empathy and compassion. As Mohammed Ali has emphasized: "I only have so much time to help as many as I can."

Spiritual Snobbery, and Humility

Spiritual snobbery – like any form of hubris – can take many forms. It connotes an attitude of 'better or holier than thou', a perspective of looking down on someone or something because it is assumed they or it are inferior. The synonyms for such behavior are arrogance, condescension, pretentiousness and conceit.

Spiritual snobbery can be a one-time thing or a pervasive way of living. Among its perpetrators are extreme fundamentalists of all religions, who think only they have access to God, making their way the only way – tolerance for diversity be damned. Such people are so smitten by a sense of righteousness that they do not hesitate – on a routine basis - to pass judgment on others. Basically, the words and actions of such spiritual snobs focus solely on their own self-centered agendas - on protecting and propagating what they consider to be unalterably right and true whether that be a creed, code of conduct or form of worship.

Examples of spiritual snobbery might include:

- Dismissing, criticizing or condemning someone for their words or behavior – and then compounding the felony by promising to pray for them.

- Assuming their way is the only way, their church or belief system the only true or correct religion.

- Condemning the views of others as blasphemous or their practices as sacrilege (as if there was only one specified way to think or behave).

- Justifying punishment or damnation for those who do not adhere to the 'evaluator's' religious creeds or practices.

Humility – of course – has a totally different rhythm and cadence. It is softer, uncritical, non-judgmental. The humble person may affirm their own spiritual preferences but never scowl or dismiss the attitudes or actions of others. Rather than criticizing the choices made by others, humble people and groups seek to honor everyone's preferences while simultaneously searching for common ground.

Examples of humble yet devoted spirituality abound.

- The calm, ease, and loving presence of the Dalai Lama.

- The loving acceptance exemplified by the demeanor of the Rev. Gene Robinson of New Hampshire, the first openly gay bishop of the Episcopal Church of America, elected and apparently adored by both his local congregation and the Governing Council of his Church.

- The loving mercies exhibited by Nelson Mandela, Bishop Tutu and the Commission on Reconciliation of South Africa, rejected retribution in favor of healing and forgiveness for those involved in their country's long history of apartheid.

- The words and actions of the many parents who listen to their children, honor their individual needs and interests, help them clarify and attain their goals, and realize that although their children came through them they are still individual Souls with their own sense of integrity, learning contracts and missions.

- Who would *you* add to the list - anyone in particular, perhaps someone in your own family or set of friends and acquaintances?

Wider and Deeper

If you want to experience a new perspective, or go beyond your limited way of viewing the universe, then borrow or buy yourself a good magnifying lens and a set of binoculars.

The magnifying lens can come with 5, 10 and 20x magnifications. Any optic firm like Bausch & Lomb will have a variety of them. The magnification of a pair of binoculars could be a low as 10 x 50, which is also the lower end of magnification of a basic telescope. Several manufacturers advertise regularly in such publications as *Astronomy*. As to seeing at the micro level, a number of firms and educational outlets also sell relatively inexpensive microscopes.

The human eye is a wonderful thing - allowing us to see up close and far away. Its wide aperture and ability to shift also enables us to see peripherally to almost 180 degrees (or almost 90 on either side). So what can a set of additional lenses do that our eyes alone cannot do? Magnification, of course, for both macro or telescopic viewing, as well as micro or microscopic explorations.

The options are numerous and mind numbing on the macro scale. With binoculars, no less a telescope, you can seemingly see *forever* - with enormous expanses of the universe becoming suddenly available. Light travels at 186,000 miles a second and most of the stars visible in the sky date from 100,000 to millions of light years away. Do the math and see the string of zeros that matches the distance your binoculars or telescope can bring into view.

If you like the vistas, wait until you rediscover the ultimate in panoramic scenery: Andromeda, Cassiopeia, the Pleiades, the Great Nebula of Orion, the periodic movement of the planets, the bright stars like Capella, Bertelgeuse, Rigel, Arcturus and Alpha Centurus, the wide path of the Milky Way, and behind them all, far distant still, are the intimations - captured in the probes of the Hubble telescope – of an ever-expanding universe filled with galaxies traveling away from us at speeds that increase with distance.

At the micro level, the entire universe of flower power is yours: pistil, stamen and even the golden-red pollen are brought into full and magnificent view. The interior of each flower is a kaleidoscope of dazzling colors arranged in a vast variety of symmetrical designs. The veins of leaves, the contours of tree barks, the tentacles of bugs, and the intricate patterns on the back of frogs and turtles suddenly become accessible. Examining the tiniest aspect of nature - including the lines of your hand with a magnifying lens or your own blood cells under a microscope - not only offers new perspectives. It opens up whole new worlds.

Perspectives change in many ways. Try sitting or kneeling down to the level of a child for ten minutes and you might better understand their 'view' of the world. Do the same in a wheel chair, or from a jail cell or hospital bed. The options are as varied as the world's circumstances, each stance awakening in us another way of seeing and experiencing another slice of reality.

Change the lens and you literally change your point of view. Adopt a new perspective and you deepen your experience. Deepen your experience, and you expand your awareness. Expand your awareness, and you broaden your appreciation of life's multiple dimensions.

Attractions and Creations

The more fearful we are, the more we attract something to fear. The more relaxed and courageous we are, the more accessible the universe becomes. Whatever we project sets off energies that inevitably boom-a-rang and circle on back to us.

So who can really be surprised when your suspicion of the person next door reverberates at your own door, and spreads down your street and throughout your neighborhood. Reverse field. Want to detect your inner energy patterns? Then examine what is happening in your life. Who and what has entered or re-entered your life recently? What kinds of energy do those people, events and experiences represent? In short, the kind of energy you are exuding is represented in the people and circumstances your attract.

The universe operates like a series of magnetic fields that attract compatible objects to it – like a series of self-fulfilling prophecies. You could, for example, strike a tuning fork and anything attuned to its pitch and tone will vibrate with it. Whatever your disposition, you will create and attract similar vibratory energies.

So ask yourself: What have I done to attract this set of positive, negative or neutral events and energies? What images, motivations and activities have I generated or propagated to account for the kinds of experiences and events I am attracting?

Obviously, there is no absolute one-to-one correspondence for there may be multiple factors involved. But over time, the patterns of experience reflect the kinds of energies we – consciously or unconsciously – have been choosing, exuding, creating and thus attracting. We receive and experience reflections of our own energy patterns. Each of us operates like a magnet or a tuning fork. In short, what we choose to send around - does indeed come around.

You Become

- What you image and project.
- A manifestation of the words, gestures and mannerisms - you choose.
- An embodiment of your dreams and visions.
- The contents of what you have been intending and imaging.
- The fulfillment of your own prophecies.
- A walking demonstration of how you smile.

- A personification of how you greet people.
- What you focus on and emphasize.
- The face and body of your energy patterns.
- A mirror of what you value.
- The persona you adopt in dealing with others.
- Whatever you affirm and celebrate.

Whatever you think, and image, and feel and do - you become, to your regret or enhancement. So be careful. You are an elongation and embodiment of your thoughts and intentions. And who you become, is the person you have chosen to be. Do your own calculations; it all adds up. You are and continually become your image of yourself. You are who and what you create. You mold yourself with your every feeling, intuition, image and activity. Choose wisely – preferably with love and joy – for you are creating the quality of both your *incarnated life* and your *Soul*.

CHAPTER 30

SACRED PARTNERS

Together

Think 'partners'. Not winning or losing. Not going it alone. Not following the tribe, 'them', or any group or organization that values assent over inquiry and discovery. Not needing to obey authority or bow to hierarchy – at least for its own sake. No, no, no. Nothing so unconscious, blind, self-negating, predetermined...as that.

Rather think of kindred spirits,

>   Coming together to share,

>   Helping each other,

Giving and receiving,

>   Highlighting what's best,

>   Honoring self and the other.

Water, mist and ice

>   The same but different,

>   Transforming as One.

You, Me and Prime Source -

>   A trinity sharing

>   Of the same essence

Made in likeness

> All mirror reflections
>
> The Whole and Its partners

The Energy and Its aspects

> Binding, Co-creating
>
> The continual unfolding.

The Pedestal

Talking with Archangel Gabriel can be an awesome experience.

Did it really happen? Was it really him?

I was literally shaking: the reading ended with a loud (and I mean very load) and sharp cracking sound that sounded like a bolt of lightning. Three times it struck: wham, wham, wham — in the space immediately next to my chair. Dumbfounded, amazed, I shared the experience with my good friend, John Hornecker of South Carolina.

John is as humble and soft-spoken a person as you would ever meet. And he is insightful; his heart and mind travel wide and deep.

"Sure it happened," he said gently. "In terms of your reactions," he added, "namely your reverence for Gabriel: you might want to bring him down from that pedestal — or climb up there with him."

I still remember those three tremors, and those words, and my shocked wonder at it all. As I absorbed John's counsel, I came to understand that it was our birth-right to also partner with the other aspects of Spirit - no matter how much we honored them and how much human history had reason to be awed by their appearance.

Gabriel is revered for being exactly who he is, a teacher and facilitator of spiritual development par excellence. He is the ultimate in the spiritual evocateur, assigned by God to remind us who we really are and thereupon willingly embrace our next assignment. Yet he is simultaneously a beloved friend.

Fundamentally, we are all part and parcel of Divinity. It makes no difference who stands where…or how high; we each play different roles. Some have truly enormous responsibilities – such as Gabriel – while smaller domains are reserved for each individual Soul. Yet each of us – an Archangel or a Soul in human clothing – is equally beloved by God.

A pedestal among partners is really no pedestal at all. Yet it does symbolize admiration, respect and great appreciation.

Creating Kosmic Consciousness

The capacity – our capacity – to co-create the universe in partnership with Prime Source is an awesome power and responsibility.

Each new incarnation, and each detailed circumstance within that incarnation, is a new opportunity to create a new experience. A person with my or your nose and interests, sensibilities, skills and outlook has never occurred before. Even our living context is unique: our feelings, thoughts and assessments may be variations on generic themes encountered by others yet are still experientially one of a kind.

Our particular way of expressing our emotions, in combination with our individual aptitudes, interests and perspectives, converging as they all do around the people, events and places of our particular life, makes each of us an original and thus the source of new data for the Prime Creator.

The creation and flow of new information does not stop there, however. Our feelings and actions intersect with the feelings and activities of many others which in turn stimulate ripples of interactions among our combined contacts. The repercussions of one word or gesture can fan out in every direction, with its intent and impact of kindness or anger – being passed from one person to another, potentially uplifting or diminishing thousands in just one day.

This is what the Buddhists mean by the web of experience: everything is related; everything is interactive and a casual expression of everything else. Very word and activity – whether motivated by love or hatred - creates a ripple effect that can influence the energies that pervade not just our immediate neighborhood. Rather it can grow exponentially and affect the entire globe – especially when reinforced by like-minded people.

So there are four major factors in the development of kosmic consciousness: (1) our personal choices create the basis for (2) the series of self-replicating energies and impacts, (3) all of which are conveyed to God (4) Who uses them to adjust the patterns of the universe as S/He continuously recreates the Kosmos.

That's the way the Kosmic system operates. It suggests we had best become aware of what we do and how we act, deliberately choosing our perspectives and activities with a mind to increasing the love and consciousness of our communities and environments.

The more aware we individual Souls become of our enormous power to create, the more consciously we become in choosing one intention or action over another. And the more conscious we are, the more we're able to create the ripple effects we prefer. Given the potential multiplying impacts of our individual choices, it is extremely important that we deliberately choose to intend spiritual essentials like love, joy, healing, gratitude and trust versus allowing our actions to be motivated willy-nilly by neutrals and negatives.

Surely God is Listening

The transmission lines from our hearts to the creative Spirit are never dependent on the weather or our vocal cords. Whatever we image and intend, whatever we do and create is registered, and whatever we pray for gets through to God. It's doubtful if God is swayed by just a majority opinion although maybe God is now allowing us to inherit the fruit of our collective labors - which might explain in part why we as individuals, communities and citizens of the same planet occasionally experience a series of setbacks or advances. If so, then it is paramount that each of us deepen and expand our spirituality. Surely God will continue to recreate a universe that reflects our individual and thus communal best intentions and behaviors. So it is wise for us to be resolute and communicate our loving intentions and actions - with regularity, devotion and focus.

What specific messages would we wish to convey to God as She ponders the next cycle of recreations? What new creations and blessings might our prayers and collective behavior earn? What additional gifts and blessings could we stimulate within the mind of God that would improve the lives of the needy, quiet the hatred and discord among people and nations, and enhance the spiritual welfare of everyone – including individuals, communities and the entire planet?

In the category of, 'wouldn't it be nice', would it not be wonderful if our cumulative efforts earned the right to have more 'Old Souls' appear on our planet, Souls with extraordinary skills, accomplished in the ways of the Spirit, able to stimulate all of us to exert our spiritual empowerments? Such an infusion of extraordinary spiritual talent might include welcoming more and more Indigo and Golden children – Souls who have, through many past incarnations, also perfected their ability to use their spiritual identities to great effectiveness. The cumulative effect of all such appearances could also help to stimulate the recognition and advancement of the very Avatars, Master Teachers and Ascended Masters we may need to guide the way…both those already in our midst as well as those about to re-enter our earthly realm.

The data about the difficult state our planet is on hand – demonstrated by the series of international difficulties and destructions that have besieged nearly every aspect of the international community during the period of 2012-2016. The emerging patterns may soon encourage God to empower the Angels to walk visibly among us as part of the grand renewal of the planet. Such a mass landing of angelic beings would certainly convince everyone that the universe is indeed One and that God's love continues to bless the Earth. Our cumulative prayers might also earn us the right to have our everyday, human consciousness elevated to the fourth, fifth and sixth dimensions. Perhaps our prayers might even hasten the emergence of a new or second planetary Earth – needed to house and nurture those who ready to move onto a higher dimension.

Who knows what will happen. Perhaps God is at this instant weighing the option to upgrade our individual and global reality by enabling the inhabitants of another dimensions to pierce the thin veil that now separates us and thus share their capacity for deeper levels of consciousness. Certainly a loving signal from a distant planet would also help to unite our people, motivate us to resolve our many wars and disputes, and transform the hearts of any who exult in only the motivations of exclusion, power and greed.

Everything we think, intend and do helps to inform God of our needs and preferences. We are Her constituent parts. Let us deliver an overwhelming message, one that will stop the bickering, shelve the guns, open the purses and enable the essence of the Special Olympics to reign supreme. When one child fell during a race at the Special Olympics a few years ago, the other participants (not 'contestants') stopped, went back, and helped the fallen boy to his feet. Then they all held hands and made sure they crossed the finish line together.

Small Details, Grand Scale

Life is an opportunity to express
the spiritual yearnings of the Soul.
The small details of daily existence
may not seem important at the time
but they are powerful
in the grand scheme of things.
Is it not awesome to realize
that each of us is helping
to construct a Kosmos
and that we are doing so
in partnership with God?!

Who Am I?

Identity. What is it? Am I merely the name on my passport, the persona pictured on my driver's license, the long list of roles and responsibilities I associate with my personal life, the set of traits I reveal in my interactions with others, the list of alleged accomplishments I affirm on my resume? Am I only the historical grooves I've recorded on an otherwise blank tape or empty caulk board?

Erase all those lists, labels, pictures and impressions that comprise 'my record' – and all that is left is the tabula, the tablet, the bulletin board, the kiosk or whatever I wish to call my original canvas.

What then? Just because the slate has been emptied and wiped clean does not mean I am without meaning. Only the historical scratching of my current biography will have been dissolved. Only the temporary stuff will have disappeared. But such ephemeral markings have always depended on the sustained presence of the substance that made such passing notations possible.

Ink dries, glue crumples, pictures fade, paint cracks, chalk marks are easily smudged, paper yellows, computer files disappear, and even tape loses its adherence. The accidental is always an add-on to the substantive. And even though many of our additions are desirable at the time – they are by their very nature temporary and fleeting. Even the body and face they adorn will fade and deteriorate. The tattered externals lack the substance of the inner essence; the peripheral cannot hold, yet the central core – ever present although invisible – does prevail.

The essence of our identity, then, is pure consciousness, awareness of the internal 'knower' and chooser who watches the embodiment do what it does, that observes it playing at the being an important person, a potential number one – scared out of its wits for fear that all the appellations it has accumulated will not last. The Soul notices everything but wisely allows none of it to stick or adhere. We attract all sorts of attributes that help as long as we remain in the Earthly domain – yet ultimately shed any and all attributes that overexert themselves and begin to act as if they were the substance itself.

So our core identity is a form of 'isness' or beingness, an immortal particle of the 'It' that creates and underlies it all. We and 'It' are one. We are manifestations of the Kosmic Soul, the Center, the Whatness. We are parts of the original and underlying rhizome because we are one of the gazillion shoots It created to spread its message and reflect Its essence. We share in the energy of 'Its' immortality. We are aspects of the sentient Being, the sine qua non of Life, the Force Field that begets history yet ultimately dissolves time and space.

We are local representatives of the Eye behind all eyes, that divine 'I' that supports the meanderings and personal accumulations we mistakenly refer to as 'you and me'. We are aspects of the Substance behind all the contingencies, the Consciousness that always was and will be, the Presence that empowers every appearance, the Life that creates our immortal Souls, The Reality that allows us to create our fleeting incarnations and lifelines and then – lessons learned – claim the fullness of our identity as immortal Souls.

Teachers All

As incarnates, we are painters, labors and accountants; fathers, mothers and children; chubby, thin and 'just right'. We are older, younger and almost forty. Some of us are learning how to become somebody and others of us are finally and deliberately learning how to be no-bodies. Some of us have finally learned how to do things with a box while others are trying to learn how to do things outside any box. Some are skilled at one thing and others really good at quite the opposite. Blue eyes, green eyes, hazel. Red-head, blond, grey. Tenor, alto, bass. High heels, flip-flops, modest and sensible. Westside, Eastside, and some other side – maybe somewhere in Queens.

All of us have lots of differences on the outside yet share a basic similarity and identity inside. We are all Souls – immortal yet in the midst of learning how to affirm our common inners while learning through our varied outers. We are - in common - immortal Souls who have placed ourselves in mortal circumstances. Thus we are – in our differences –

excellent students...for we have so much to learn. And we are – in our similarities – superb teachers...for we have so much to share.

If...

If the world understood and truly honored the fact that:

1. We are immortal Souls

2. Who have chosen to incarnate

3. In order complete a set of challenges and commissions

4. So we might learn how to love

5. And extend our capacity for compassion

6. We thereby deepen and expand our consciousness

7. As we serve God and each other as we co-create and re-create the universe.

Then it would have ample reason to:

1. Stop WORRYING,

2. Get rid of HURRYING,

3. Abandon DENYING,

4. Cease WHINING,

5. Give up REGRETTING,

6. Diminish the STRIVING, and

7. Let go of the biggest obstacle of all: FEAR.

In place of those negative dynamics, wouldn't be nice and natural to:

1. Begin serious bouts of celebrating,

2. Spend more time meditating and contemplating,

3. Be trusting of ourselves, others and the universe,

4. Open ourselves to learning from everyone and everything,

5. Express unconditional love for everyone we encounter,

6. Embrace our spiritual empowerments, and

7. Live each day with outrageous displays of gratitude and joy.

Representative

A reminder – again - of an everyday reality: you are the representative...perhaps of a number of affiliations and values. Everywhere you go, you represent something to someone: male-female, north-south, presumed citizen-presumed immigrant, rich-poor, white-black-latino-oriential-native-indian, Presbyterian-Jewish, whoever-whatever. Wherever you go, however you dress and behave, there will be somebody who will experience it as a commentary on your gender, age, ethnic affiliation, nationality or host of other real or presumed identities.

People in military dress, for example, are perceived as representatives of the armed forces. Men wearing a collar or woman donned in a habit – despite their individual traits – are assessed to be representatives of a religious class or grouping. Carry a cane, wheel a baby carriage, wear a carpenter's belt, drive a Cadillac - and it is assumed you possess the traits or identities that many associate with such accouterments or paraphernalia.

Try it: as you encounter others, be aware of the traits you usually associate with some particular identity. You may not know the person walking toward you but you probably make assumptions about him/her as you superimpose on them your interpretation of their associated traits.

Note how many of your assessments, for example, are descriptive ('he is probably from the suburbs', 'a Canadian' or 'from down south'). And despite your desire to stop judging others or indulging in negative stereotypes, note how many of your assessments are exactly that: 'he's probably a rich snob', 'a high school dropout', 'won't she make a lovely teenager'.

Now, let's raise the stakes. What is it about others that makes you suspect they are 'Representatives of God'? Is it their dress, words, attitude or tone? If many of the things that suggest 'God's Representative' are overtly religious, try minimizing if not eliminating those things from your assessment, and see what happens. Either way, do you assume that religion and the overt signs of religious affiliation automatically qualify that person to be a 'Representative of God'? Conversely, do you assume that spirituality is an attribute, a perspective or a lifestyle that is independent of one's vocabulary, dress or affiliation?

More pointedly, do you think there is something about you – your words and values, your activities and associations, the books you read, the ways in which you honor a religious tradition or spiritual perspective – which if they were fully known would elicit from others the conclusion that you probably were one of 'God's Representatives'?

Would that association bother you or would you be honored by it? Besides making you a bit self-conscious, would you act any differently - at least some of the time - simply because someone associated you with God? Would you be more careful? Would you be more aware of what you say and do, and how you say and do it? Would you become more conscious of how you present yourself and the associations your words and actions activate?

By the way, what things, traits, perspectives or activities do you associate with anyone being perceived as 'God's Representative'? Do you think Gandhi, Helen Keller, Black Elk, Martin Luther King – or any figure in modern or ancient history – was an Ambassador of God? Are there members of your community, family or neighborhood you think would qualify?

If so, how and why do you reach such a conclusion? Why do they 'feel' like or 'seem' like a spiritual being? In your experience, what do 'Representatives of God' say and do that clarifies their divine identity? Are their traits, dress, perspectives, language or behavior aligned with whatever you associate with being an 'image of', a 'reflection of', or a 'spokesperson for God'?

Among those associations, are there any you personally would prefer not to exhibit? Are there any you would be happy to exemplify? Putting it bluntly, do you know and realize you are an 'Immortal Soul' and a 'Representative of the Creator'? Like it or not - that's who and what you are, and like it or not, there probably are some people who already associate you with that role. What will you do now? Do you want to make some changes in your profile, perhaps affirming your role, even wishing you were a more identifiable and positive force for the all things you and others associate with being totally loving and God-like?

Summary Reminders

Just in case you have started to forget what was in Chapters 1-29, we offer some summary reminders – to be viewed not as destination points but as perspectives and ways of traveling.

- Give thanks everyday for your life and the opportunity to contribute to your own welfare and that of others.

- Ask for enlightenment and understanding to flow to and within you.

- State your intentions each day by choosing a word or phase that summarizes the kinds of energy you wish to attract and create.

- Be aware of the ways in which your intentions are manifest throughout the day.

- Pause every once in a while - no matter how busy your agenda - and just breathe in the fullness and stillness that surrounds you.

- Claim your personal empowerment by affirming that you - your intentions, thoughts, images and daydreams - create your reality.

- Sense the presence throughout the day of another dimension, one of angelic energy - that hovers around you, guides you, helps to tilt events in your direction.

- Imagine your Guardian Angel at your side – ready and able to assist – as soon as you explicitly request Her/His guidance.

- Give thanks to God for inviting you to partner in the on-going creation of the universe.

- Remind yourself throughout the day to stay in the now, live in the moment, see the person before you, and attend to whoever is in view and to whatever is at hand.

- Avoid the toxic. Seek the joyful.

- Pray, Meditate, Contemplate. Stop, now, and just do it. Rushed? Unclear? Then just sit or walk alone and tune into the silence for a minute or two.

- Express your opinion? Of course. Judge another? No - especially not yourself.

- Be playful everyday – not just during designated times but as a general and pervasive attitude, a way of living that brings zest, surprise and warmth to everything you encounter.

- End the day as you begin it – with an act of reverence and a word of thanksgiving.

APPENDIX

OUTLINE OF OUR SOUL IDENTITY

The following is a potential outline of our Soul identity. Please revise and adapt as experience, insight and consciousness suggest.

1. I am *an immortal Soul who has * chosen to incarnate on Earth * for a finite number of years. * I contracted to appear on Earth * in bodily form * in order to * experience the challenges and learn the lessons * I chose prior to incarnating and while my Soul still resided fully in the realm of Pure Spirit.

2. I have also chosen to incarnate to learn how to transform the spiritual energies of love, empathy and understanding into material expression and form.

3. Before incarnating I choose the general terms of my incarnation in the form of a contract or learning agreement. That agreement outlines my overall purpose or mission, placement, parents, personality traits and abilities, major issues, challenges and the kinds of contributions I wish to make.

4. I have incarnated many, many times before on Earth and elsewhere in the universe. Many Souls have incarnated numerous times, some as many as 20,000 or more, each in a different setting, and each time with a different set of characteristics, skills, issues, mission and desired learning.

5. My Soul, like all Souls, is immortal: it cannot die. It is not eternal like God, however, for it was created by God to serve a divine purpose, the general outlines of which are summarized here.

6. I have deliberately filled my current contract with challenges so I may learn more about the deeper levels of consciousness, understanding and creativity.

7. In my material identity, I possess or reside in a mind-body that is equipped with a sufficient range of sensate, mental, intuitive and emotional abilities to meet the challenges I, as an immortal Soul, have selected.

8. The focus of this and all lifelines is to learn. The experience of being incarnated is like going to school. It represents an opportunity to grow in the awareness of God's abiding presence and emulate His/Her capacity for unconditional love.

9. All life is a partnership with God. This God-Soul connection continues unabated whether we incarnate in material form or remain in the state of Pure Spirit.

10. During any given incarnation, our ego-bodies can invoke the guidance of Prime Source (or God) and the various angelic presences (including our Guardian Angel).

11. During incarnation, I can fulfil, modify or ignore the mission and objectives I outlined in my learning agreement. Free will always reigns.

12. When we return to the realm of Pure State, we are not judged as sinful for not achieving parts of our learning agreement. Rather, we are counseled and made aware of those missed opportunities to increase our state of consciousness. Such unfinished business then often becomes the theme (again) of the desired learning outlined for the next incarnation.

13. Each of us lives in a given incarnational state for as long as we wish – usually long enough to complete all or at least a substantial portion of our original intentions. A given incarnation is the creation of the individual Soul who is free to choose when and how it wants to surrender its temporary embodiment and return to the realm of Pure Spirit.

14. There are no accidents or 'real' tragedies. The challenges and difficulties experienced by the incarnate were chosen by it's Soul in order to broaden the Soul's experience, and both deepen and expand it's state of consciousness.

15. When we let go of the body that we have inhabited, we – as immortal Souls – are escorted by angels back to the realm of Pure Spirit where we are greeted by loved ones in a setting that reflects the beliefs and traditions of our earthly experience. If we had lived in Polynesia, for example, the initial setting will be Polynesian – and will remain so until we have adjusted to being back in the realm of Pure Spirit and It's totally inclusive scenario of love.

16. None of us will be judged for any of the choices we make in the incarnated state for there is no such thing as sin, the devil, an avenging God, or heaven and hell. Once we have returned to Pure Spirit, however, spiritual tutors will help us assess and debrief our behavior during the preceding incarnation. If we hurt others through insensitivity, callousness or insufficient love and compassion, we'll undergo those experiences during our debriefing in order to learn how our actions or inactions were harmful to others.

17. The principle guiding the assessment of any incarnation is not vengeance but learning – learning empathy through greater understanding, as well as learning how to love and empower oneself in the face of challenges that can jeopardize one's spiritual identity and mission.

18. The lessons gleaned from our life reviews usually become the basis for study and reflection in the Pure State. Thus it is not unusual for us to include variations on those themes in the learning agreement we adopt for the next incarnation.

19. Choice, free and open choice are central to the entire process of learning As Souls – whether in the state of a Pure Soul or one of incarnation - we choose what we wish to learn, at what pace and

in what set of circumstances. Each choice – in either state - is a test of our capacity to create and attract a reality that is both empowering and loving. And each choice is part of the continual and abiding goal to be as loving and enlightened as the All-Loving God.

20. As an immortal Soul and aspect of the divine, we are always encouraged to increase our

    a. Ability to live in the timeless and eternal moment,

    b. Consciousness of the loving presence of God in all situations and things,

    c. Trust in our power to express and create spiritual realities in the material realm,

    d. Capacity to fear nothing and overcome all obstacles as we fulfill our spiritual missions,

    e. Awareness that there are no accidents or tragedies, only Souls attempting to learn the lessons they outlined in their contracts and thereby fulfill their missions.

21. We are co-creators of the evolving Kosmos: all our intentions and experiences are communicated directly to God and figure in Prime Source's continuous creation and re-creation of the universe. Thus our thoughts and actions, our roles, missions and learnings, all have an impact on how the Earth fairs and how the universe evolves.

22. We have ample reason to thank the Creator for including us in this great adventure.

Surely God said it first - so we end this book with Her everlasting tribute:

"Namaste: The divinity in me bows to the divinity in you."

Melozzo d Forli, *Dome of St. Mark's Sacristy, Venice*, c. 1480
Everything is united - for everything converges to and extends from the Center.

THE AUTHOR

William Francis Sturner, Ph.D., is the author of twelve books, father of two children, playmate of six grandchildren, lover of art and music, international consultant and facilitator, psychotherapist, and very spirited and joyful facilitator.

His work combines the perspective of growing up in the Bronx with the disciplines of Jungian, Gestalt and spiritual psychology. His university appointments have included full professorships at three American universities and vice presidencies at two. He has also been awarded visiting appointments at the universities of Limerick, Ireland; Istanbul Technical, Turkey; Buffalo State, USA; Santiago de Compostela, Spain; and Moscow State, Russia.

He has offered workshops and consulting throughout the USA, Europe, the Middle East, Africa and Latin America, and is a regular presenter at international conferences on Creativity and Innovation.

Sturner moved his 'Open Heart Sanctuary' in 2015 - from East Aurora, NY to Sarasota-Osprey, Florida – close to the shores of the Bay of Mexico. He continues to spend his time communing with nature, offering counselling and workshops on personal and spiritual development, and writing books on mythic tales, reincarnation, angels and mystic healing.

wfsturner@mac.com

www.KindredSpirits.Us

Made in the USA
Columbia, SC
05 July 2017